DRIFTING DRAGONS

Taku Kuwabara

8

DRIFTING DRAGONS

Table of Contents

SHIP NAME

Quin Zaza

SHIP MARK

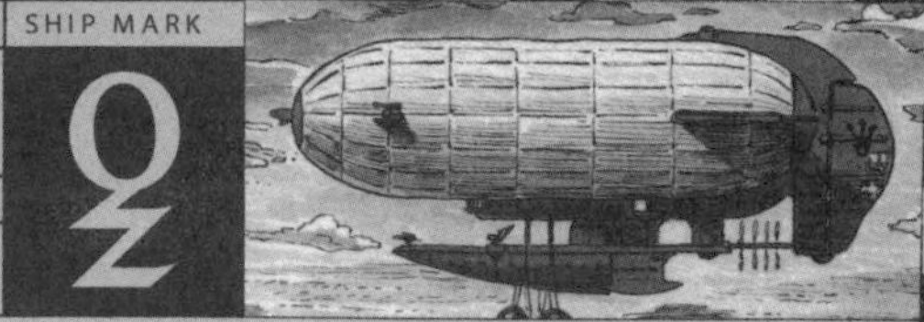

CHARACTER LIST

Crew	TOTAL 19

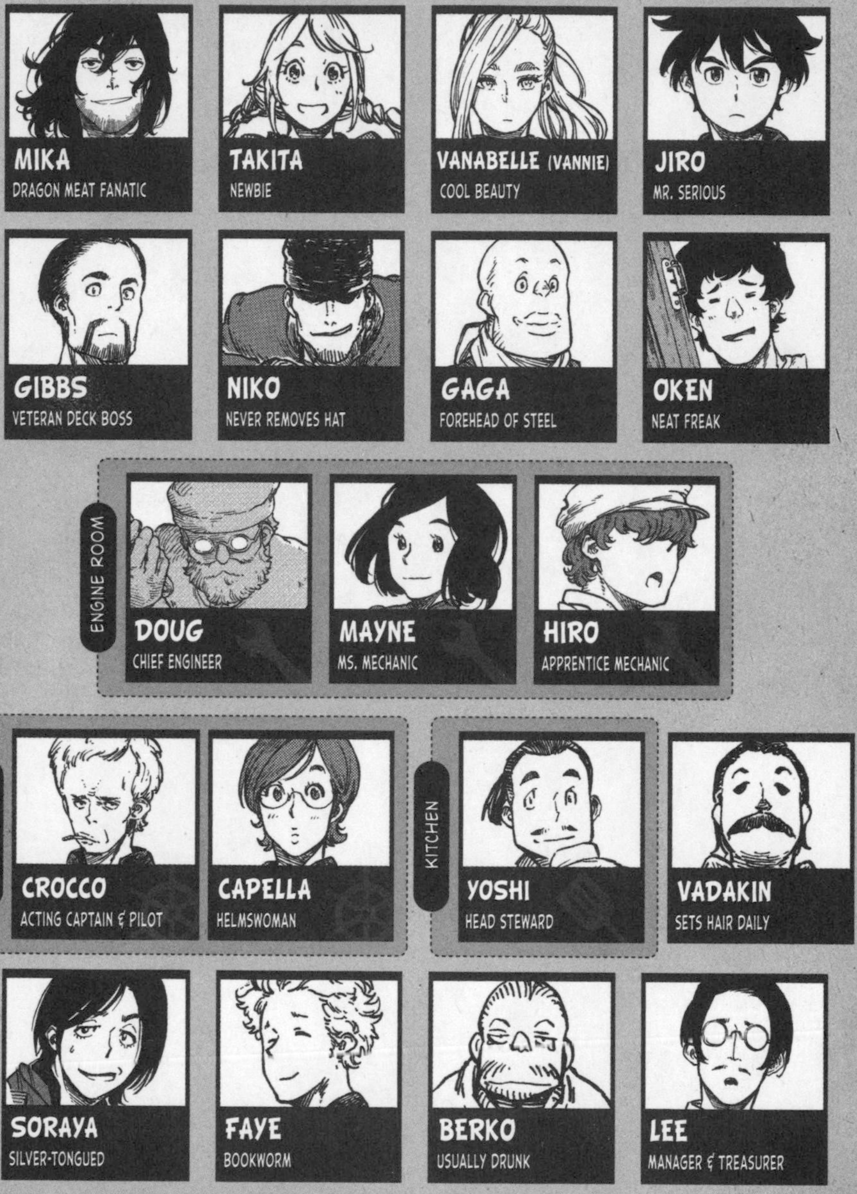
MIKA
DRAGON MEAT FANATIC
TAKITA
NEWBIE
VANABELLE (VANNIE)
COOL BEAUTY
JIRO
MR. SERIOUS
GIBBS
VETERAN DECK BOSS
NIKO
NEVER REMOVES HAT
GAGA
FOREHEAD OF STEEL
OKEN
NEAT FREAK
ENGINE ROOM
DOUG
CHIEF ENGINEER
MAYNE
MS. MECHANIC
HIRO
APPRENTICE MECHANIC
BRIDGE
CROCCO
ACTING CAPTAIN & PILOT
CAPELLA
HELMSWOMAN
KITCHEN
YOSHI
HEAD STEWARD
VADAKIN
SETS HAIR DAILY
SORAYA
SILVER-TONGUED
FAYE
BOOKWORM
BERKO
USUALLY DRUNK
LEE
MANAGER & TREASURER

*This is a work of fiction. Any resemblances to real people, groups, and events are purely coincidental.

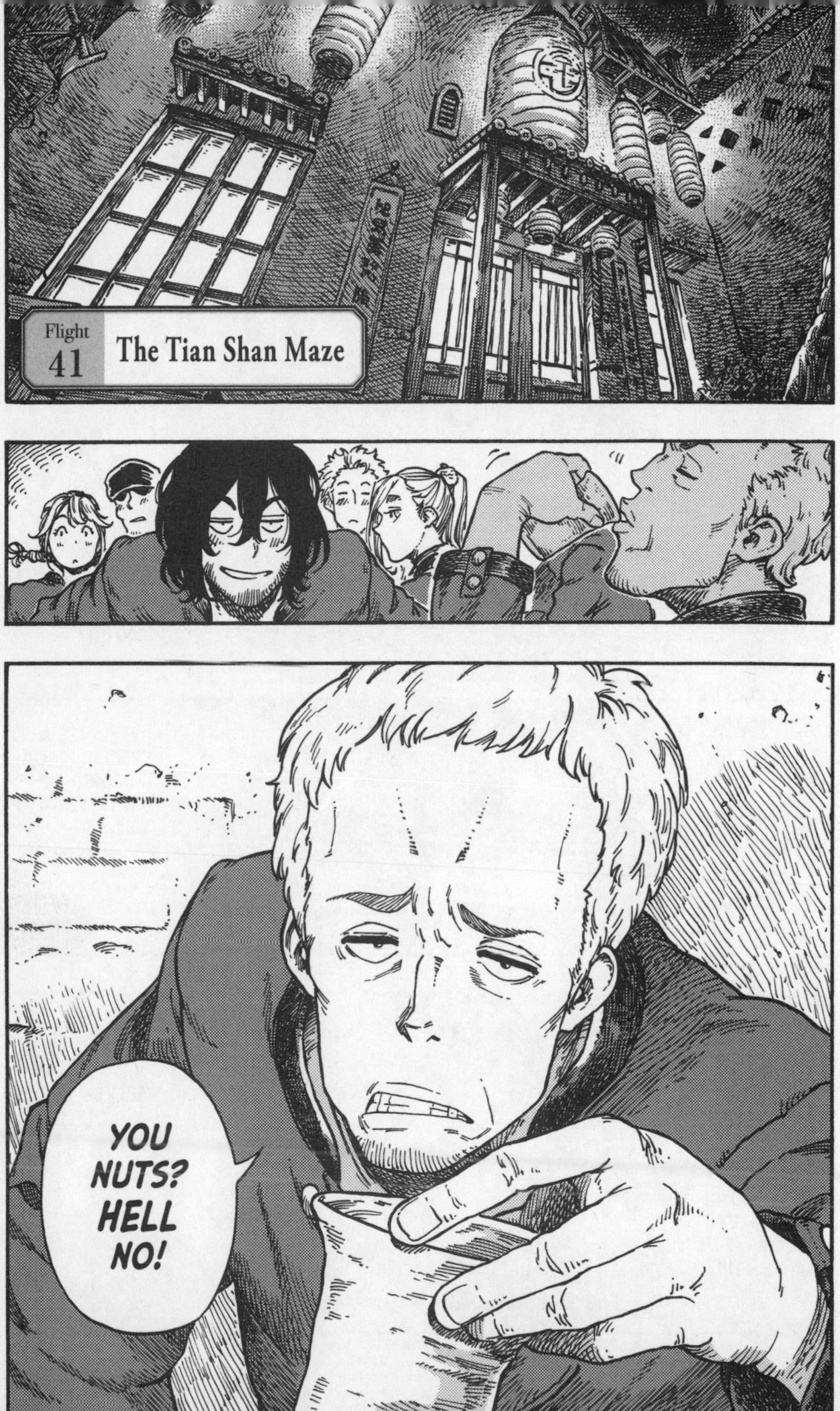
Flight 41 The Tian Shan Maze
YOU NUTS? HELL NO!

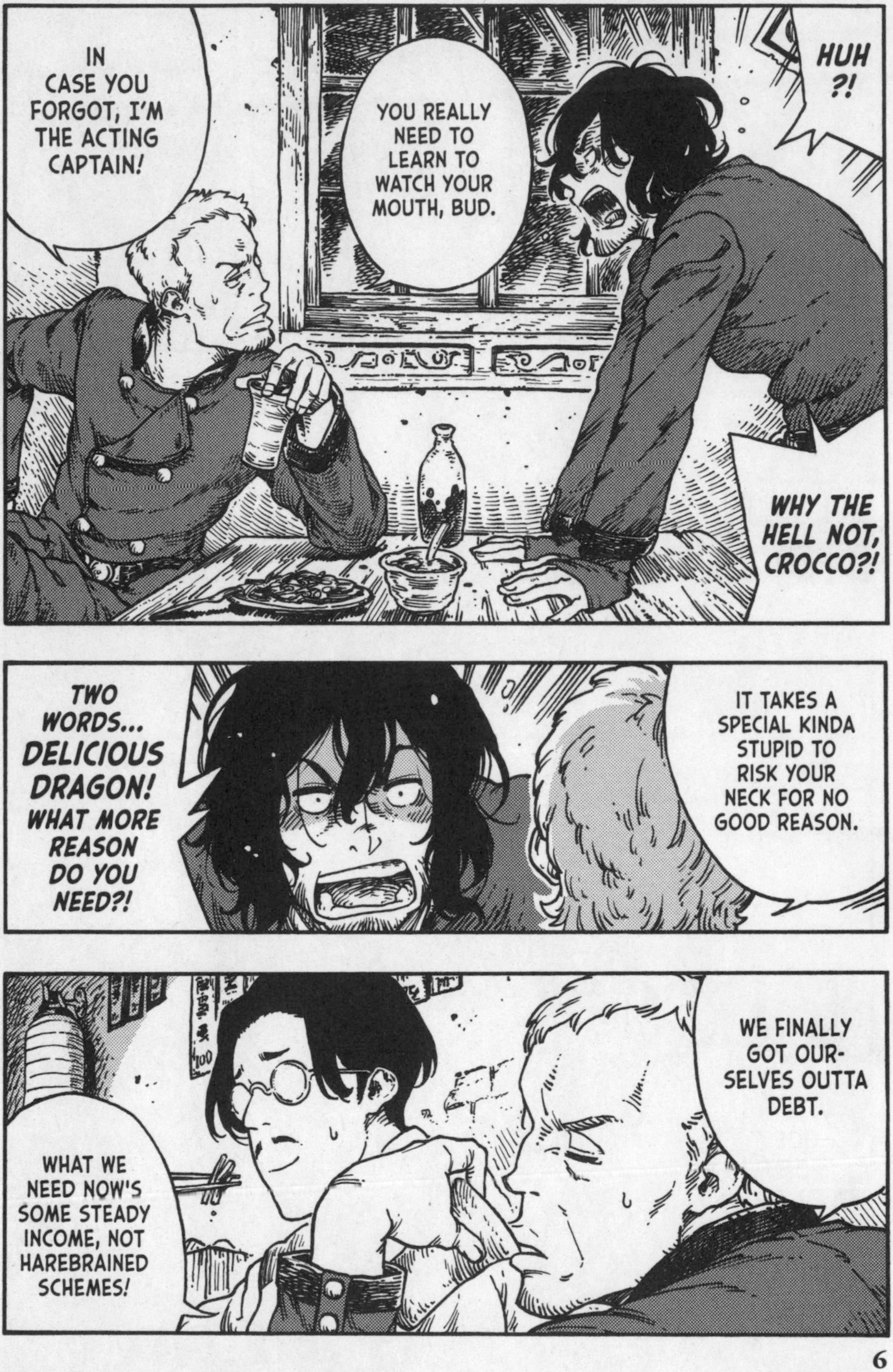
HUH ?!
WHY THE HELL NOT, CROCCO?!
YOU REALLY NEED TO LEARN TO WATCH YOUR MOUTH, BUD.
IN CASE YOU FORGOT, I'M THE ACTING CAPTAIN!
IT TAKES A SPECIAL KINDA STUPID TO RISK YOUR NECK FOR NO GOOD REASON.
TWO WORDS... DELICIOUS DRAGON! WHAT MORE REASON DO YOU NEED?!
WE FINALLY GOT OUR-SELVES OUTTA DEBT.
WHAT WE NEED NOW'S SOME STEADY INCOME, NOT HAREBRAINED SCHEMES!

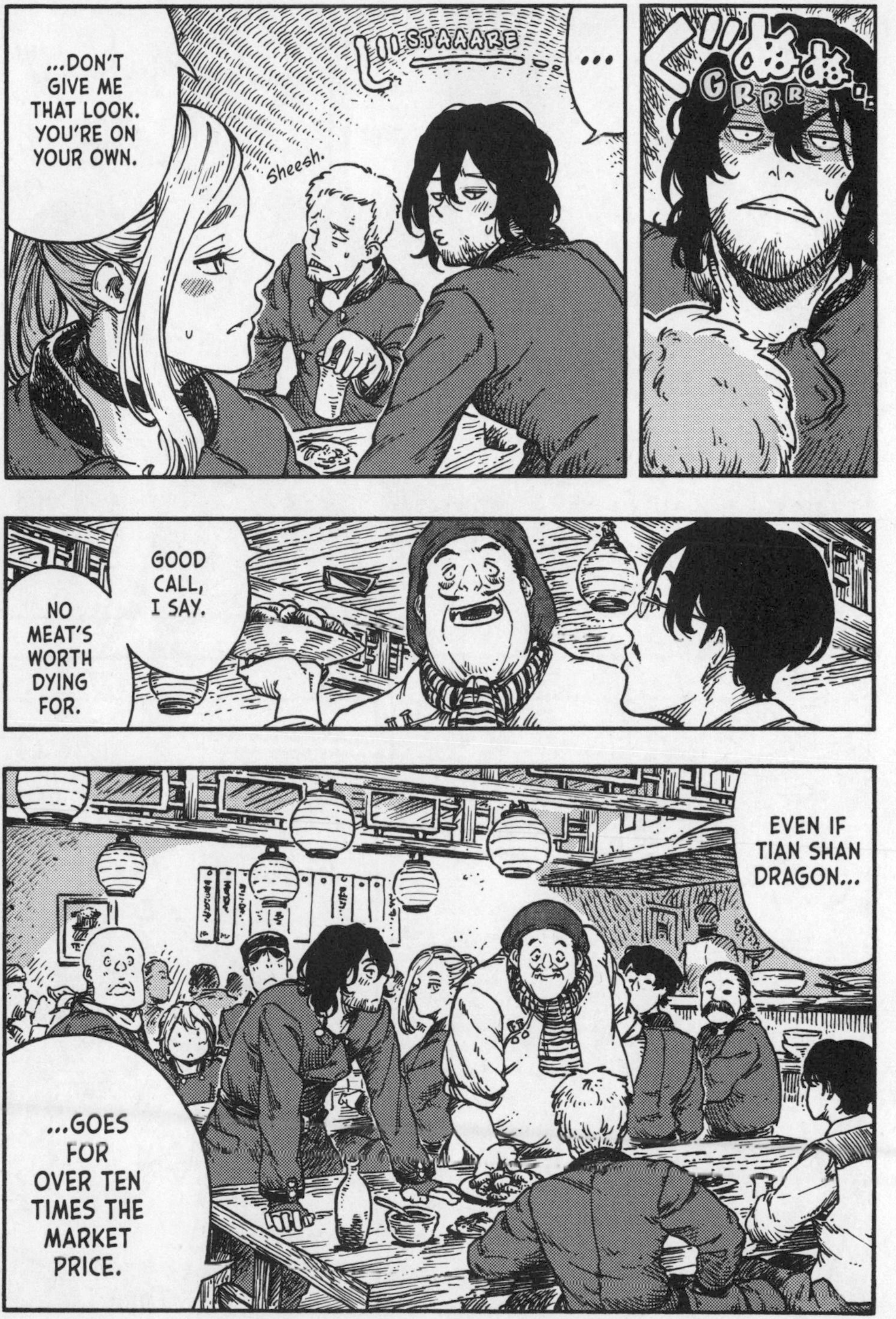
GRRR
...
STAAARE
Sheesh.
...DON'T GIVE ME THAT LOOK. YOU'RE ON YOUR OWN.
GOOD CALL, I SAY.
NO MEAT'S WORTH DYING FOR.
EVEN IF TIAN SHAN DRAGON...
...GOES FOR OVER TEN TIMES THE MARKET PRICE.

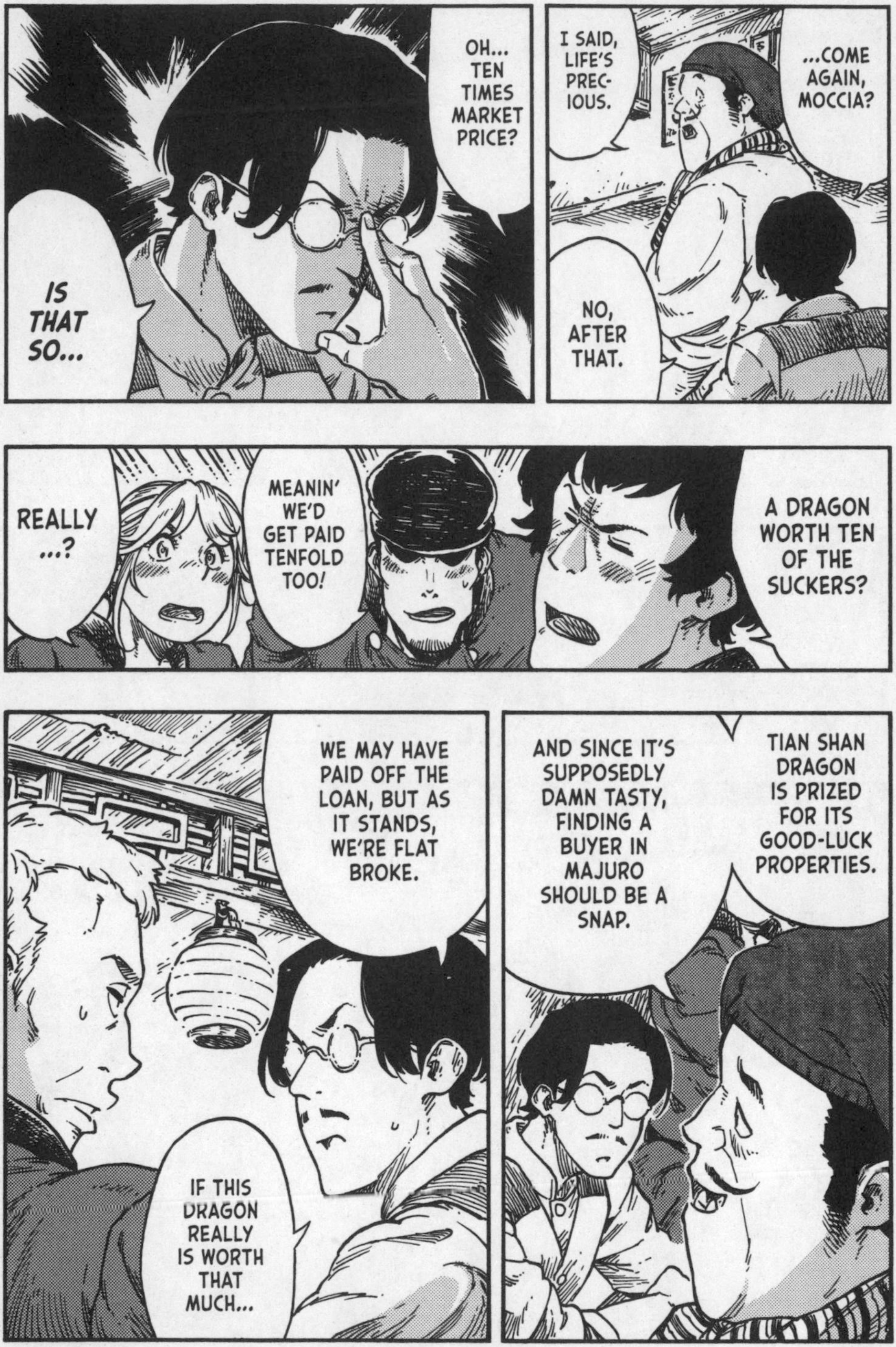
...COME AGAIN, MOCCIA?
I SAID, LIFE'S PREC-IOUS.
NO, AFTER THAT.
OH... TEN TIMES MARKET PRICE?
IS THAT SO...
A DRAGON WORTH TEN OF THE SUCKERS?
MEANIN' WE'D GET PAID TENFOLD TOO!
REALLY ...?
TIAN SHAN DRAGON IS PRIZED FOR ITS GOOD-LUCK PROPERTIES.
AND SINCE IT'S SUPPOSEDLY DAMN TASTY, FINDING A BUYER IN MAJURO SHOULD BE A SNAP.
WE MAY HAVE PAID OFF THE LOAN, BUT AS IT STANDS, WE'RE FLAT BROKE.
IF THIS DRAGON REALLY IS WORTH THAT MUCH...

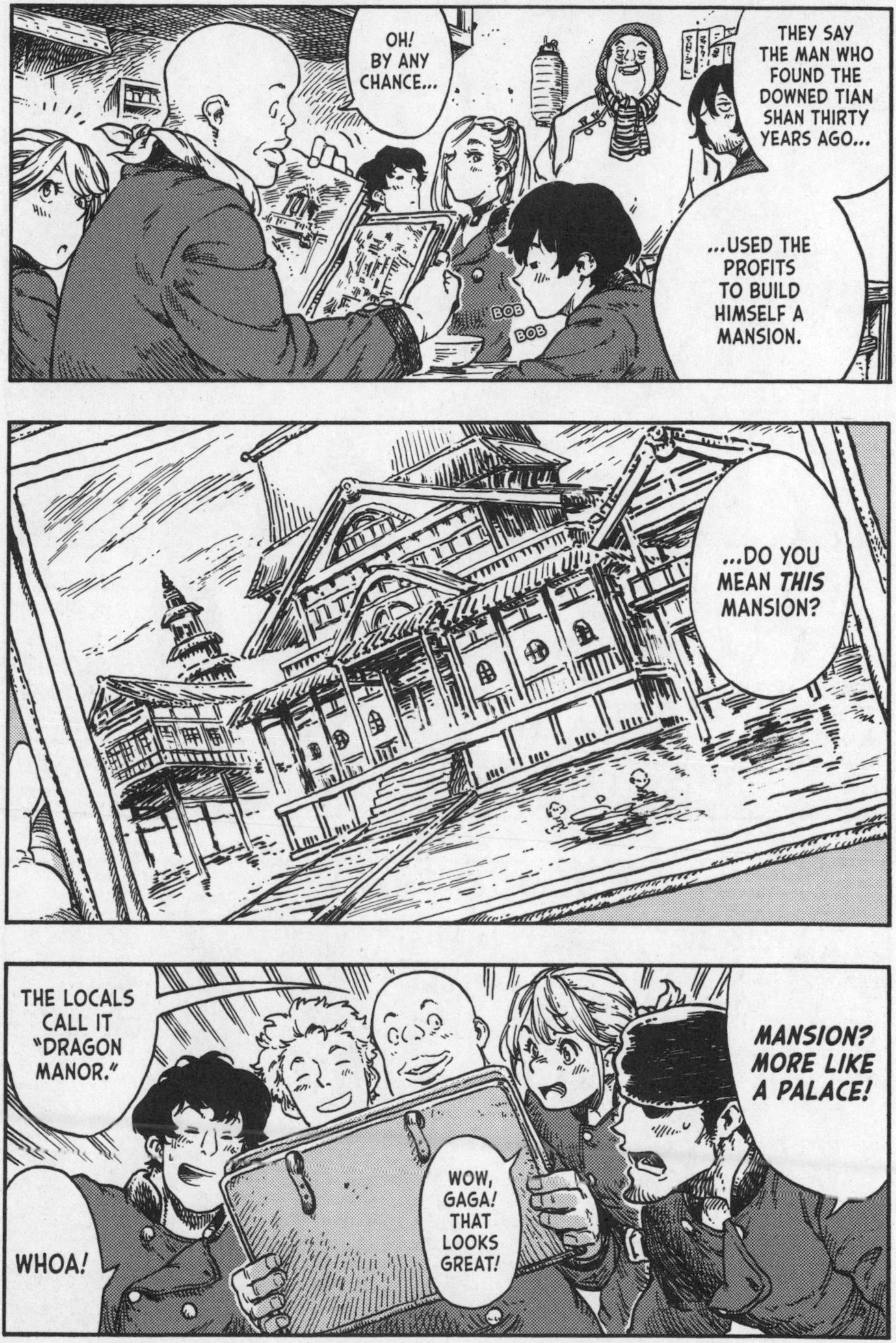
THEY SAY THE MAN WHO FOUND THE DOWNED TIAN SHAN THIRTY YEARS AGO...
...USED THE PROFITS TO BUILD HIMSELF A MANSION.
OH! BY ANY CHANCE...
BOB
BOB
...DO YOU MEAN THIS MANSION?
MANSION? MORE LIKE A PALACE!
WOW, GAGA! THAT LOOKS GREAT!
THE LOCALS CALL IT "DRAGON MANOR."
WHOA!

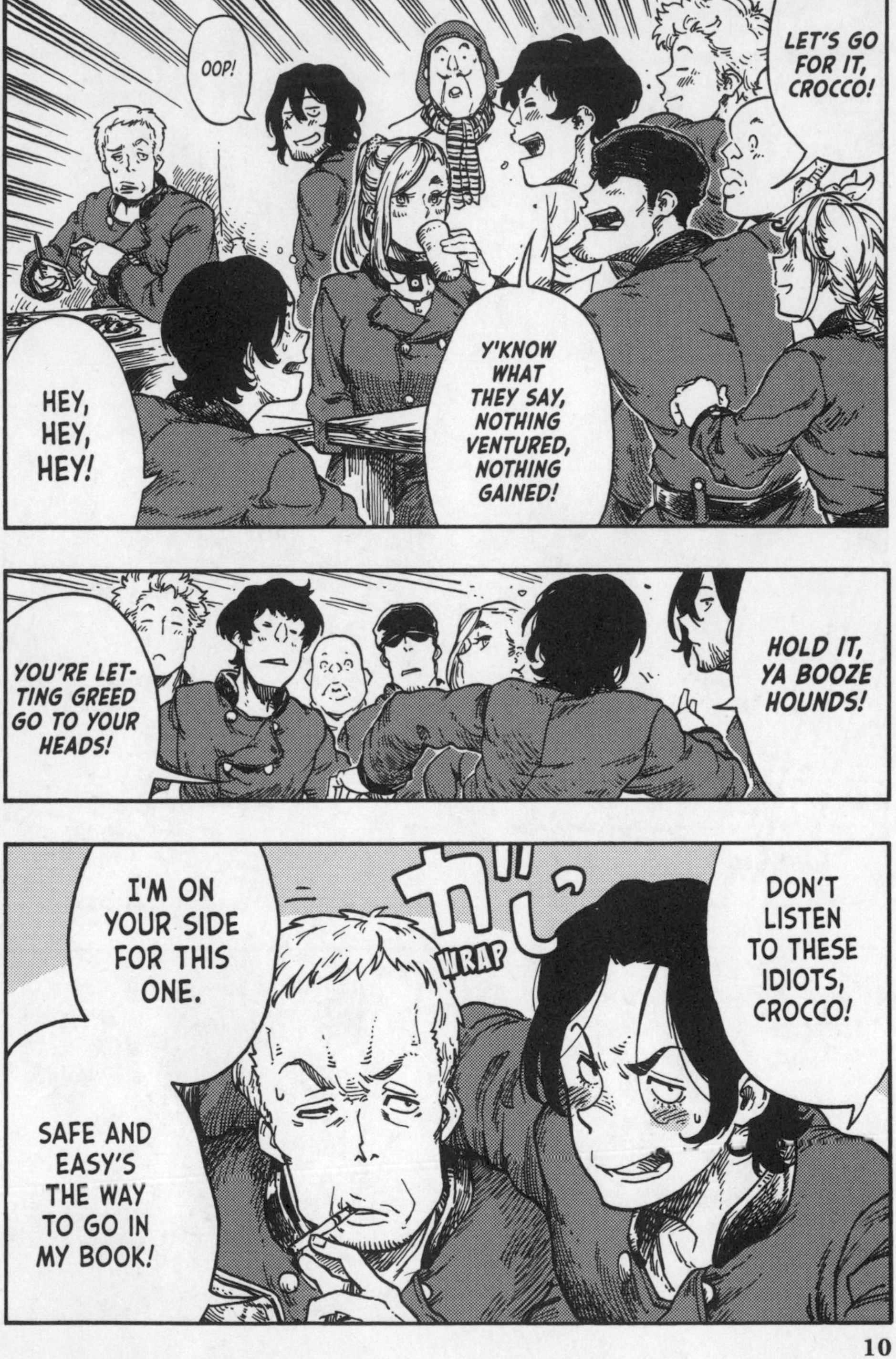
LET'S GO FOR IT, CROCCO!
OOP!
Y'KNOW WHAT THEY SAY, NOTHING VENTURED, NOTHING GAINED!
HEY, HEY, HEY!
HOLD IT, YA BOOZE HOUNDS!
YOU'RE LET-TING GREED GO TO YOUR HEADS!
DON'T LISTEN TO THESE IDIOTS, CROCCO!
ガしっ
WRAP
I'M ON YOUR SIDE FOR THIS ONE.
SAFE AND EASY'S THE WAY TO GO IN MY BOOK!

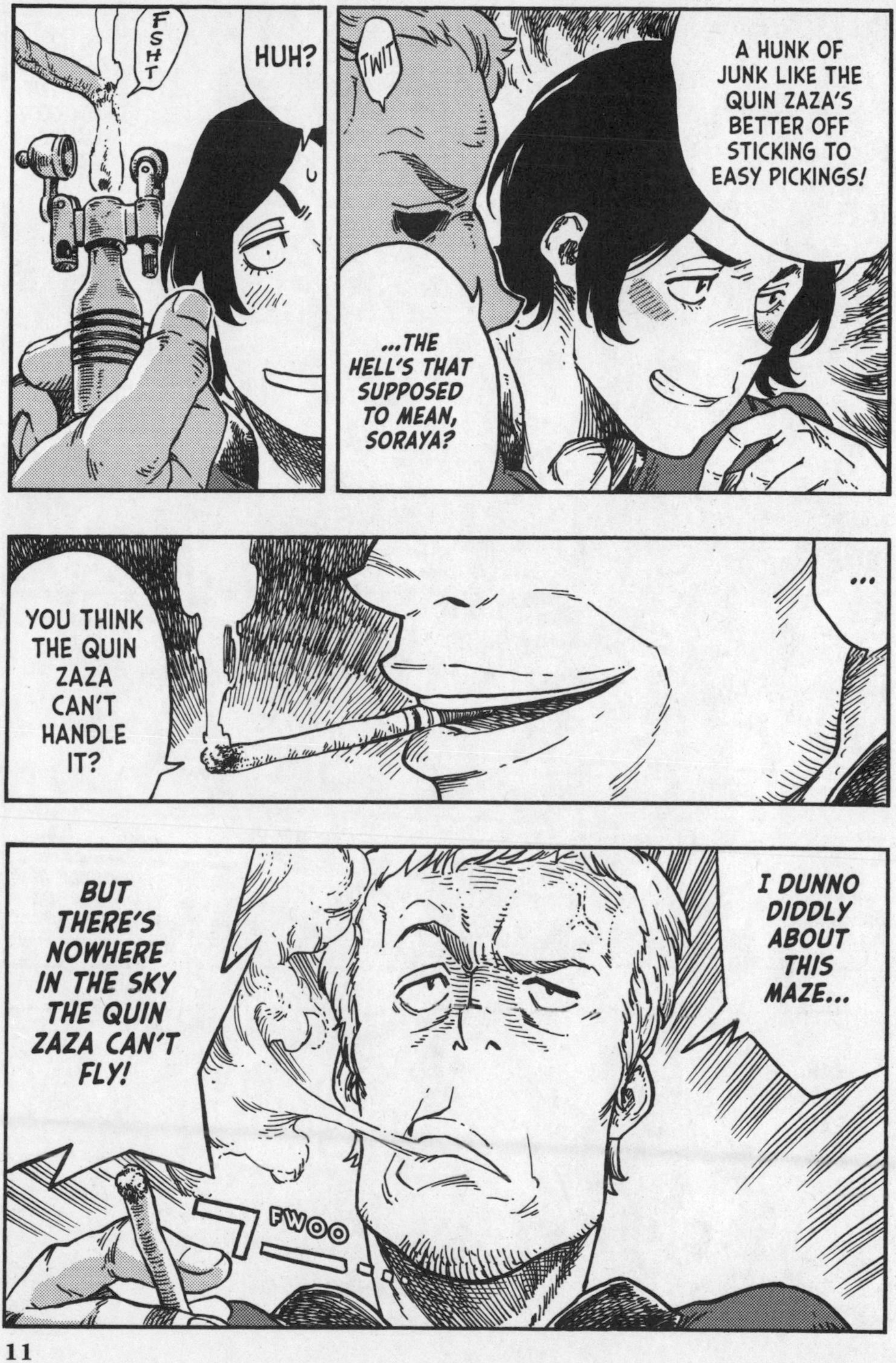
A HUNK OF JUNK LIKE THE QUIN ZAZA'S BETTER OFF STICKING TO EASY PICKINGS!
TWIT
...THE HELL'S THAT SUPPOSED TO MEAN, SORAYA?
HUH?
FSHT
...
YOU THINK THE QUIN ZAZA CAN'T HANDLE IT?
I DUNNO DIDDLY ABOUT THIS MAZE...
BUT THERE'S NOWHERE IN THE SKY THE QUIN ZAZA CAN'T FLY!
FWOO

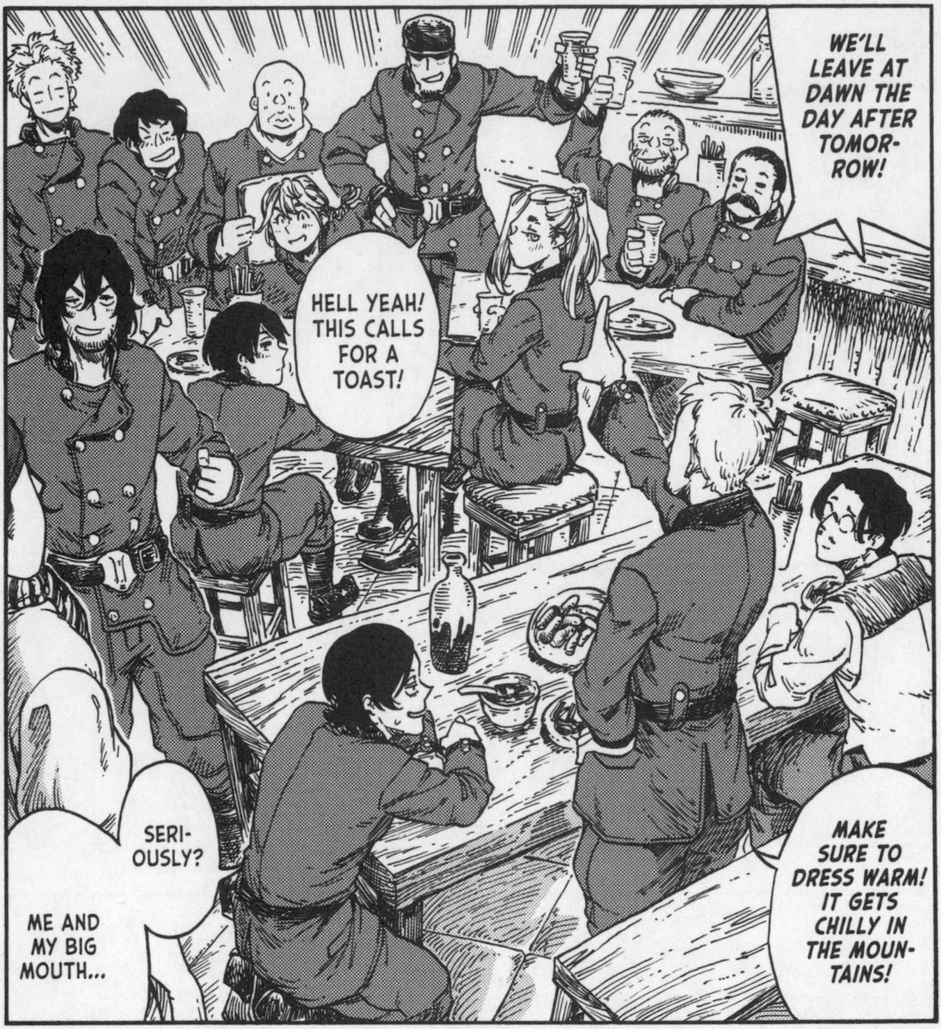
WE'LL LEAVE AT DAWN THE DAY AFTER TOMORROW!
HELL YEAH! THIS CALLS FOR A TOAST!
MAKE SURE TO DRESS WARM! IT GETS CHILLY IN THE MOUNTAINS!
SERIOUSLY?
ME AND MY BIG MOUTH...

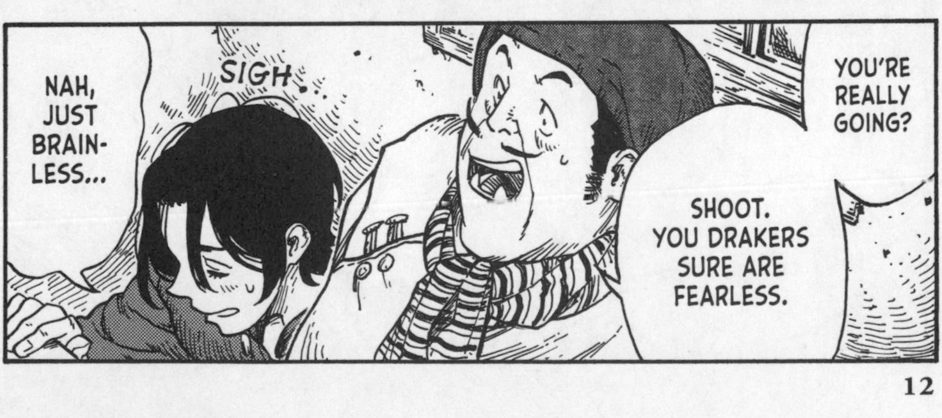
YOU'RE REALLY GOING?
SHOOT. YOU DRAKERS SURE ARE FEARLESS.
SIGH
NAH, JUST BRAINLESS...

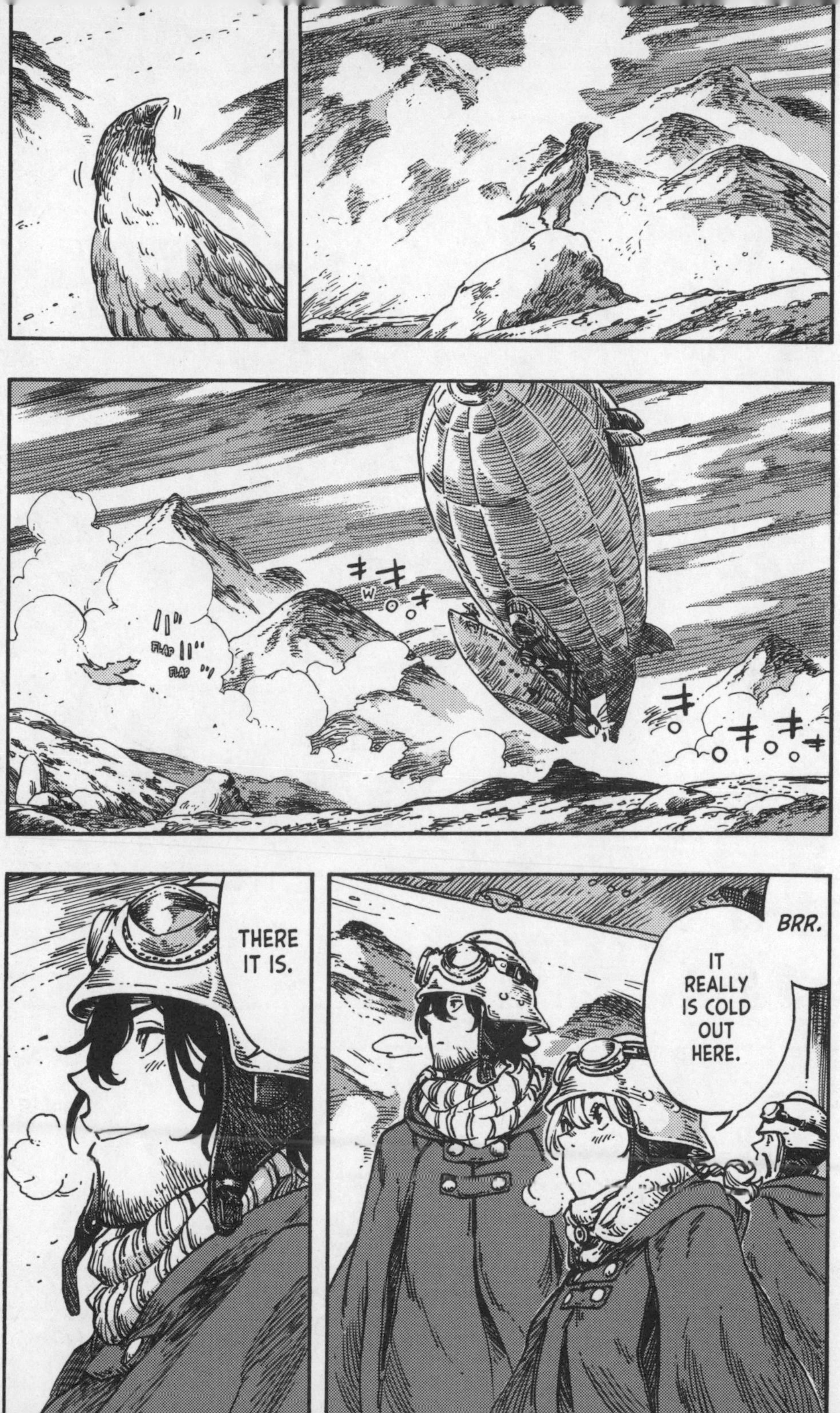
FLAP
FLAP
BRR.
IT REALLY IS COLD OUT HERE.
THERE IT IS.

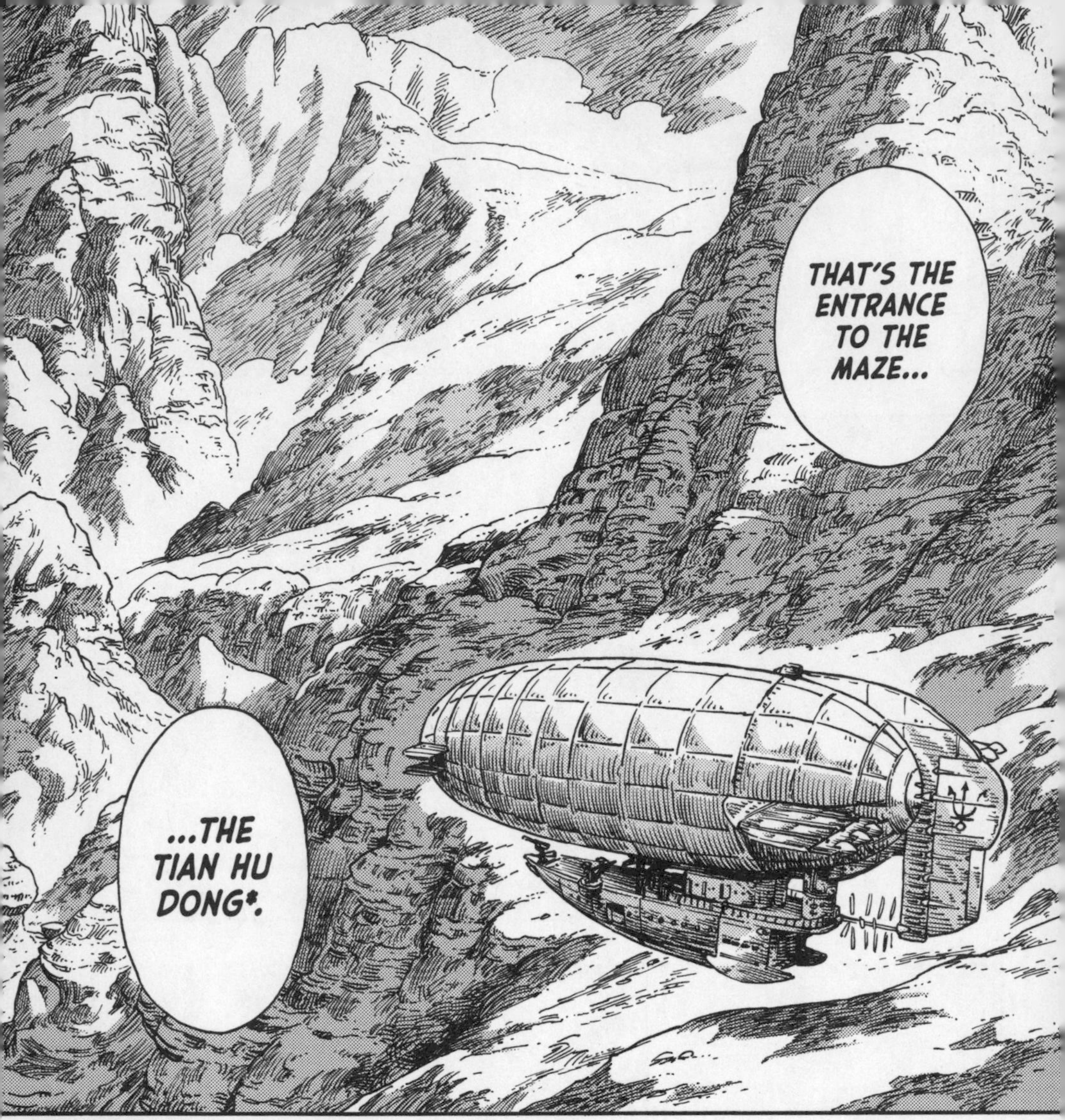
THAT'S THE ENTRANCE TO THE MAZE...
...THE TIAN HU DONG*.

*The Heavenly Hollow

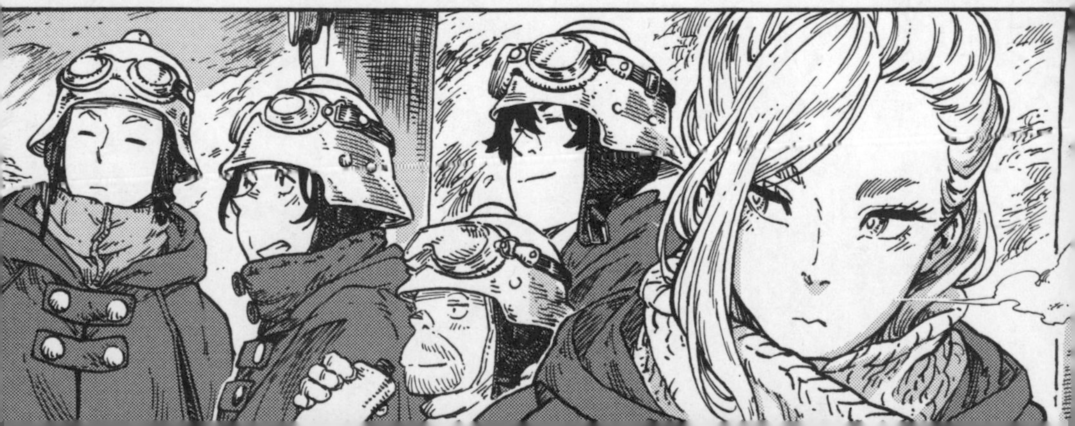

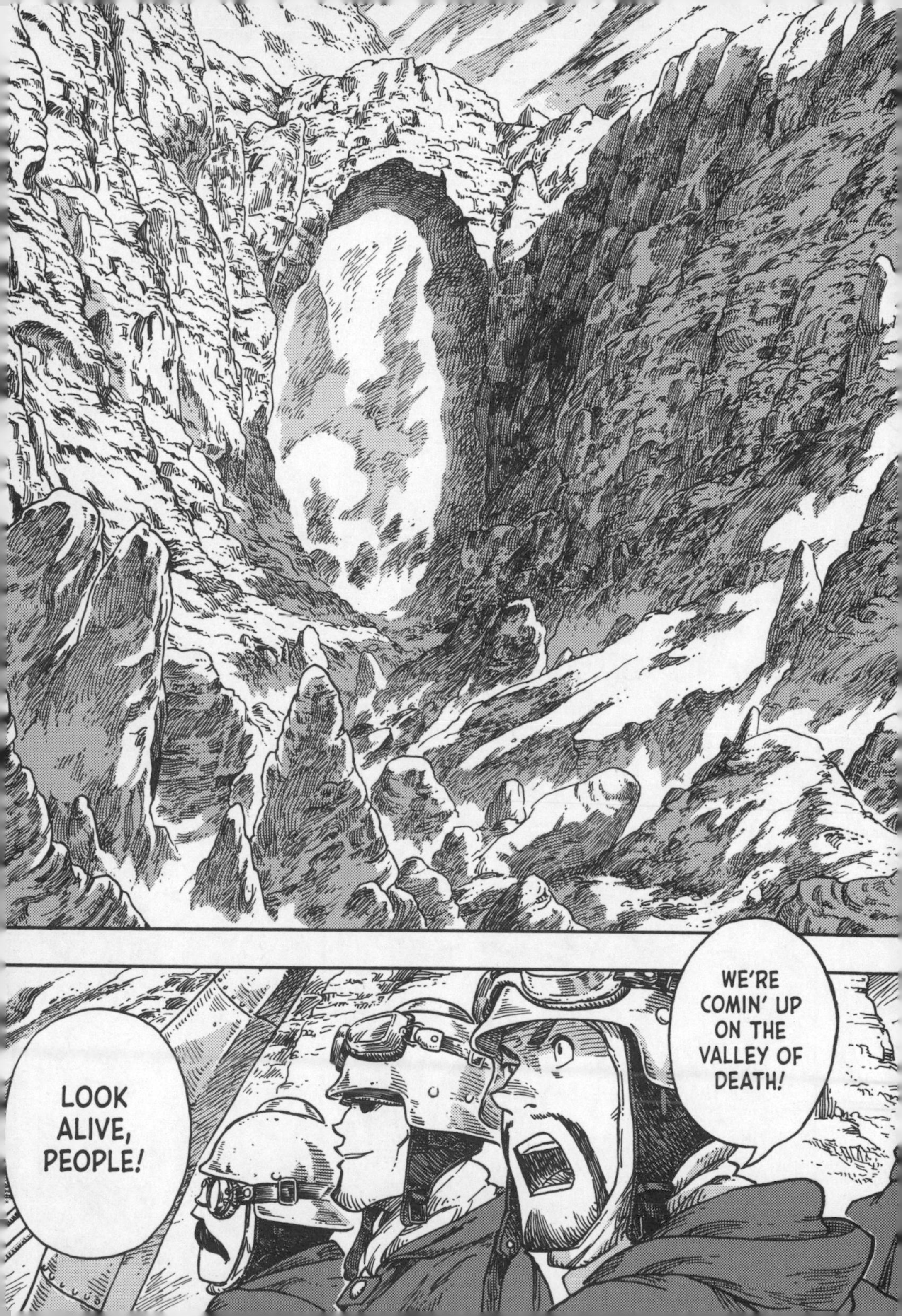
WE'RE COMIN' UP ON THE VALLEY OF DEATH!
LOOK ALIVE, PEOPLE!

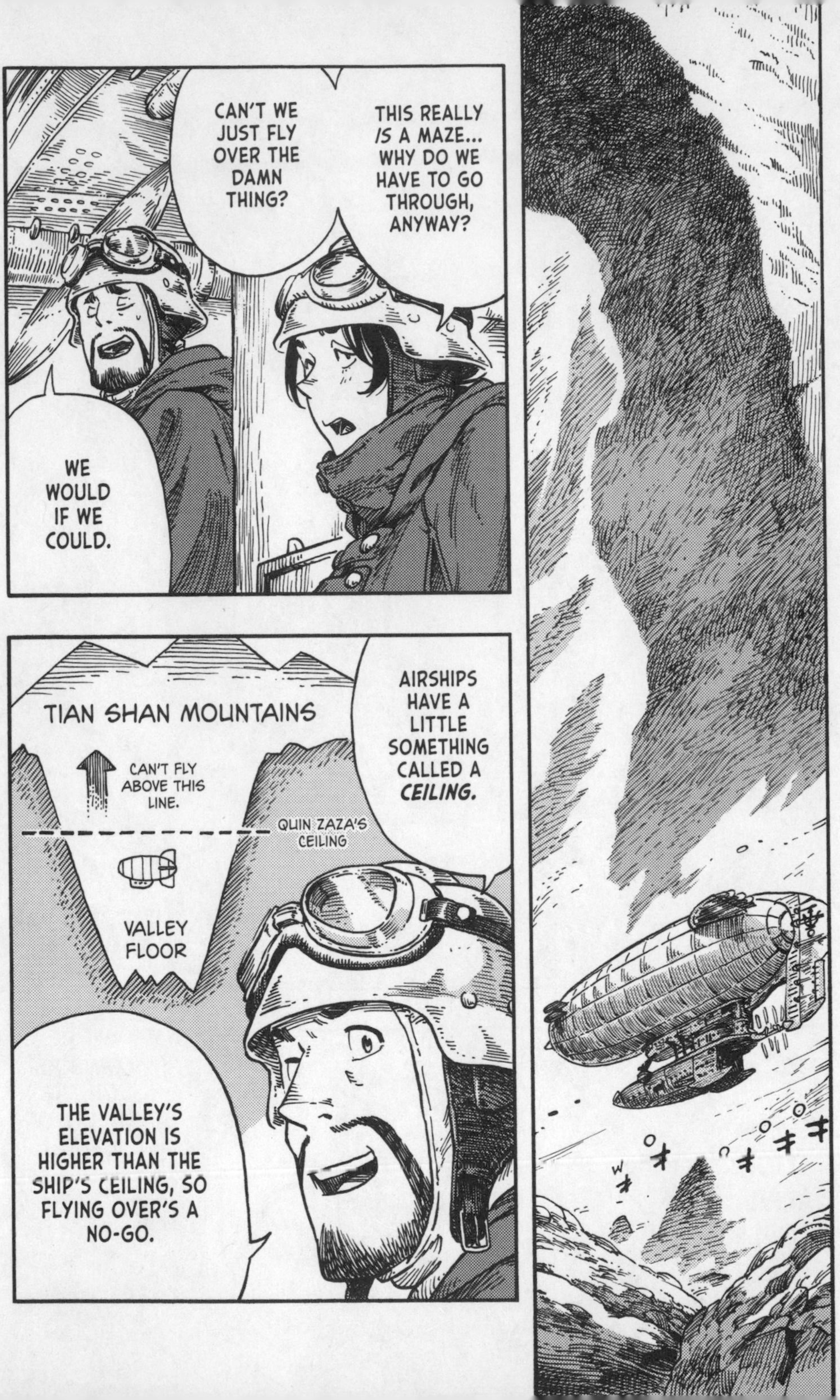
THIS REALLY *IS* A MAZE... WHY DO WE HAVE TO GO THROUGH, ANYWAY?
CAN'T WE JUST FLY OVER THE DAMN THING?
WE WOULD IF WE COULD.
AIRSHIPS HAVE A LITTLE SOMETHING CALLED A ***CEILING.***
TIAN SHAN MOUNTAINS
CAN'T FLY ABOVE THIS LINE.
QUIN ZAZA'S CEILING
VALLEY FLOOR
THE VALLEY'S ELEVATION IS HIGHER THAN THE SHIP'S CEILING, SO FLYING OVER'S A NO-GO.

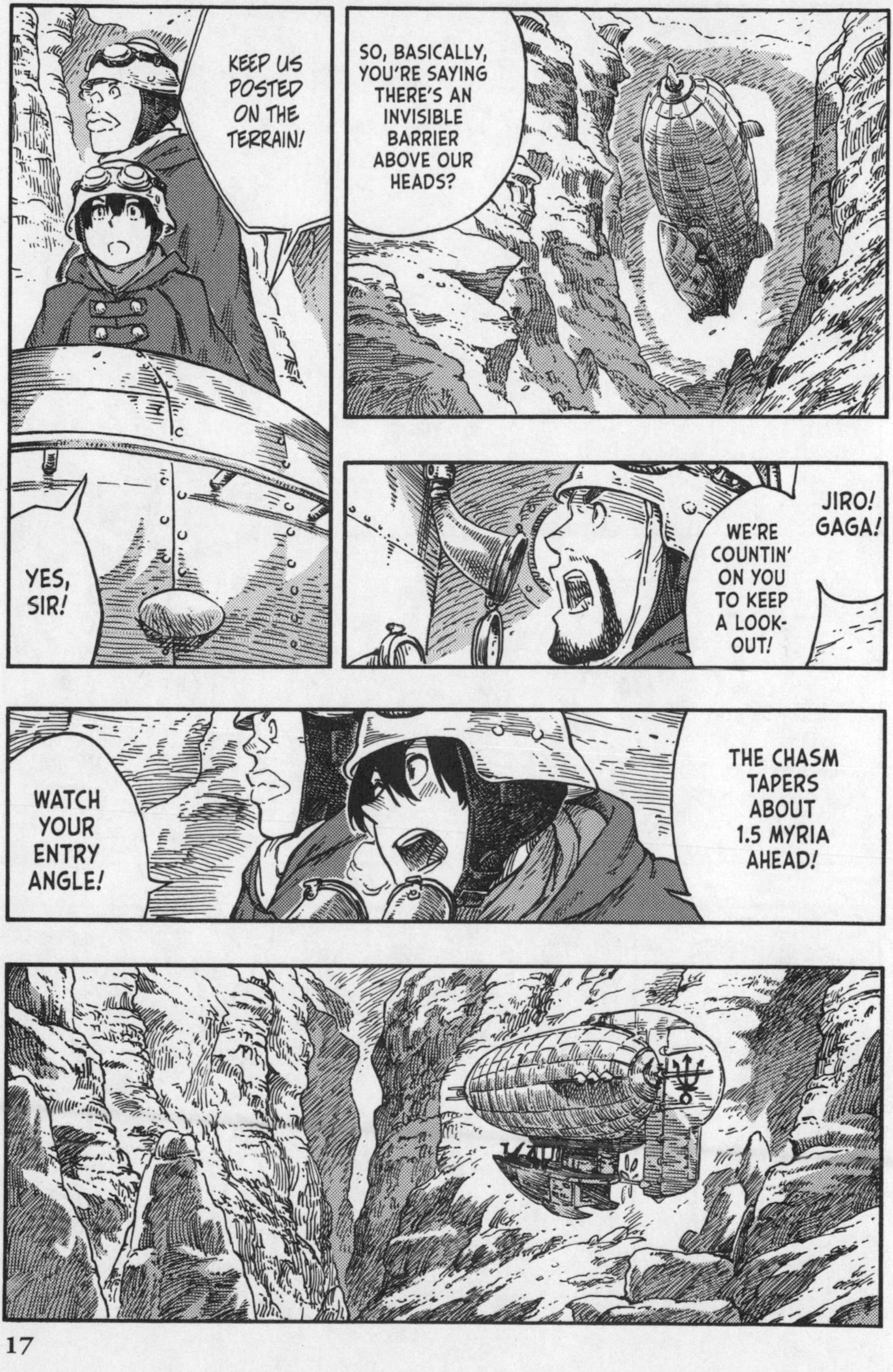
SO, BASICALLY, YOU'RE SAYING THERE'S AN INVISIBLE BARRIER ABOVE OUR HEADS?
JIRO! GAGA!
WE'RE COUNTIN' ON YOU TO KEEP A LOOK-OUT!
KEEP US POSTED ON THE TERRAIN!
YES, SIR!
THE CHASM TAPERS ABOUT 1.5 MYRIA AHEAD!
WATCH YOUR ENTRY ANGLE!

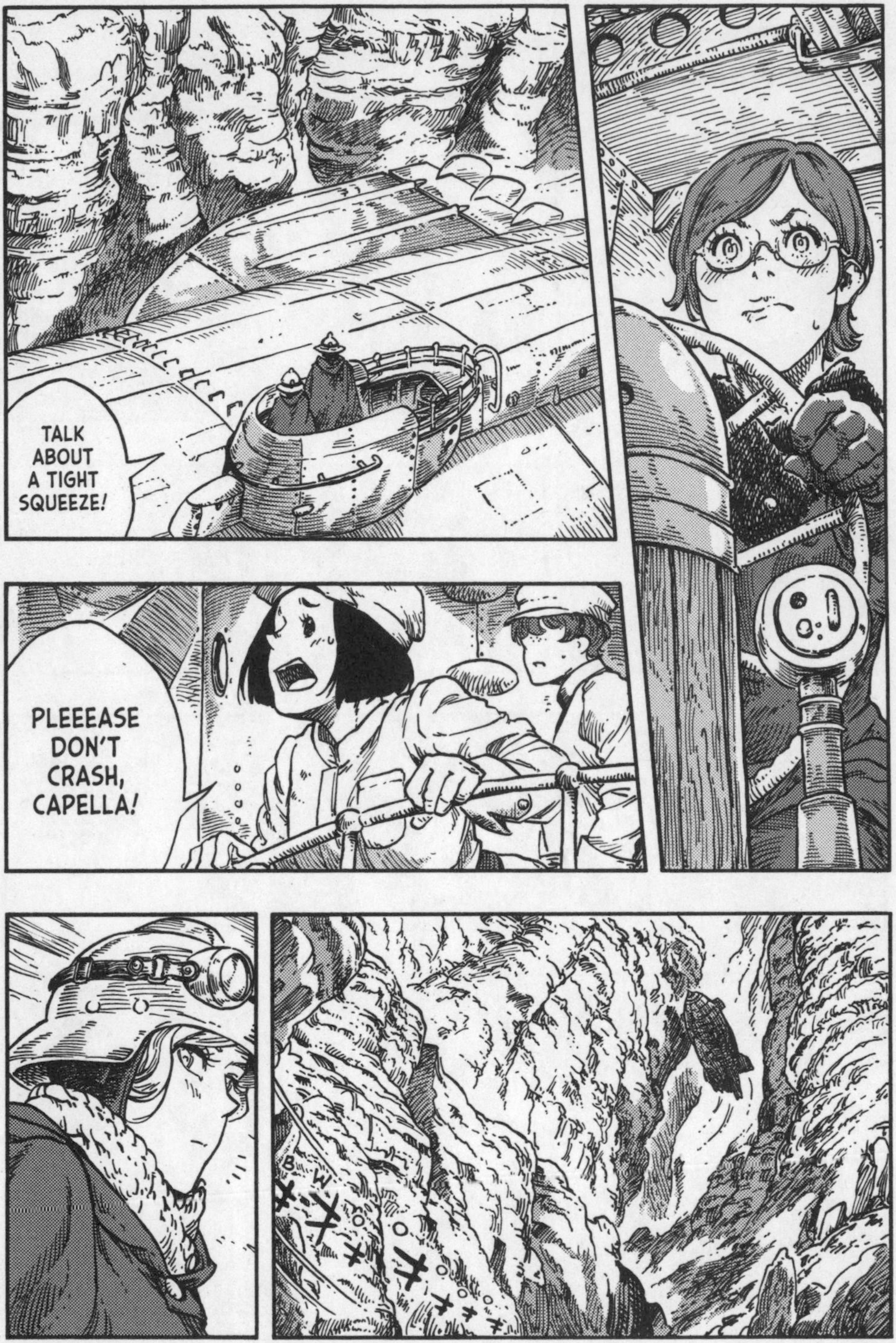
TALK ABOUT A TIGHT SQUEEZE!
PLEEEASE DON'T CRASH, CAPELLA!

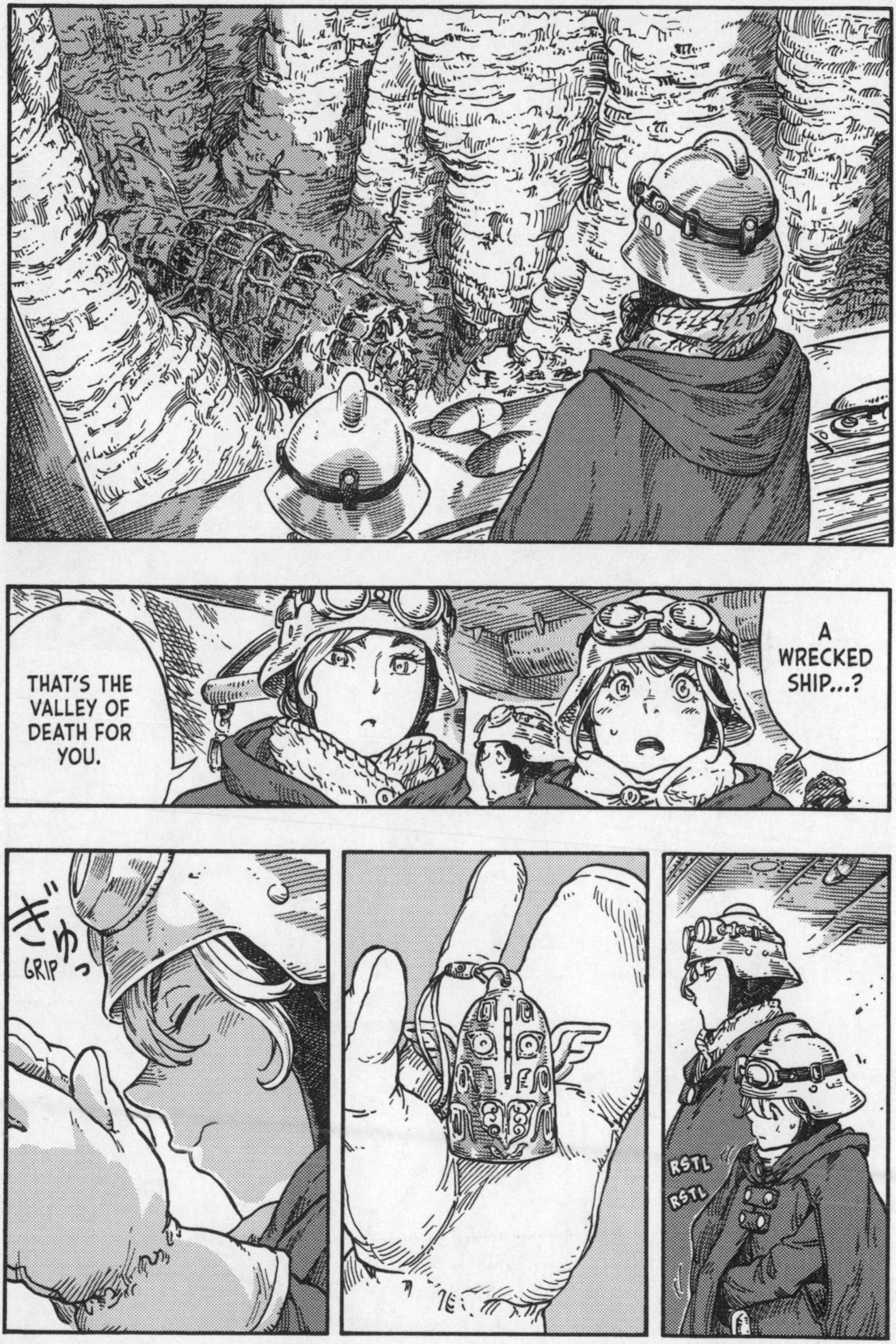
A WRECKED SHIP...?
THAT'S THE VALLEY OF DEATH FOR YOU.
RSTL
RSTL
ぎゅっ
GRIP

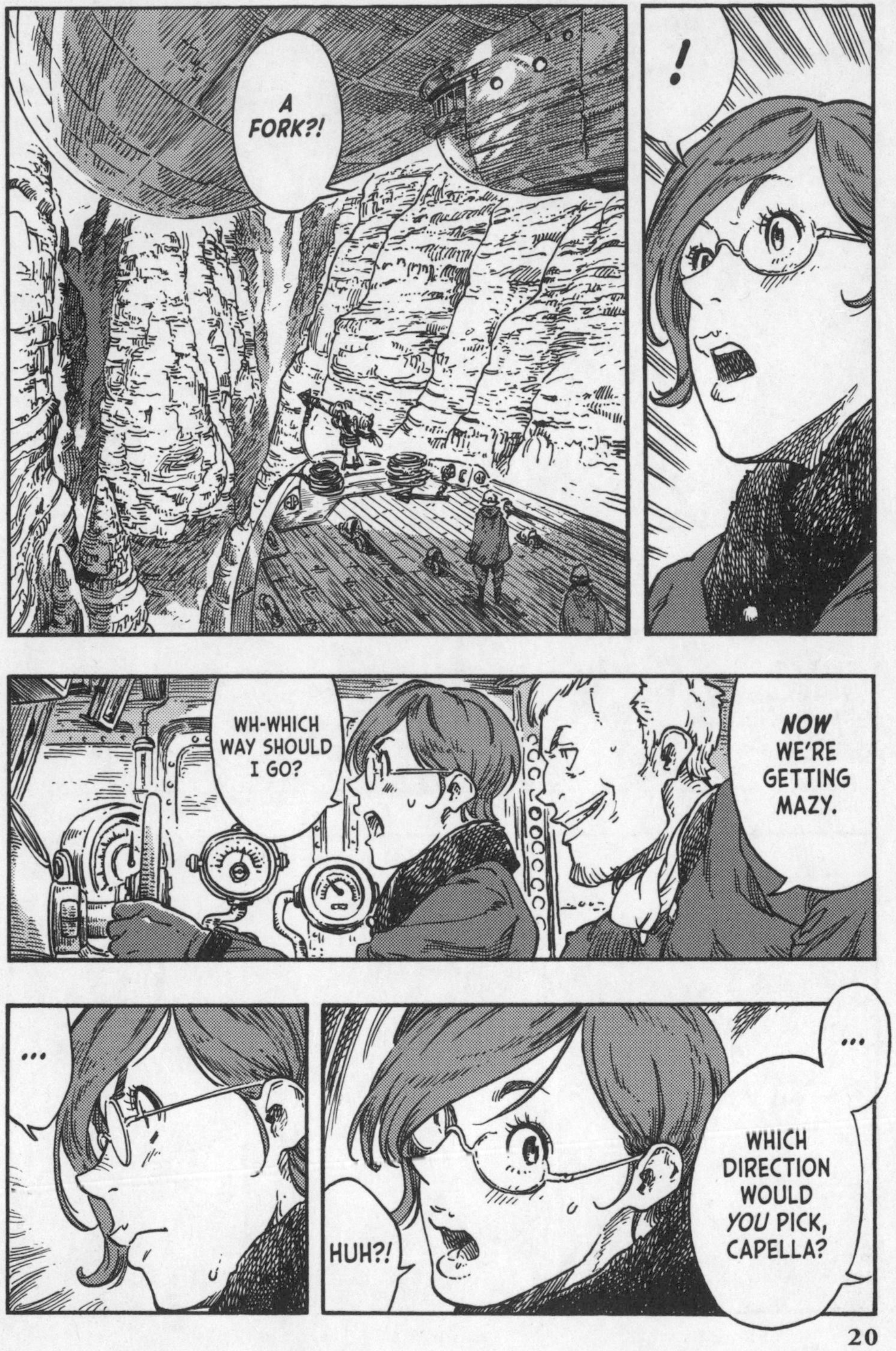
!
A FORK?!
NOW WE'RE GETTING MAZY.
WH-WHICH WAY SHOULD I GO?
...
WHICH DIRECTION WOULD YOU PICK, CAPELLA?
HUH?!
...

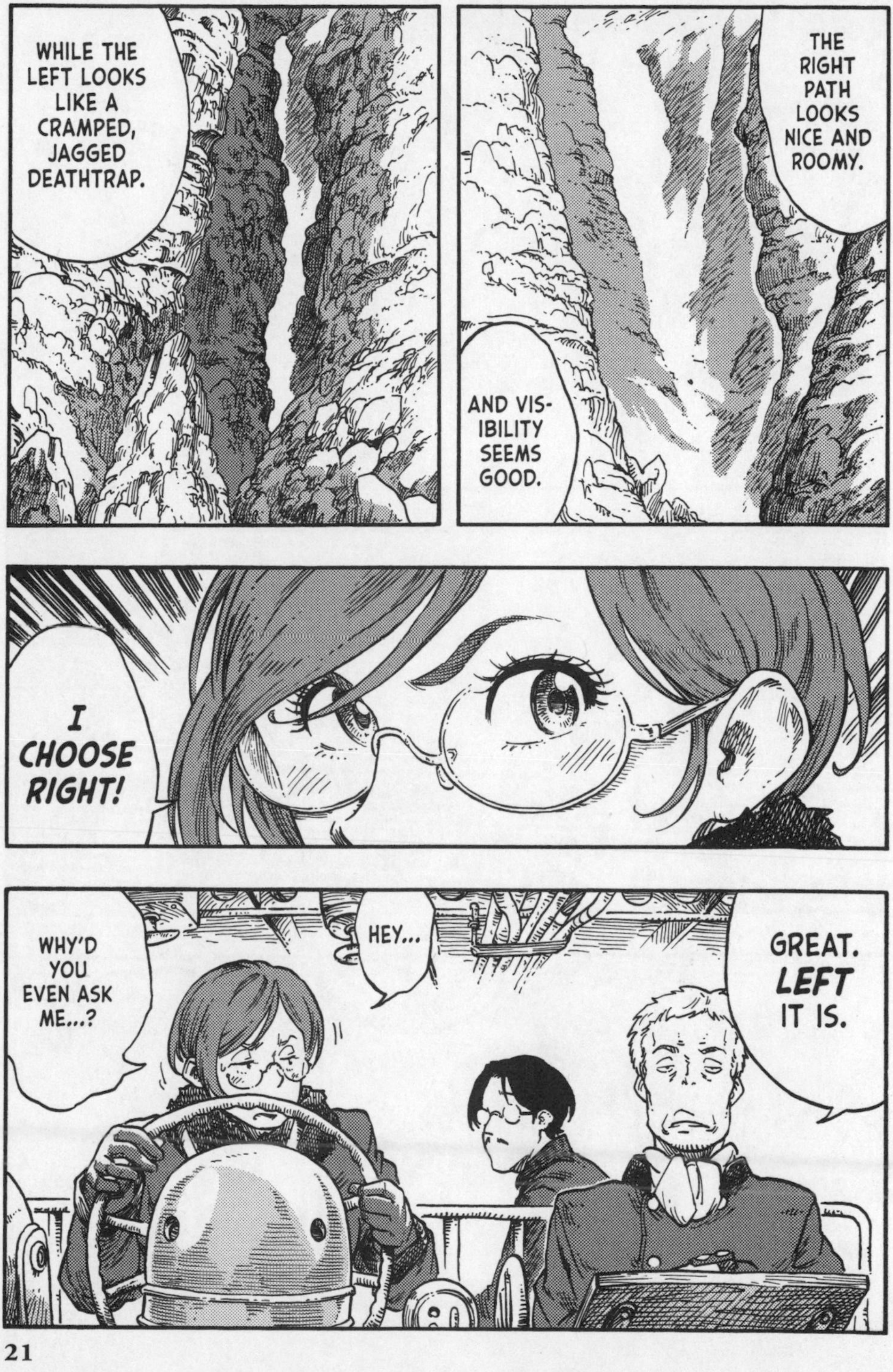
THE RIGHT PATH LOOKS NICE AND ROOMY.
AND VISIBILITY SEEMS GOOD.
WHILE THE LEFT LOOKS LIKE A CRAMPED, JAGGED DEATHTRAP.
I CHOOSE RIGHT!
GREAT. LEFT IT IS.
HEY...
WHY'D YOU EVEN ASK ME...?

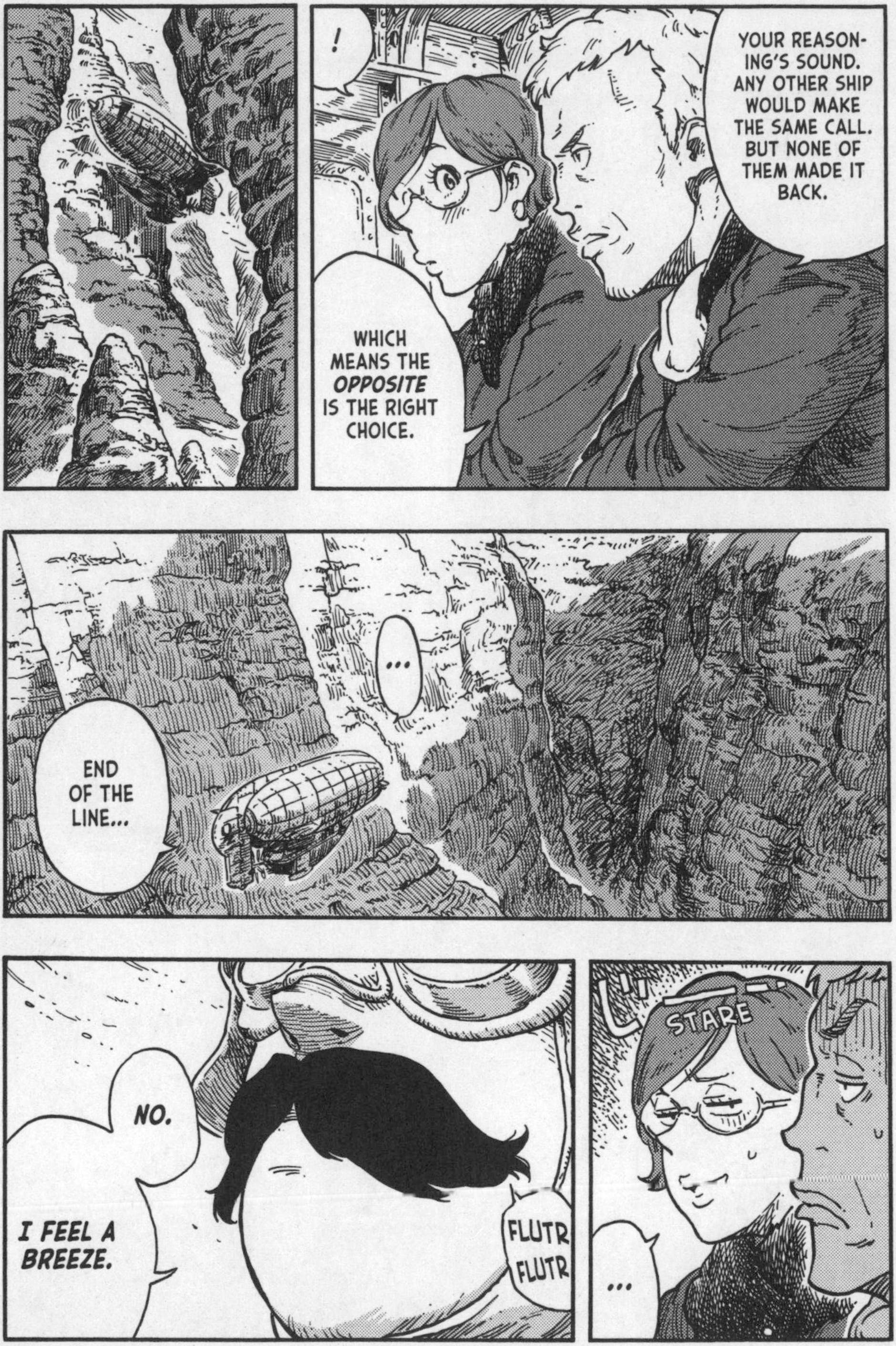
YOUR REASONING'S SOUND. ANY OTHER SHIP WOULD MAKE THE SAME CALL. BUT NONE OF THEM MADE IT BACK.
!
WHICH MEANS THE *OPPOSITE* IS THE RIGHT CHOICE.
...
END OF THE LINE...
STARE
...
NO.
I FEEL A BREEZE.
FLUTR FLUTR

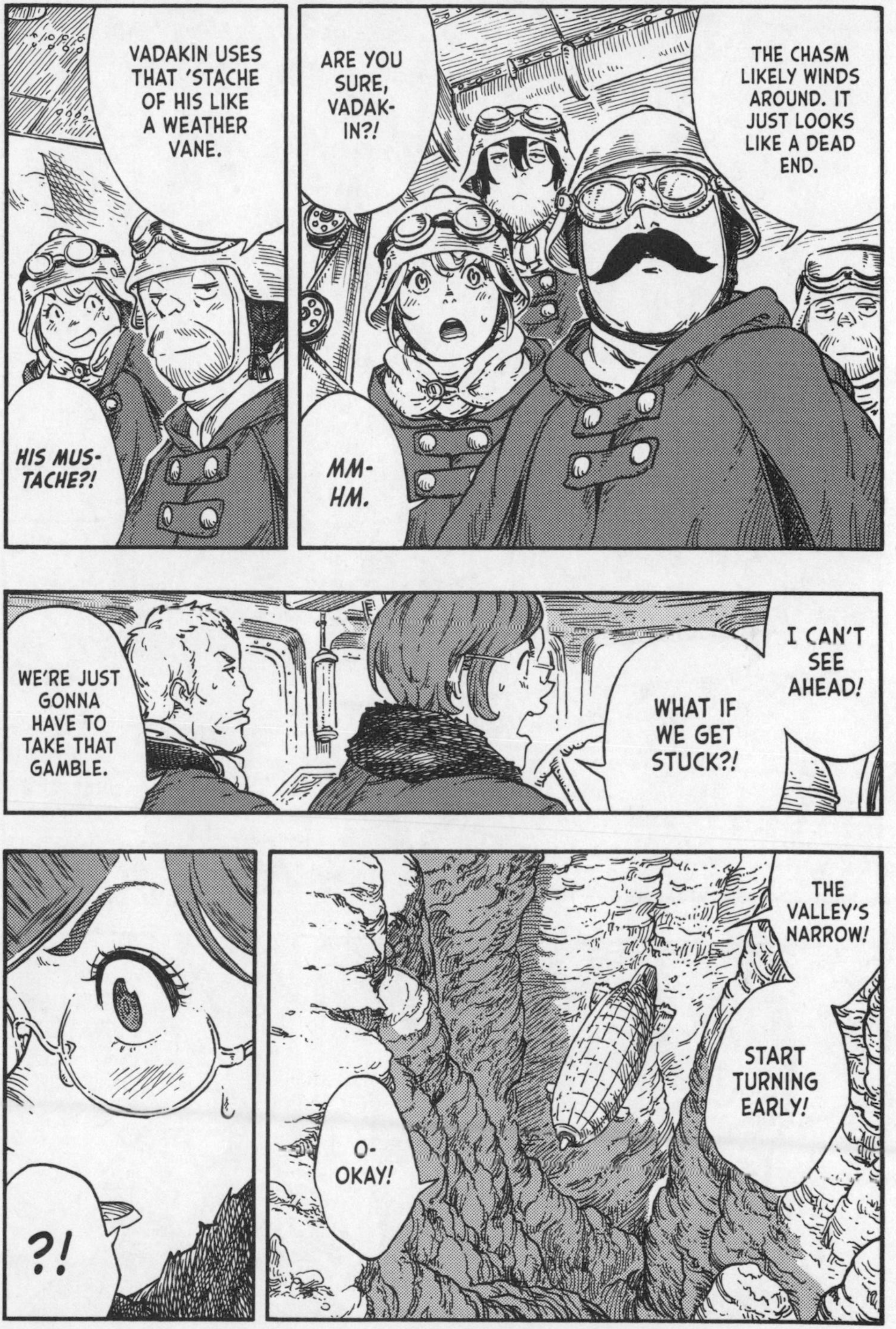
THE CHASM LIKELY WINDS AROUND. IT JUST LOOKS LIKE A DEAD END.
ARE YOU SURE, VADAKIN?!
MM-HM.
VADAKIN USES THAT 'STACHE OF HIS LIKE A WEATHER VANE.
HIS MUSTACHE?!
I CAN'T SEE AHEAD!
WHAT IF WE GET STUCK?!
WE'RE JUST GONNA HAVE TO TAKE THAT GAMBLE.
THE VALLEY'S NARROW!
START TURNING EARLY!
O-OKAY!
?!

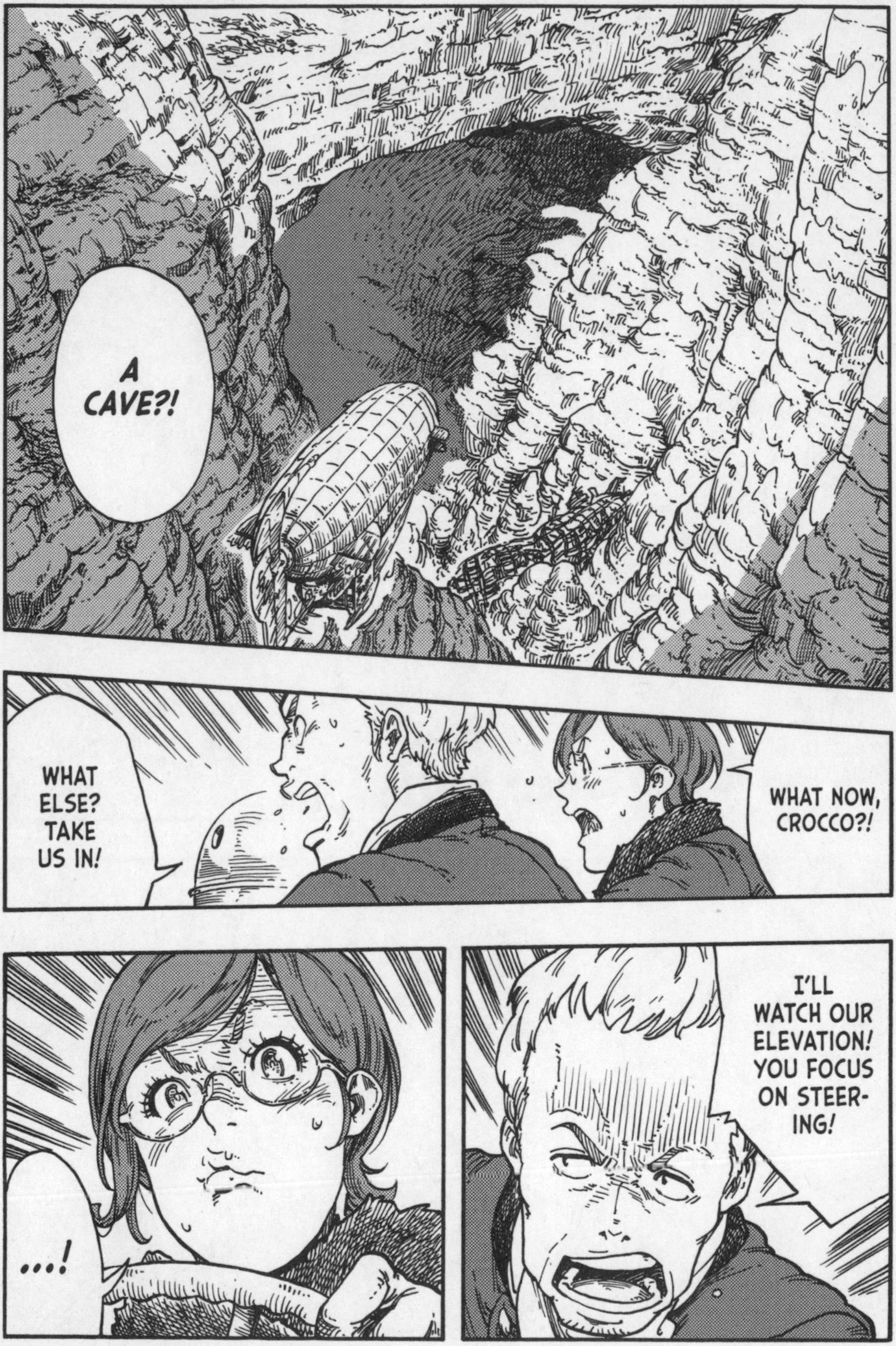
A CAVE?!
WHAT NOW, CROCCO?!
WHAT ELSE? TAKE US IN!
I'LL WATCH OUR ELEVATION! YOU FOCUS ON STEER-ING!
...!

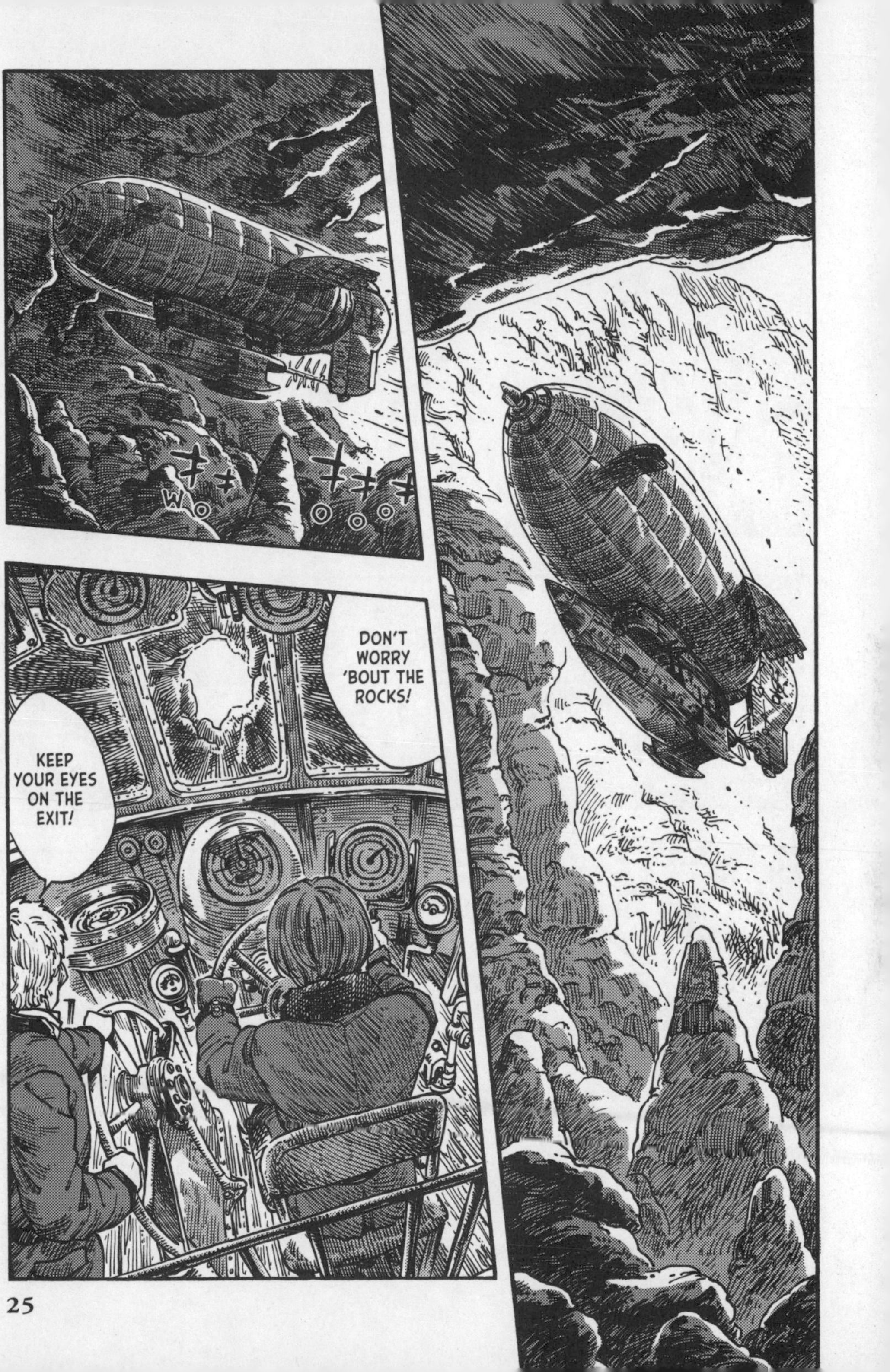
DON'T WORRY 'BOUT THE ROCKS!
KEEP YOUR EYES ON THE EXIT!

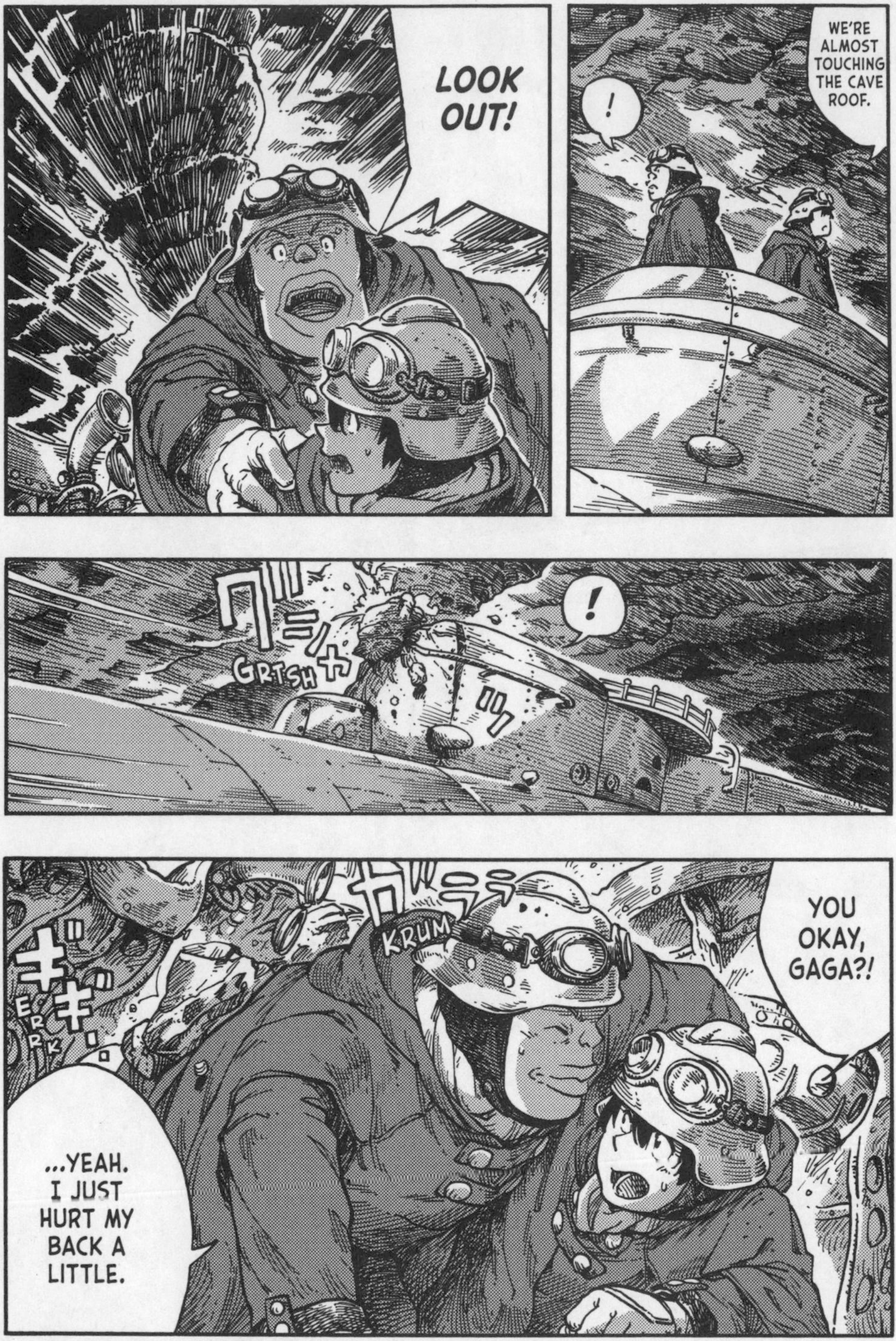
WE'RE ALMOST TOUCHING THE CAVE ROOF.
!
LOOK OUT!
!
GRTSH
YOU OKAY, GAGA?!
KRUM
ERK
...YEAH. I JUST HURT MY BACK A LITTLE.

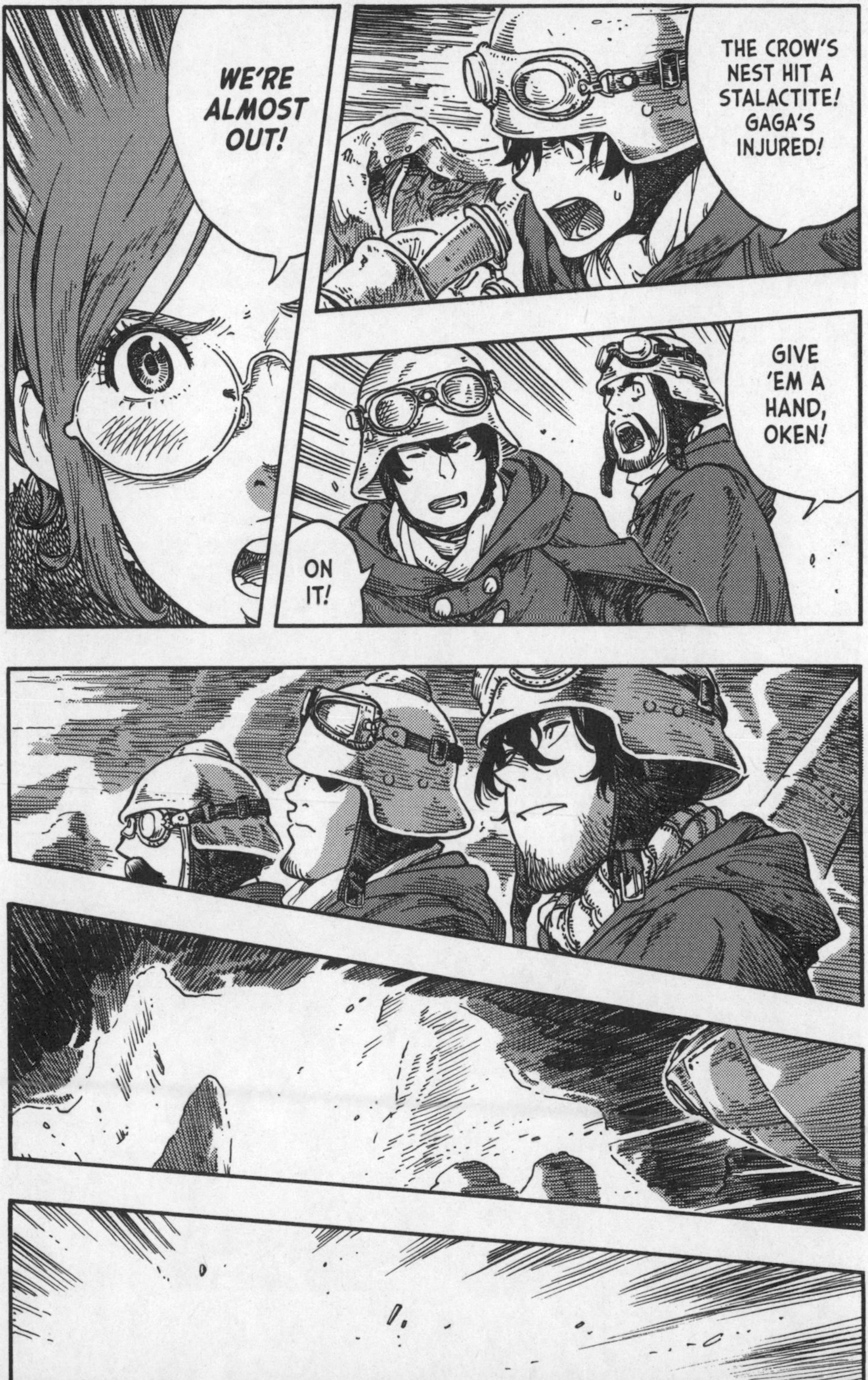
THE CROW'S NEST HIT A STALACTITE! GAGA'S INJURED!
GIVE 'EM A HAND, OKEN!
ON IT!
WE'RE ALMOST OUT!

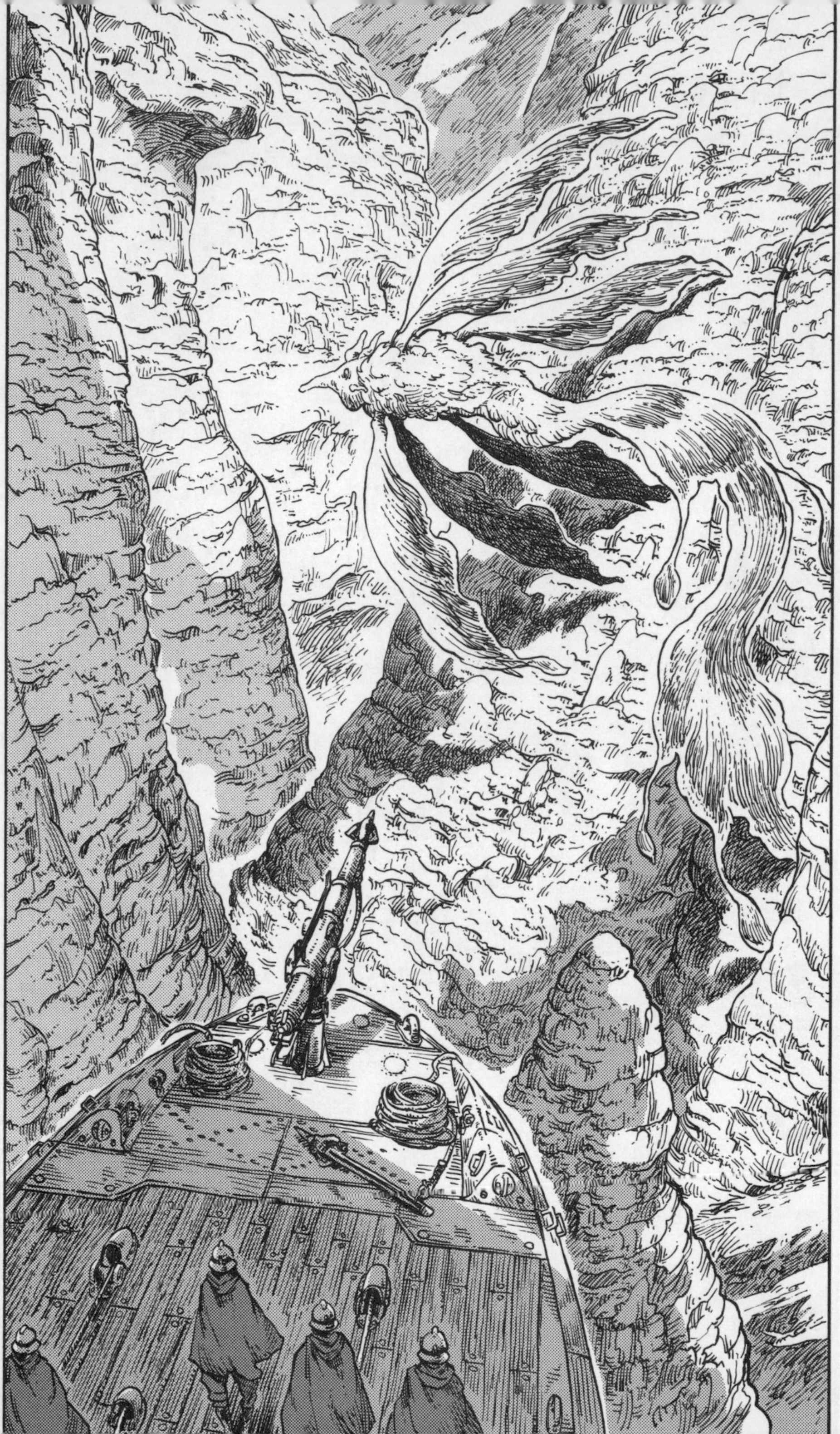

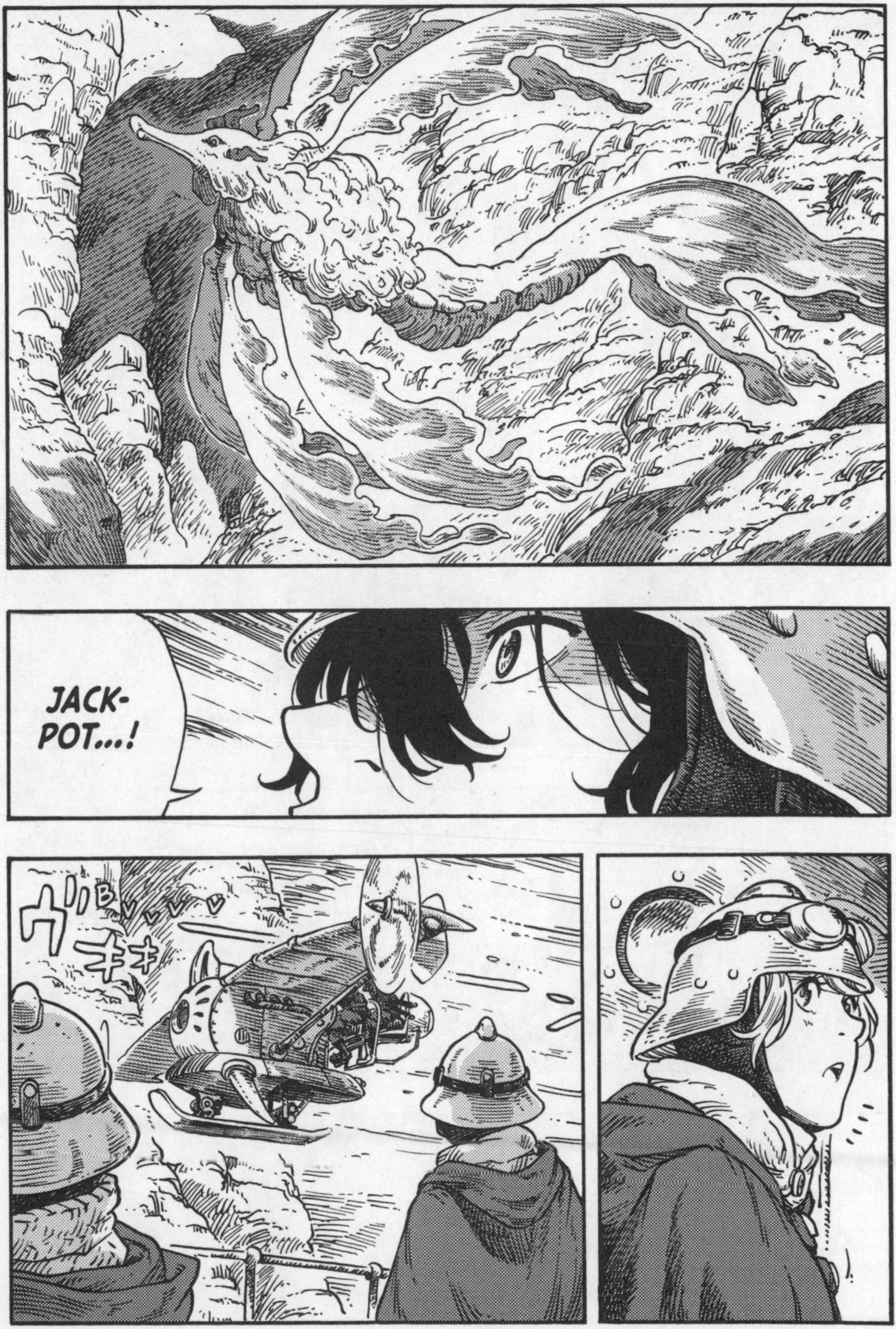
JACK-
POT...!
ヴィキキ
BVVVV

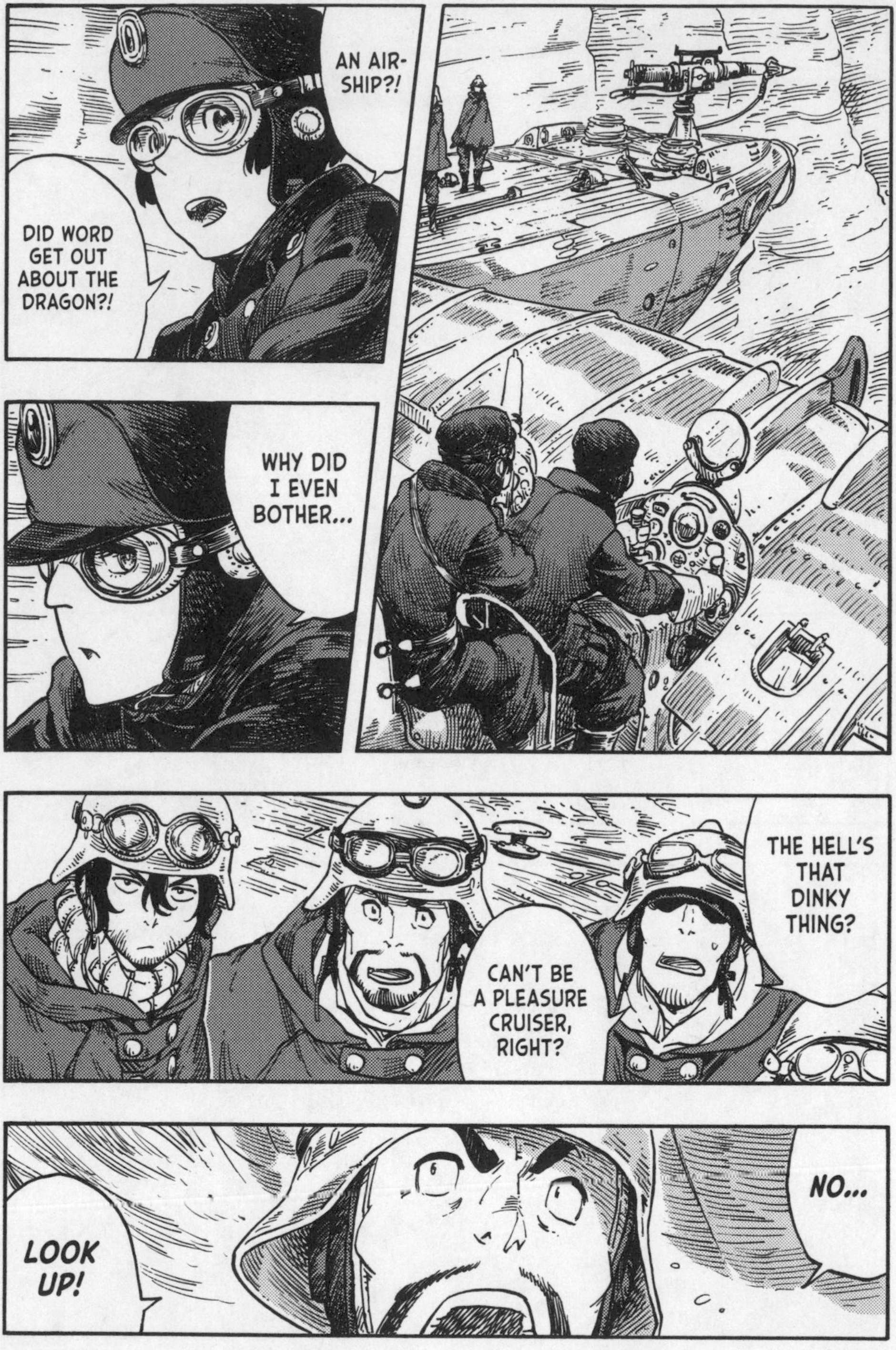
AN AIR-SHIP?!
DID WORD GET OUT ABOUT THE DRAGON?!
WHY DID I EVEN BOTHER...
THE HELL'S THAT DINKY THING?
CAN'T BE A PLEASURE CRUISER, RIGHT?
NO...
LOOK UP!

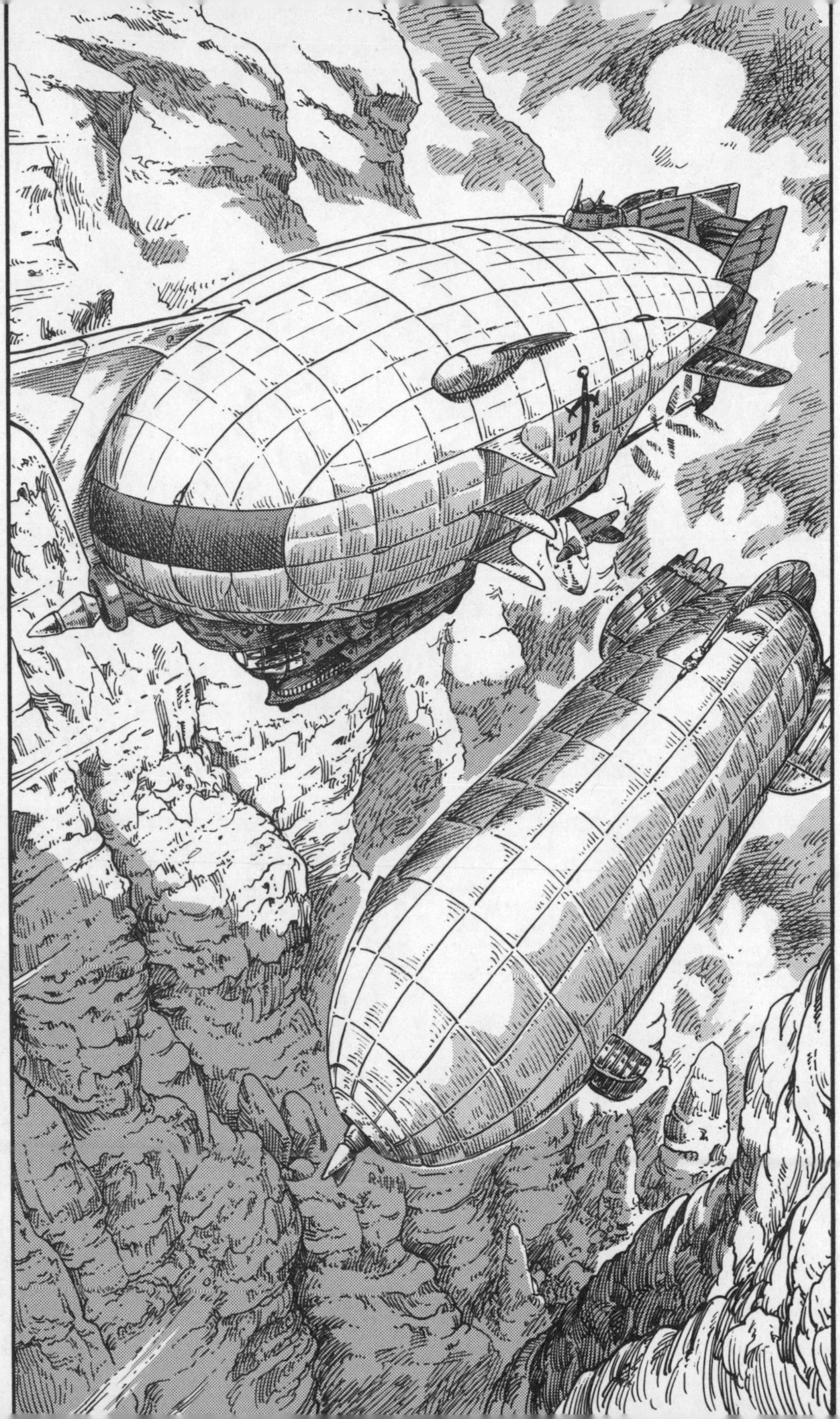

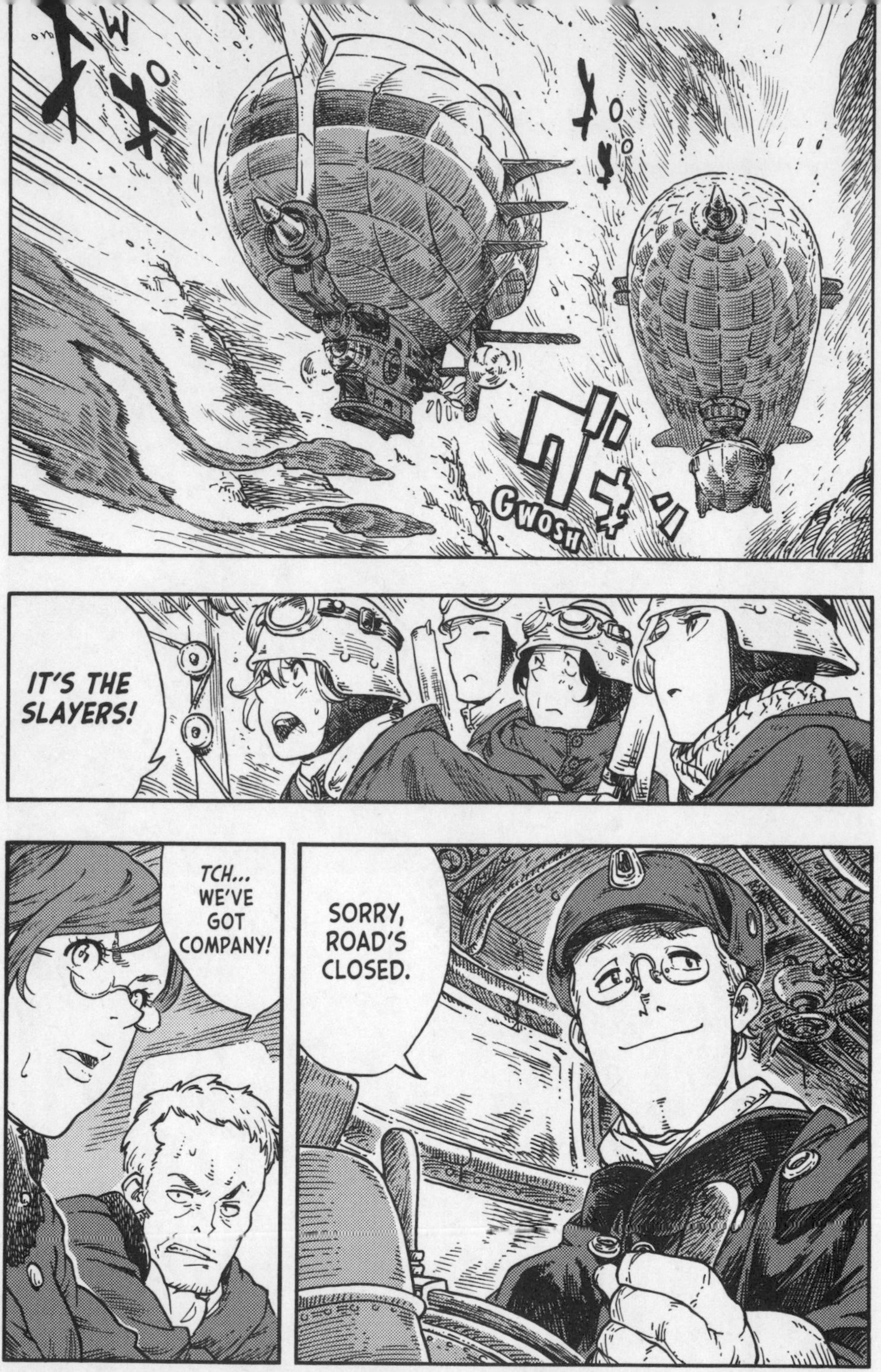
GWOSH
IT'S THE SLAYERS!
SORRY, ROAD'S CLOSED.
TCH... WE'VE GOT COMPANY!

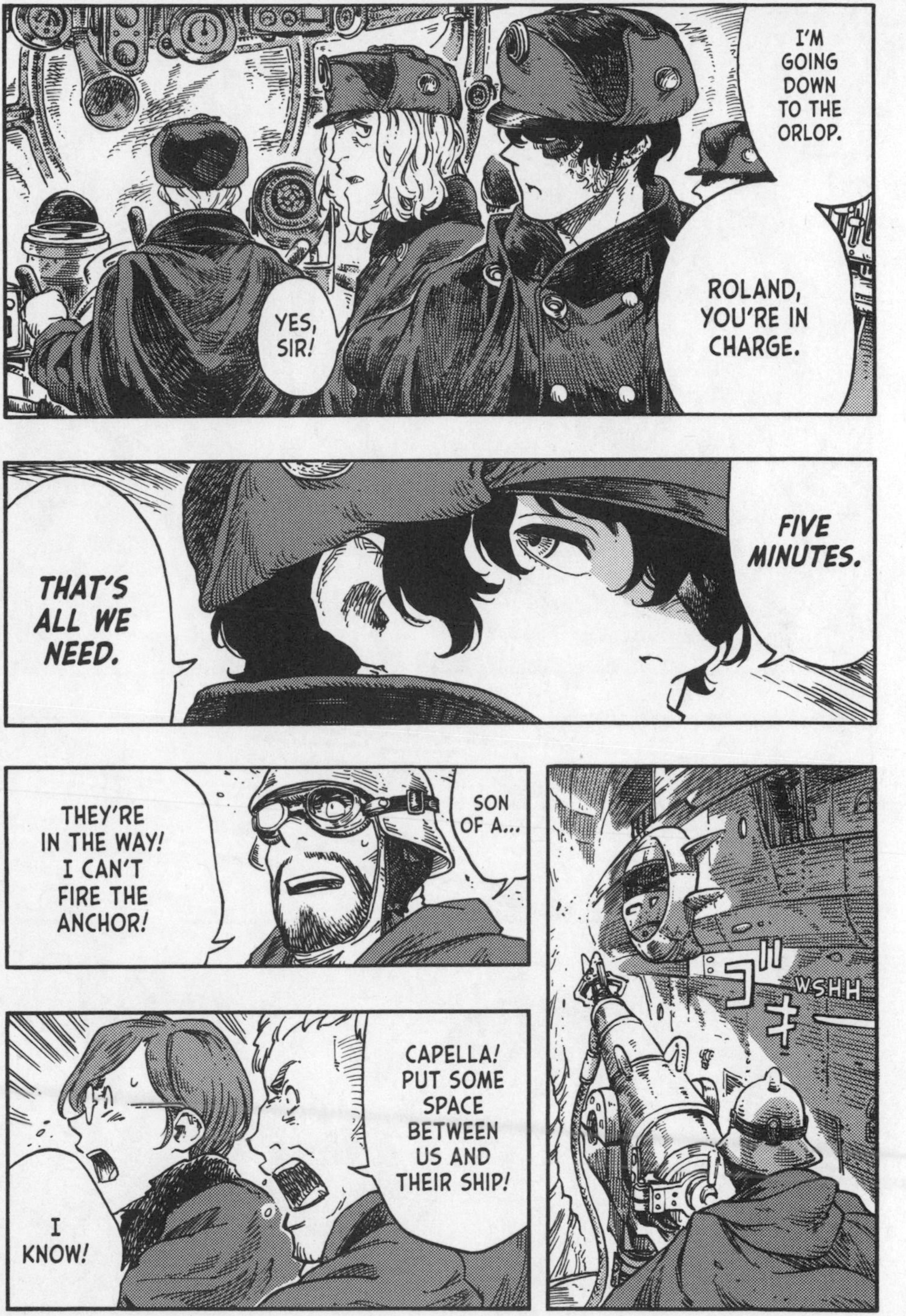
I'M GOING DOWN TO THE ORLOP.
ROLAND, YOU'RE IN CHARGE.
YES, SIR!
FIVE MINUTES.
THAT'S ALL WE NEED.
ゴキー
WSHH
SON OF A...
THEY'RE IN THE WAY! I CAN'T FIRE THE ANCHOR!
CAPELLA! PUT SOME SPACE BETWEEN US AND THEIR SHIP!
I KNOW!

I'M TRYING, BUT...
...THE CHASM'S JUST TOO NARROW!
BOOF
THERE'S THE SIGNAL.
ALL RIGHT.
LET'S GET CRACKING!

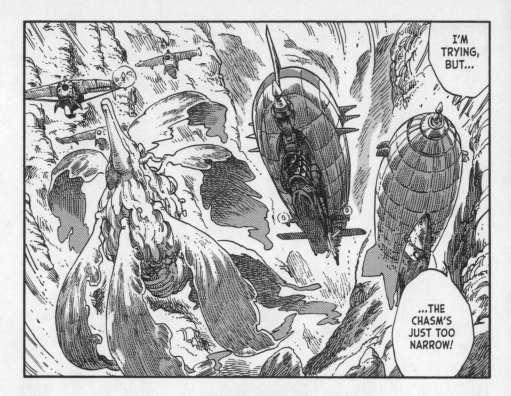

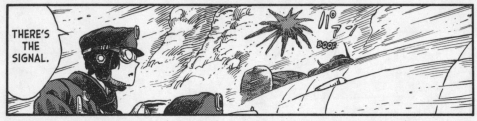

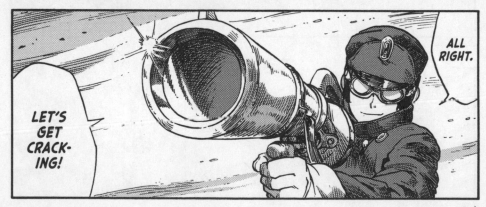

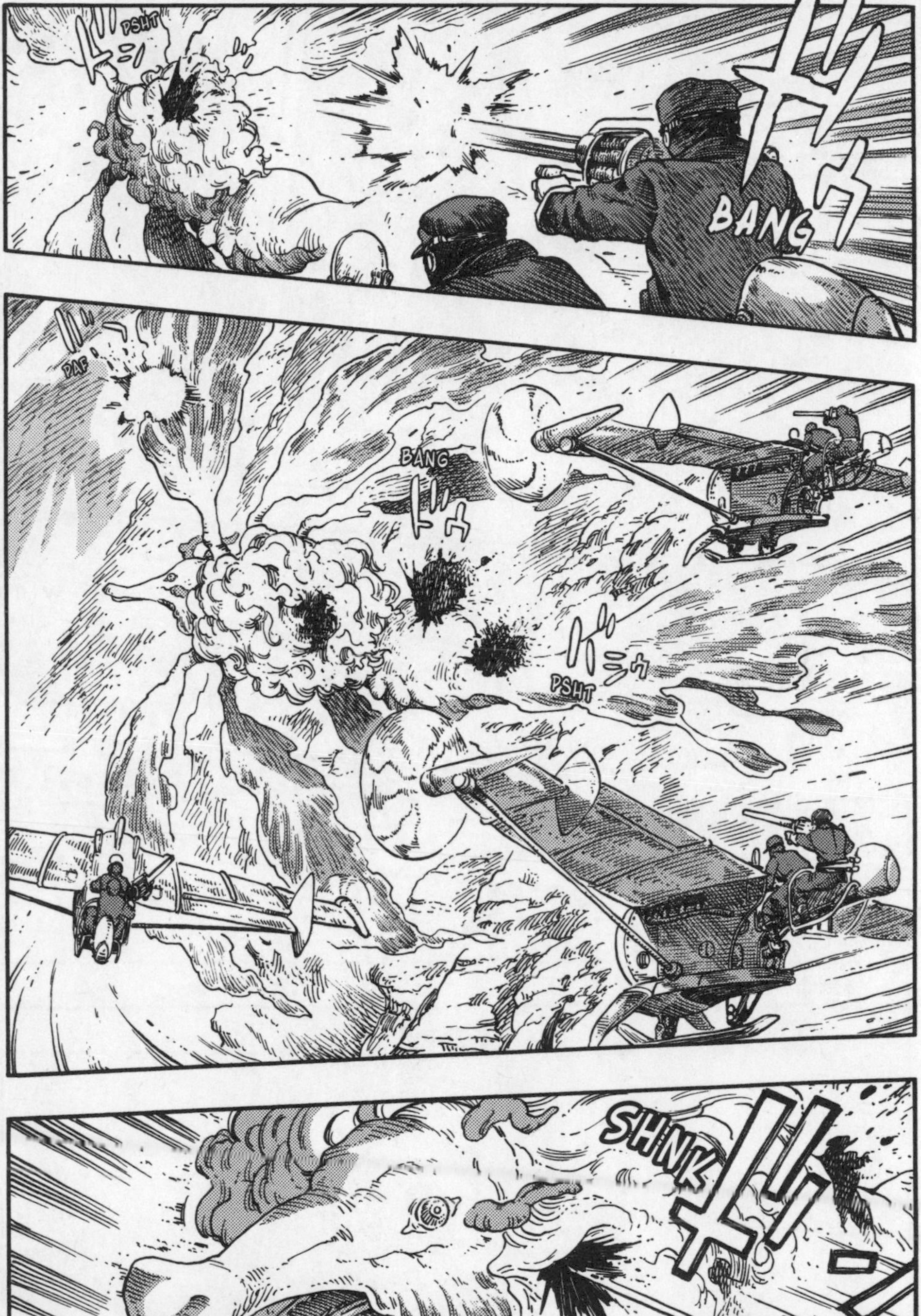
BANG
PSHT
BANG
PSHT
DAF
SHINK

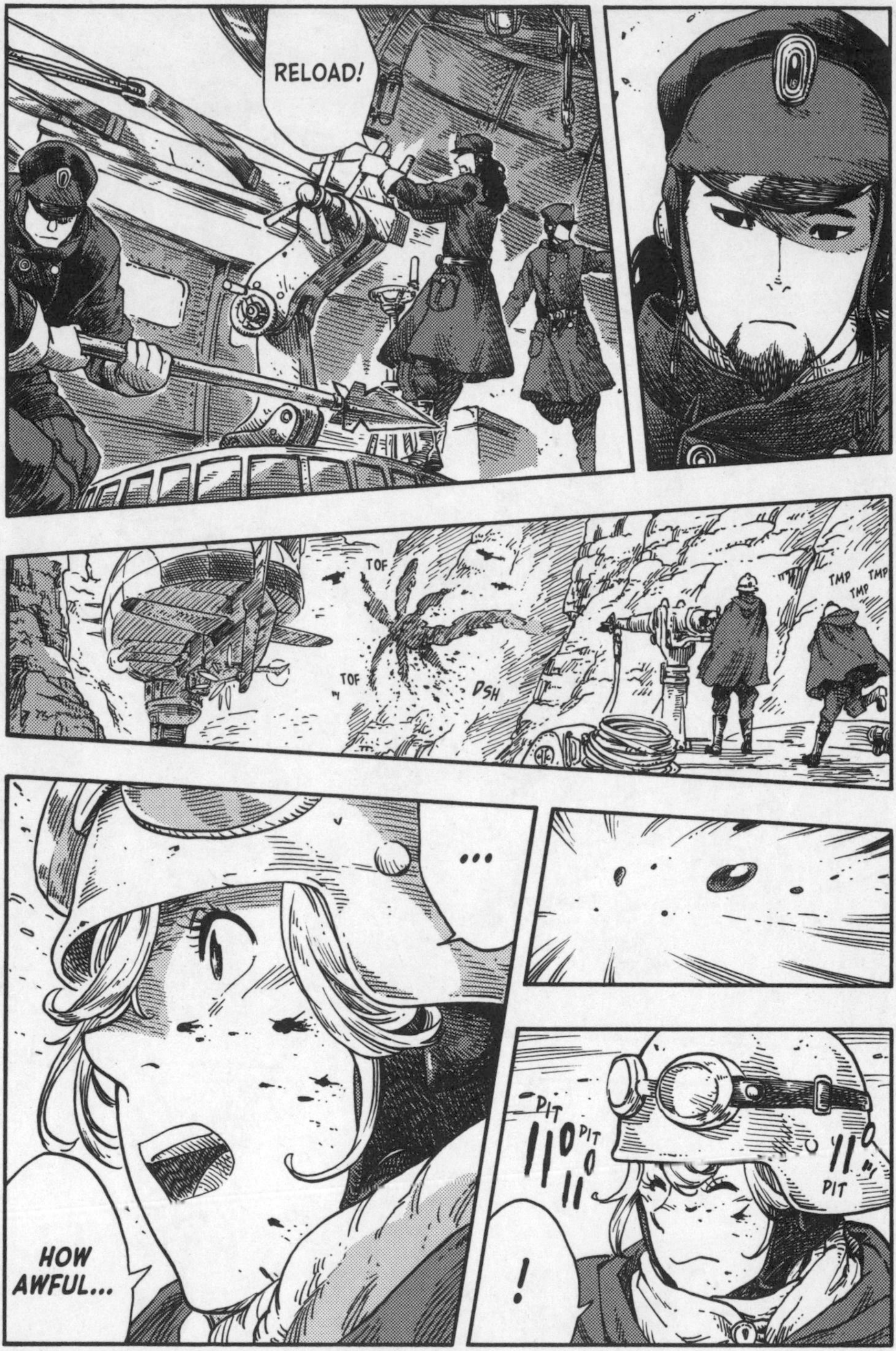
RELOAD!
TOF
TOF
DSH
TMP TMP TMP
PIT PIT PIT
!
...
HOW AWFUL...

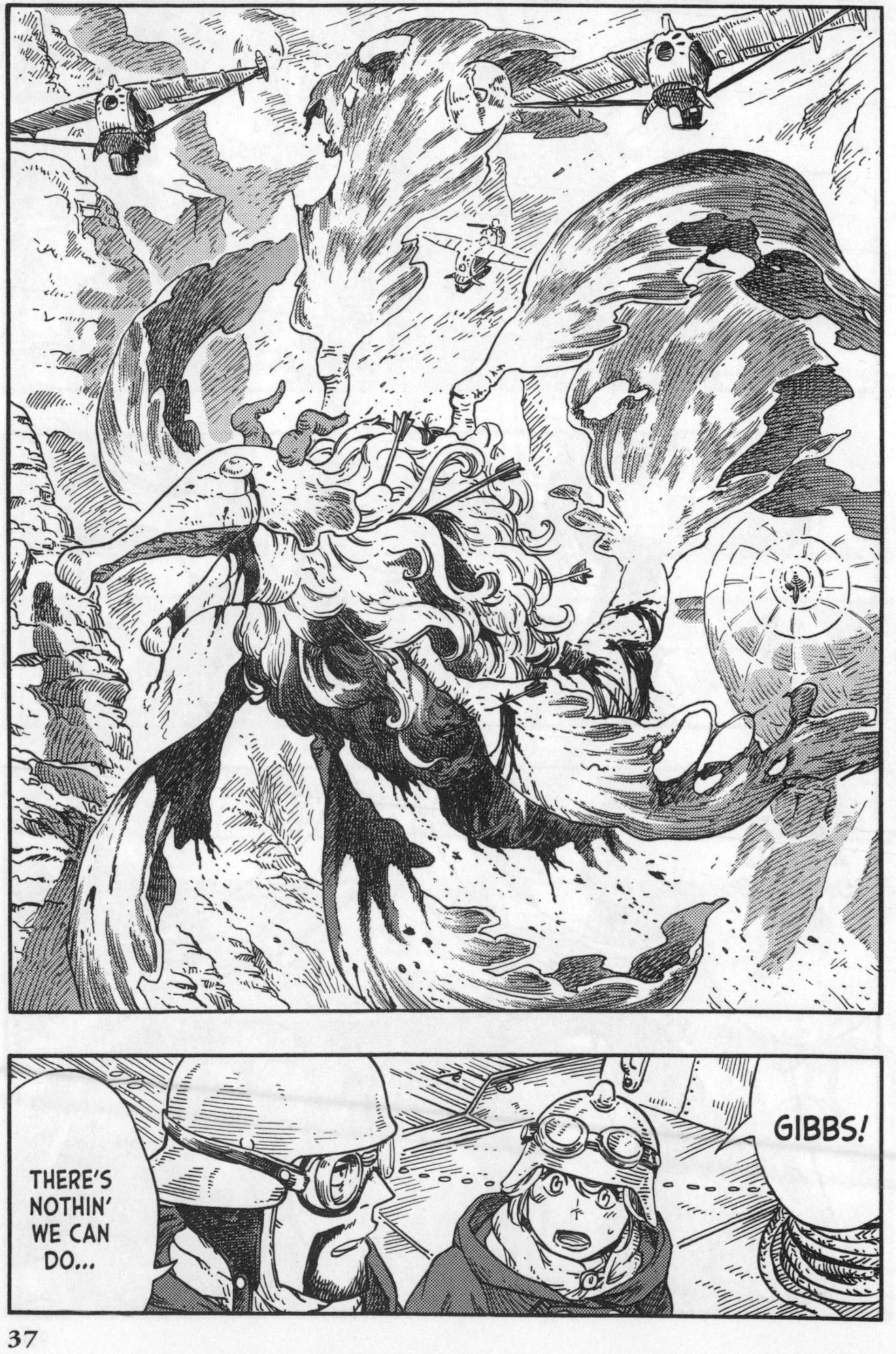
GIBBS!
THERE'S NOTHIN' WE CAN DO...

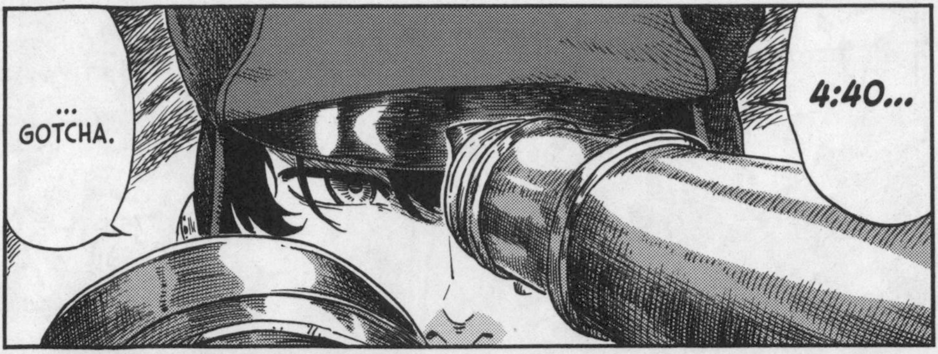
4:40...
... GOTCHA.

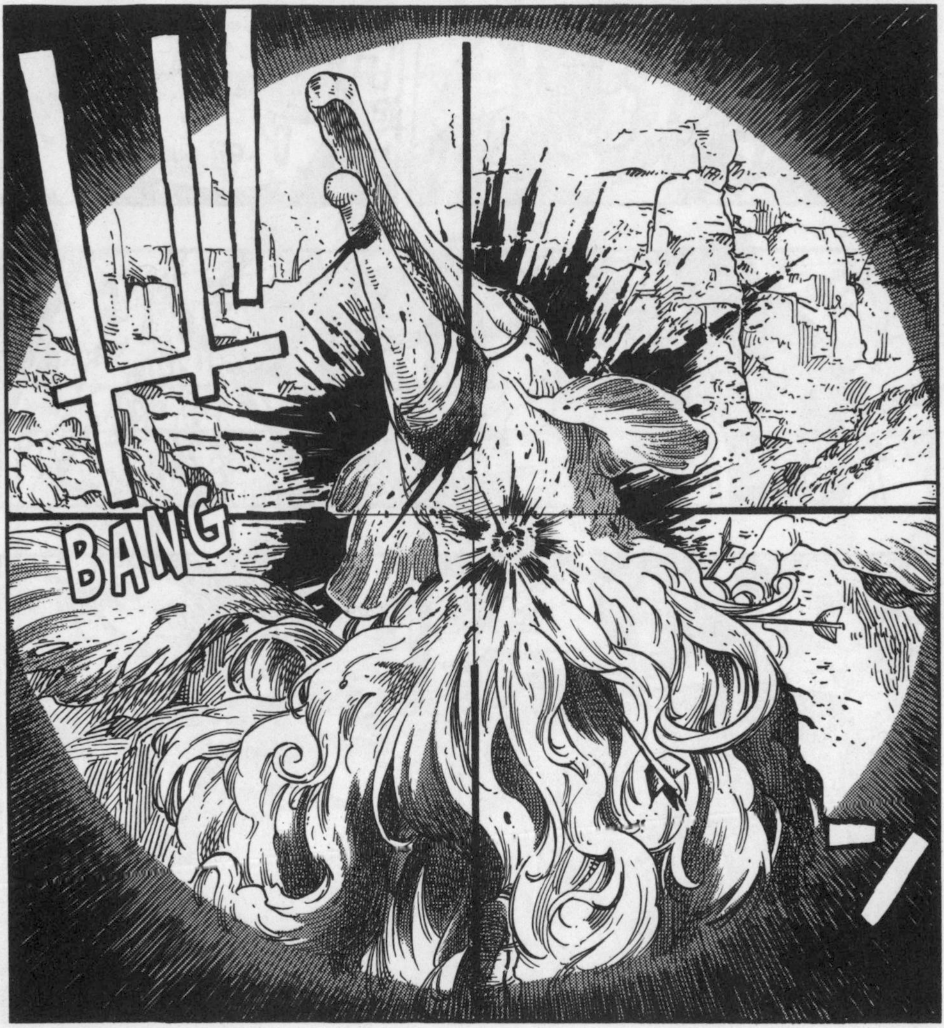
BANG

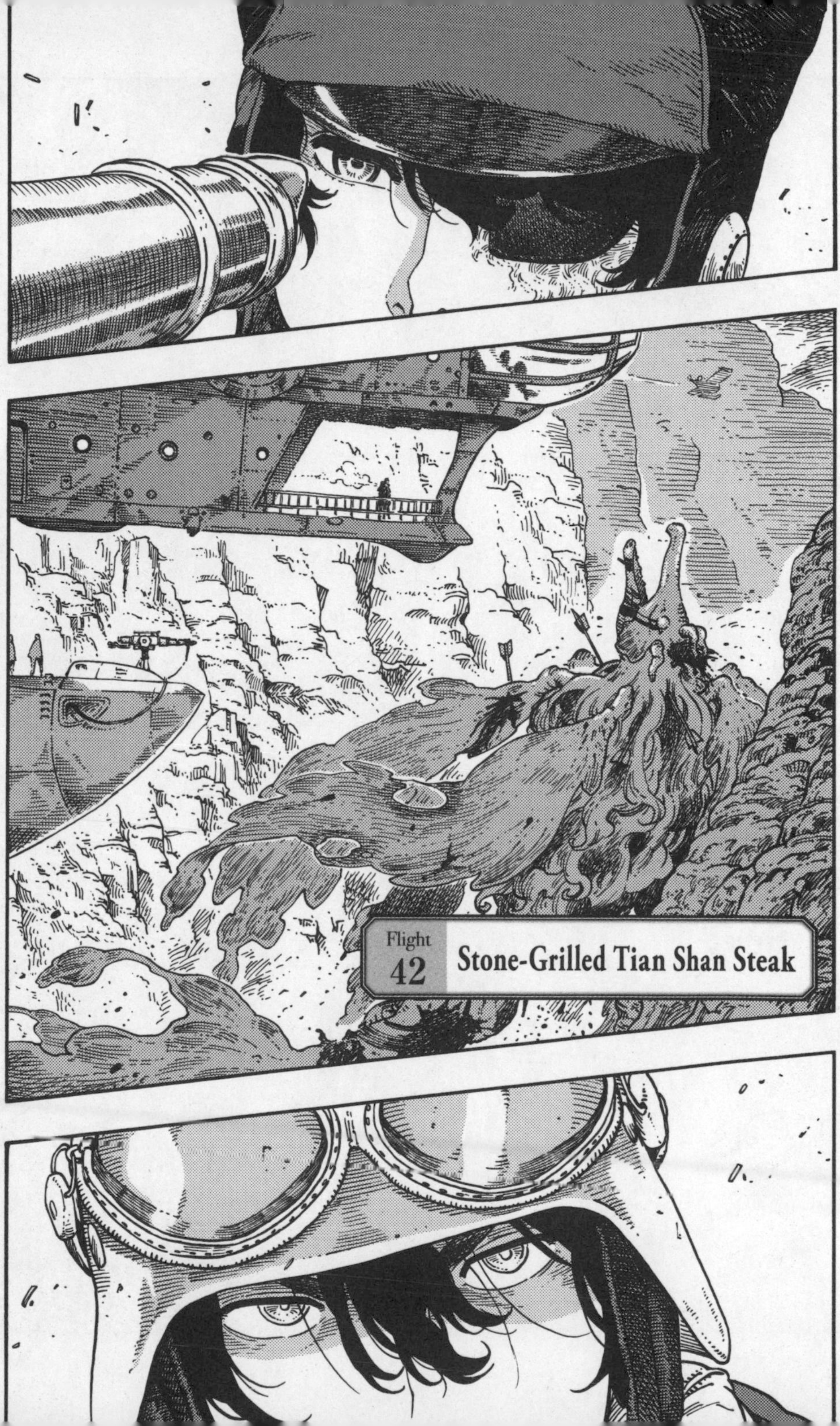
Flight 42
Stone-Grilled Tian Shan Steak

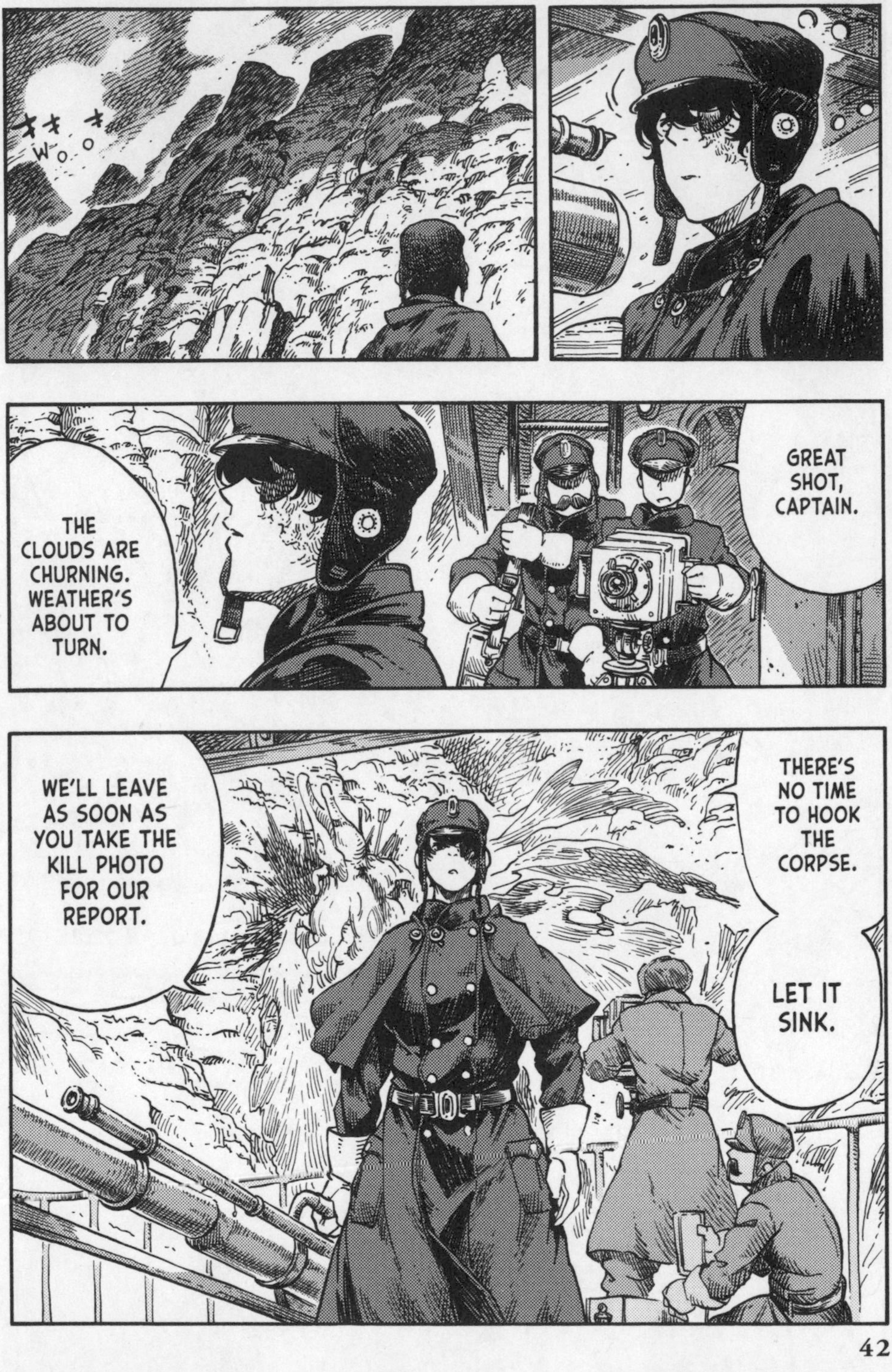
WOO
GREAT SHOT, CAPTAIN.
THE CLOUDS ARE CHURNING. WEATHER'S ABOUT TO TURN.
THERE'S NO TIME TO HOOK THE CORPSE.
LET IT SINK.
WE'LL LEAVE AS SOON AS YOU TAKE THE KILL PHOTO FOR OUR REPORT.

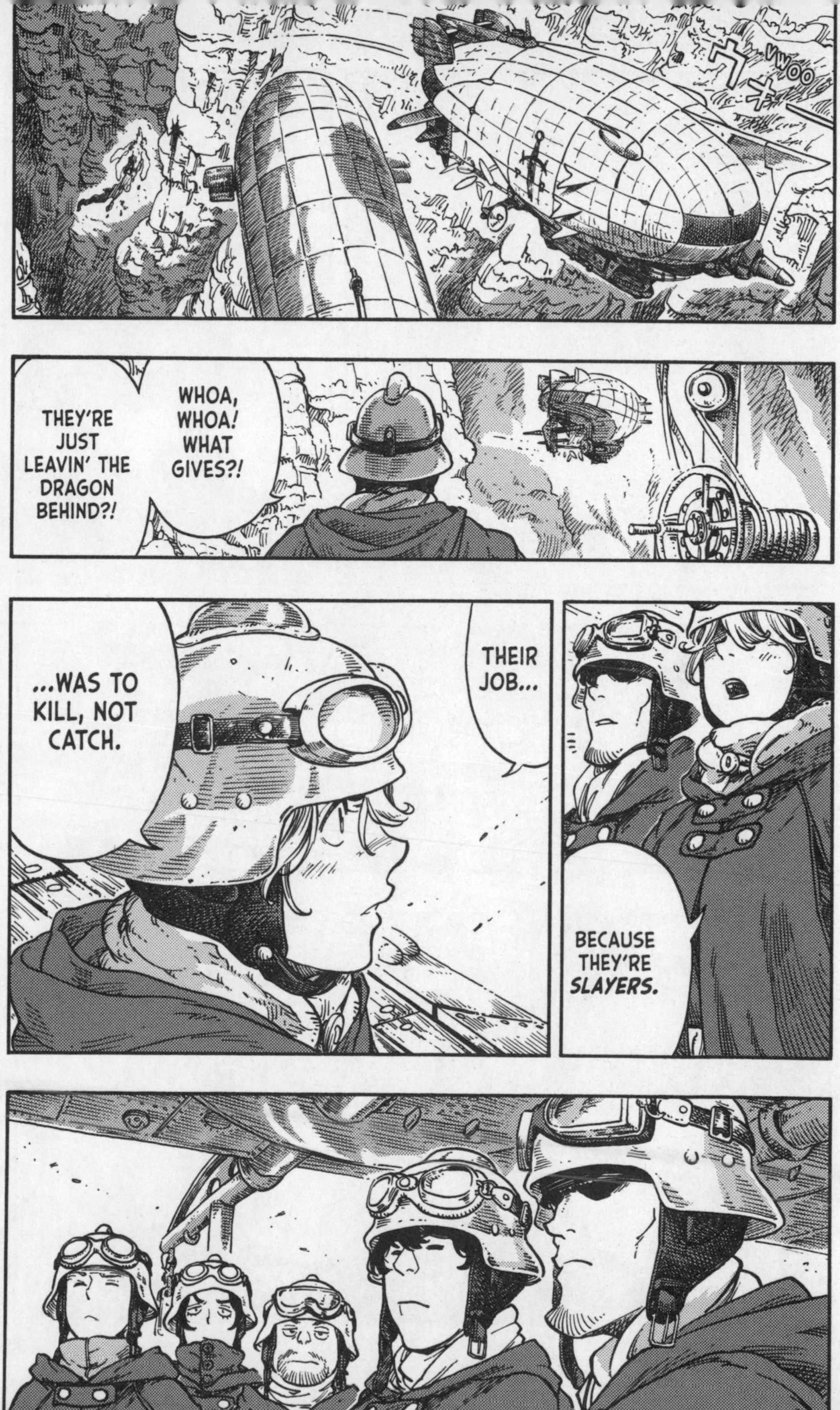
VWOO
WHOA, WHOA! WHAT GIVES?!
THEY'RE JUST LEAVIN' THE DRAGON BEHIND?!
BECAUSE THEY'RE *SLAYERS.*
THEIR JOB...
...WAS TO KILL, NOT CATCH.

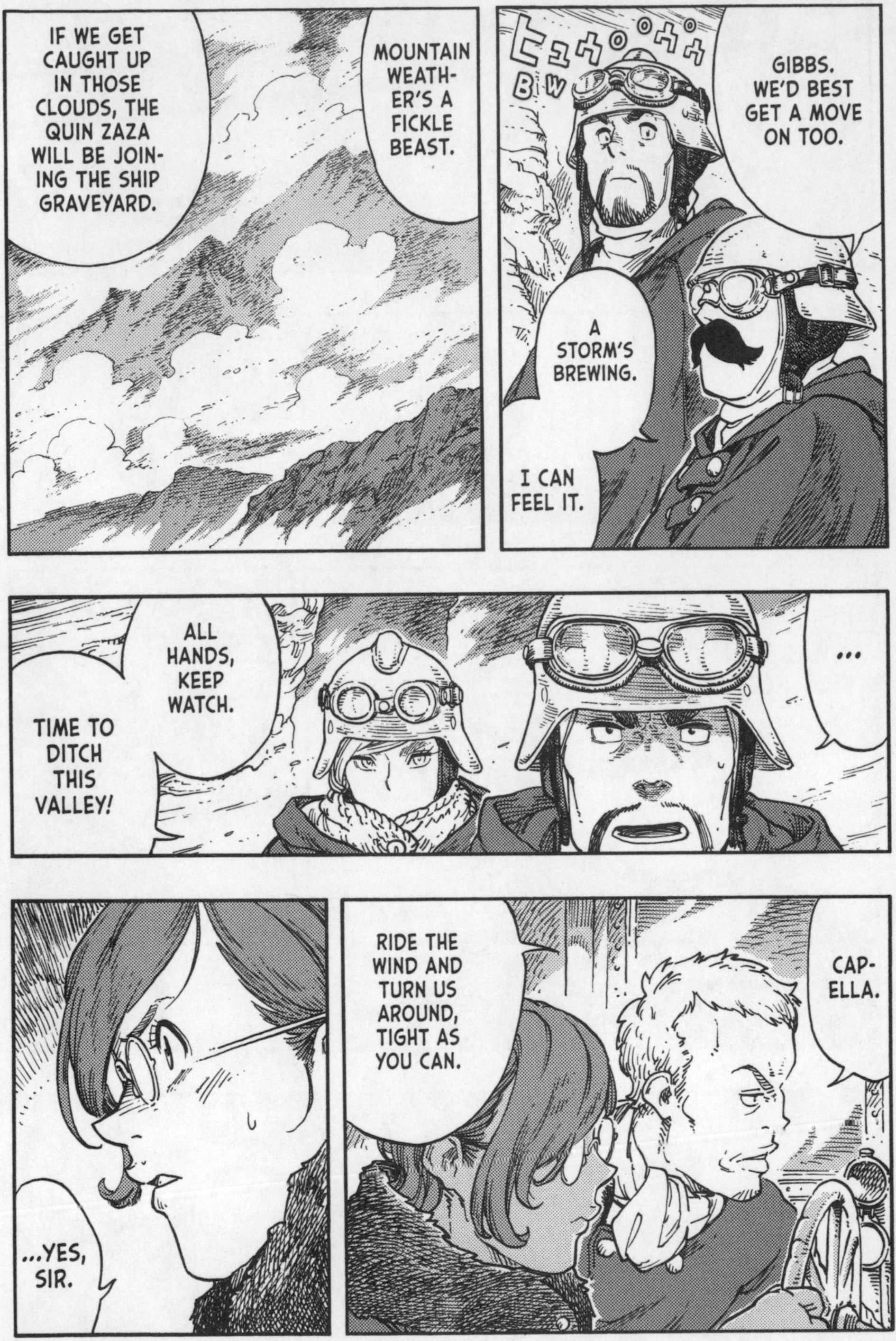
BW
GIBBS. WE'D BEST GET A MOVE ON TOO.
A STORM'S BREWING.
I CAN FEEL IT.
MOUNTAIN WEATHER'S A FICKLE BEAST.
IF WE GET CAUGHT UP IN THOSE CLOUDS, THE QUIN ZAZA WILL BE JOINING THE SHIP GRAVEYARD.
...
ALL HANDS, KEEP WATCH.
TIME TO DITCH THIS VALLEY!
CAPELLA.
RIDE THE WIND AND TURN US AROUND, TIGHT AS YOU CAN.
...YES, SIR.

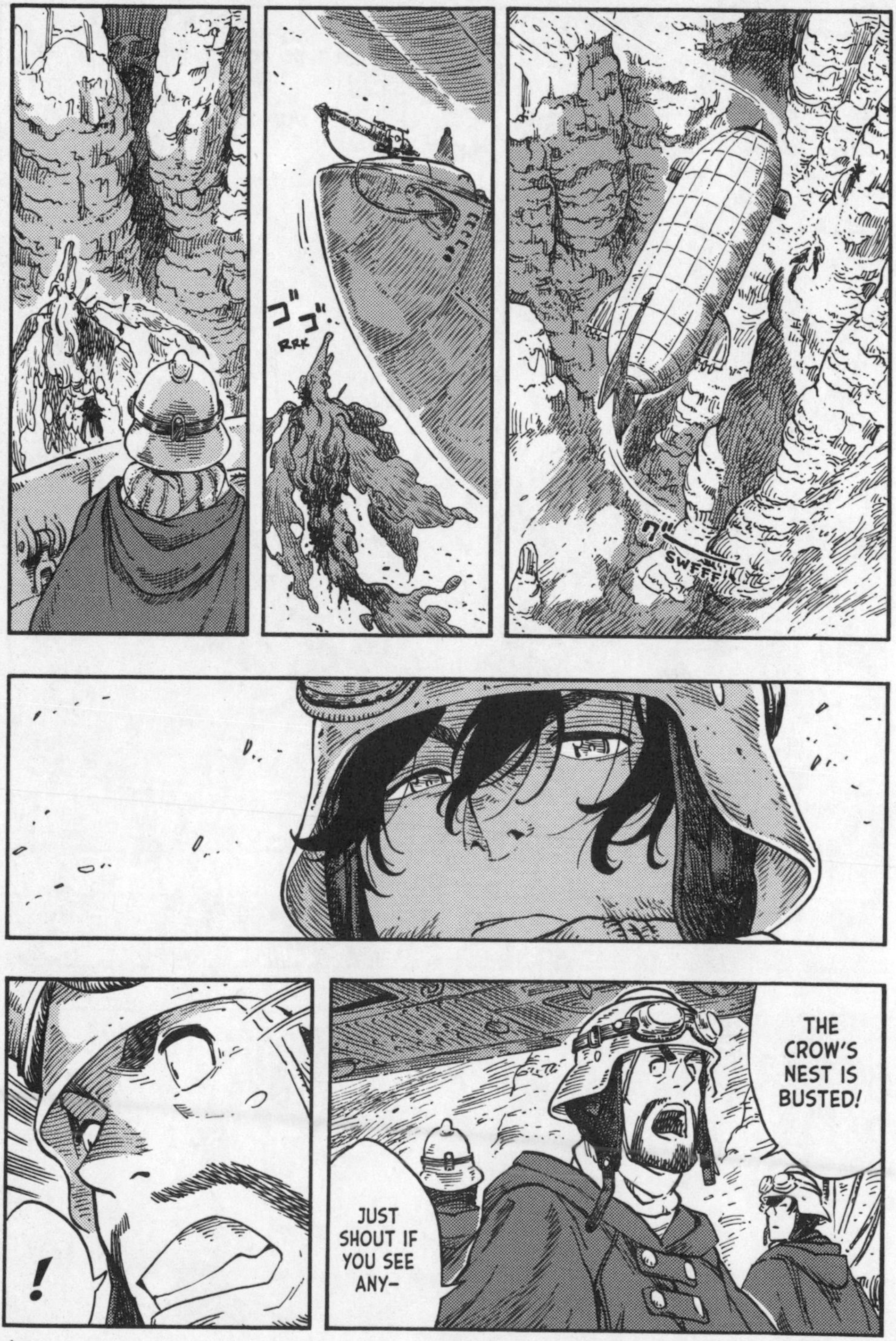
ヷ
SWFFF
ゴゴ
RRK
THE CROW'S NEST IS BUSTED!
JUST SHOUT IF YOU SEE ANY–
!

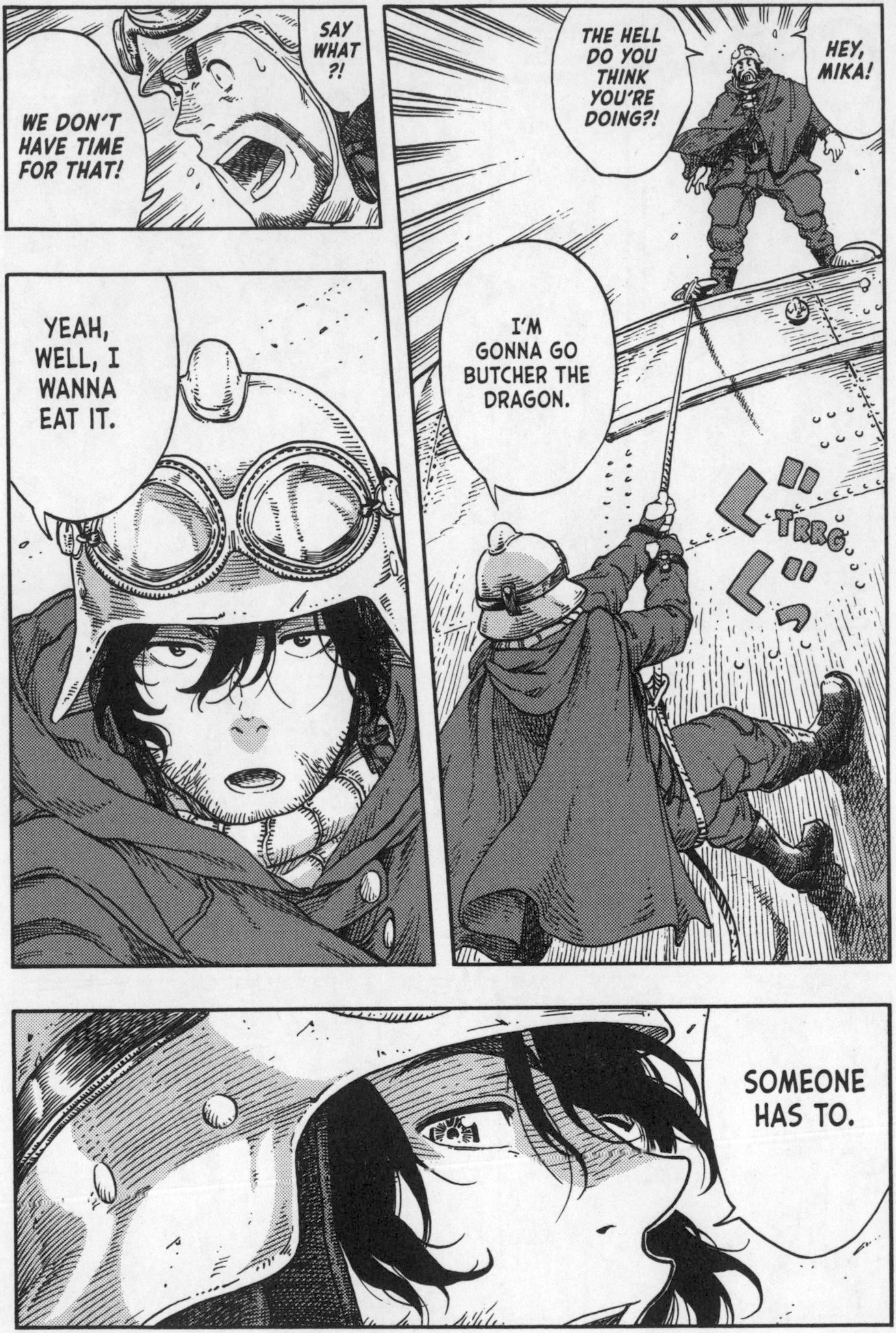
HEY, MIKA!
THE HELL DO YOU THINK YOU'RE DOING?!
I'M GONNA GO BUTCHER THE DRAGON.
TRRG
SAY WHAT?!
WE DON'T HAVE TIME FOR THAT!
YEAH, WELL, I WANNA EAT IT.
SOMEONE HAS TO.

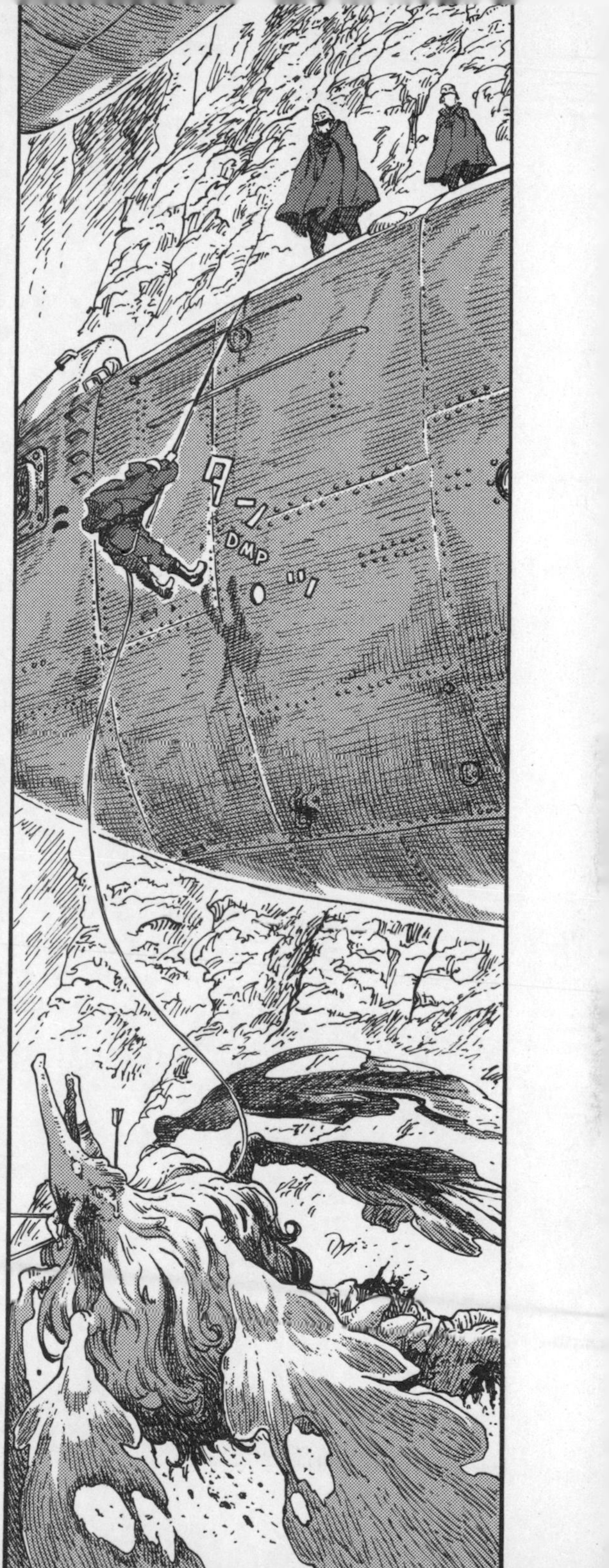
DMP

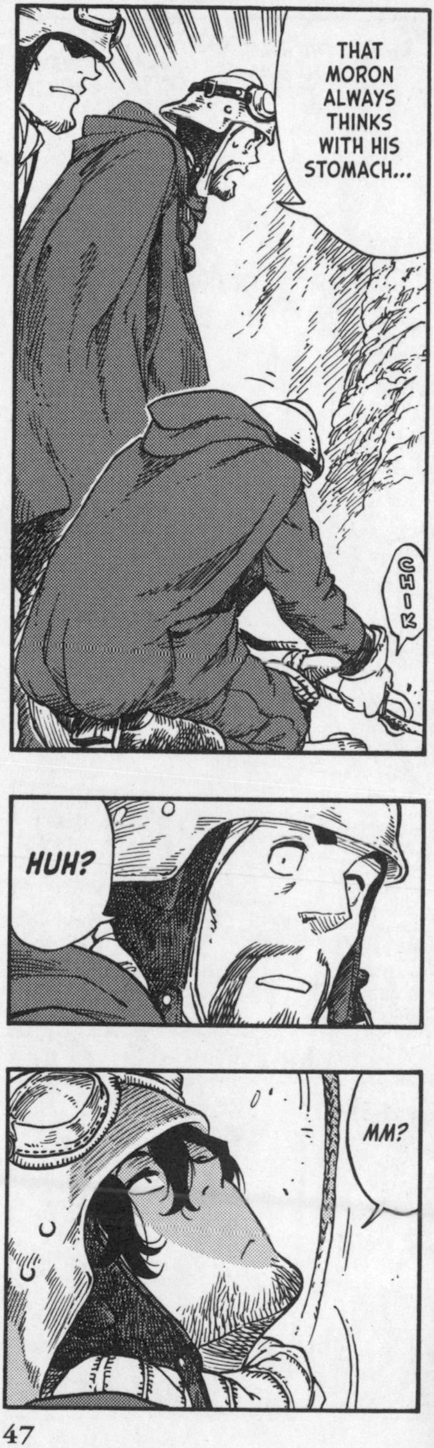
THAT MORON ALWAYS THINKS WITH HIS STOMACH...
CHIK
HUH?
MM?

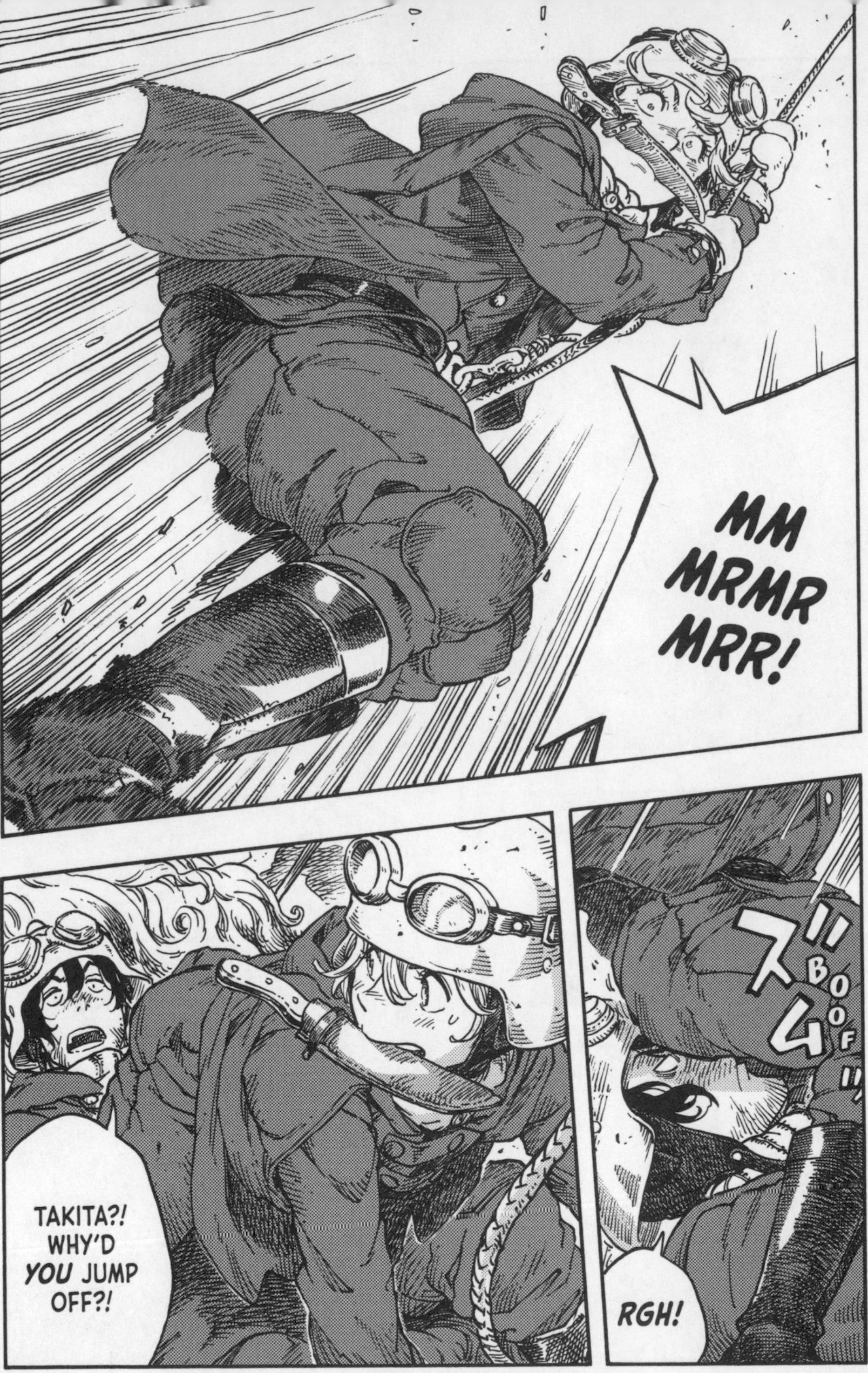
MM MRMR MRR!
ズム
BOOF
RGH!
TAKITA?! WHY'D *YOU* JUMP OFF?!

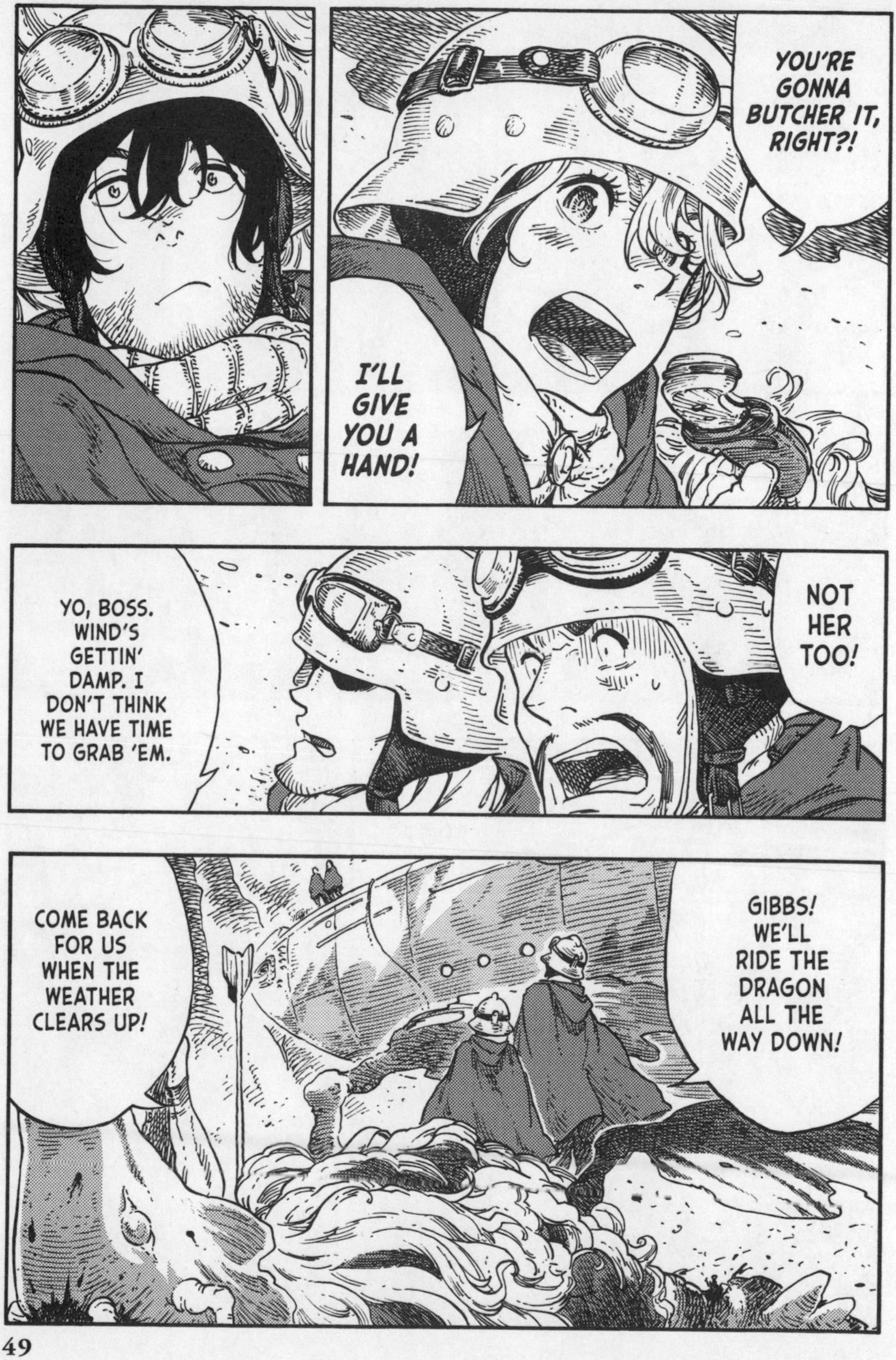
YOU'RE GONNA BUTCHER IT, RIGHT?!
I'LL GIVE YOU A HAND!
NOT HER TOO!
YO, BOSS. WIND'S GETTIN' DAMP. I DON'T THINK WE HAVE TIME TO GRAB 'EM.
GIBBS! WE'LL RIDE THE DRAGON ALL THE WAY DOWN!
COME BACK FOR US WHEN THE WEATHER CLEARS UP!

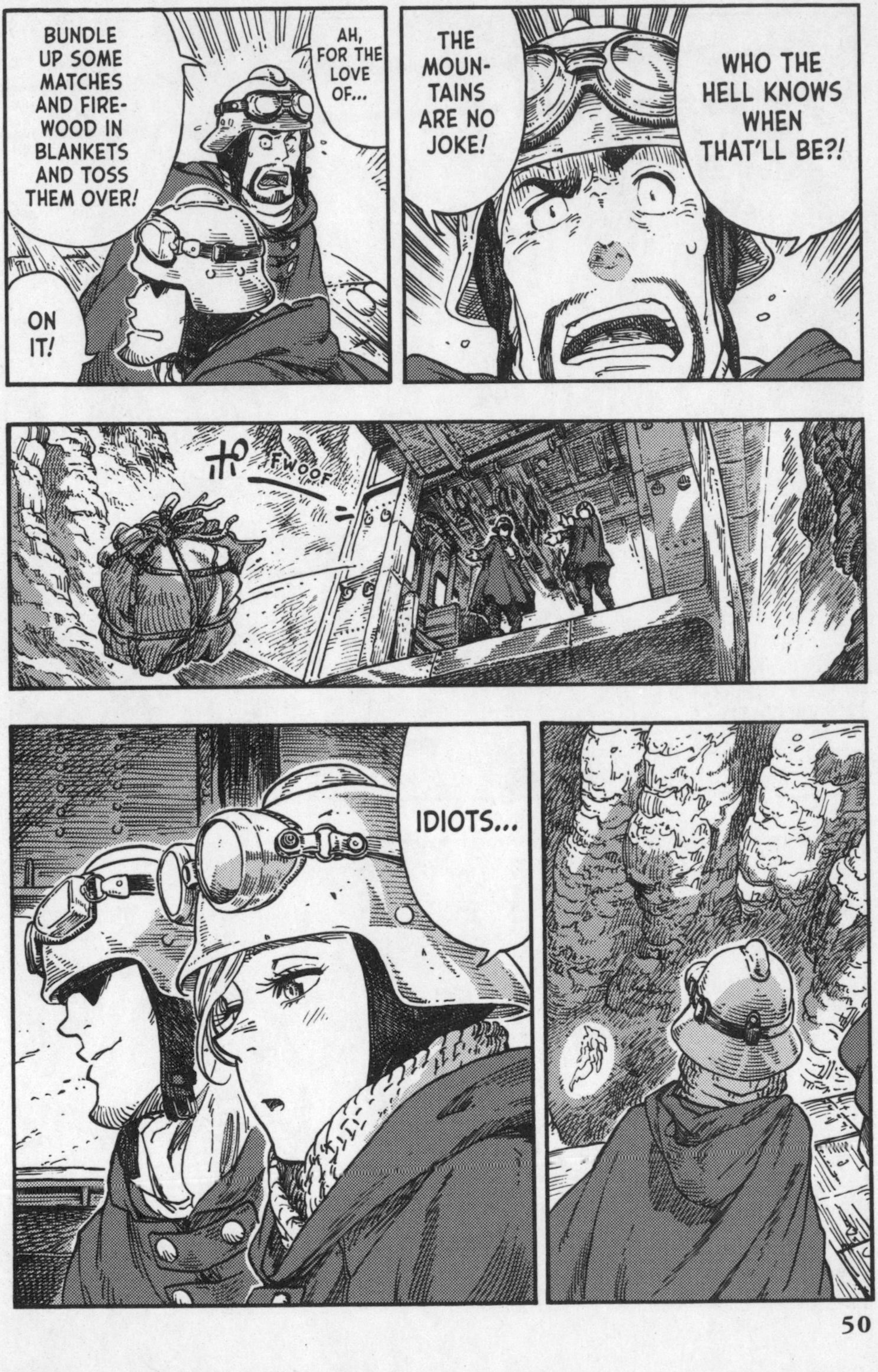
WHO THE HELL KNOWS WHEN THAT'LL BE?!
THE MOUN-TAINS ARE NO JOKE!
AH, FOR THE LOVE OF...
BUNDLE UP SOME MATCHES AND FIRE-WOOD IN BLANKETS AND TOSS THEM OVER!
ON IT!
ポ
FWOOF
IDIOTS...

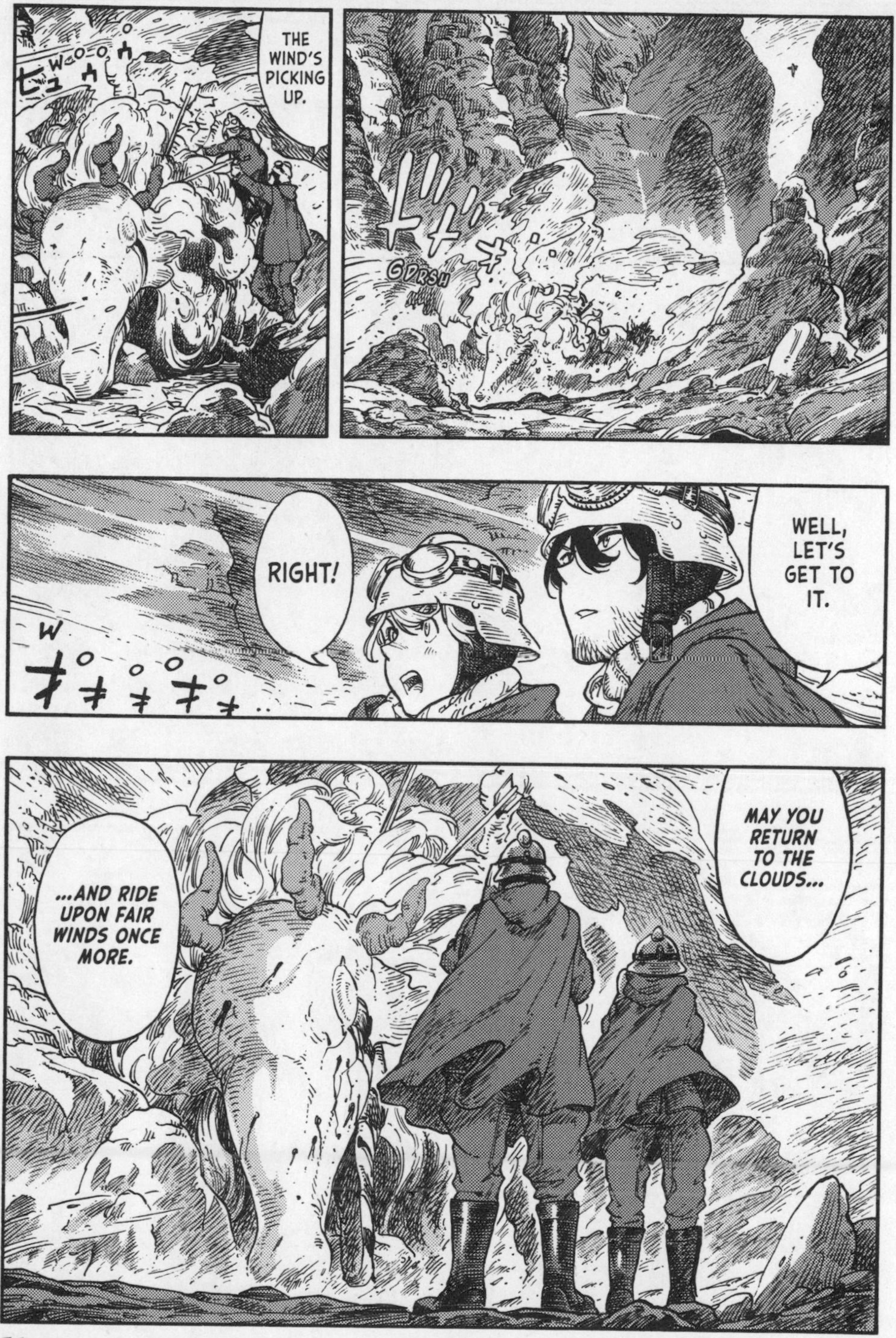
GDRSH
THE WIND'S PICKING UP.
W-O-O-O
WELL, LET'S GET TO IT.
RIGHT!
W
MAY YOU RETURN TO THE CLOUDS...
...AND RIDE UPON FAIR WINDS ONCE MORE.

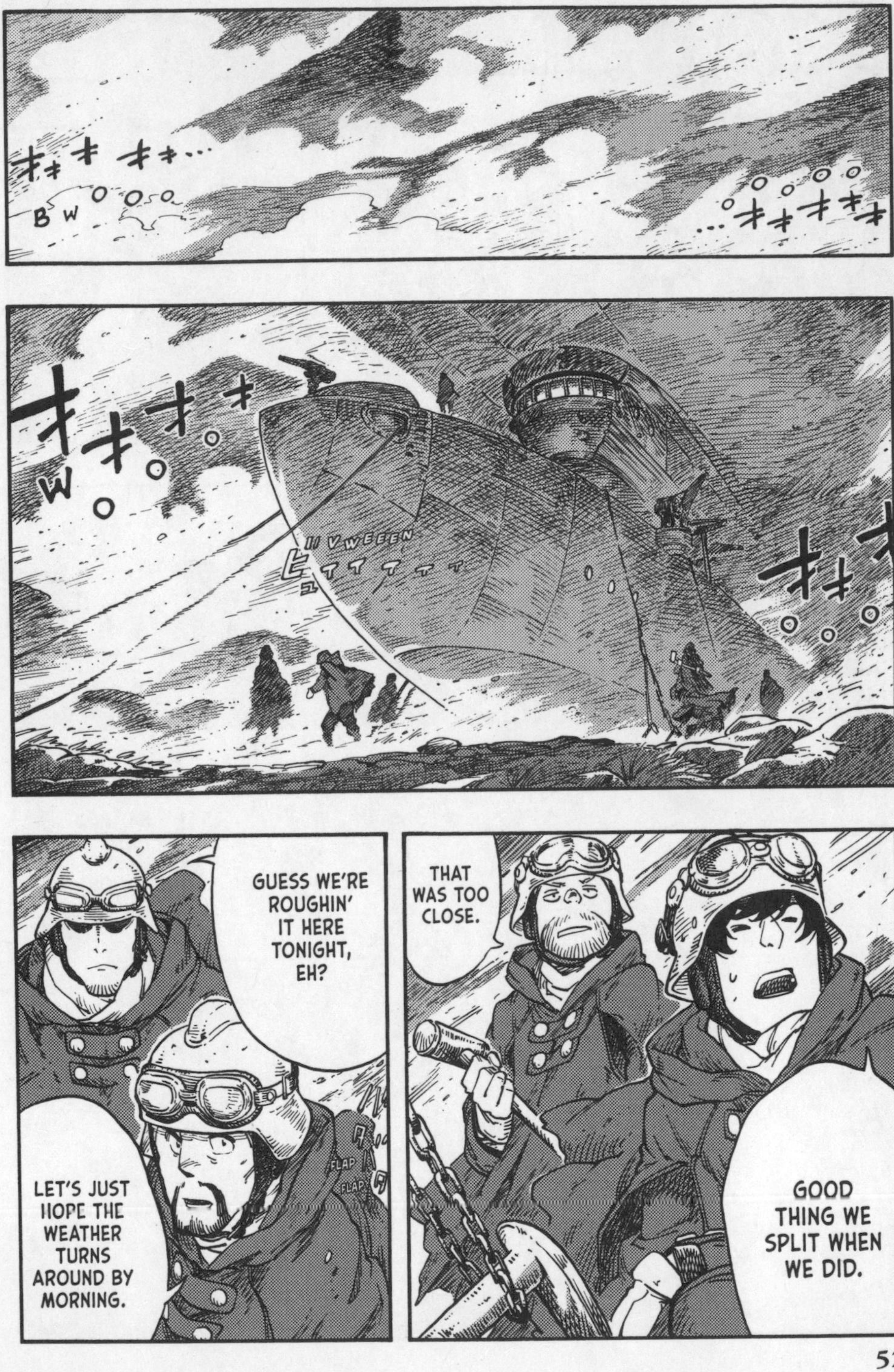
BWOOOO
VWEEEN
THAT WAS TOO CLOSE.
GOOD THING WE SPLIT WHEN WE DID.
GUESS WE'RE ROUGHIN' IT HERE TONIGHT, EH?
FLAP FLAP
LET'S JUST HOPE THE WEATHER TURNS AROUND BY MORNING.

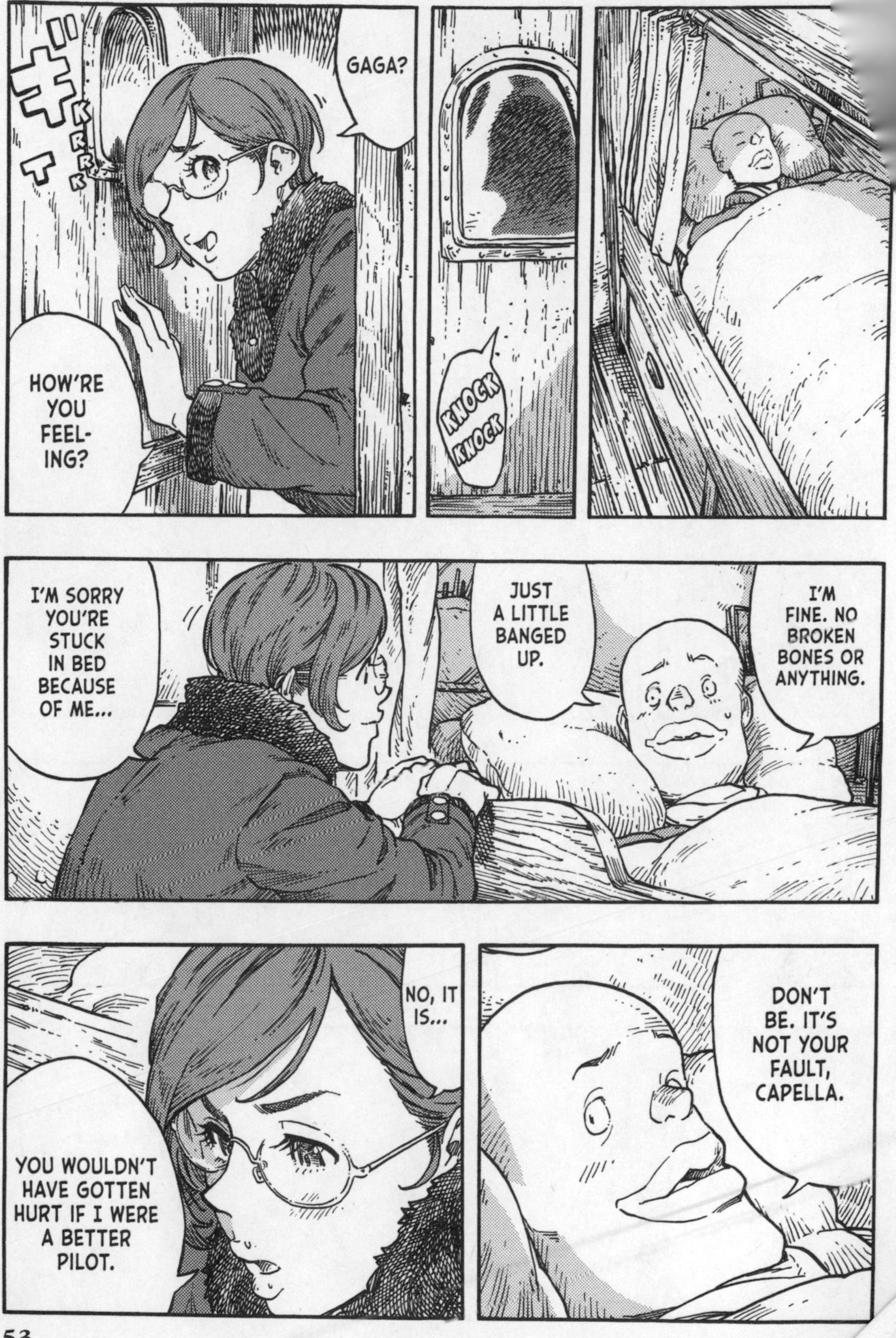
KNOCK KNOCK
GAGA?
ギイ
KRRK
HOW'RE YOU FEELING?
I'M FINE. NO BROKEN BONES OR ANYTHING.
JUST A LITTLE BANGED UP.
I'M SORRY YOU'RE STUCK IN BED BECAUSE OF ME...
DON'T BE. IT'S NOT YOUR FAULT, CAPELLA.
NO, IT IS...
YOU WOULDN'T HAVE GOTTEN HURT IF I WERE A BETTER PILOT.

...I'M SORRY.

TO BE HONEST, MY HANDS ARE *STILL* SHAKING.

HOW SILLY IS THAT?

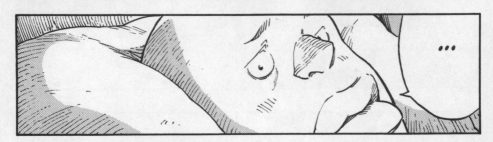

...

...WE MADE IT OUT, DIDN'T WE?

B-BUT...

54

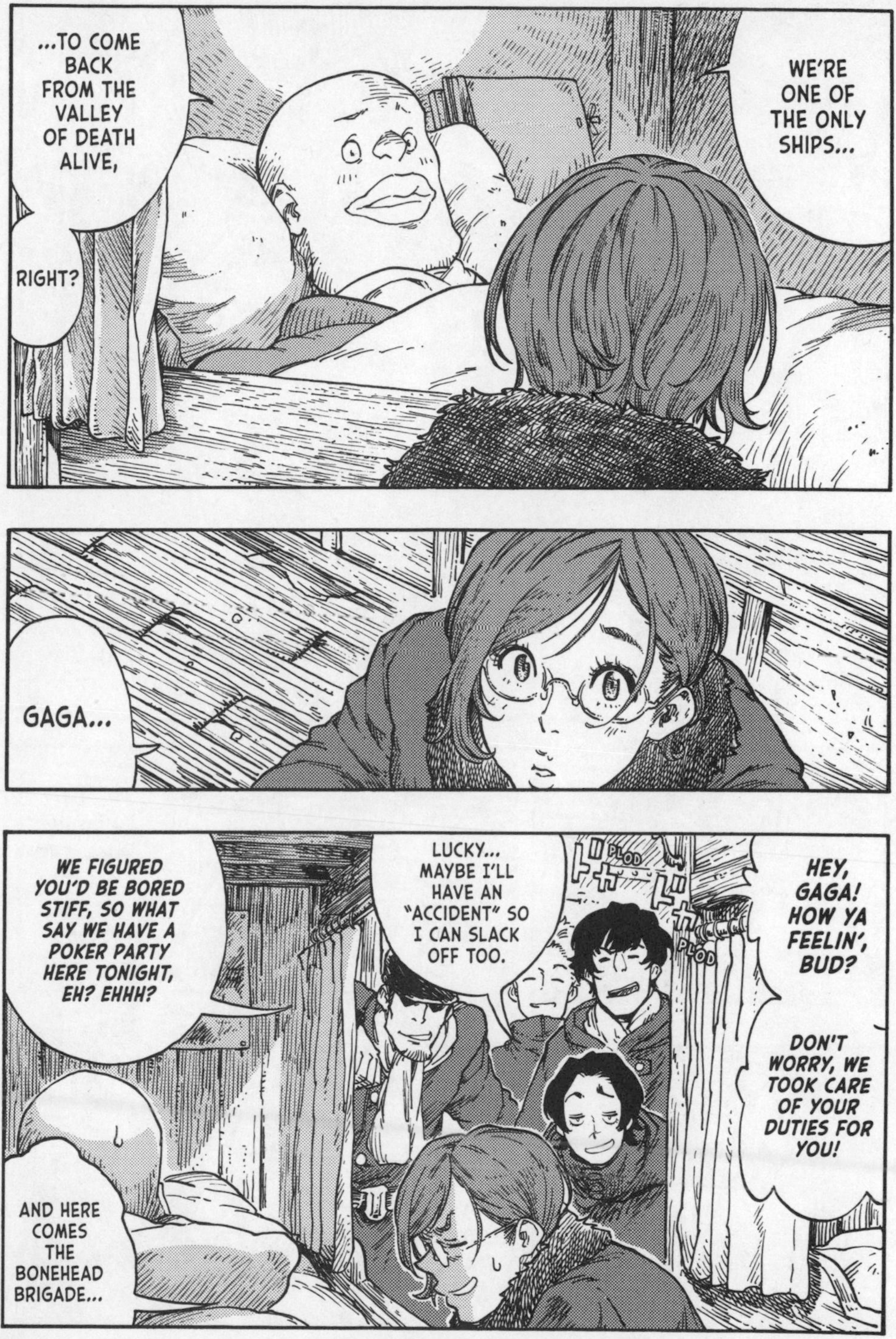
WE'RE ONE OF THE ONLY SHIPS...
...TO COME BACK FROM THE VALLEY OF DEATH ALIVE,
RIGHT?
GAGA...
HEY, GAGA! HOW YA FEELIN', BUD?
DON'T WORRY, WE TOOK CARE OF YOUR DUTIES FOR YOU!
PLOD
PLOD
LUCKY... MAYBE I'LL HAVE AN "ACCIDENT" SO I CAN SLACK OFF TOO.
WE FIGURED YOU'D BE BORED STIFF, SO WHAT SAY WE HAVE A POKER PARTY HERE TONIGHT, EH? EHHH?
AND HERE COMES THE BONEHEAD BRIGADE...

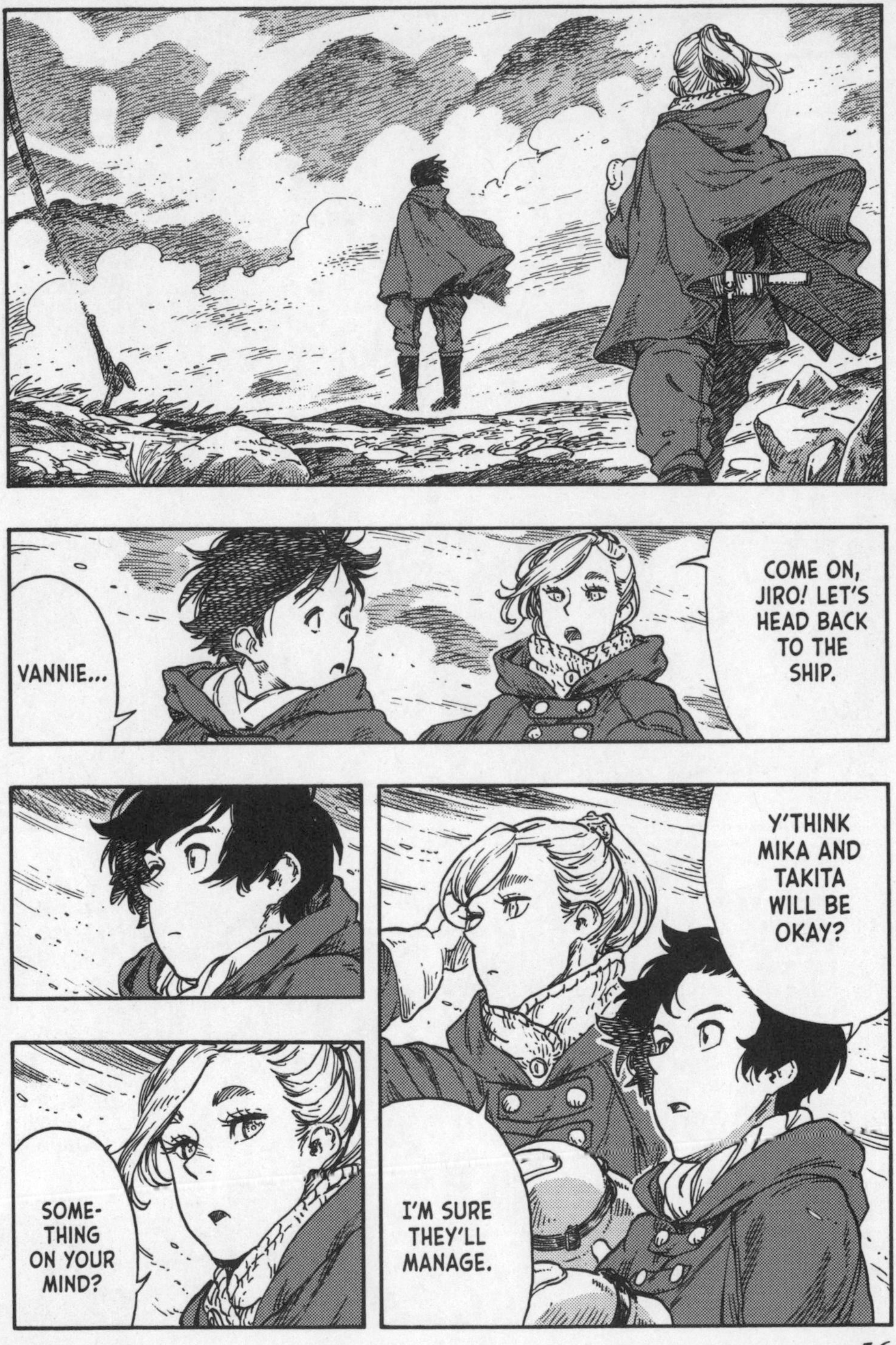
COME ON, JIRO! LET'S HEAD BACK TO THE SHIP.
VANNIE...
Y'THINK MIKA AND TAKITA WILL BE OKAY?
I'M SURE THEY'LL MANAGE.
SOME-THING ON YOUR MIND?

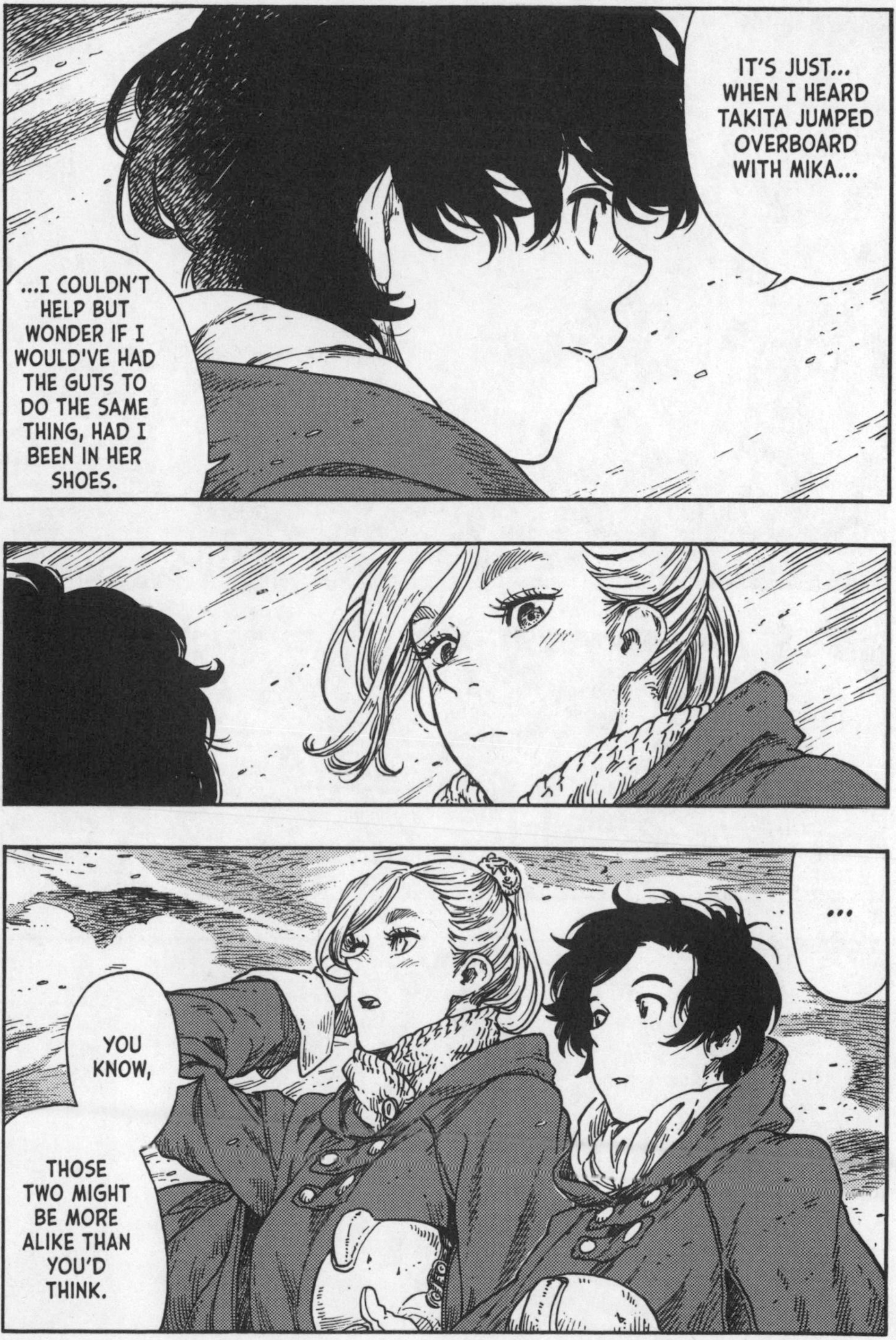
IT'S JUST... WHEN I HEARD TAKITA JUMPED OVERBOARD WITH MIKA...
...I COULDN'T HELP BUT WONDER IF I WOULD'VE HAD THE GUTS TO DO THE SAME THING, HAD I BEEN IN HER SHOES.
...
YOU KNOW,
THOSE TWO MIGHT BE MORE ALIKE THAN YOU'D THINK.

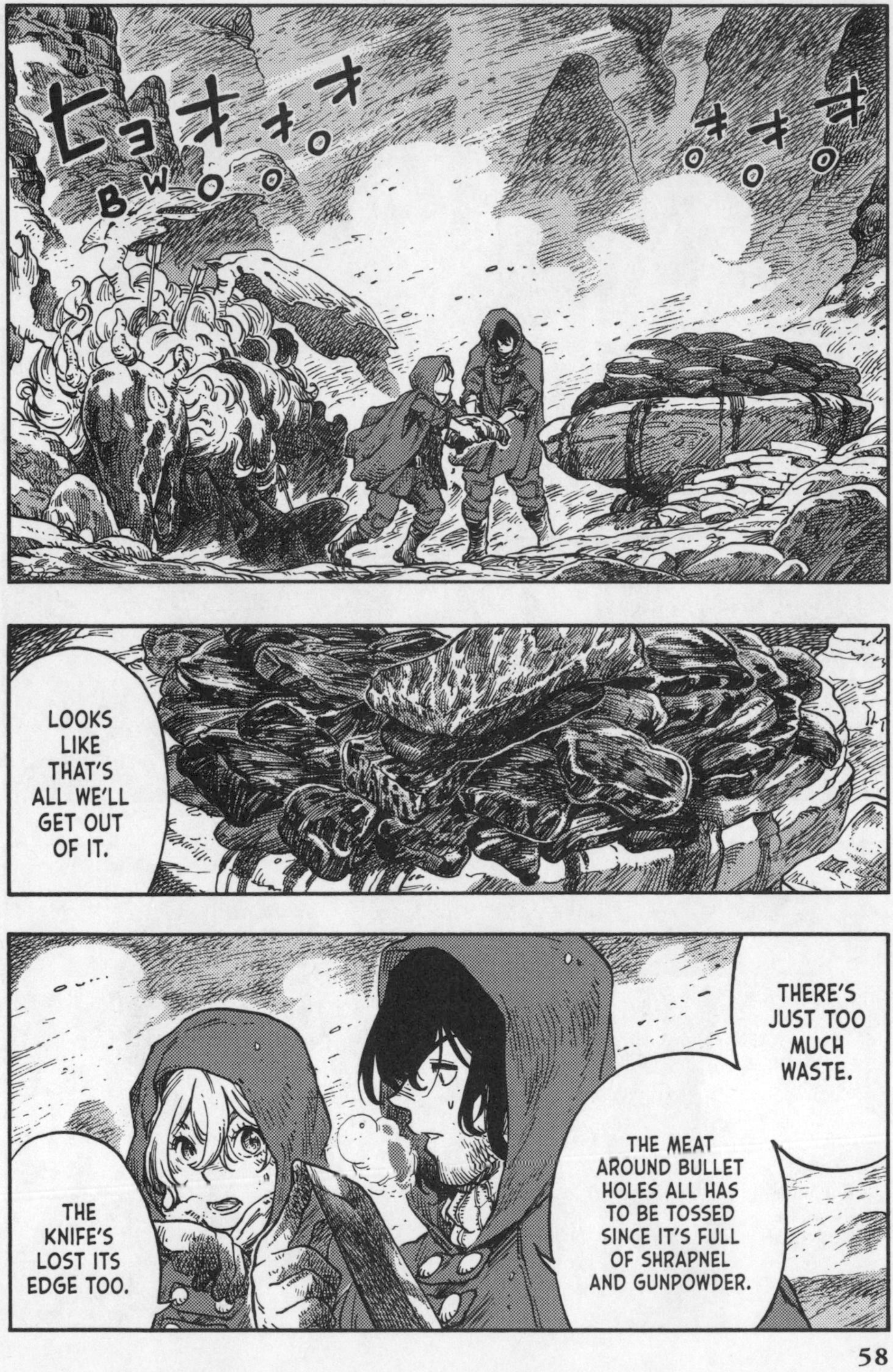
ヒョオォォ
BWOOOO
ォォォ
LOOKS LIKE THAT'S ALL WE'LL GET OUT OF IT.
THERE'S JUST TOO MUCH WASTE.
THE MEAT AROUND BULLET HOLES ALL HAS TO BE TOSSED SINCE IT'S FULL OF SHRAPNEL AND GUNPOWDER.
THE KNIFE'S LOST ITS EDGE TOO.

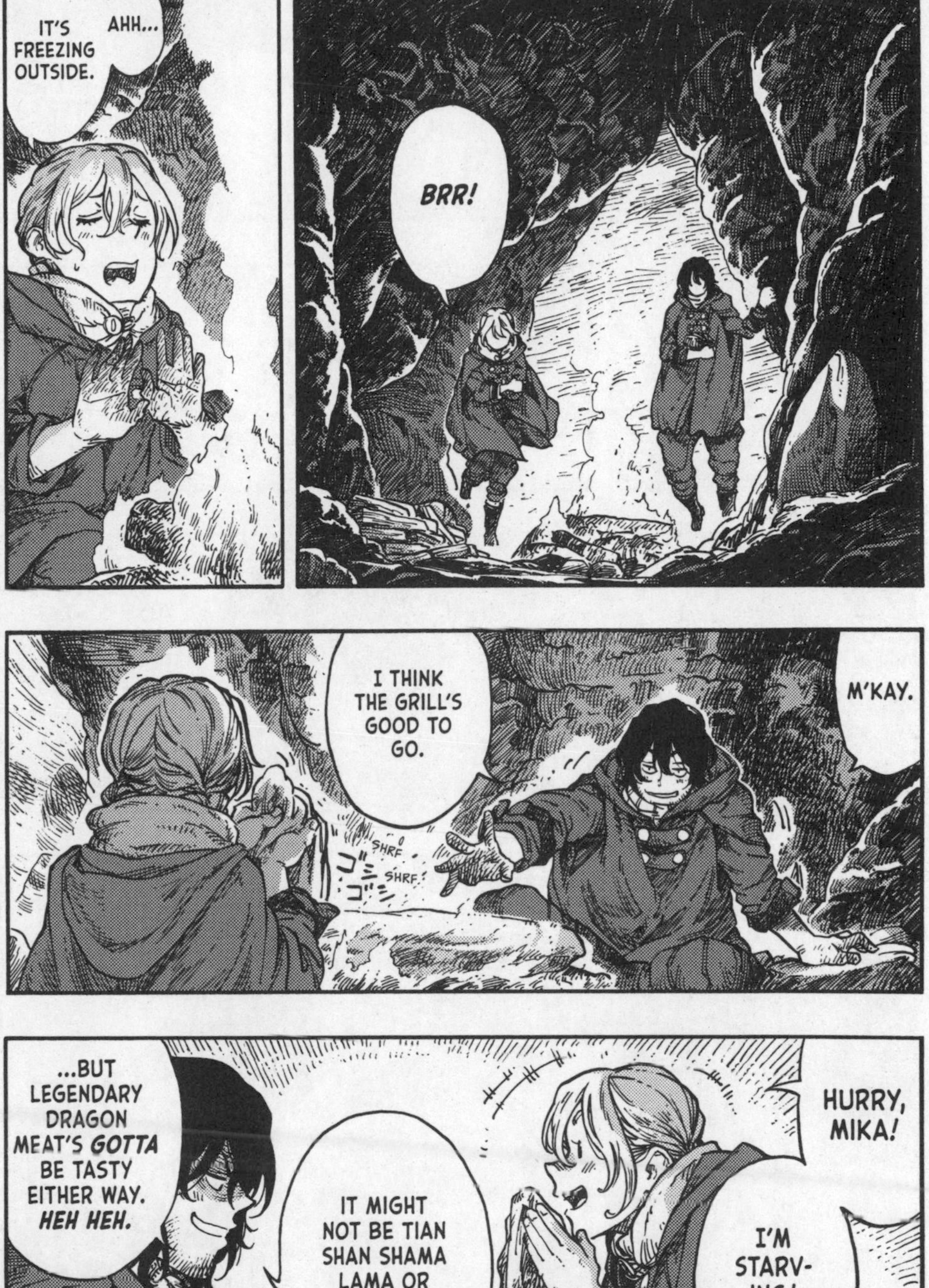
BRR!
AHH... IT'S FREEZING OUTSIDE.
M'KAY.
I THINK THE GRILL'S GOOD TO GO.
SHRF SHRF
HURRY, MIKA!
I'M STARVING!
IT MIGHT NOT BE TIAN SHAN SHAMA LAMA OR WHATEVER...
...BUT LEGENDARY DRAGON MEAT'S GOTTA BE TASTY EITHER WAY. HEH HEH.

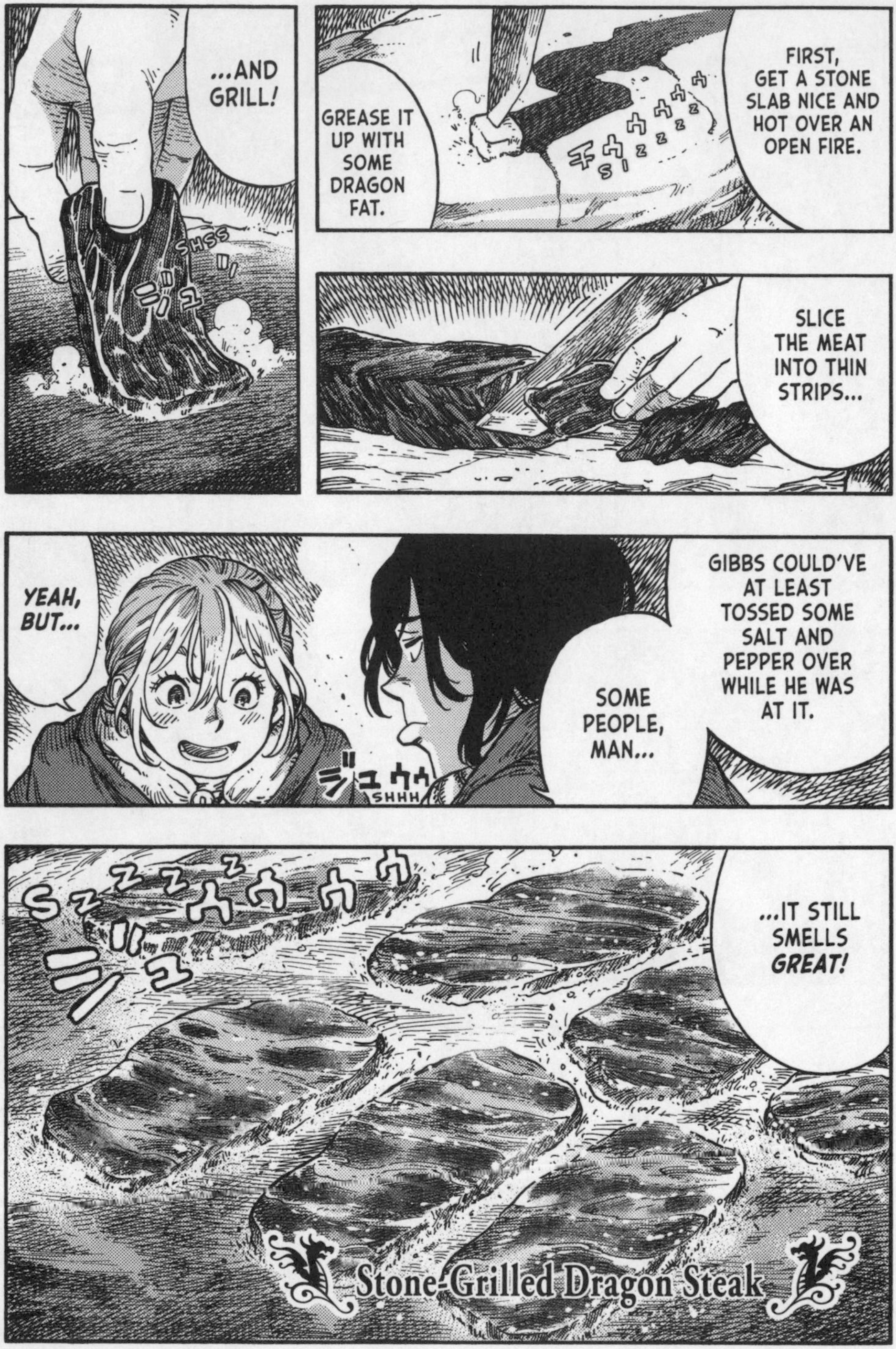
FIRST, GET A STONE SLAB NICE AND HOT OVER AN OPEN FIRE.
GREASE IT UP WITH SOME DRAGON FAT.
SLICE THE MEAT INTO THIN STRIPS...
...AND GRILL!
SHSS
GIBBS COULD'VE AT LEAST TOSSED SOME SALT AND PEPPER OVER WHILE HE WAS AT IT.
SOME PEOPLE, MAN...
YEAH, BUT...
SHHH
...IT STILL SMELLS GREAT!
Stone-Grilled Dragon Steak

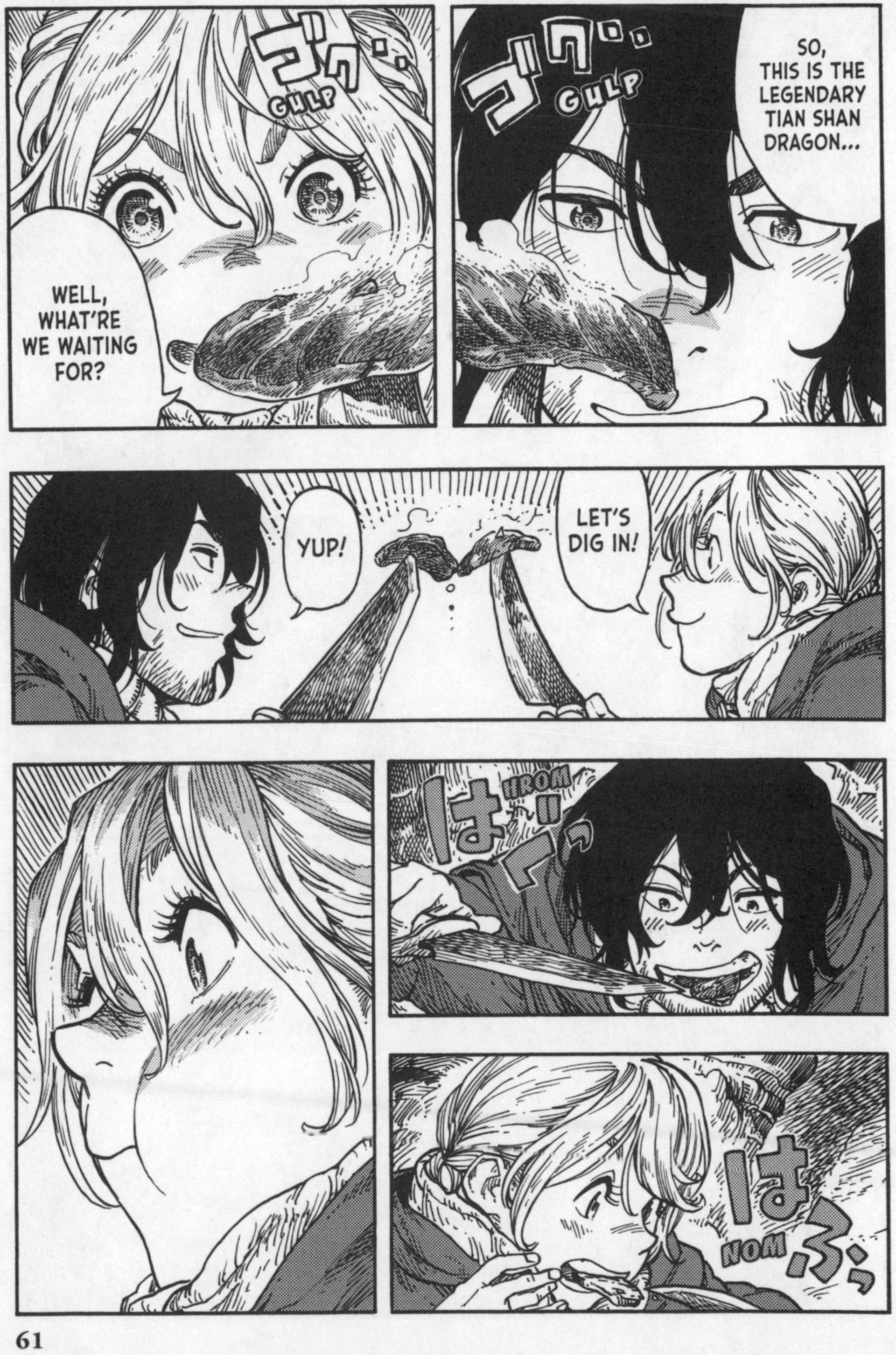
ゴクッ
GULP
SO, THIS IS THE LEGENDARY TIAN SHAN DRAGON...
ゴクッ
GULP
WELL, WHAT'RE WE WAITING FOR?
LET'S DIG IN!
YUP!
はぐっ
HROM
はふっ
NOM

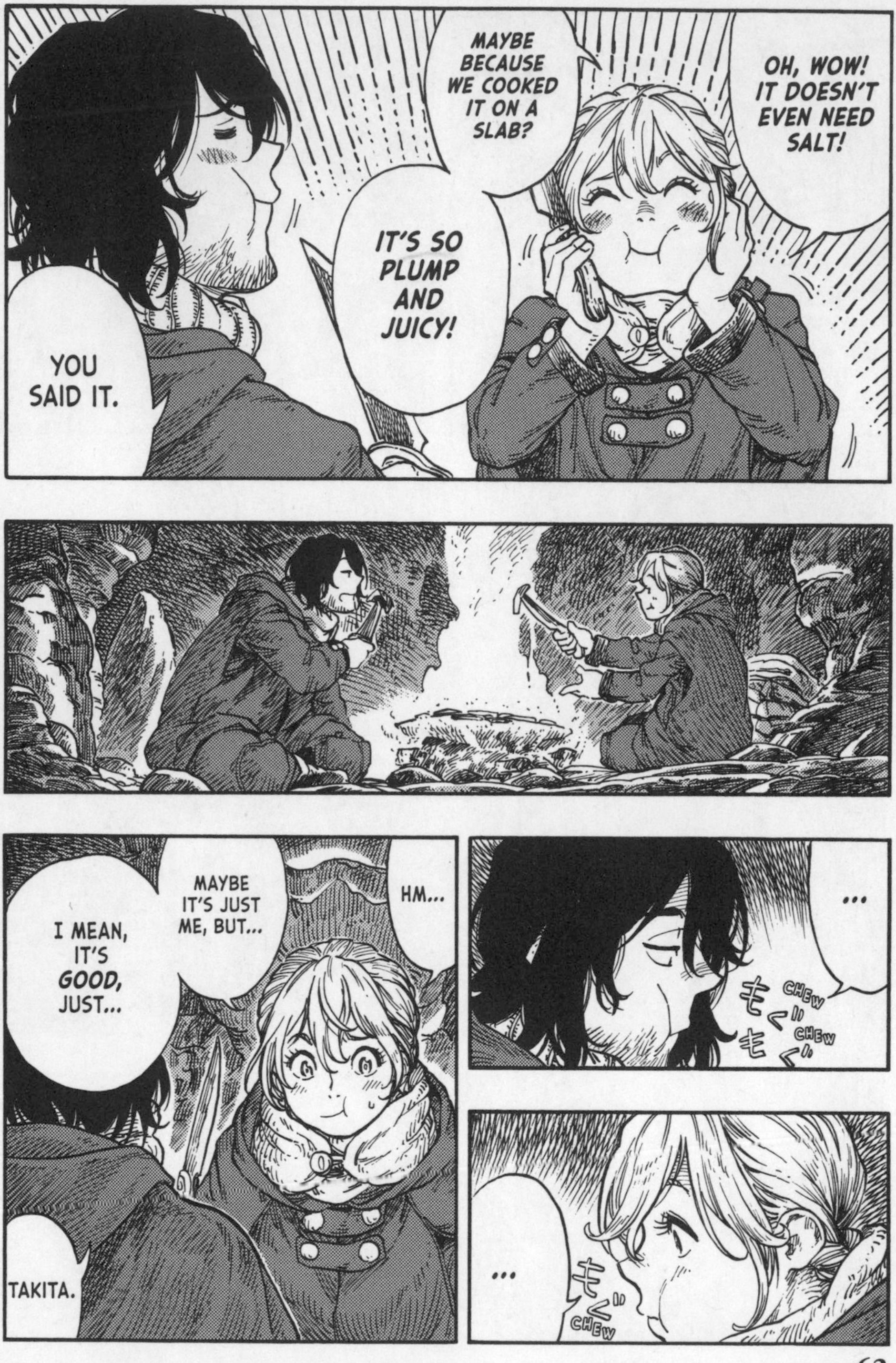
OH, WOW! IT DOESN'T EVEN NEED SALT!
MAYBE BECAUSE WE COOKED IT ON A SLAB?
IT'S SO PLUMP AND JUICY!
YOU SAID IT.
...
もぐもぐ
CHEW CHEW
...
もぐ
CHEW
HM...
MAYBE IT'S JUST ME, BUT...
I MEAN, IT'S *GOOD*, JUST...
TAKITA.

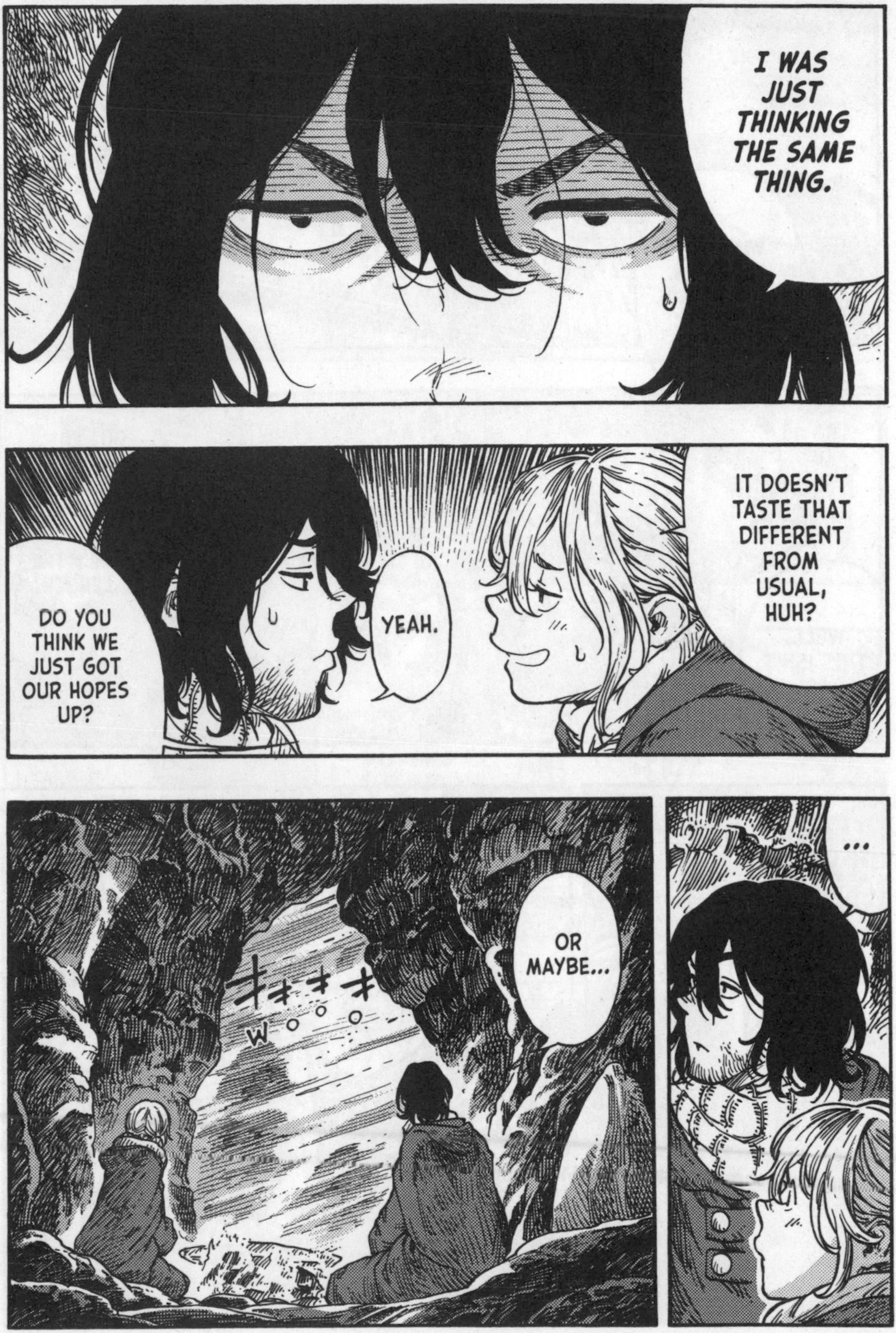
I WAS JUST THINKING THE SAME THING.
IT DOESN'T TASTE THAT DIFFERENT FROM USUAL, HUH?
YEAH.
DO YOU THINK WE JUST GOT OUR HOPES UP?
...
OR MAYBE...
WOOO

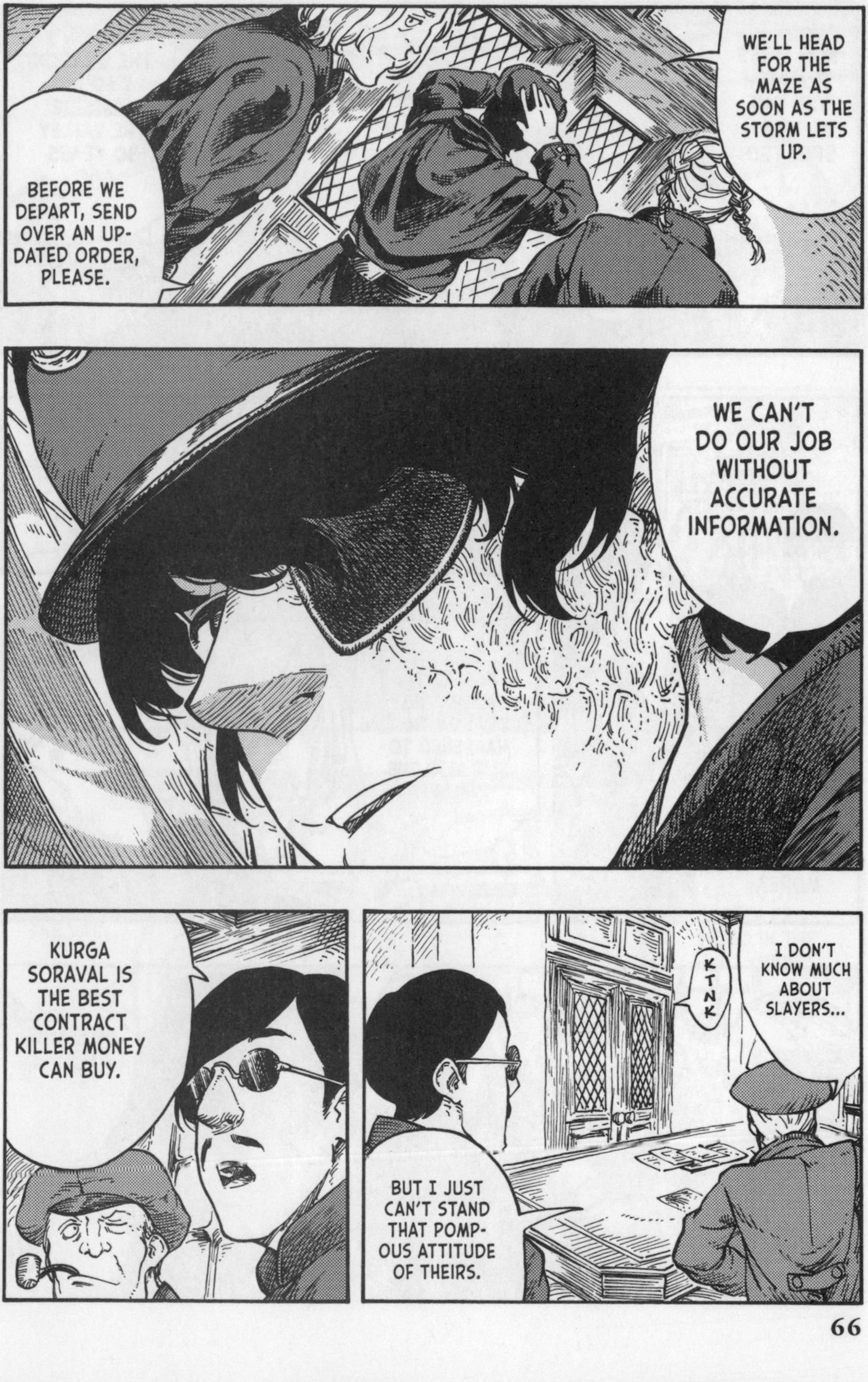
WE'LL HEAD FOR THE MAZE AS SOON AS THE STORM LETS UP.
BEFORE WE DEPART, SEND OVER AN UPDATED ORDER, PLEASE.
WE CAN'T DO OUR JOB WITHOUT ACCURATE INFORMATION.
I DON'T KNOW MUCH ABOUT SLAYERS...
KTNK
BUT I JUST CAN'T STAND THAT POMPOUS ATTITUDE OF THEIRS.
KURGA SORAVAL IS THE BEST CONTRACT KILLER MONEY CAN BUY.

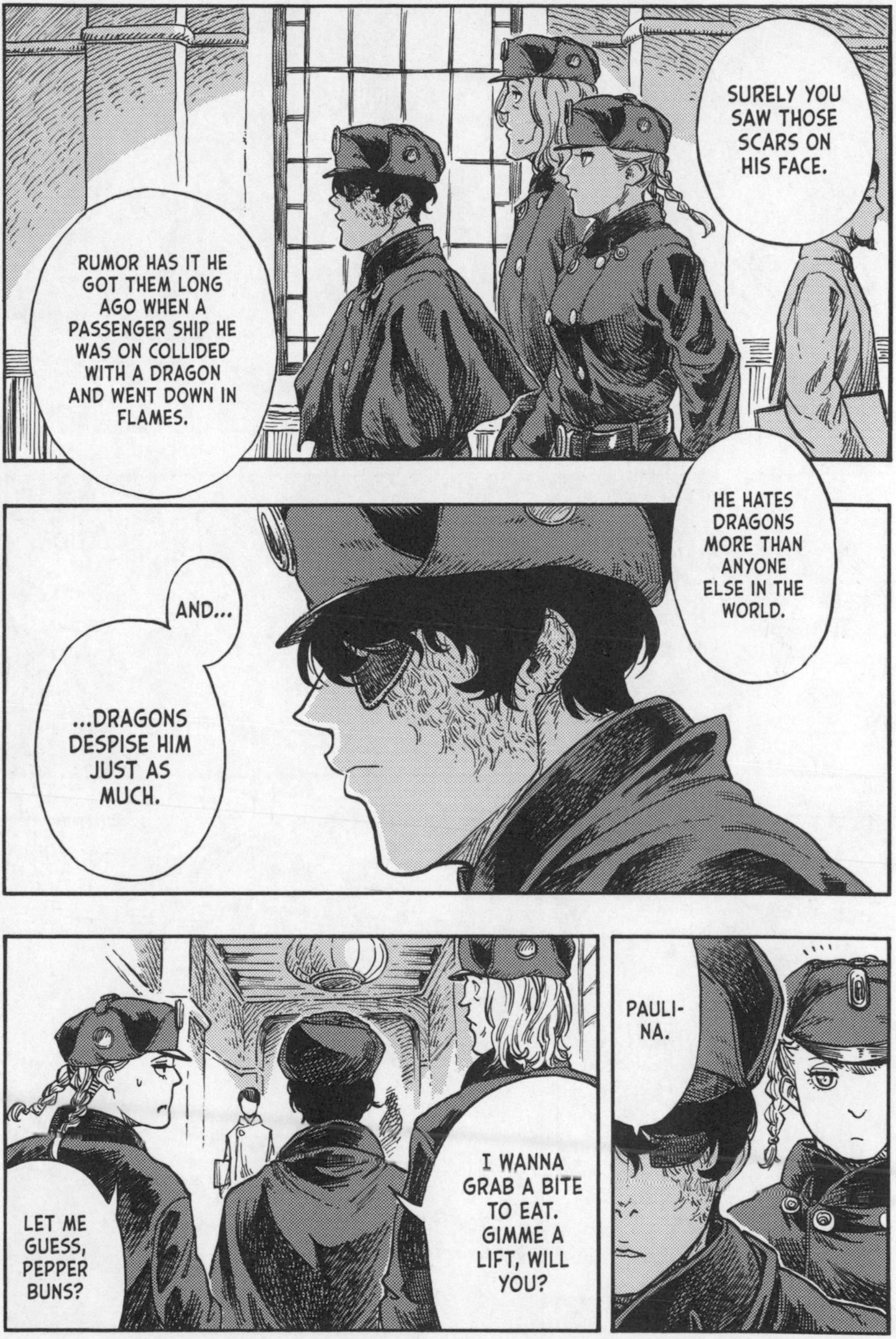
SURELY YOU SAW THOSE SCARS ON HIS FACE.
RUMOR HAS IT HE GOT THEM LONG AGO WHEN A PASSENGER SHIP HE WAS ON COLLIDED WITH A DRAGON AND WENT DOWN IN FLAMES.
HE HATES DRAGONS MORE THAN ANYONE ELSE IN THE WORLD.
AND...
...DRAGONS DESPISE HIM JUST AS MUCH.
PAULI-NA.
I WANNA GRAB A BITE TO EAT. GIMME A LIFT, WILL YOU?
LET ME GUESS, PEPPER BUNS?

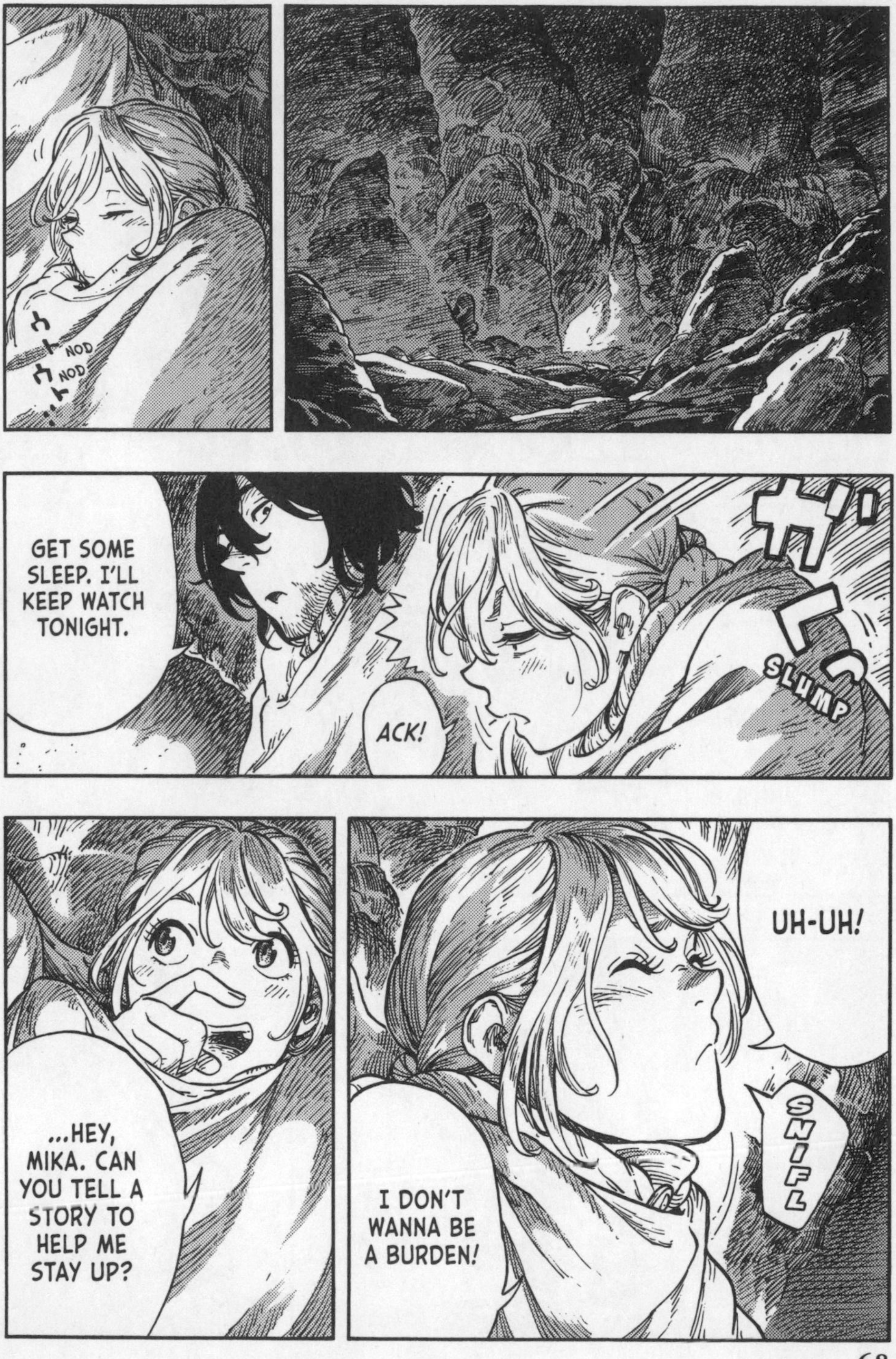
ウトウト…
NOD
NOD
ガクッ
SLUMP
ACK!
GET SOME SLEEP. I'LL KEEP WATCH TONIGHT.
UH-UH!
SNIFL
I DON'T WANNA BE A BURDEN!
...HEY, MIKA. CAN YOU TELL A STORY TO HELP ME STAY UP?

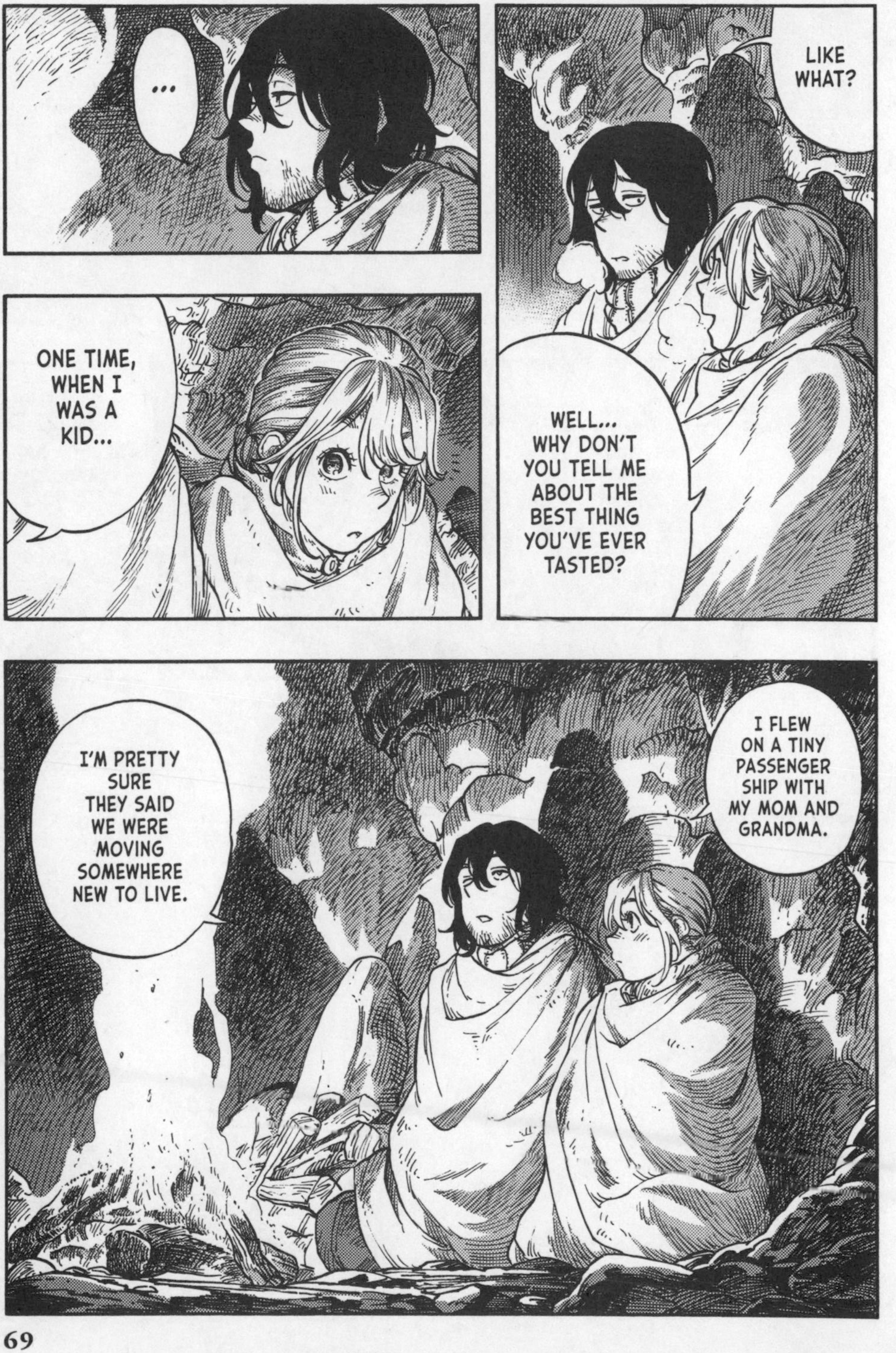
LIKE WHAT?
WELL... WHY DON'T YOU TELL ME ABOUT THE BEST THING YOU'VE EVER TASTED?
...
ONE TIME, WHEN I WAS A KID...
I FLEW ON A TINY PASSENGER SHIP WITH MY MOM AND GRANDMA.
I'M PRETTY SURE THEY SAID WE WERE MOVING SOMEWHERE NEW TO LIVE.

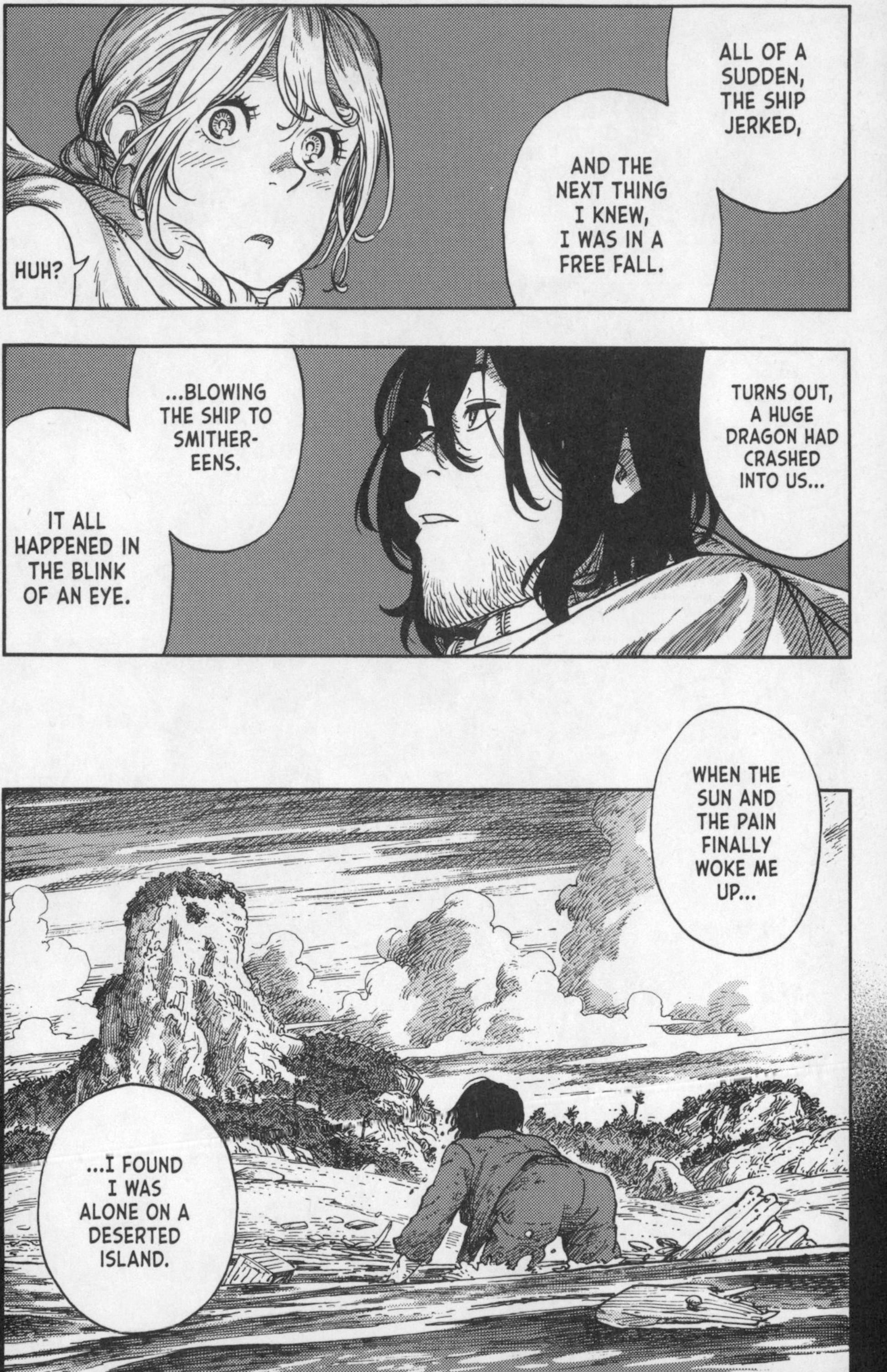
ALL OF A SUDDEN, THE SHIP JERKED,
AND THE NEXT THING I KNEW, I WAS IN A FREE FALL.
HUH?
TURNS OUT, A HUGE DRAGON HAD CRASHED INTO US...
...BLOWING THE SHIP TO SMITHER-EENS.
IT ALL HAPPENED IN THE BLINK OF AN EYE.
WHEN THE SUN AND THE PAIN FINALLY WOKE ME UP...
...I FOUND I WAS ALONE ON A DESERTED ISLAND.

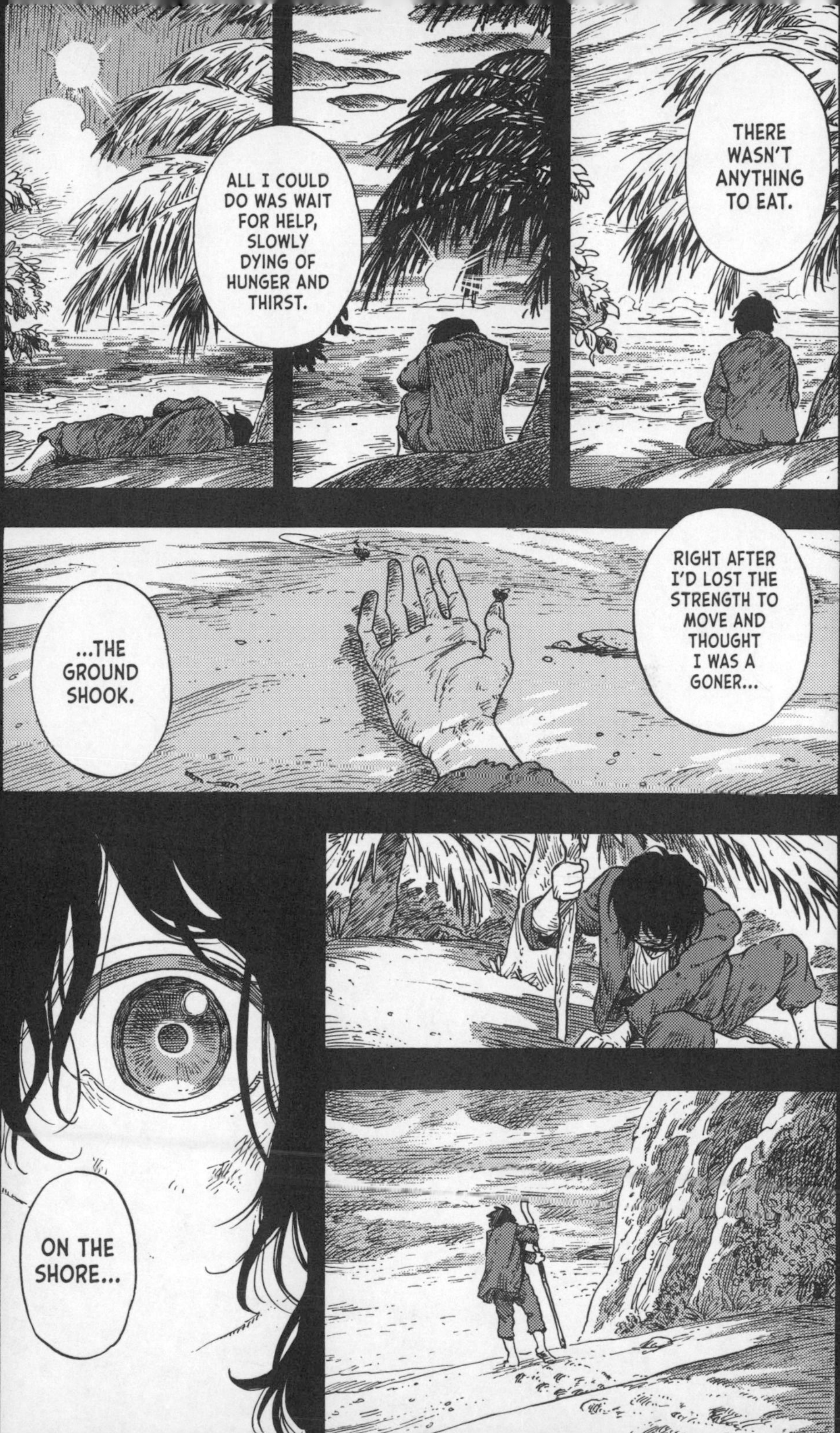
THERE WASN'T ANYTHING TO EAT.
ALL I COULD DO WAS WAIT FOR HELP, SLOWLY DYING OF HUNGER AND THIRST.
RIGHT AFTER I'D LOST THE STRENGTH TO MOVE AND THOUGHT I WAS A GONER...
...THE GROUND SHOOK.
ON THE SHORE...

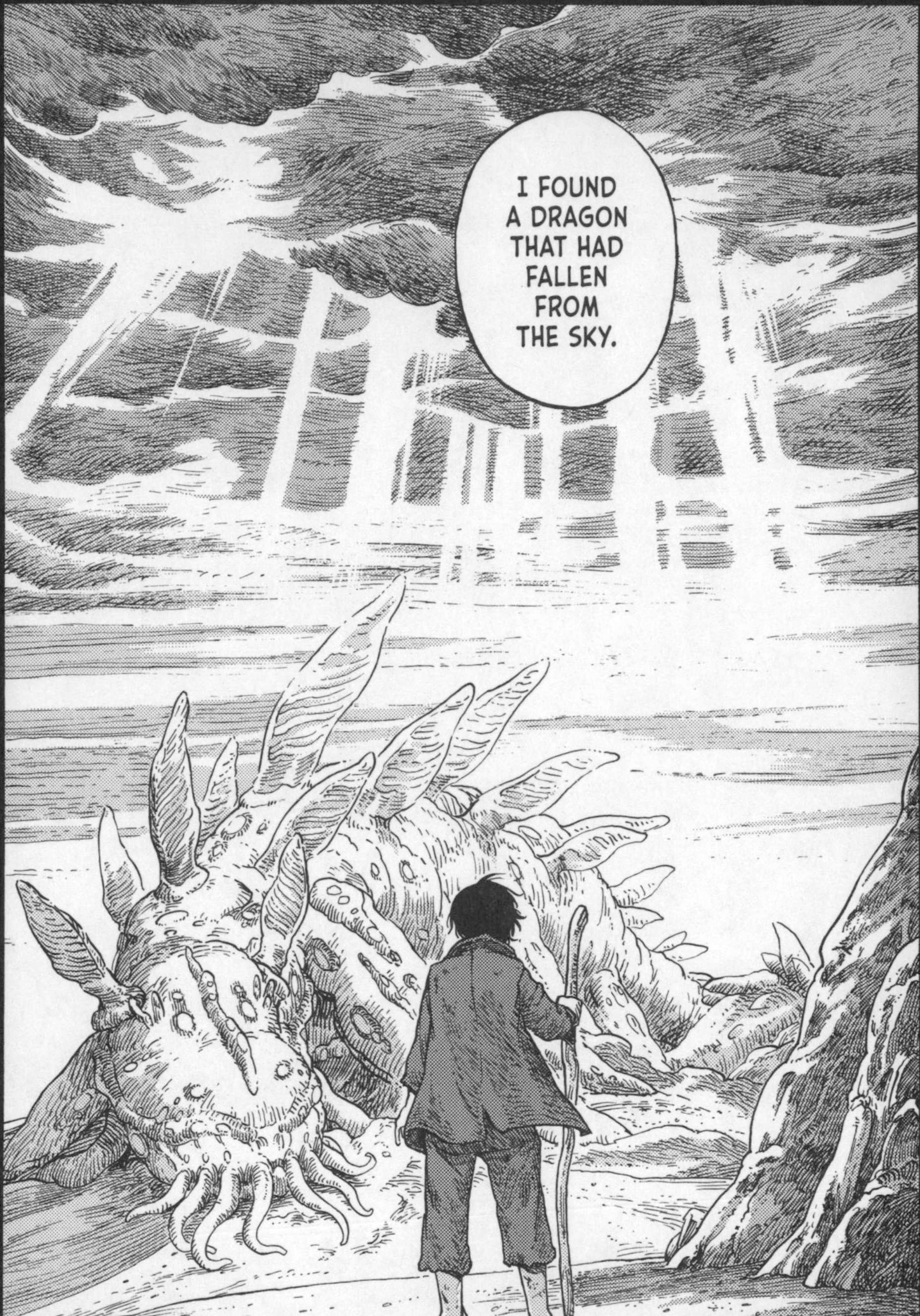
I FOUND A DRAGON THAT HAD FALLEN FROM THE SKY.

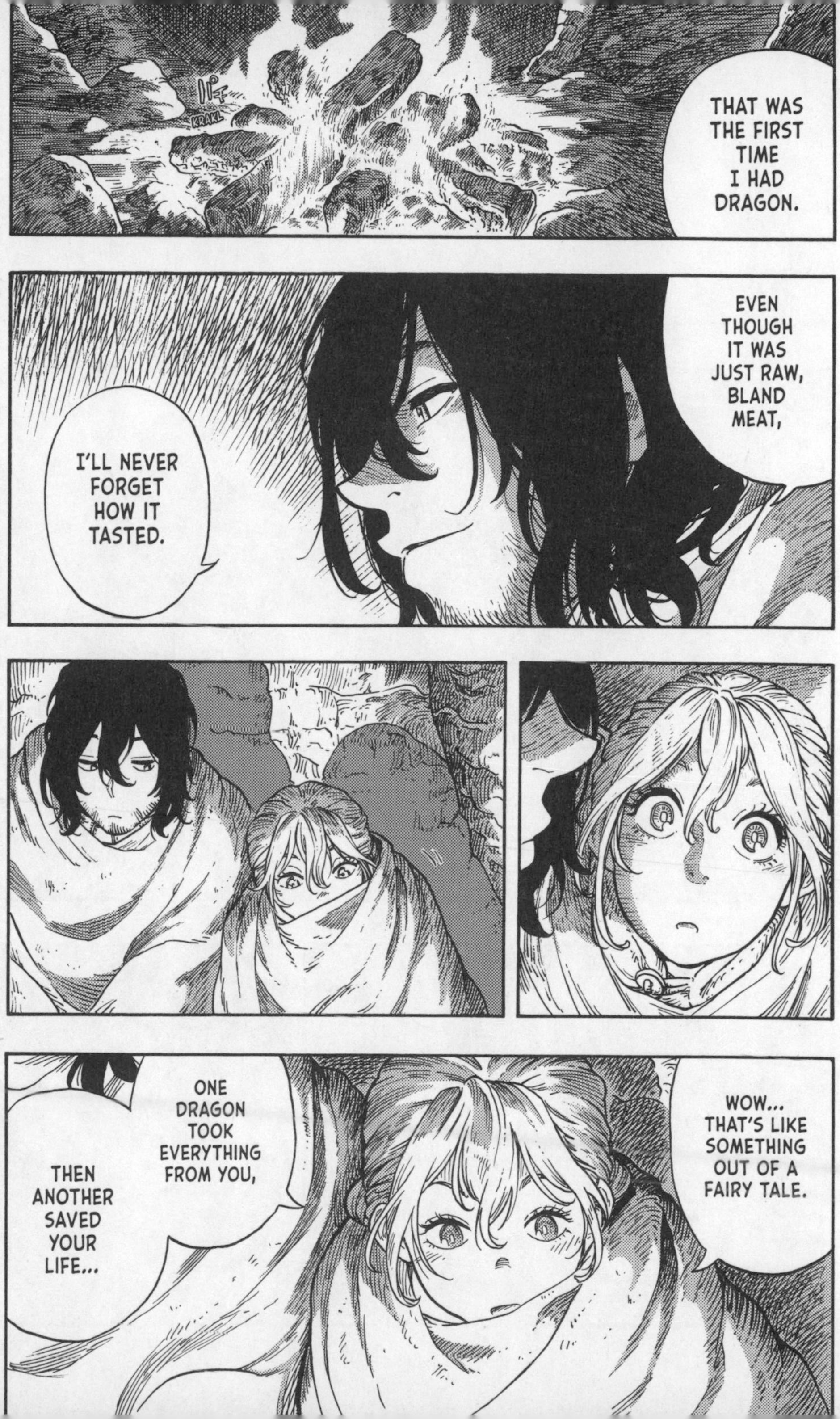

パチ
KRAKL
THAT WAS THE FIRST TIME I HAD DRAGON.
EVEN THOUGH IT WAS JUST RAW, BLAND MEAT,
I'LL NEVER FORGET HOW IT TASTED.
WOW... THAT'S LIKE SOMETHING OUT OF A FAIRY TALE.
ONE DRAGON TOOK EVERYTHING FROM YOU,
THEN ANOTHER SAVED YOUR LIFE...

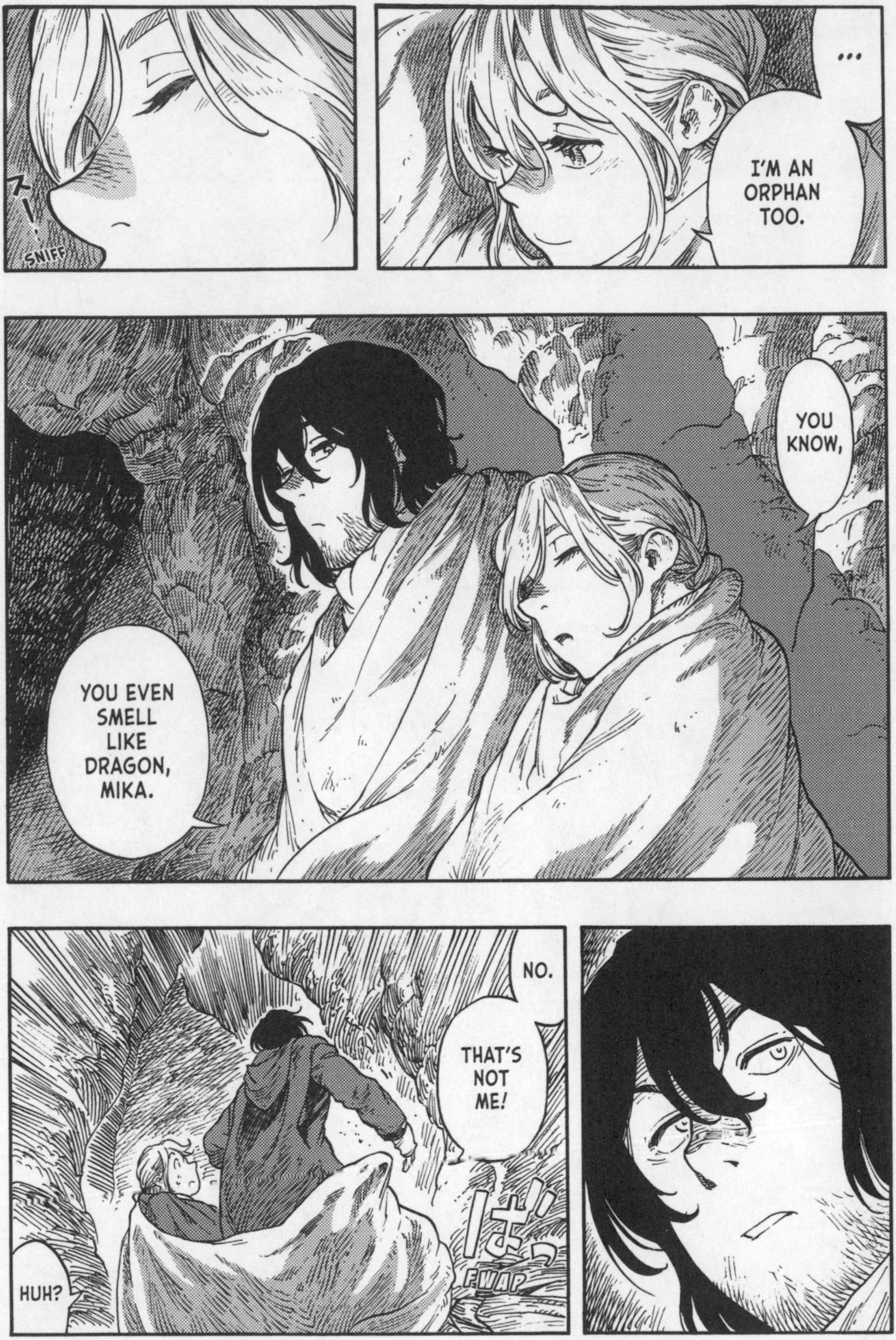
...
I'M AN ORPHAN TOO.
スー
SNIFF
YOU KNOW,
YOU EVEN SMELL LIKE DRAGON, MIKA.
NO.
THAT'S NOT ME!
ぱっ
FWAP
HUH?

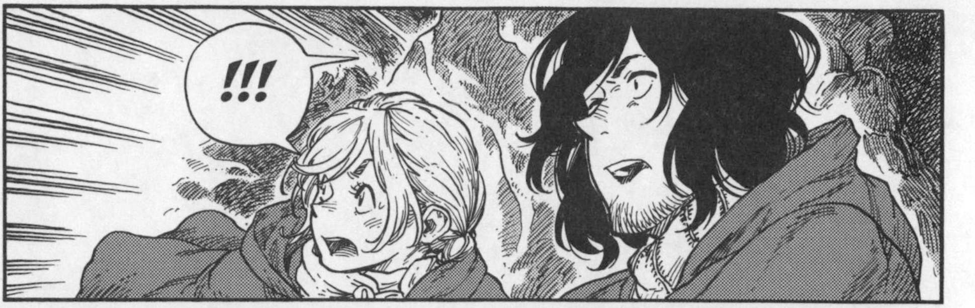
!!!
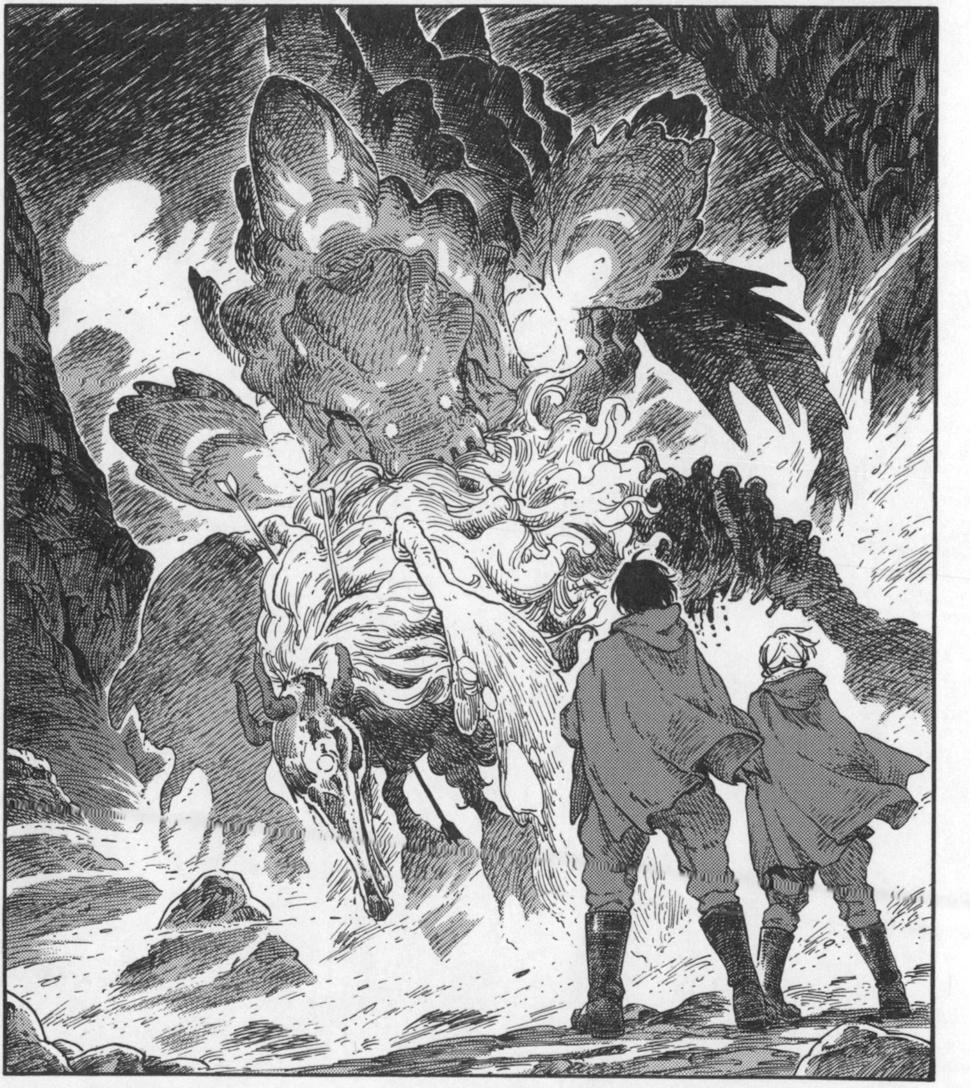

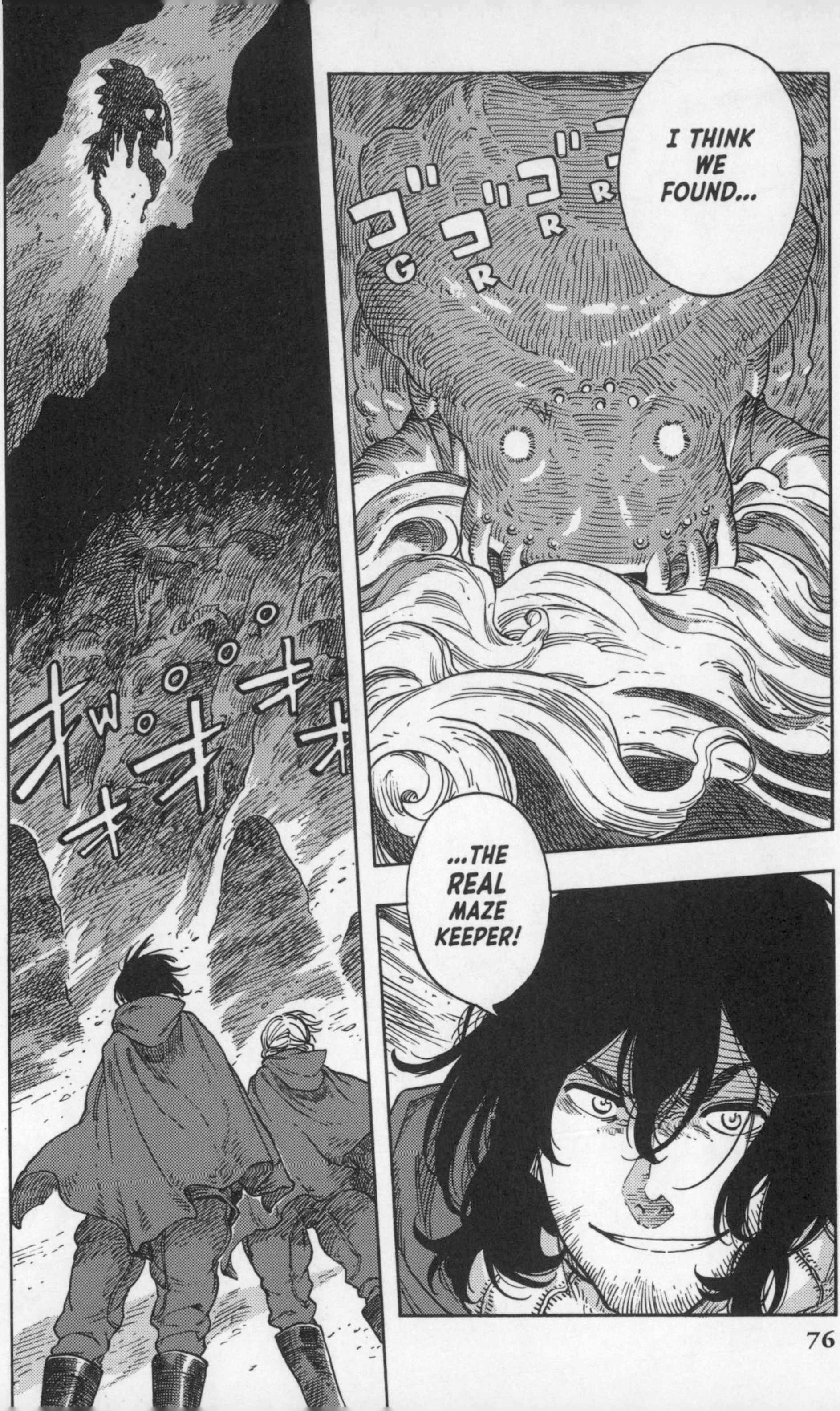
I THINK WE FOUND...
GRRRR
...THE REAL MAZE KEEPER!
WOOOO

Stone-Grilled Steak

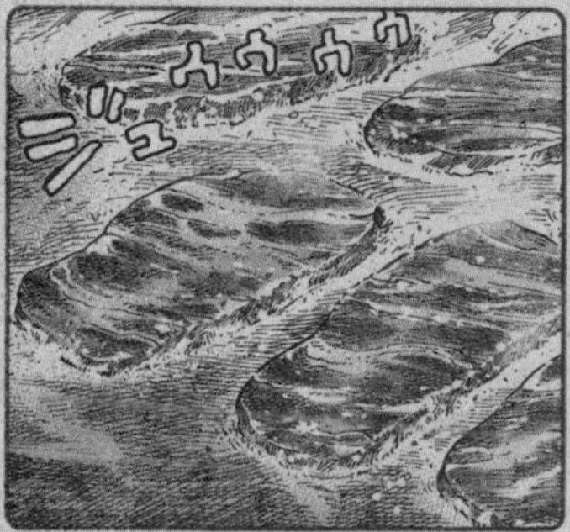

Ingredients

✦ Dragon meat

[Preparation]

Examine the meat carefully to determine the direction of the grain.

With a kitchen knife, slice the meat against the grain into 5-7 mm-thick strips. This results in tender morsels with a pleasant mouthfeel, while also creating a more voluminous eating experience.

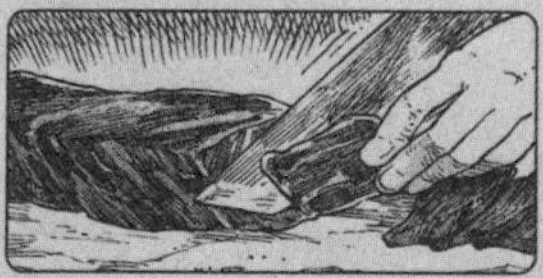

[Grilling]

Grill the strips of meat on the center of a well-heated stone slab. Once the strips are seared on both sides, transfer to a warm rock and let rest for a couple minutes, allowing the residual heat to cook the meat the rest of the way through.

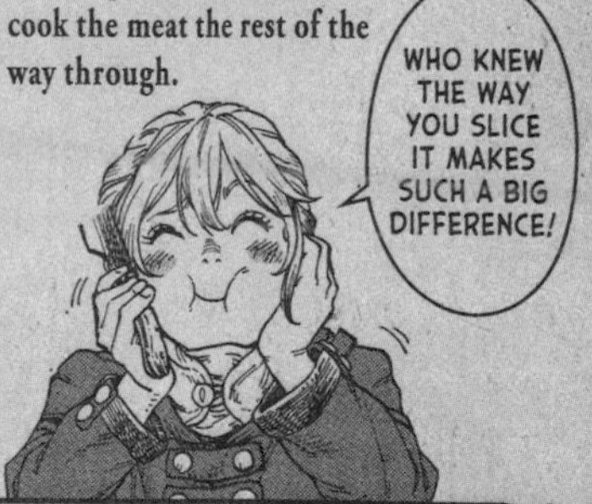
WHO KNEW THE WAY YOU SLICE IT MAKES SUCH A BIG DIFFERENCE!

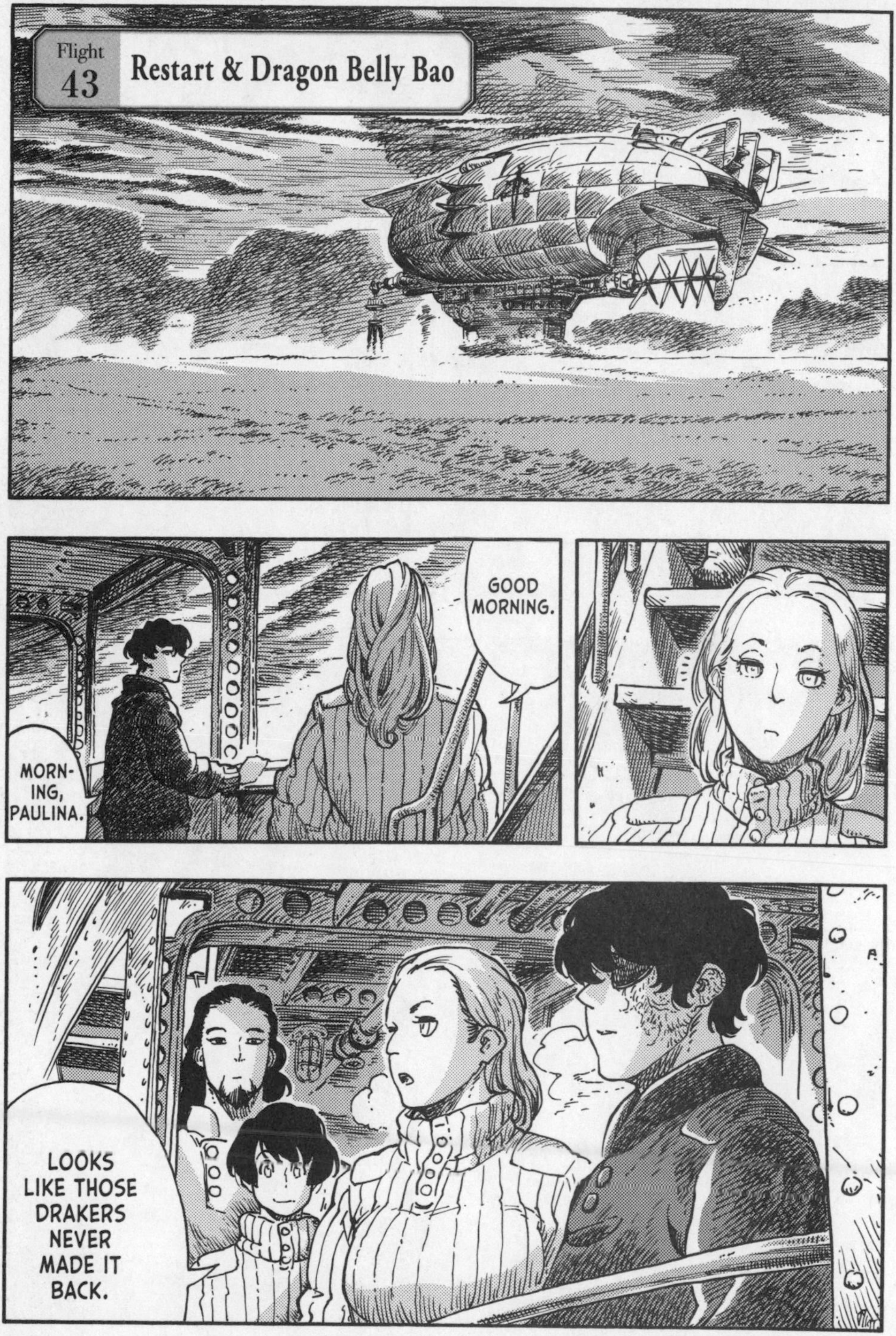
Flight 43
Restart & Dragon Belly Bao
GOOD MORNING.
MORNING-ING, PAULINA.
LOOKS LIKE THOSE DRAKERS NEVER MADE IT BACK.

SOME-
THING
WRONG
?

UH-OH.
ANOTHER
SHIP BITES
THE DUST...

HEY, THEY
MIGHT BE
OUR RIVALS,
BUT YOU
SHOULDN'T
SPEAK ILL
OF THEM.

HUNT ORDER

MAYBE...

HUH?

YES,
SIR.

GET READY
FOR TAKE-
OFF. WE'RE
LEAVING.
NOW.

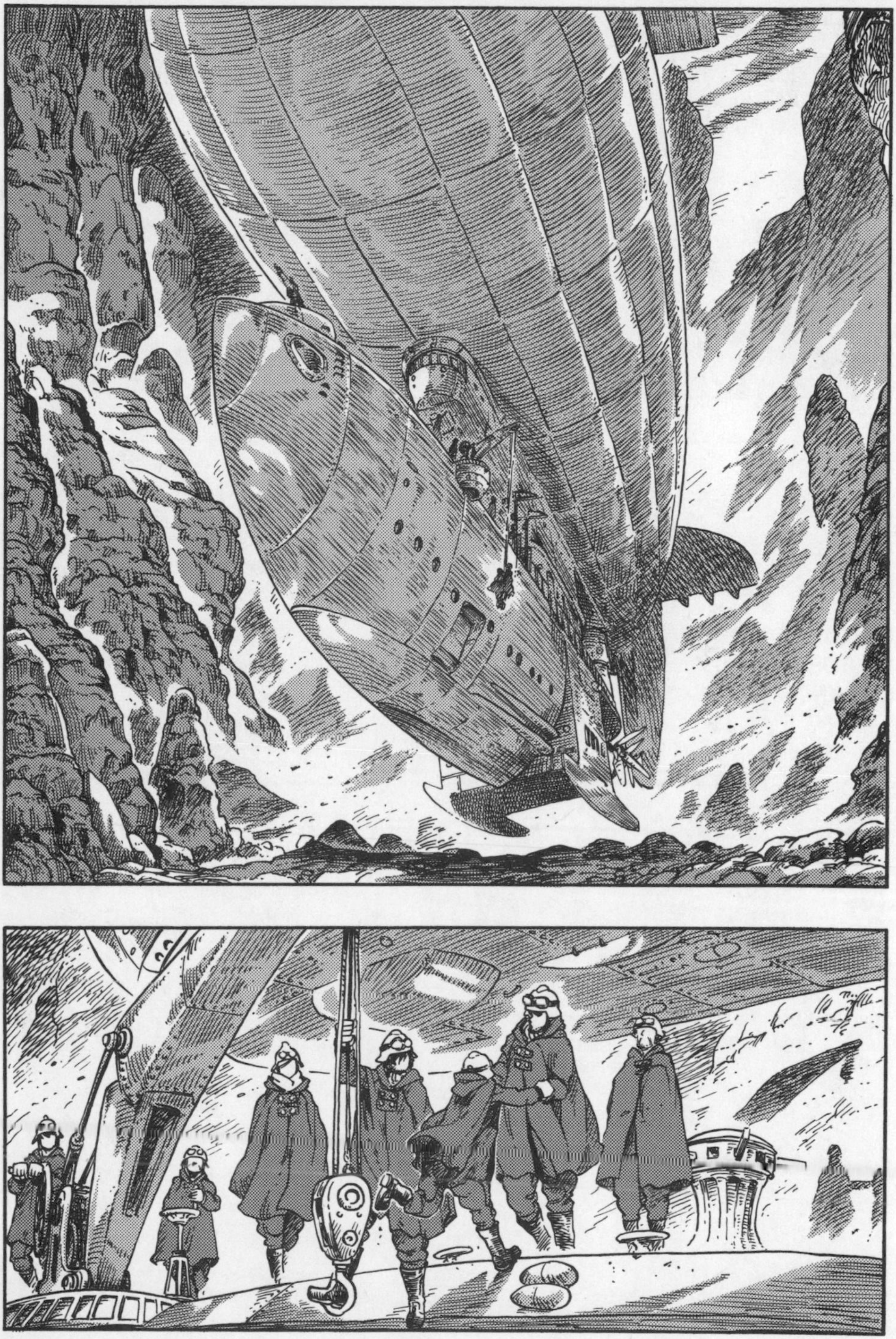

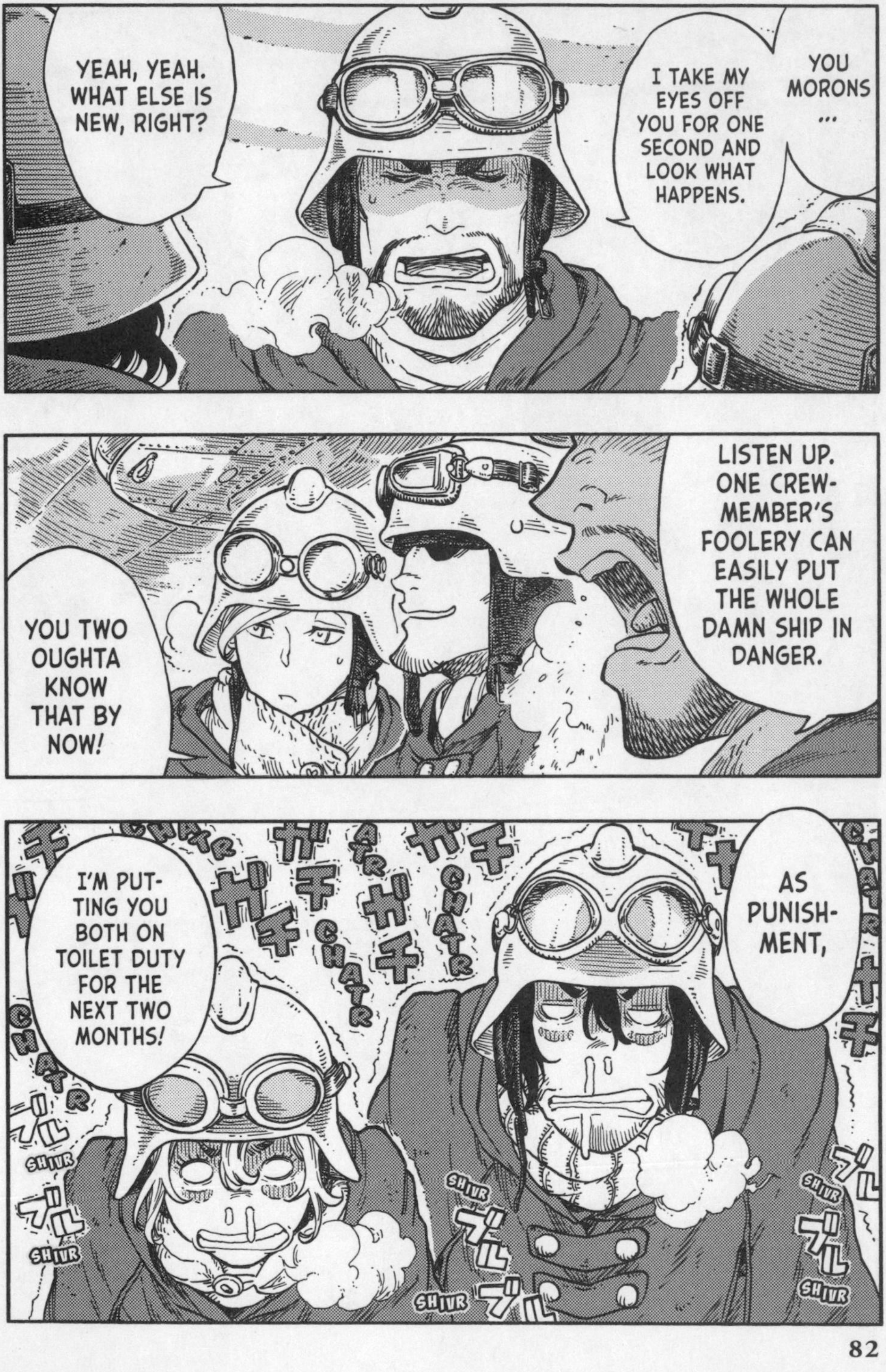
YOU MORONS ...
I TAKE MY EYES OFF YOU FOR ONE SECOND AND LOOK WHAT HAPPENS.
YEAH, YEAH. WHAT ELSE IS NEW, RIGHT?
LISTEN UP. ONE CREW-MEMBER'S FOOLERY CAN EASILY PUT THE WHOLE DAMN SHIP IN DANGER.
YOU TWO OUGHTA KNOW THAT BY NOW!
AS PUNISH-MENT,
I'M PUT-TING YOU BOTH ON TOILET DUTY FOR THE NEXT TWO MONTHS!
CHATR
SHIVR

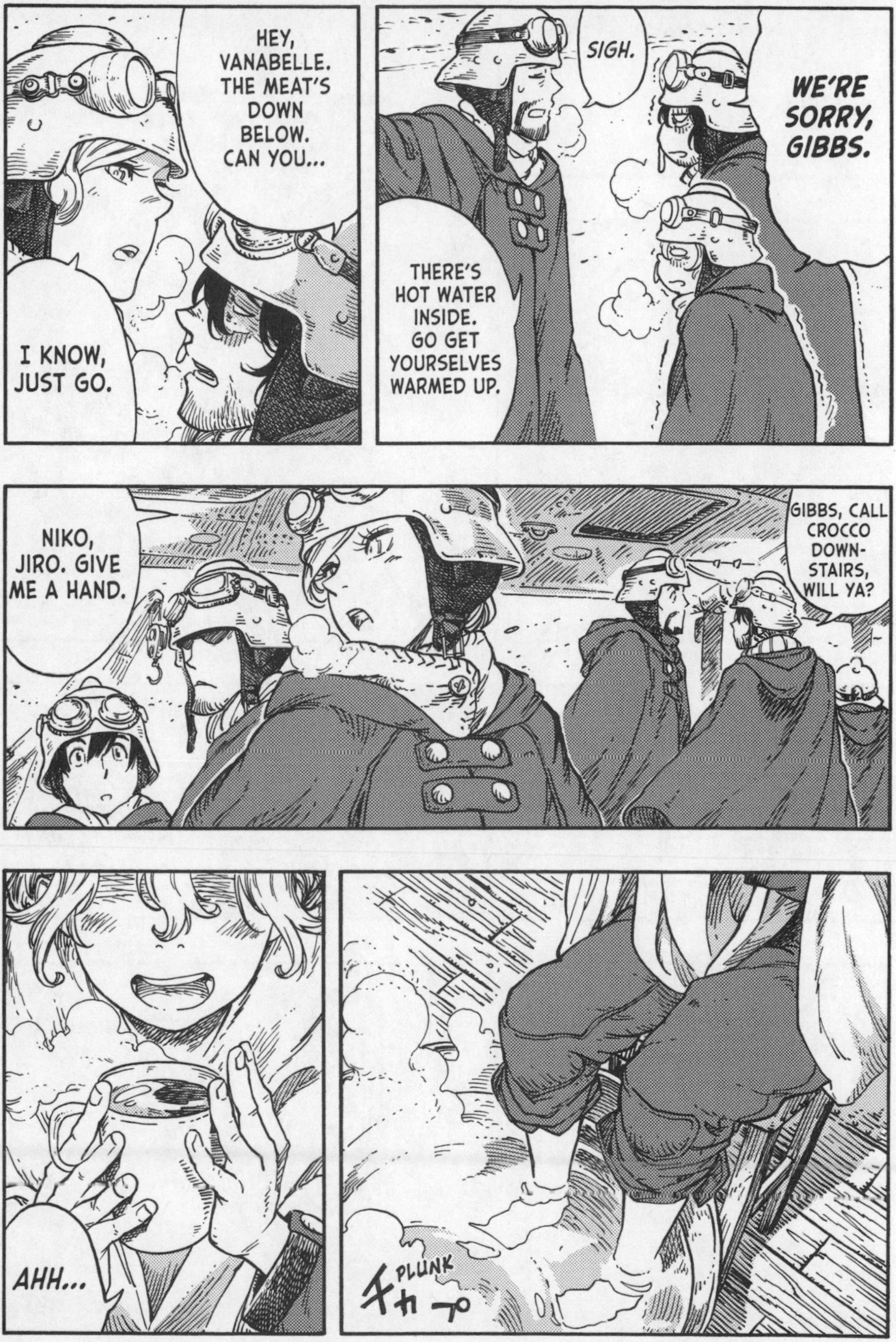
WE'RE SORRY, GIBBS.
SIGH.
THERE'S HOT WATER INSIDE. GO GET YOURSELVES WARMED UP.
HEY, VANABELLE. THE MEAT'S DOWN BELOW. CAN YOU...
I KNOW, JUST GO.
GIBBS, CALL CROCCO DOWN-STAIRS, WILL YA?
NIKO, JIRO. GIVE ME A HAND.
PLUNK
AHH...

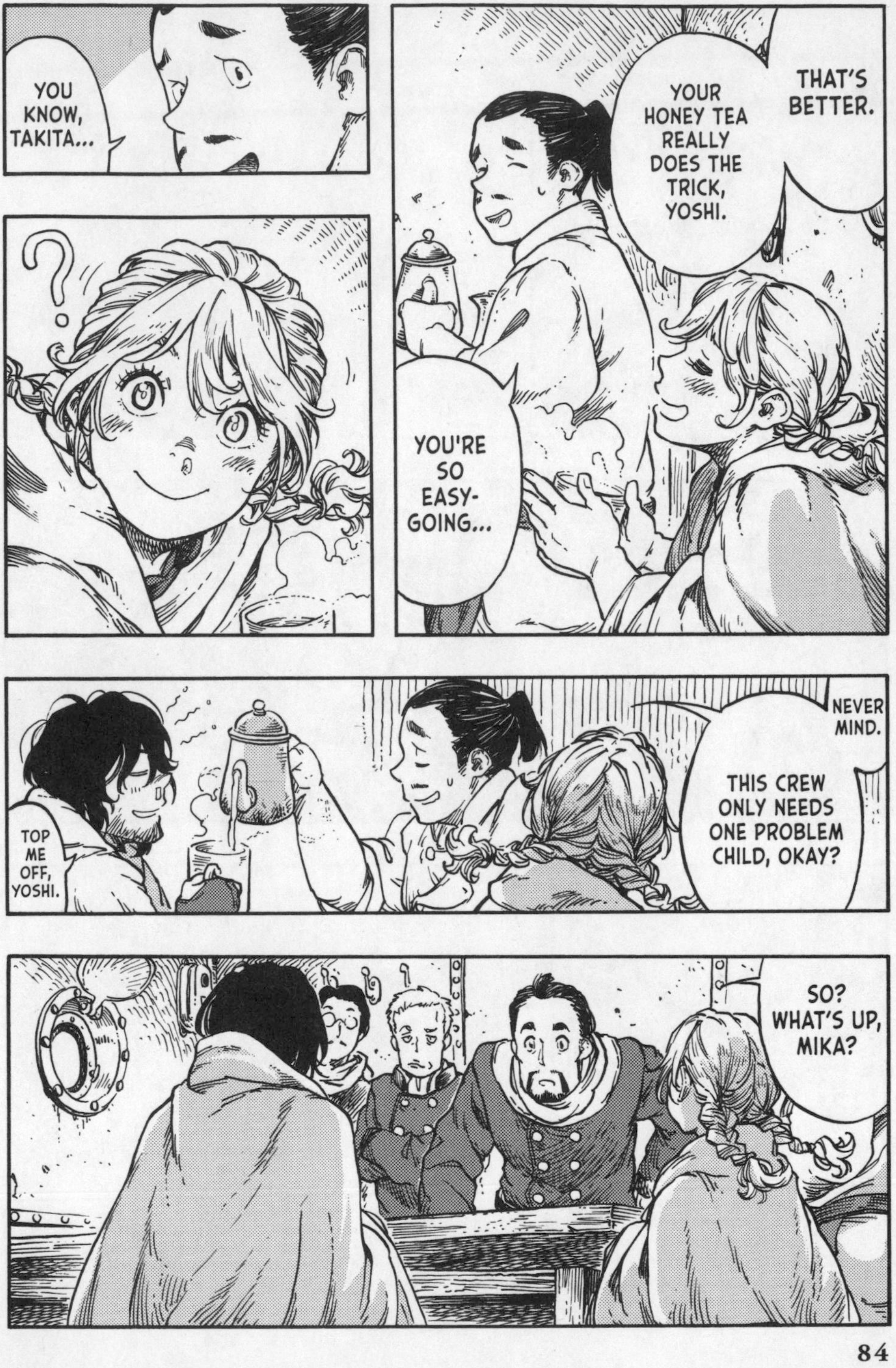
THAT'S BETTER.
YOUR HONEY TEA REALLY DOES THE TRICK, YOSHI.
YOU'RE SO EASY-GOING...
YOU KNOW, TAKITA...
?
NEVER MIND.
THIS CREW ONLY NEEDS ONE PROBLEM CHILD, OKAY?
TOP ME OFF, YOSHI.
SO? WHAT'S UP, MIKA?

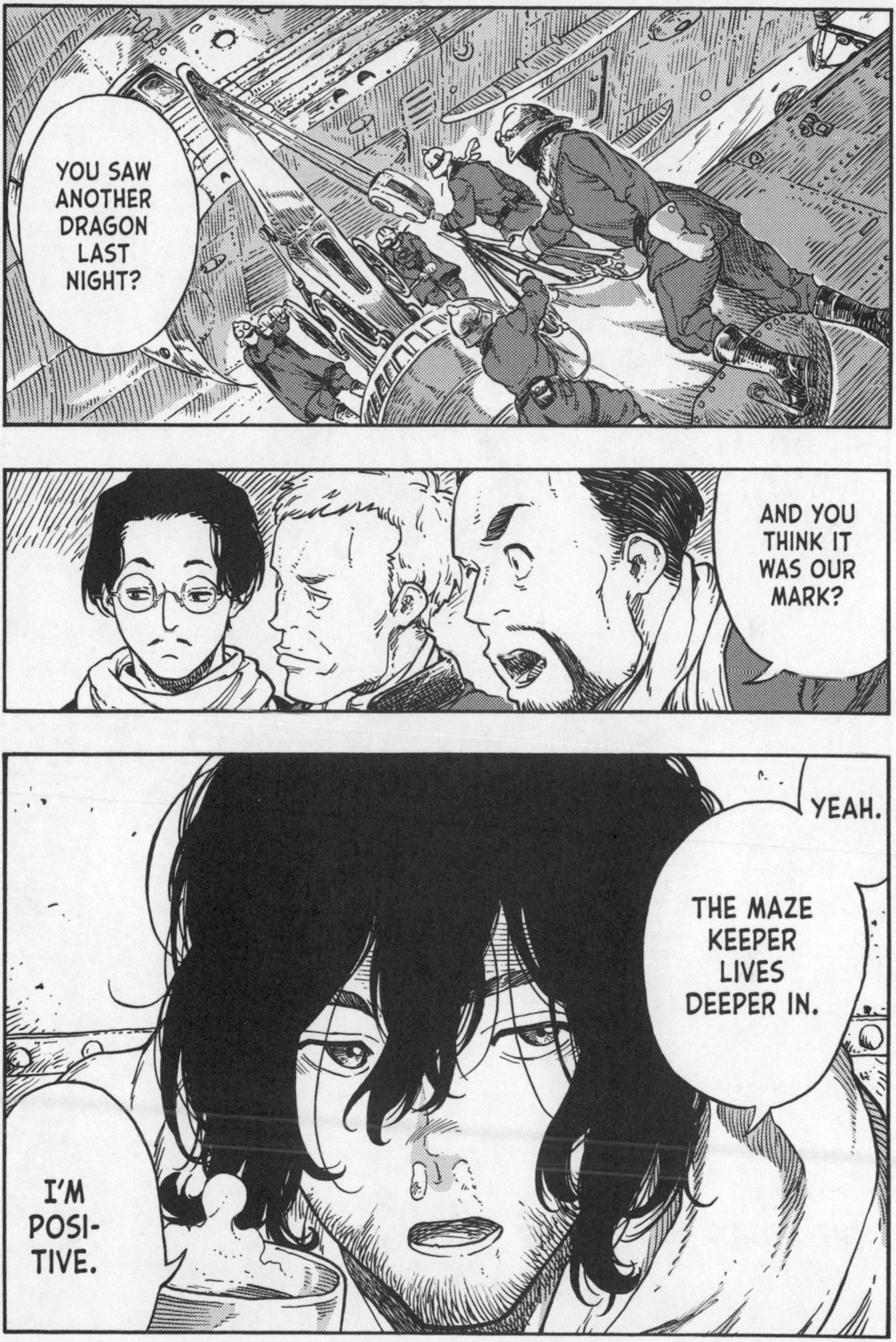
YOU SAW ANOTHER DRAGON LAST NIGHT?
AND YOU THINK IT WAS OUR MARK?
YEAH.
THE MAZE KEEPER LIVES DEEPER IN.
I'M POSI-TIVE.

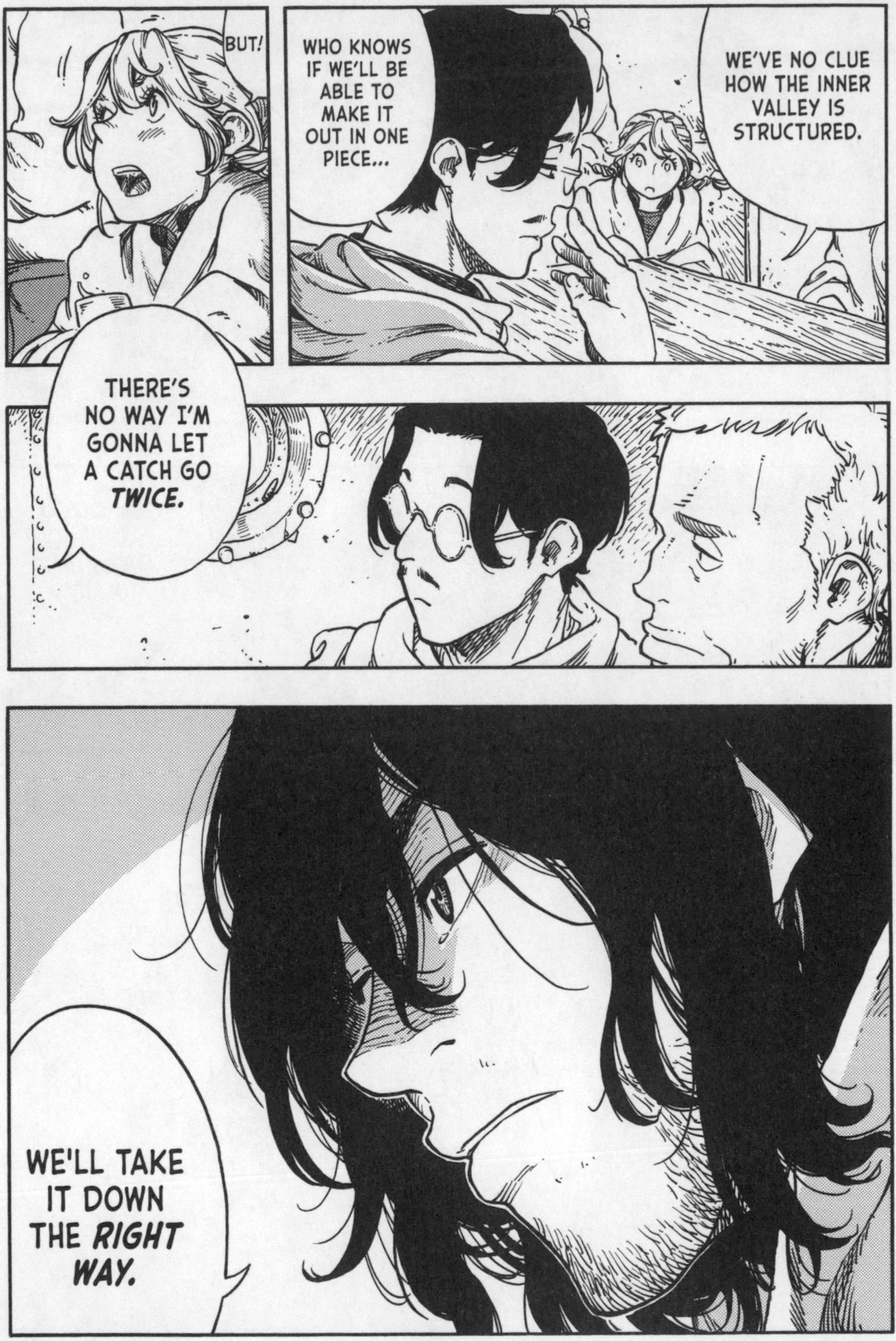
WE'VE NO CLUE HOW THE INNER VALLEY IS STRUCTURED.
WHO KNOWS IF WE'LL BE ABLE TO MAKE IT OUT IN ONE PIECE...
BUT!
THERE'S NO WAY I'M GONNA LET A CATCH GO *TWICE.*
WE'LL TAKE IT DOWN THE *RIGHT WAY.*

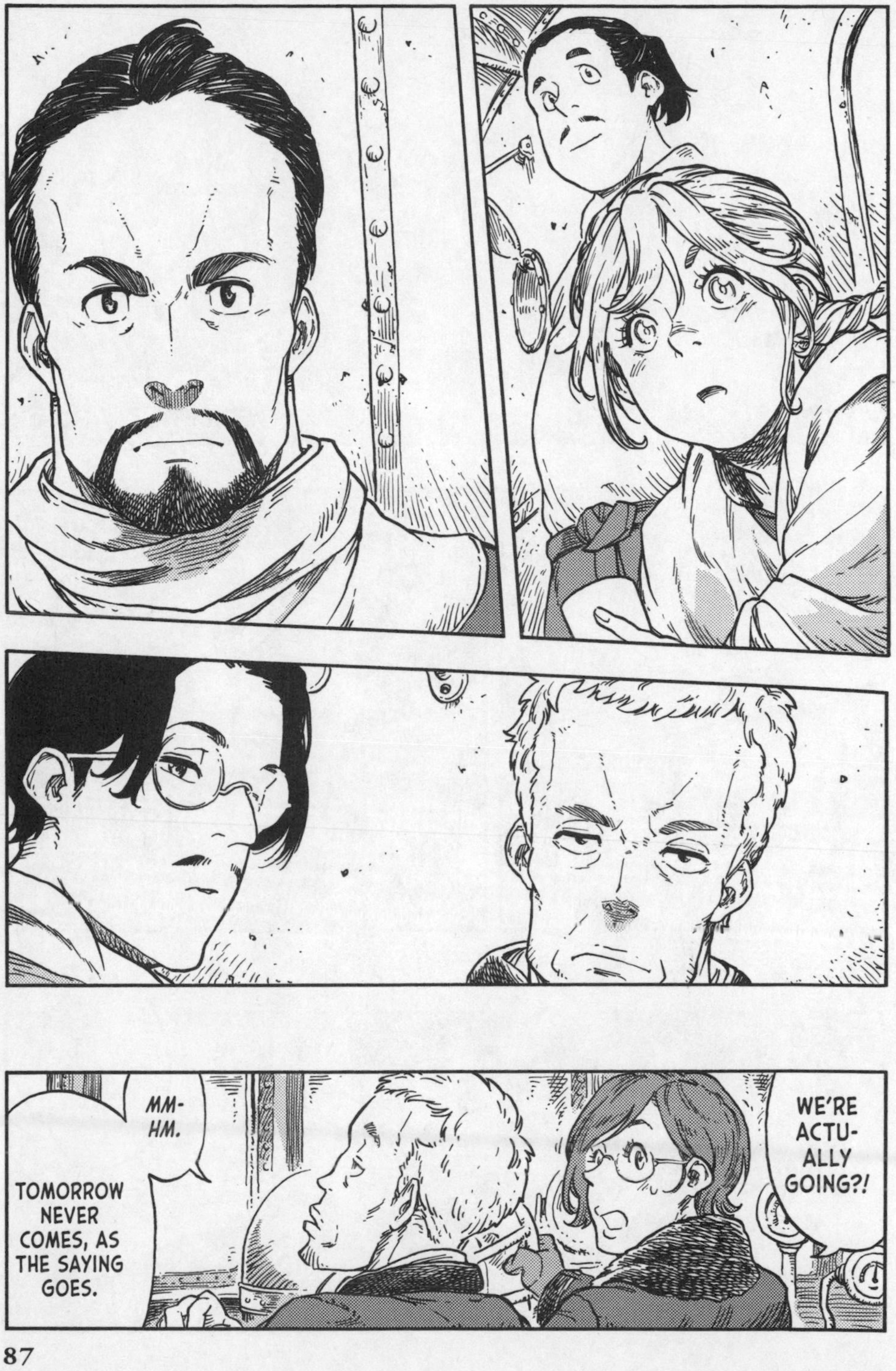
WE'RE ACTU-ALLY GOING?!
MM-HM.
TOMORROW NEVER COMES, AS THE SAYING GOES.

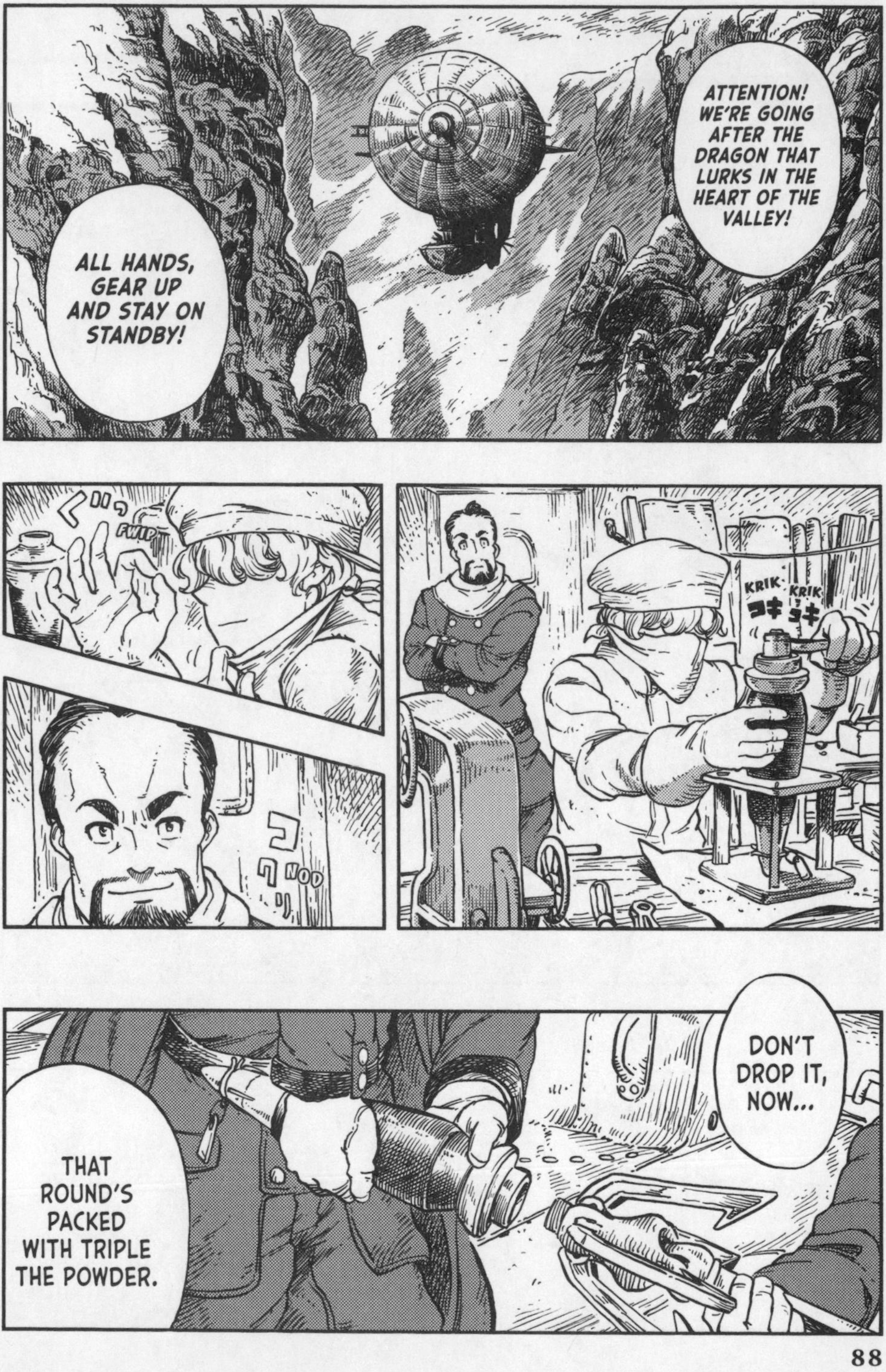
ATTENTION! WE'RE GOING AFTER THE DRAGON THAT LURKS IN THE HEART OF THE VALLEY!
ALL HANDS, GEAR UP AND STAY ON STANDBY!
KRIK KRIK
FWIP
NOD
DON'T DROP IT, NOW...
THAT ROUND'S PACKED WITH TRIPLE THE POWDER.

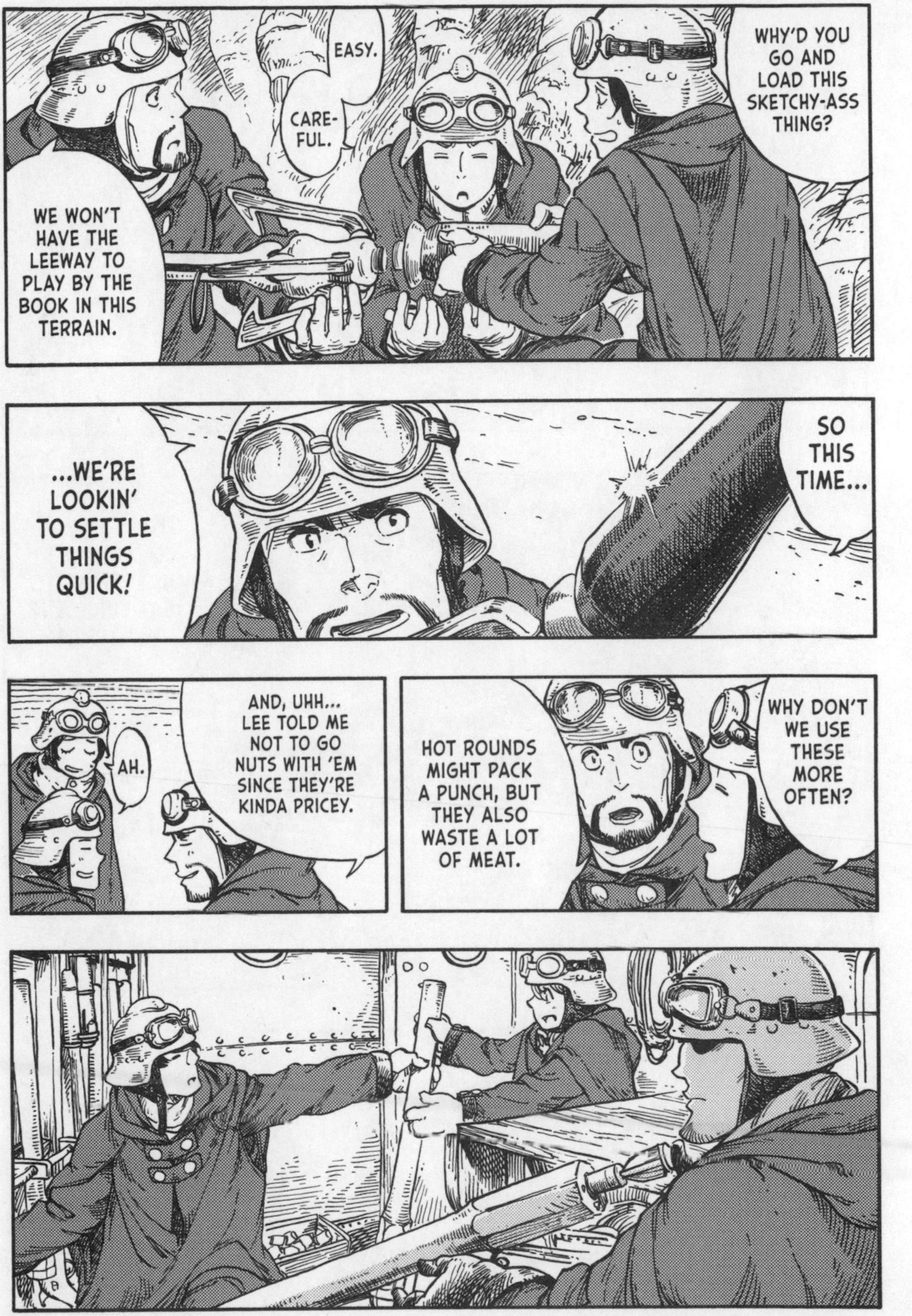
WHY'D YOU GO AND LOAD THIS SKETCHY-ASS THING?
EASY.
CARE-FUL.
WE WON'T HAVE THE LEEWAY TO PLAY BY THE BOOK IN THIS TERRAIN.
SO THIS TIME...
...WE'RE LOOKIN' TO SETTLE THINGS QUICK!
WHY DON'T WE USE THESE MORE OFTEN?
HOT ROUNDS MIGHT PACK A PUNCH, BUT THEY ALSO WASTE A LOT OF MEAT.
AND, UHH... LEE TOLD ME NOT TO GO NUTS WITH 'EM SINCE THEY'RE KINDA PRICEY.
AH.

FOOD'S READY, GANG! DIG IN NOW WHILE YOU HAVE A CHANCE!

AW, YEAH!

CHACK

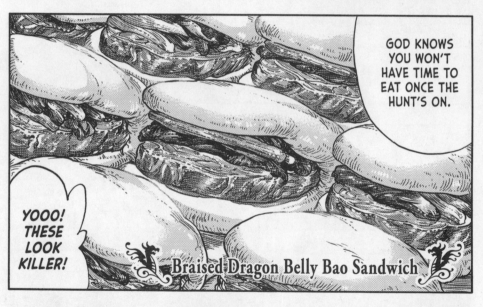

GOD KNOWS YOU WON'T HAVE TIME TO EAT ONCE THE HUNT'S ON.

YOOO! THESE LOOK KILLER!

Braised Dragon Belly Bao Sandwich

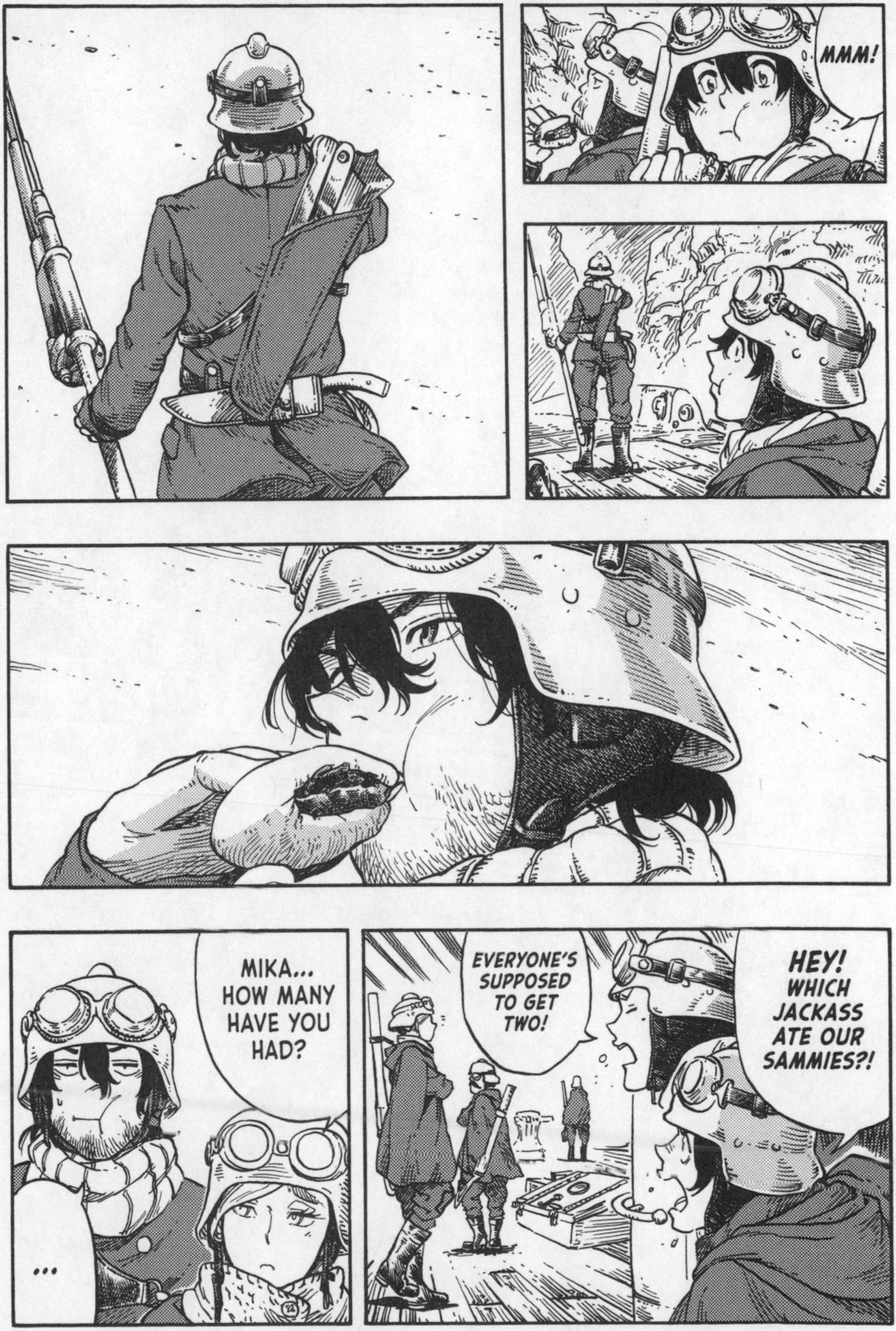
MMM!
HEY! WHICH JACKASS ATE OUR SAMMIES?!
EVERYONE'S SUPPOSED TO GET TWO!
MIKA... HOW MANY HAVE YOU HAD?
...

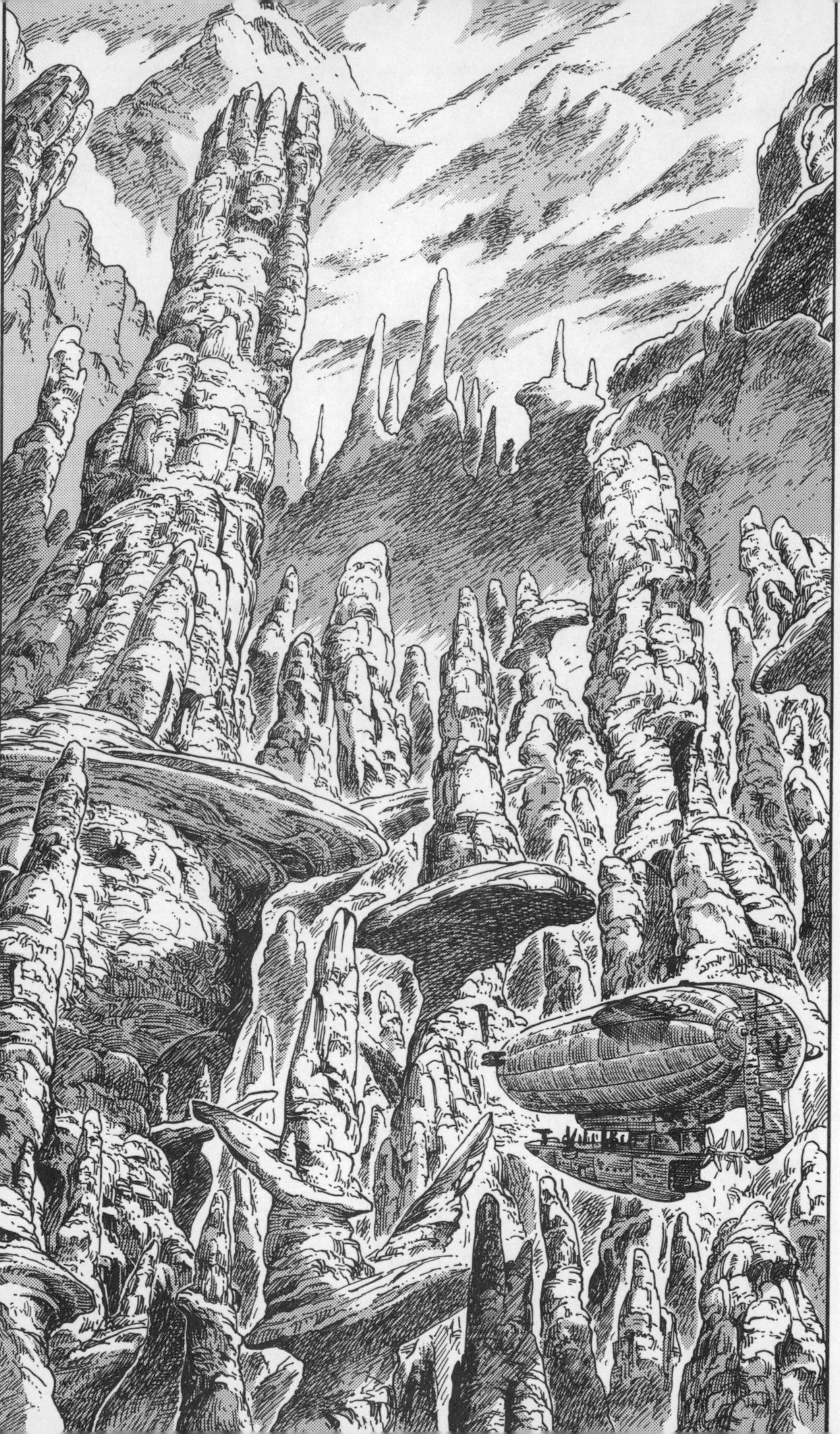

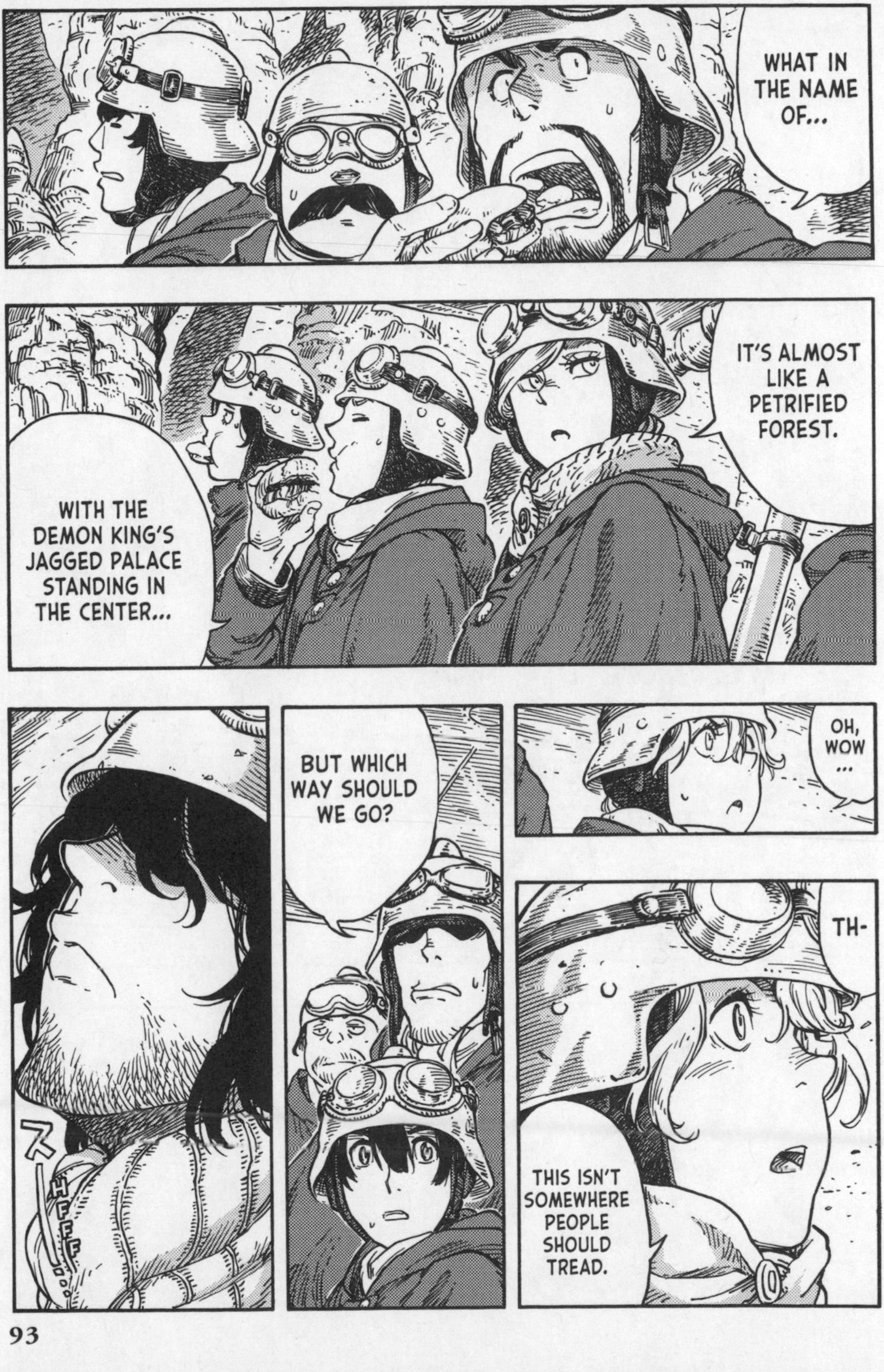
WHAT IN THE NAME OF...
IT'S ALMOST LIKE A PETRIFIED FOREST.
WITH THE DEMON KING'S JAGGED PALACE STANDING IN THE CENTER...
OH, WOW ...
TH-
THIS ISN'T SOMEWHERE PEOPLE SHOULD TREAD.
BUT WHICH WAY SHOULD WE GO?
ス
HFFF...

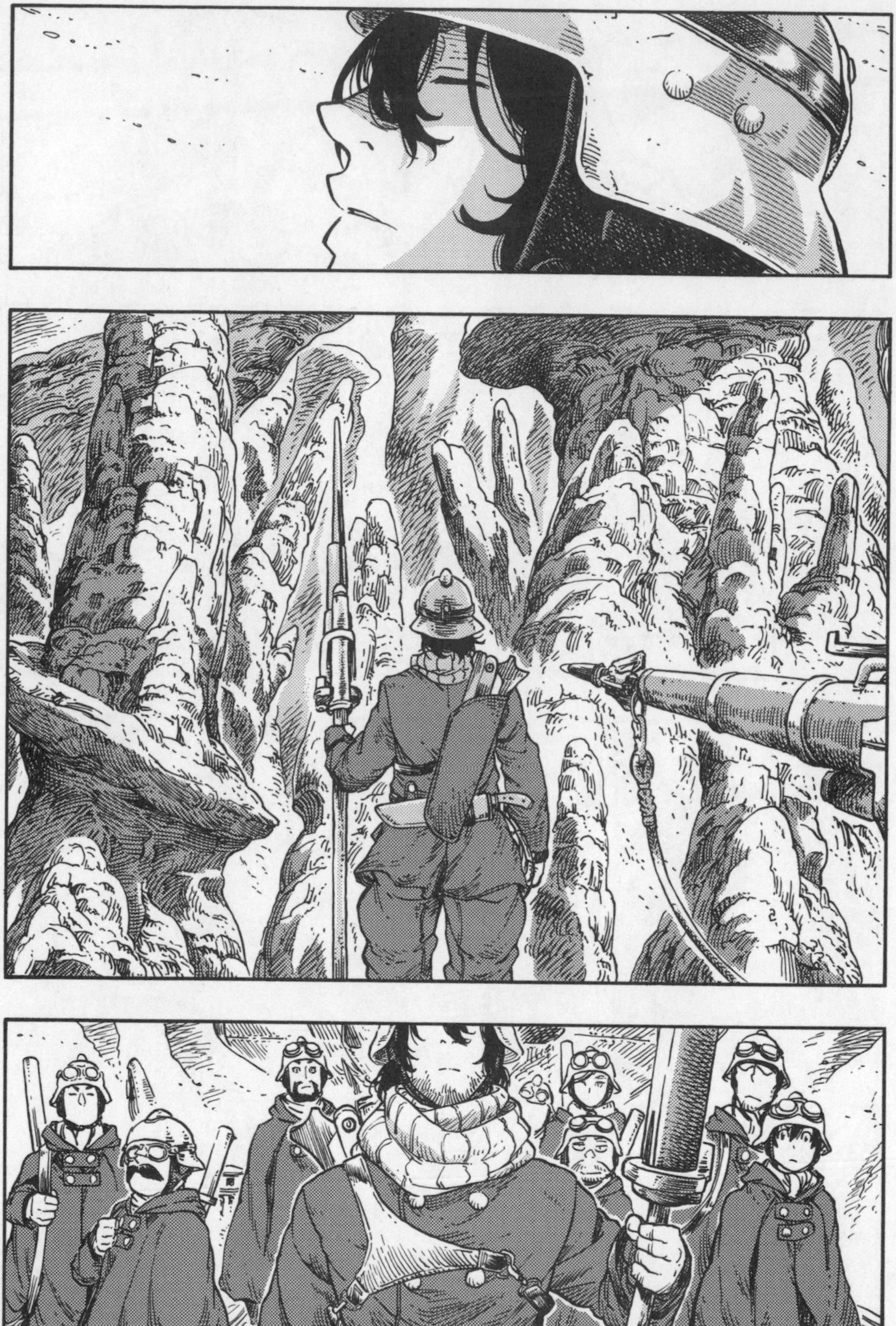

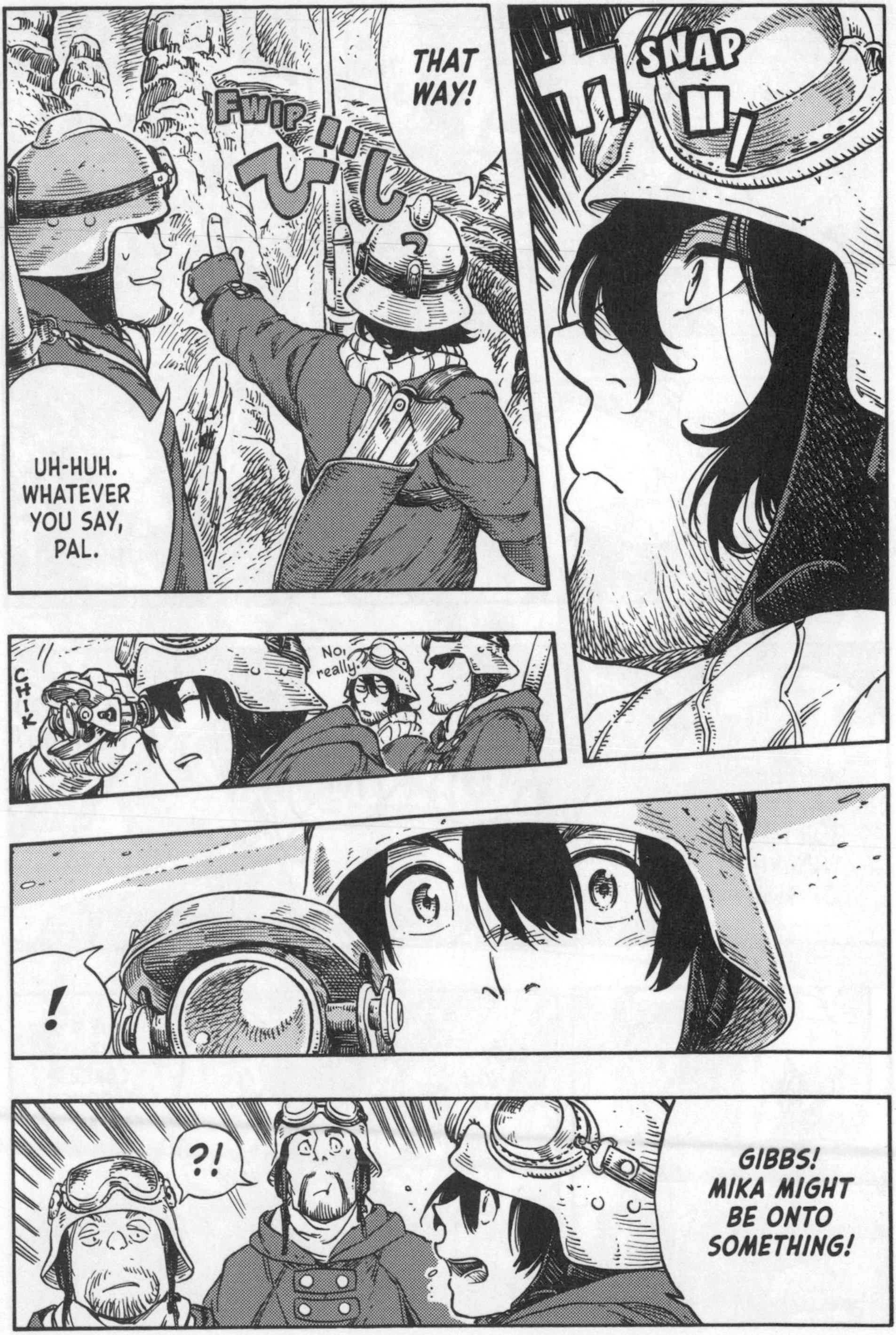
SNAP
THAT WAY!
FWIP
UH-HUH. WHATEVER YOU SAY, PAL.
No, really.
CHIK
!
GIBBS! MIKA MIGHT BE ONTO SOMETHING!
?!

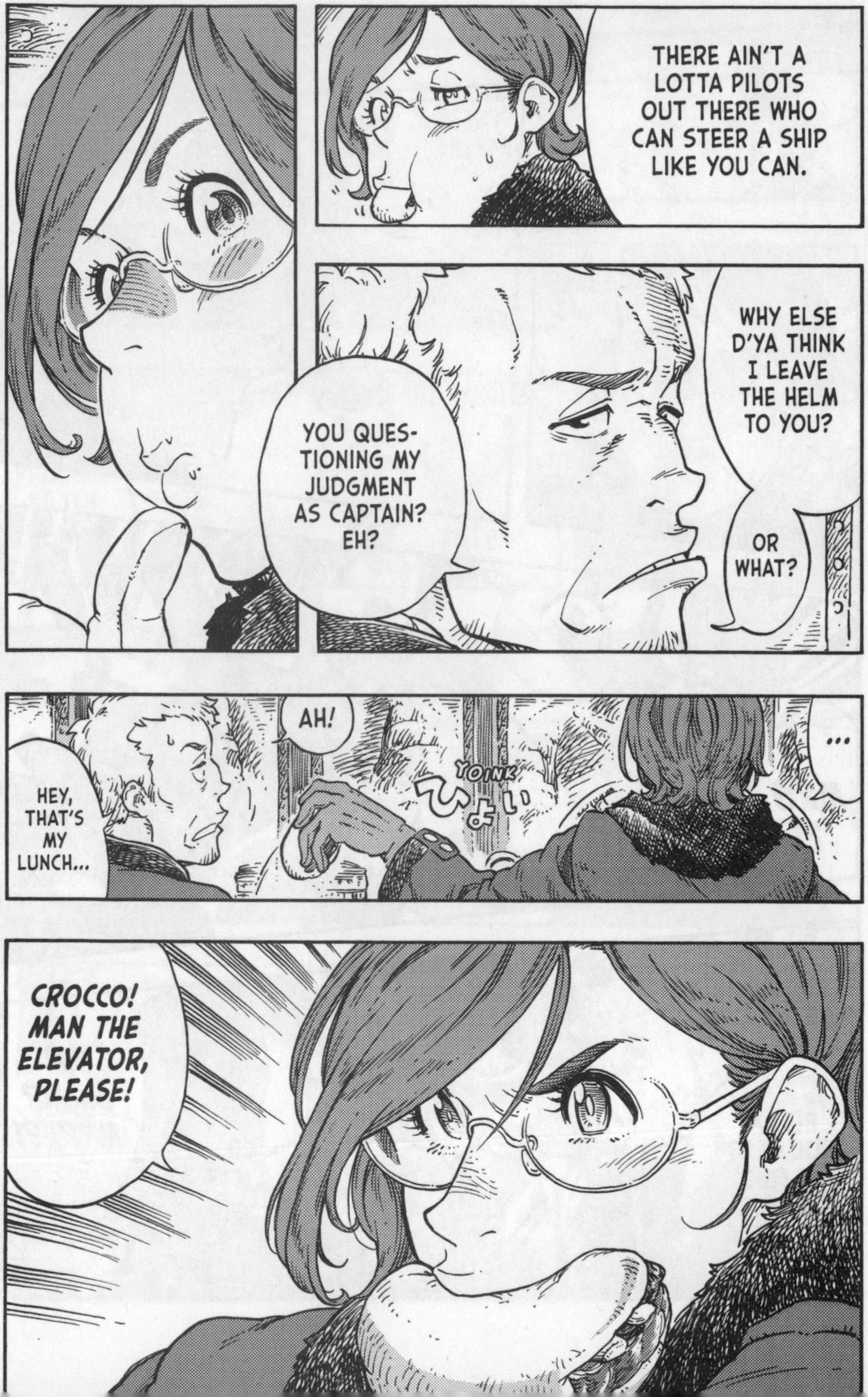
THERE AIN'T A LOTTA PILOTS OUT THERE WHO CAN STEER A SHIP LIKE YOU CAN.
WHY ELSE D'YA THINK I LEAVE THE HELM TO YOU?
OR WHAT?
YOU QUES-TIONING MY JUDGMENT AS CAPTAIN? EH?
...
YOINK
ひょい
AH!
HEY, THAT'S MY LUNCH...
CROCCO! MAN THE ELEVATOR, PLEASE!

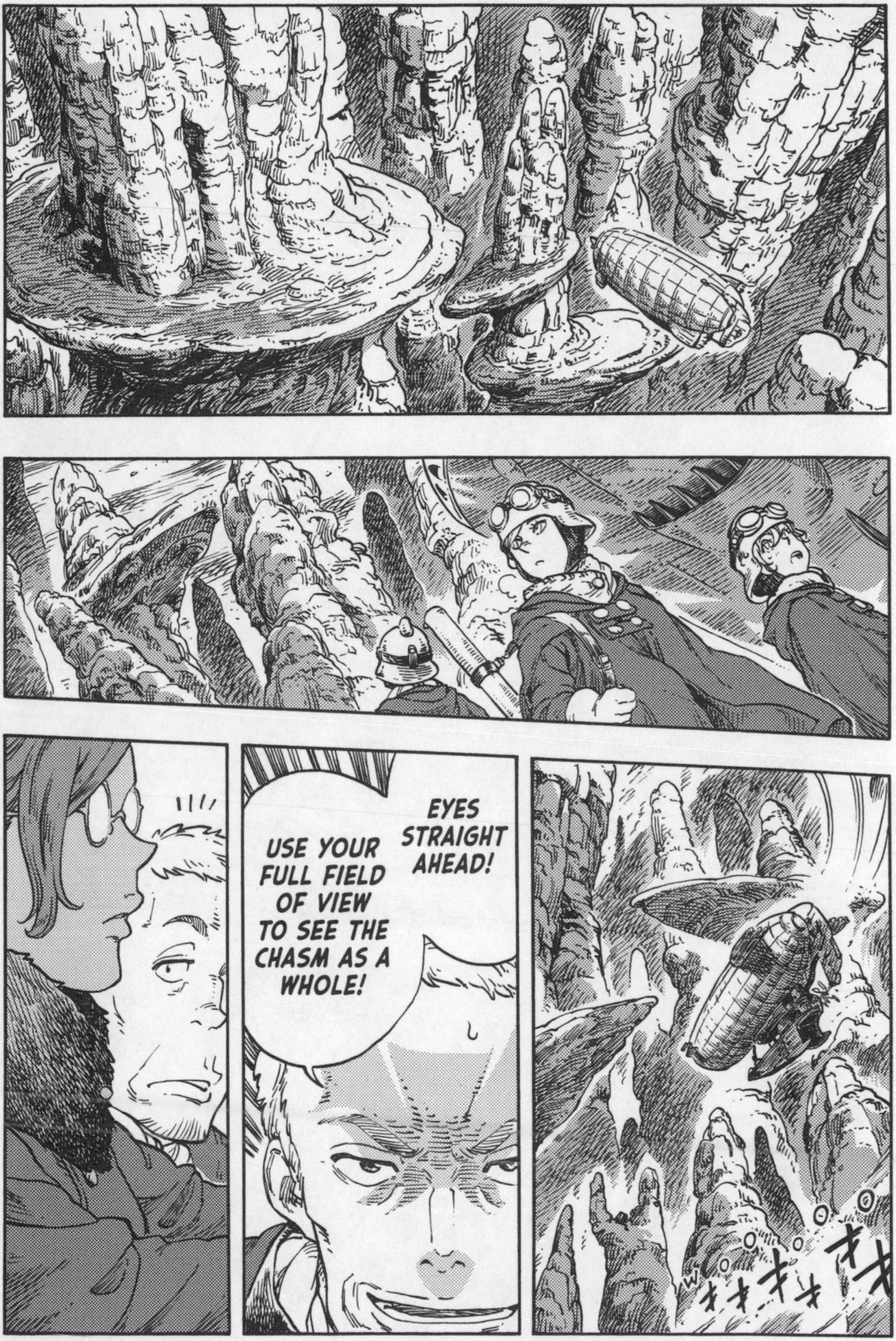
EYES STRAIGHT AHEAD!
USE YOUR FULL FIELD OF VIEW TO SEE THE CHASM AS A WHOLE!

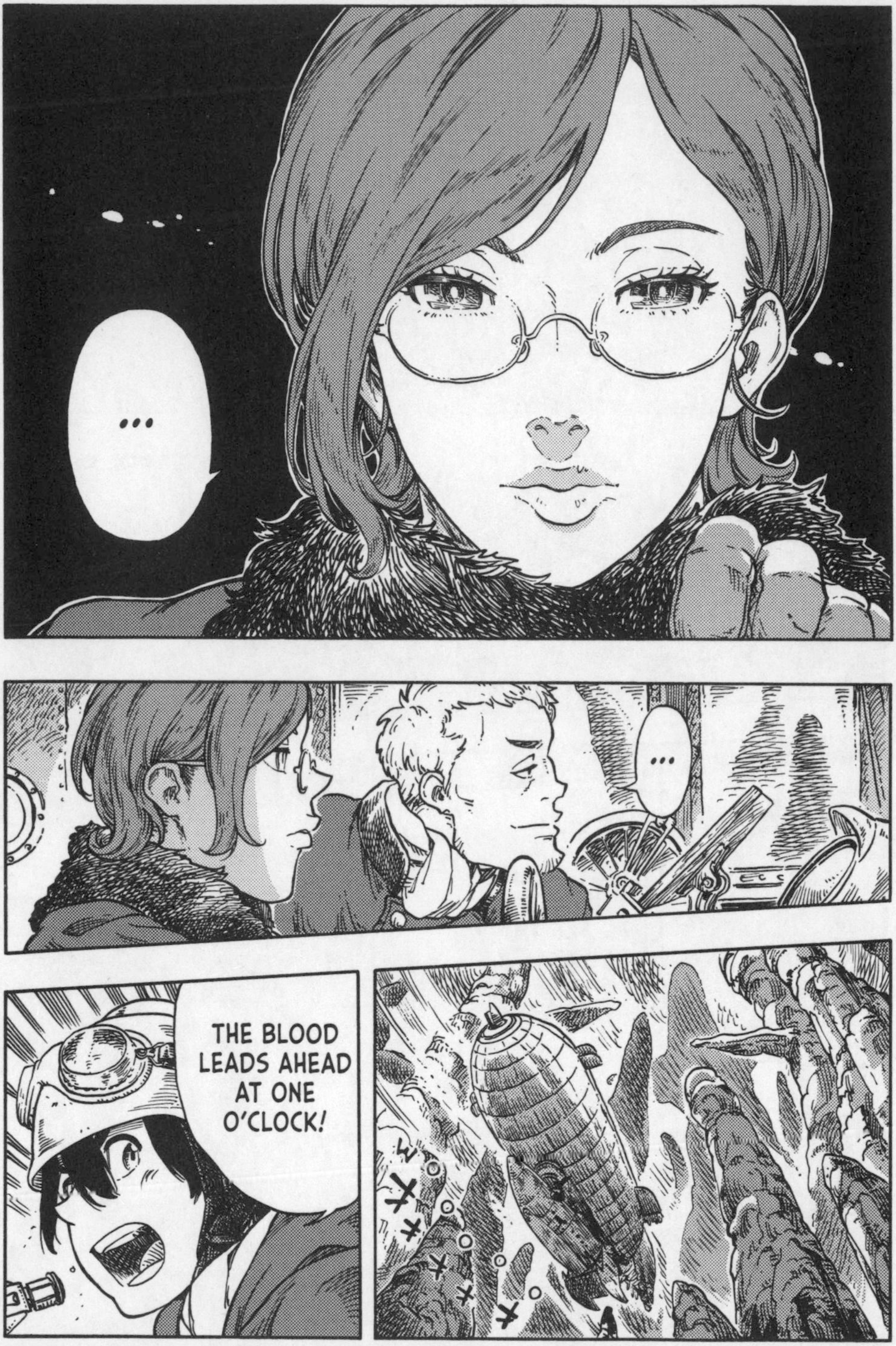
…
…
THE BLOOD LEADS AHEAD AT ONE O'CLOCK!

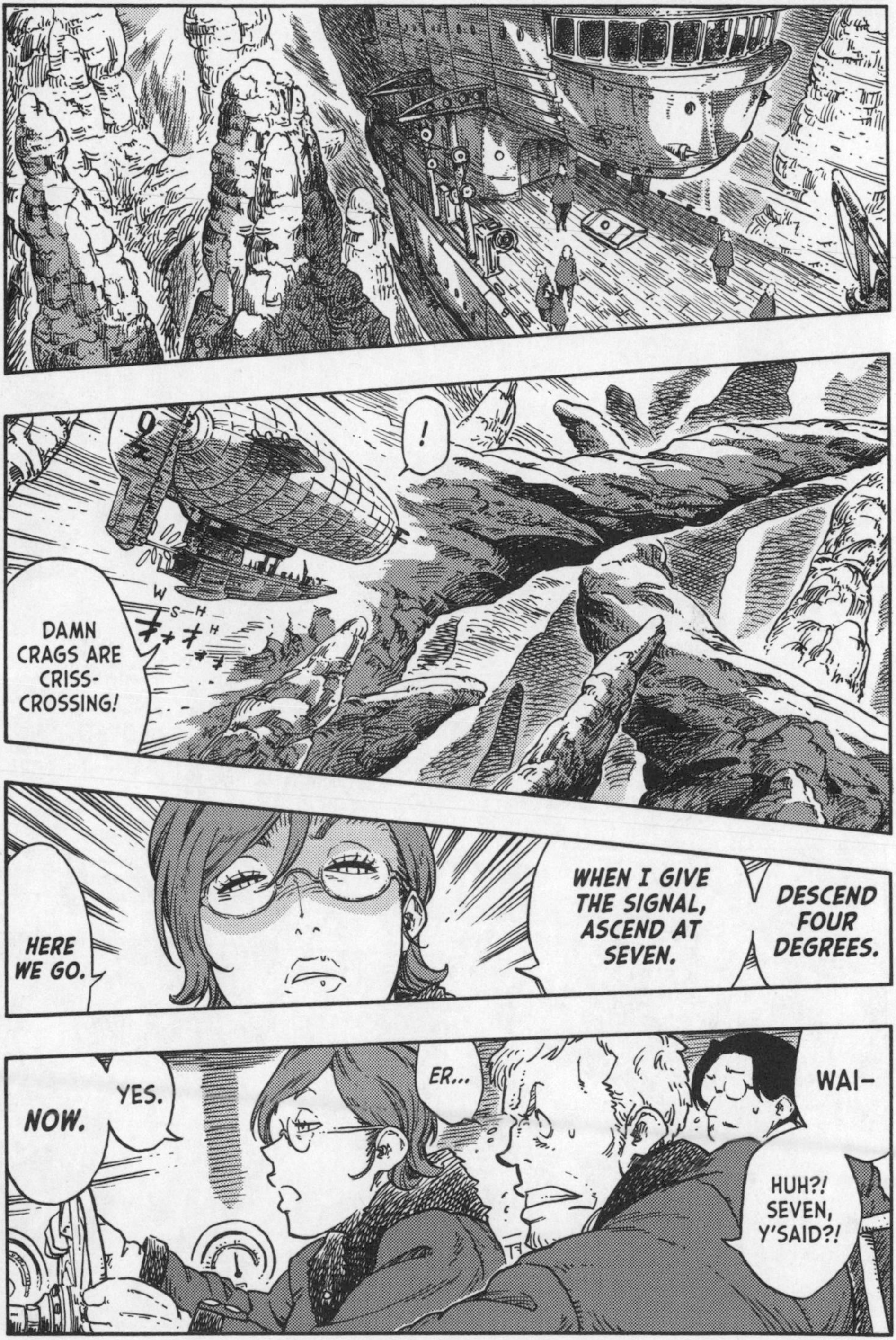
!
DAMN CRAGS ARE CRISS-CROSSING!
DESCEND FOUR DEGREES.
WHEN I GIVE THE SIGNAL, ASCEND AT SEVEN.
HERE WE GO.
WAI-
HUH?! SEVEN, Y'SAID?!
ER...
YES.
NOW.

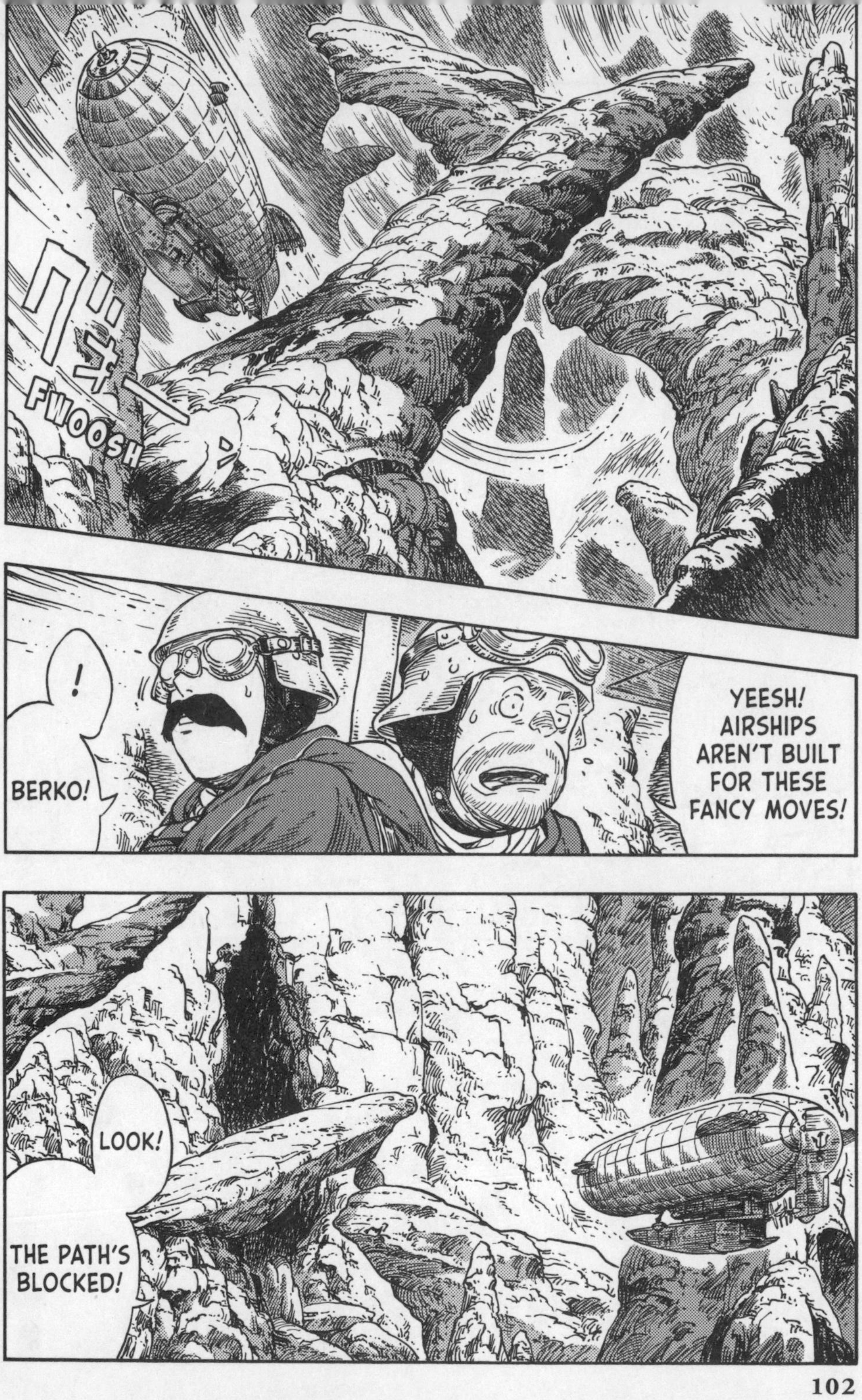
FWOOSH
YEESH! AIRSHIPS AREN'T BUILT FOR THESE FANCY MOVES!
!
BERKO!
LOOK!
THE PATH'S BLOCKED!

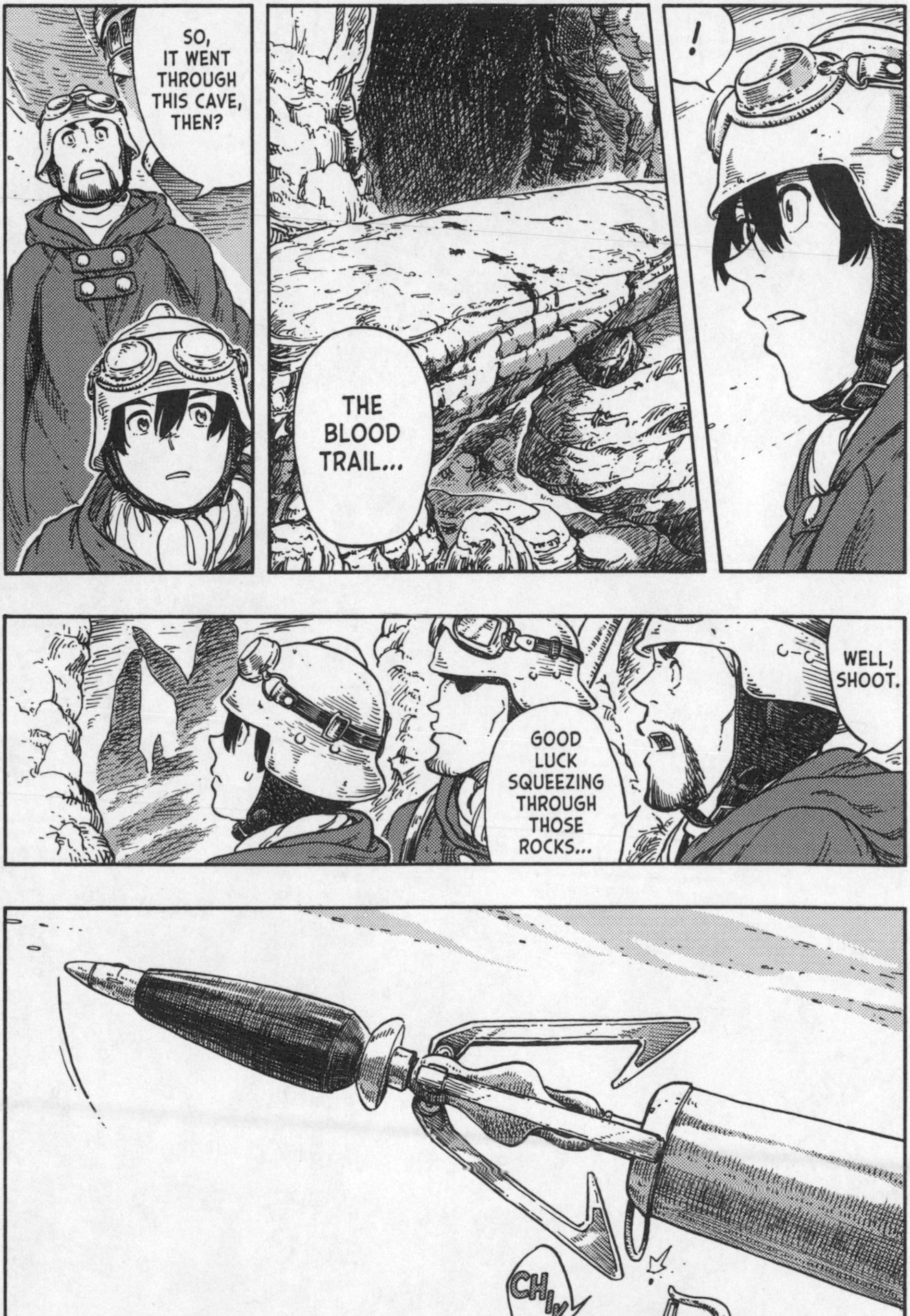
!
THE BLOOD TRAIL...
SO, IT WENT THROUGH THIS CAVE, THEN?
WELL, SHOOT.
GOOD LUCK SQUEEZING THROUGH THOSE ROCKS...
CHIK

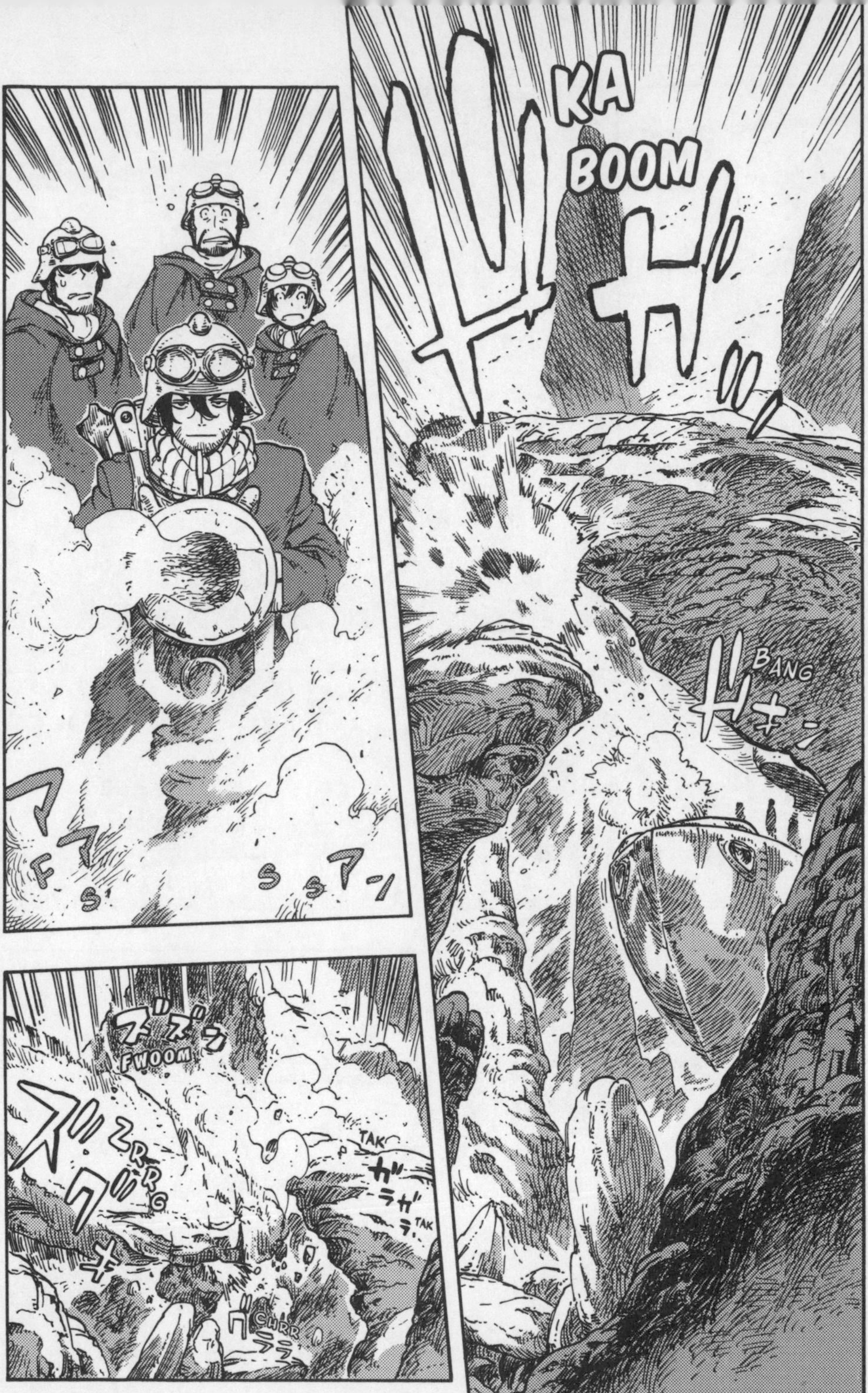
KA
BOOM
BANG
F
S
S
S
FWOOM
ZRRRG
TAK
TAK
CHRR

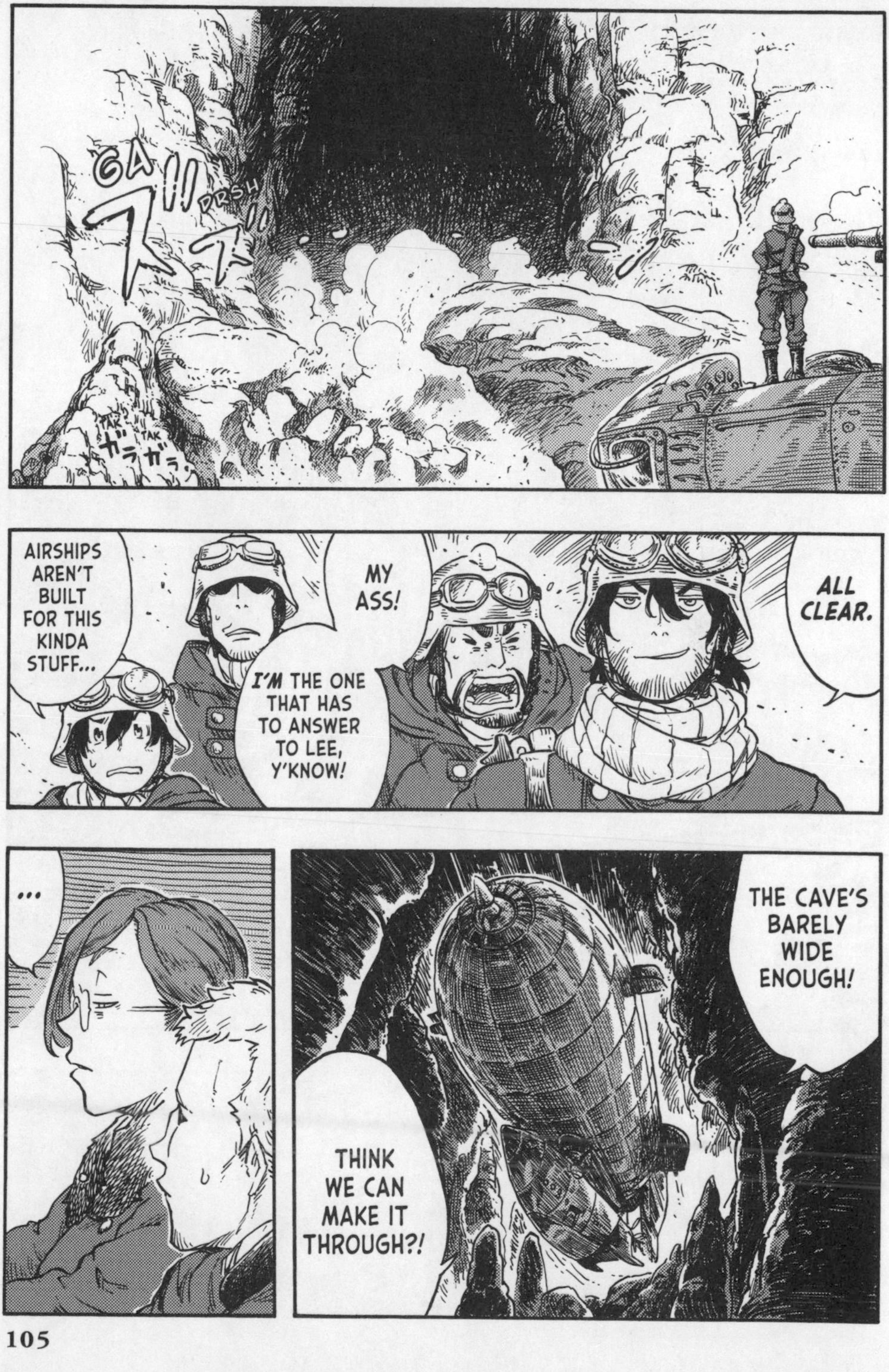
GA
DRSH
TAK TAK
ALL CLEAR.
MY ASS!
I'M THE ONE THAT HAS TO ANSWER TO LEE, Y'KNOW!
AIRSHIPS AREN'T BUILT FOR THIS KINDA STUFF...
THE CAVE'S BARELY WIDE ENOUGH!
THINK WE CAN MAKE IT THROUGH?!
...

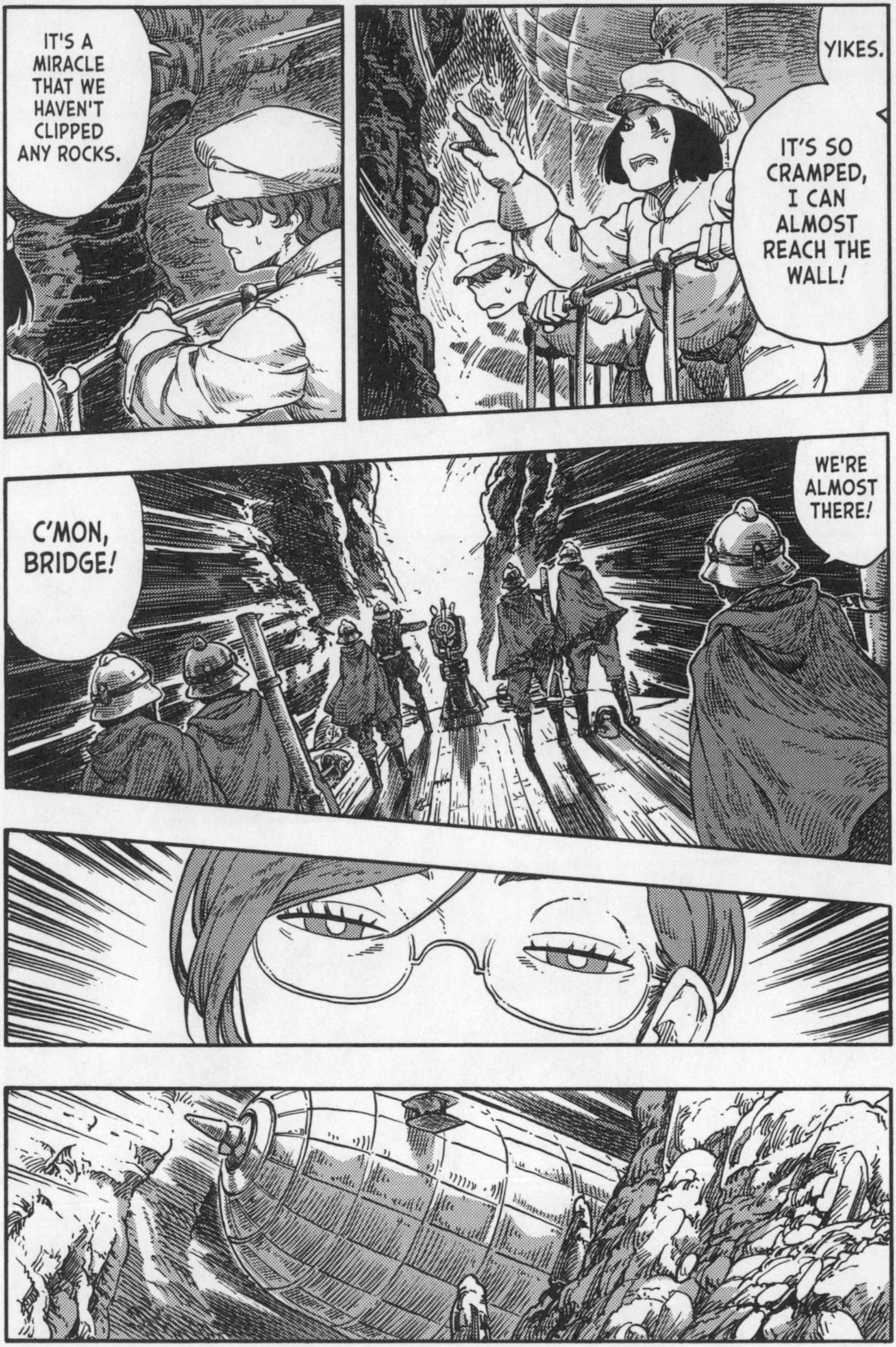
YIKES.
IT'S SO CRAMPED, I CAN ALMOST REACH THE WALL!
IT'S A MIRACLE THAT WE HAVEN'T CLIPPED ANY ROCKS.
WE'RE ALMOST THERE!
C'MON, BRIDGE!

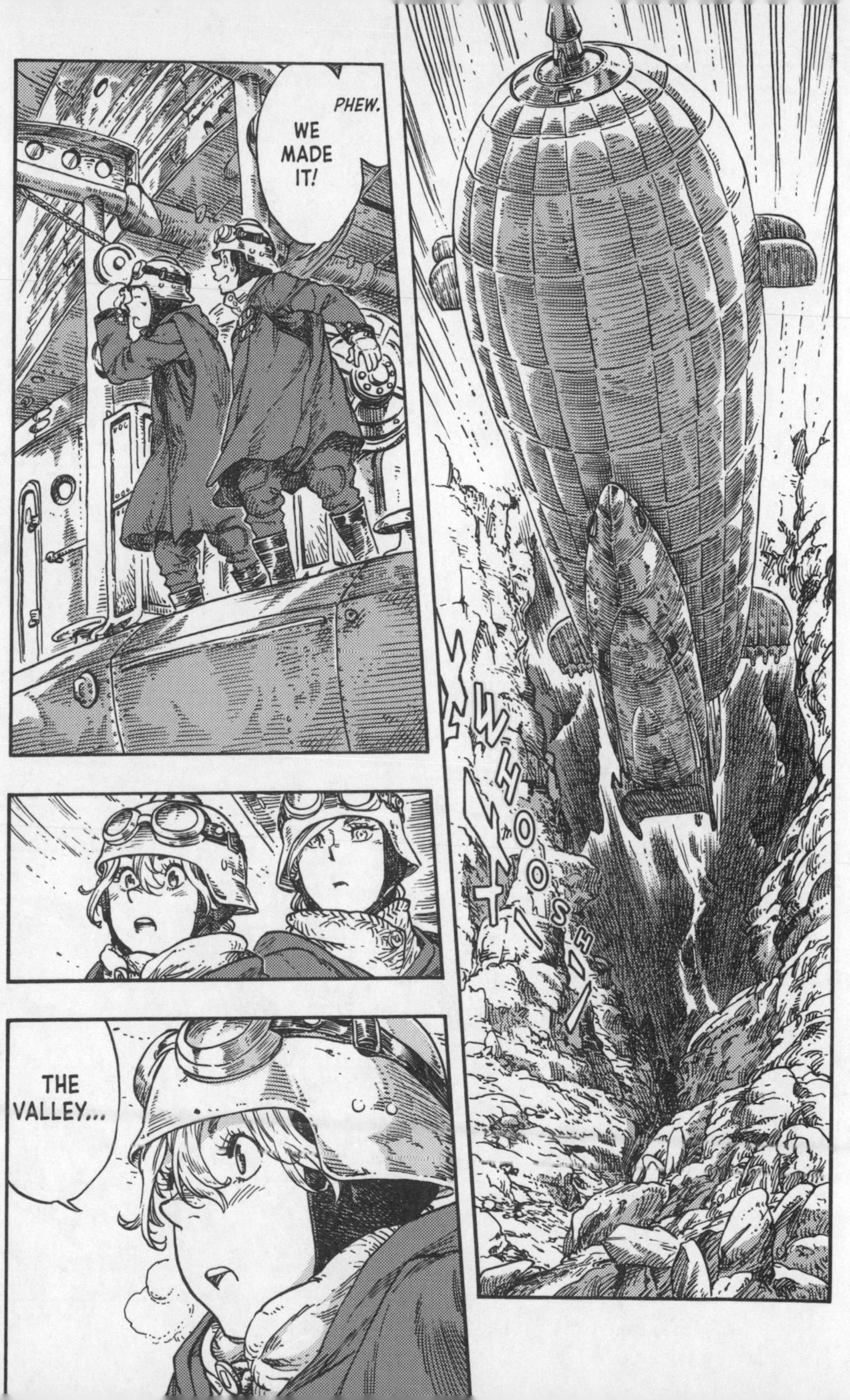
WHOOSH
PHEW.
WE MADE IT!
THE VALLEY...

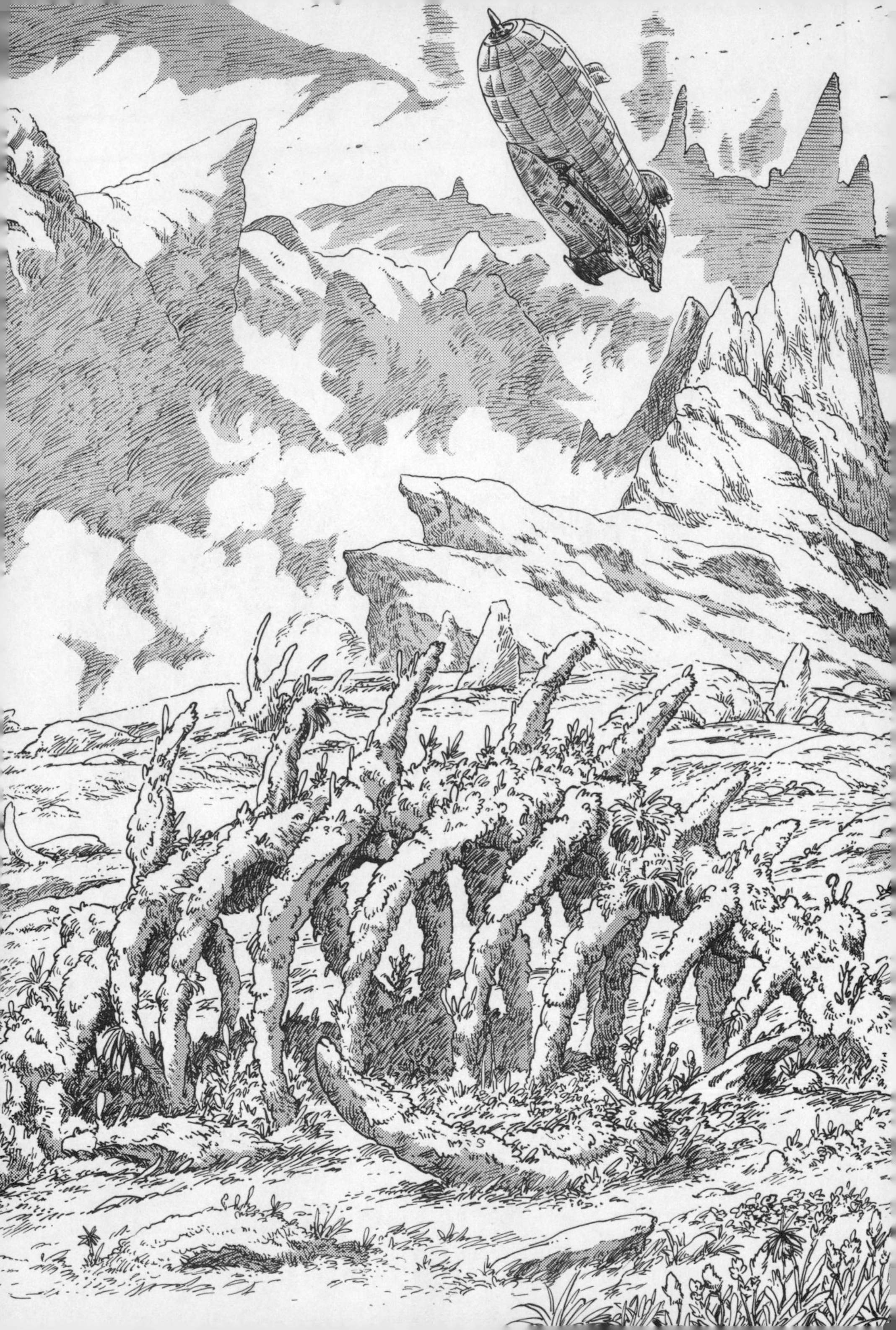

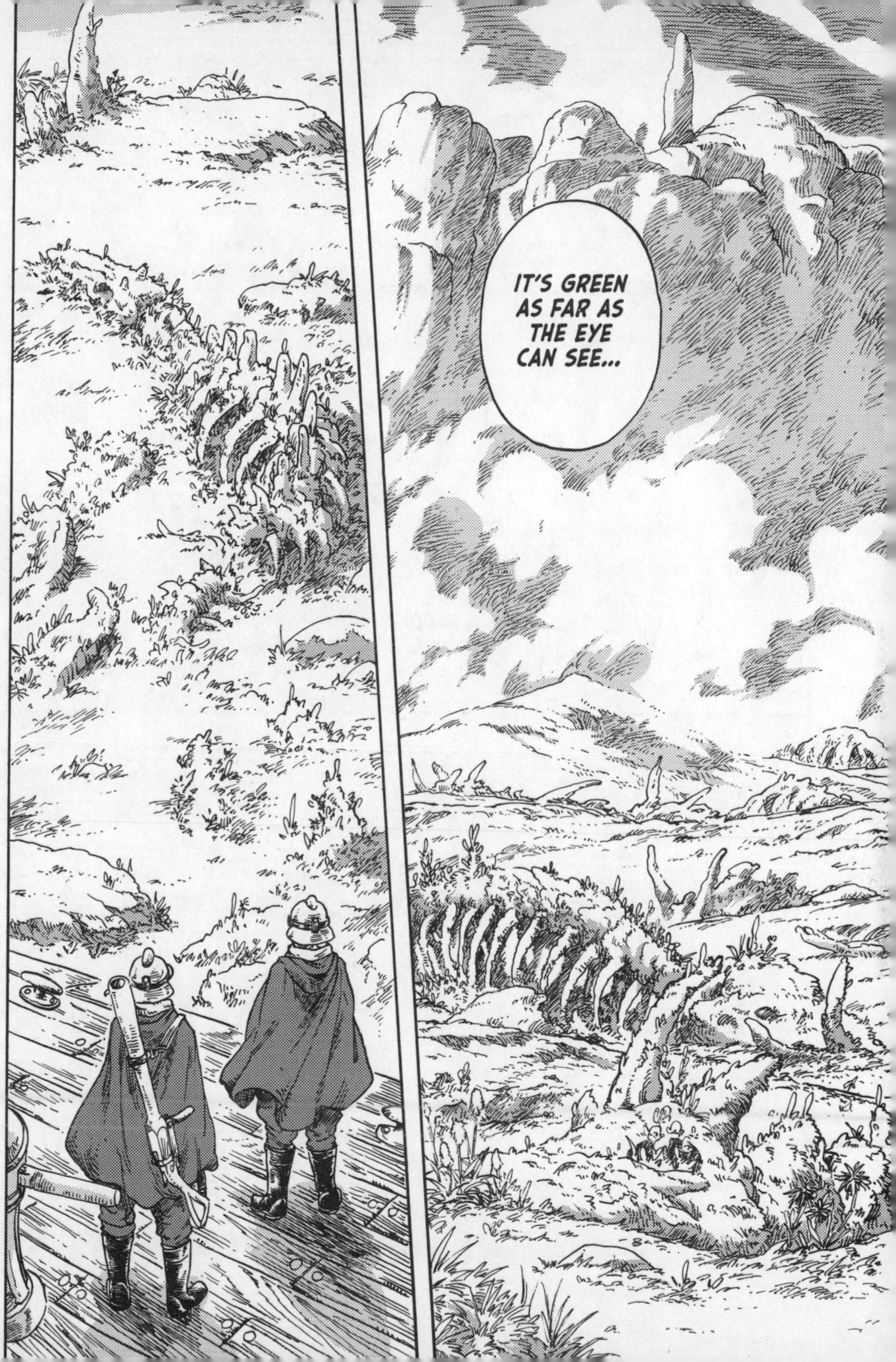
IT'S GREEN AS FAR AS THE EYE CAN SEE...

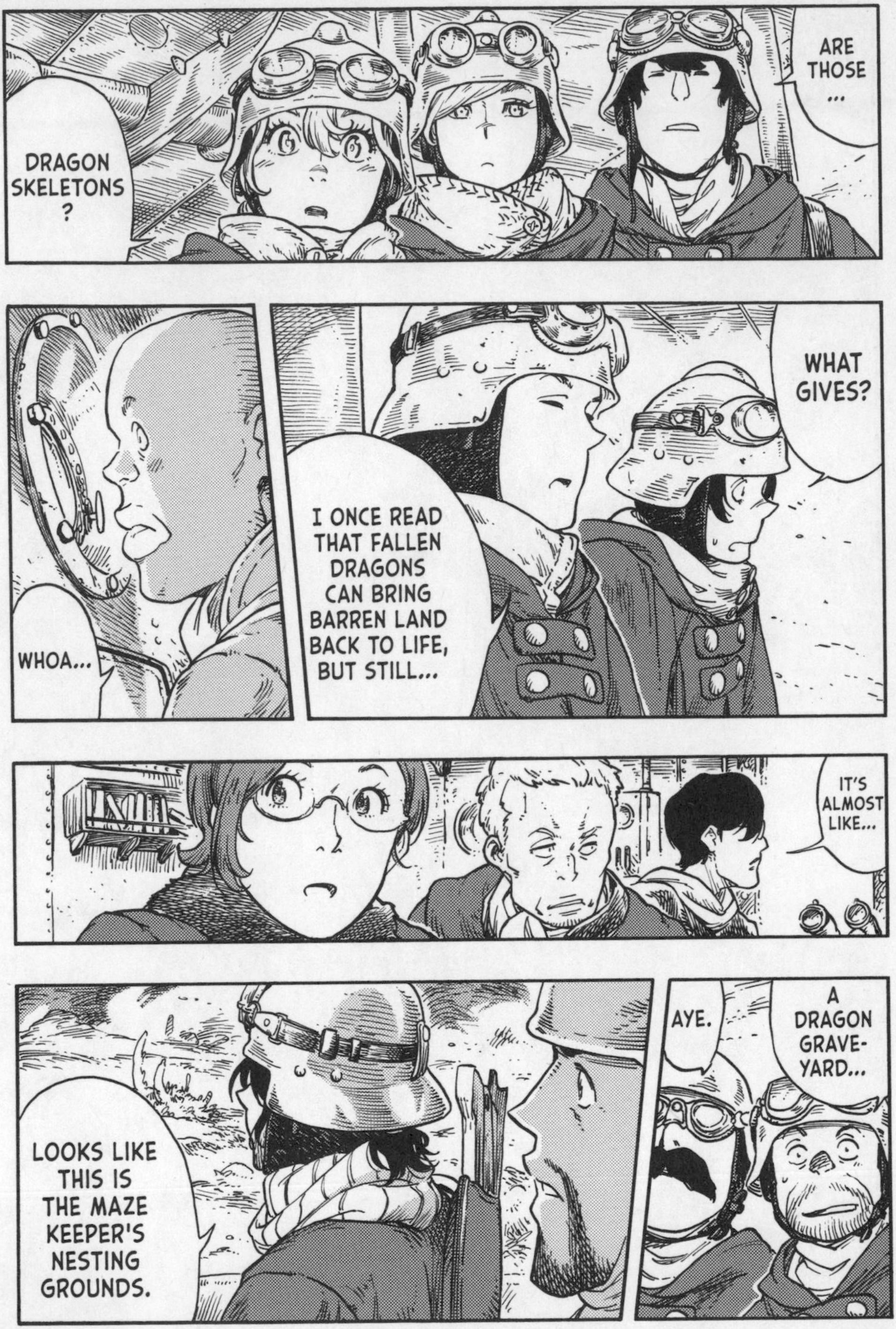
ARE THOSE ...
DRAGON SKELETONS ?
WHAT GIVES?
I ONCE READ THAT FALLEN DRAGONS CAN BRING BARREN LAND BACK TO LIFE, BUT STILL...
WHOA...
IT'S ALMOST LIKE...
A DRAGON GRAVE-YARD...
AYE.
LOOKS LIKE THIS IS THE MAZE KEEPER'S NESTING GROUNDS.

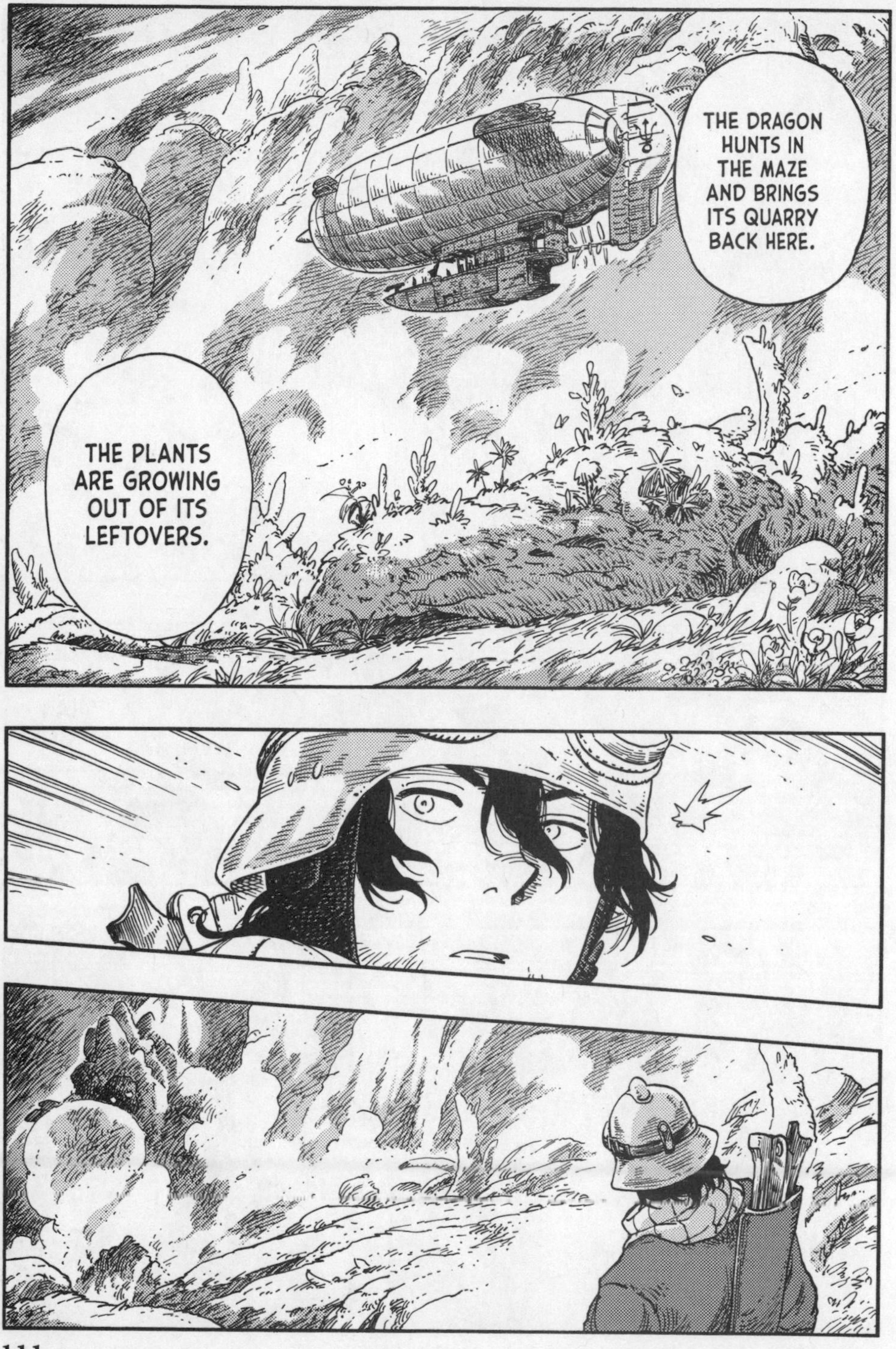
THE DRAGON HUNTS IN THE MAZE AND BRINGS ITS QUARRY BACK HERE.
THE PLANTS ARE GROWING OUT OF ITS LEFTOVERS.

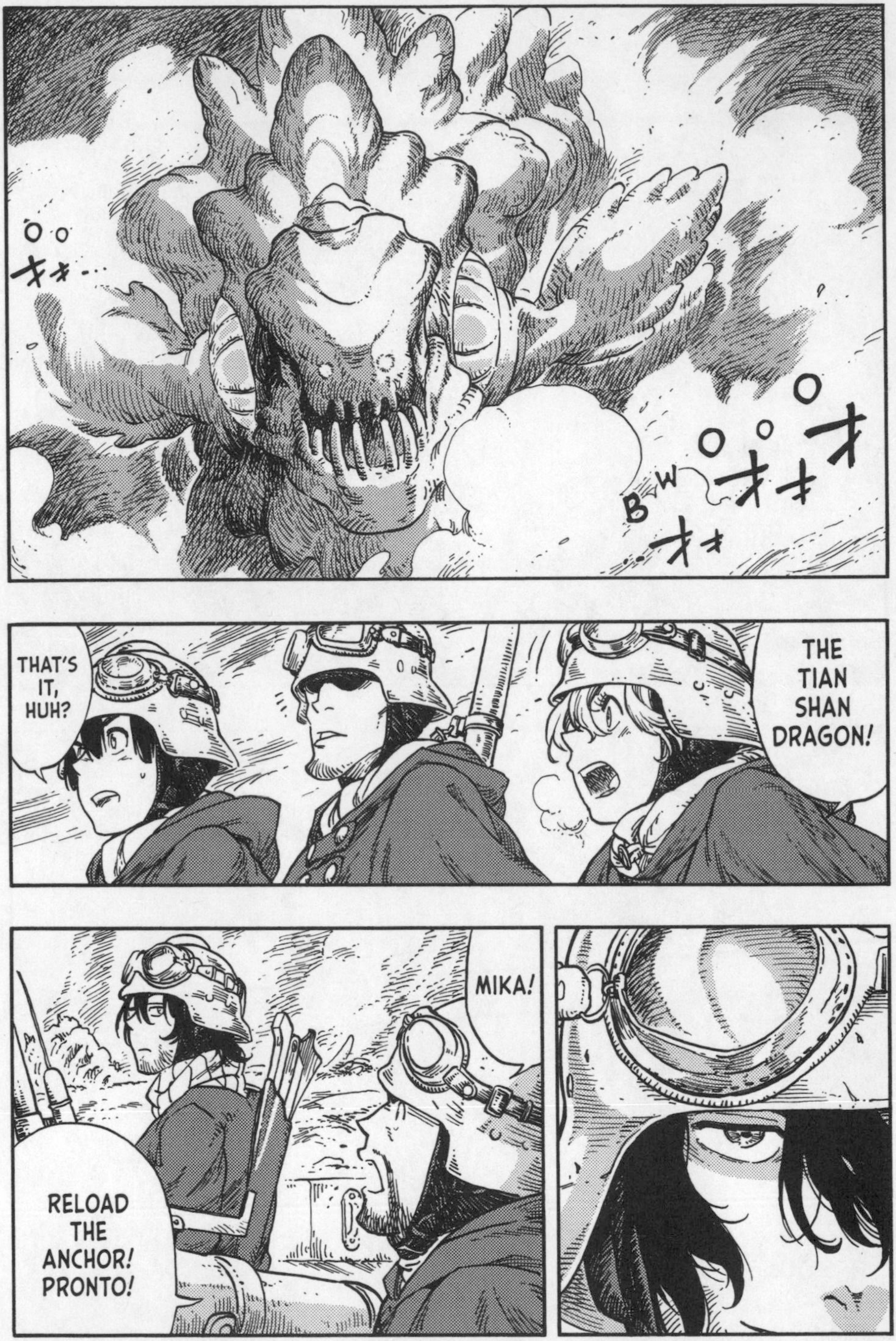
OO
BWOOO
THE TIAN SHAN DRAGON!
THAT'S IT, HUH?
MIKA!
RELOAD THE ANCHOR! PRONTO!

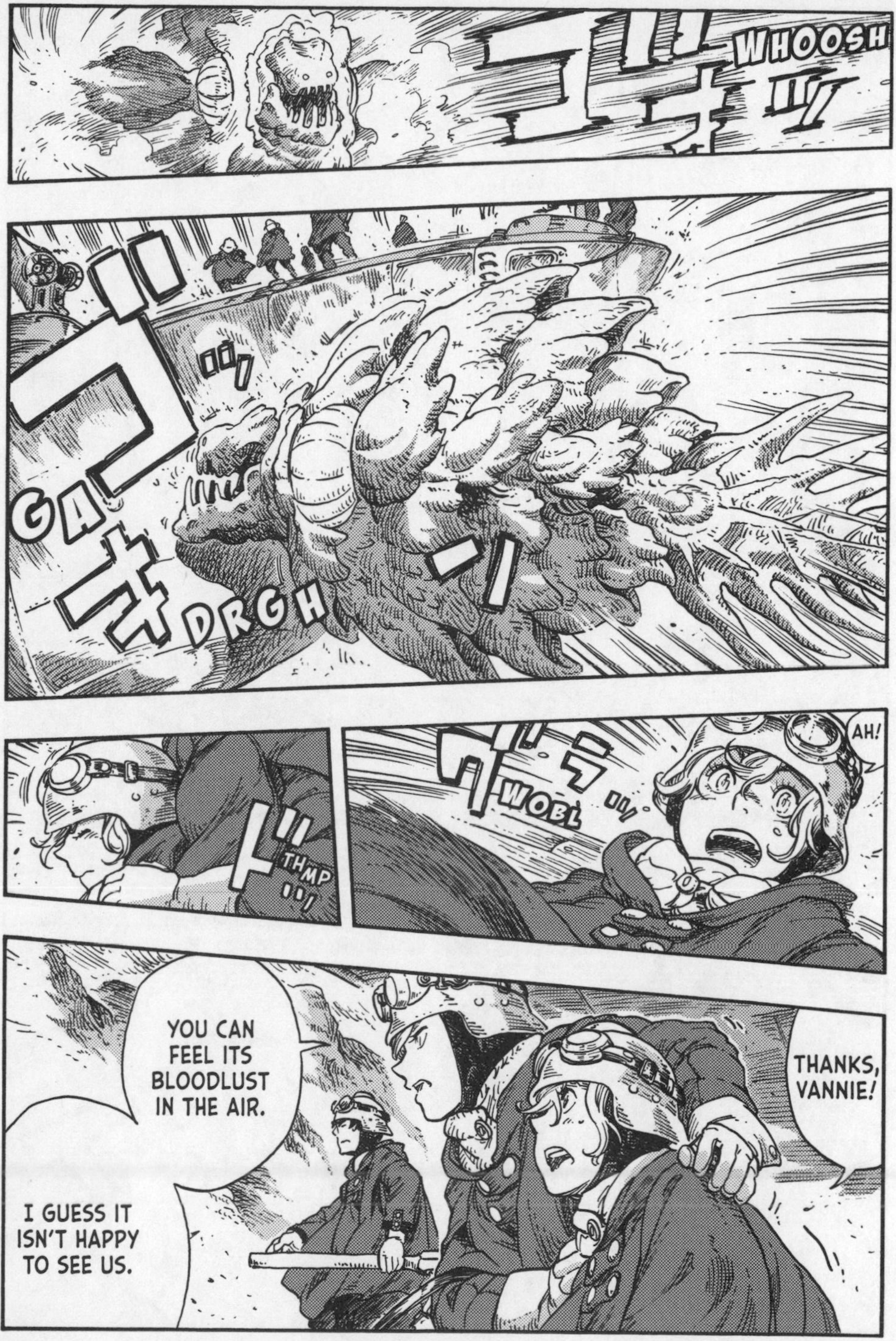
WHOOSH
GA
DRGH
AH!
WOBL
THMP
THANKS, VANNIE!
YOU CAN FEEL ITS BLOODLUST IN THE AIR.
I GUESS IT ISN'T HAPPY TO SEE US.

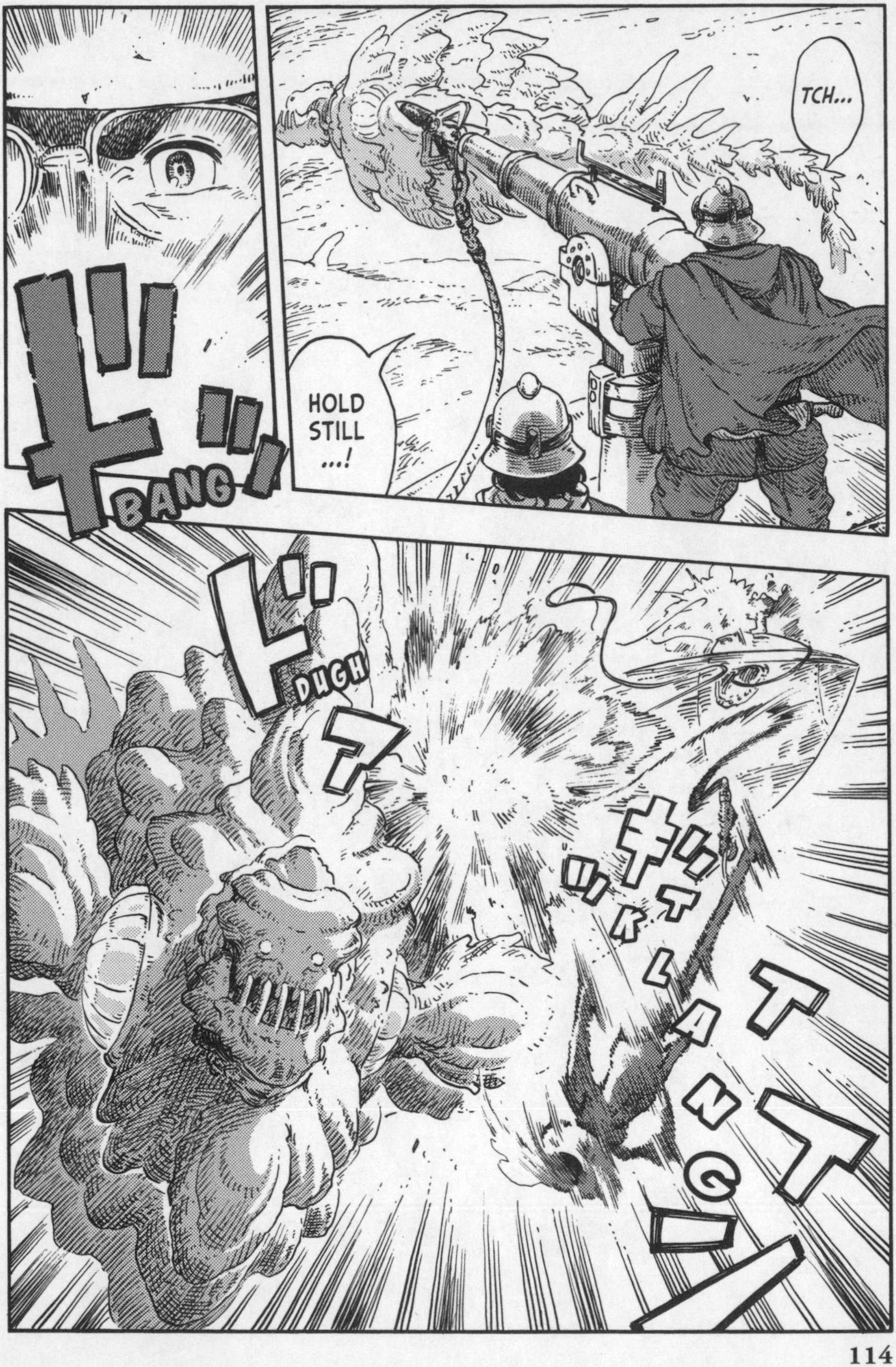
TCH...
HOLD STILL ...!
BANG
DUGH
KLANG

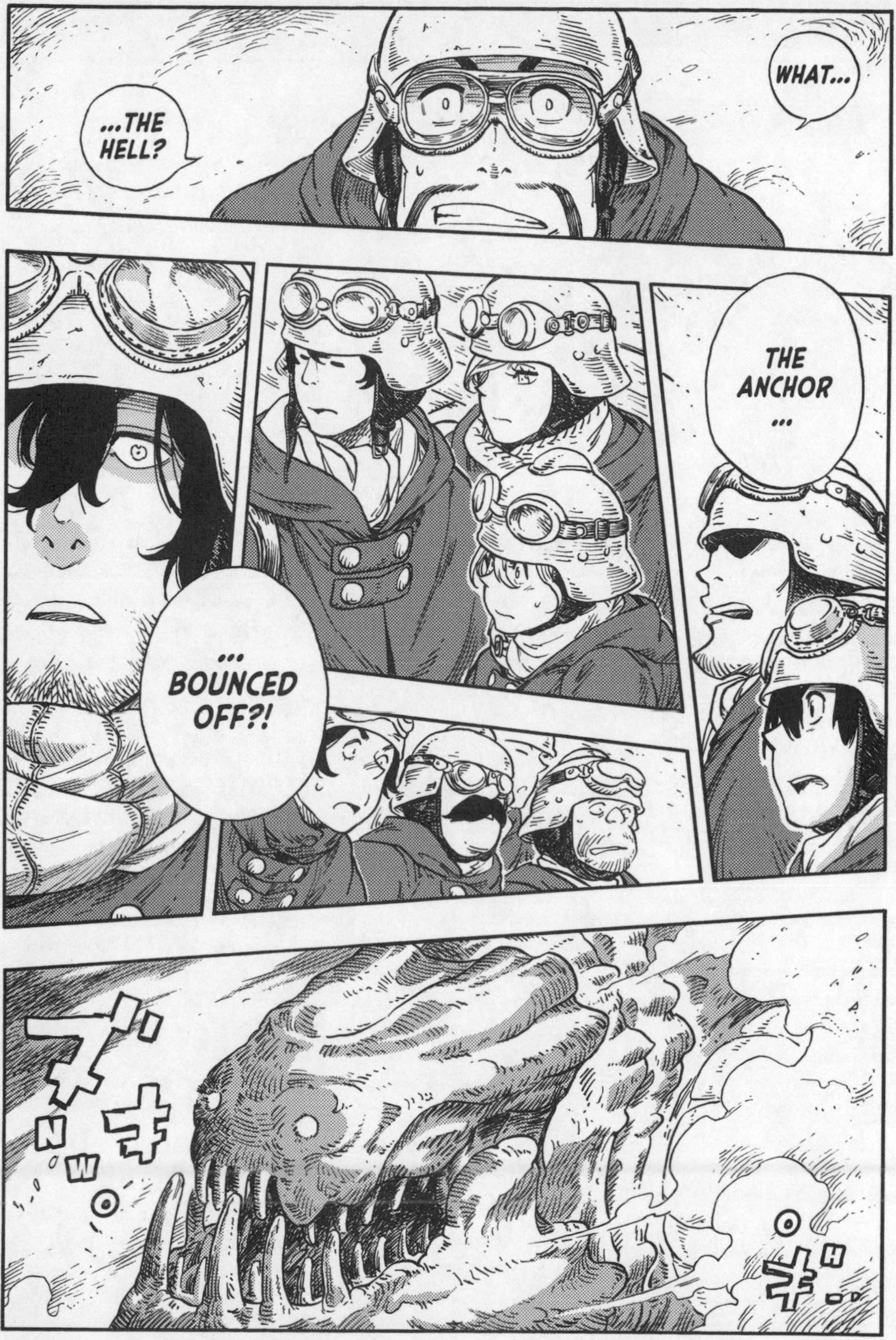
WHAT...
...THE HELL?
THE ANCHOR ...
... BOUNCED OFF?!

Dragon Belly Bao

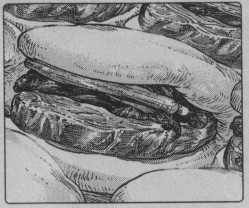

Ingredients (Serves 4)

★ Bao:

Cake flour: 100 g	Bread flour: 50 g	Baking powder: 1 tsp
Yeast (fresh or dried): 1 tsp	Salt: ½ tsp	Sugar: 1 tbsp
Sesame seed oil: 2 tsp	Milk (or warm water): 5-6 tbsp	

★ Braised dragon belly:

Dragon meat (preferably a fatty cut such as the belly): 400 g	
Sugar: 40 g	Soy sauce: 3 tbsp
Shaoxing wine: 3 tbsp	Water: 2 cups
Green onion: 1 bulb	Ginger root: 1 small piece
Star anise: 1 pod	Bok choy: half a bulb

01

First, we'll make the buns. Place all of the bao ingredients except the sesame oil and milk in a large bowl and mix together thoroughly with a whisk or other utensil. While stirring, slowly add milk, a little at a time. Once a shaggy dough forms, mix in sesame oil.

02

Turn the dough onto a lightly floured surface and knead until smooth. Return the dough ball to the bowl and let rest at room temperature for one hour.

03

Divide the dough into fourths, roll each section into a ball, and flatten into disks with a rolling pin. Lightly grease the tops of the disks with reserved oil and fold over.

04

Steam the buns in a steamer for 10-12 minutes.

05

Next, we'll make the braised dragon belly. Slice the dragon meat into sandwich-sized pieces and place on a plate.

06

Heat an unoiled pan over high heat and sear the dragon meat until golden brown and a fair amount of fat renders out. Add sugar to the pan and mix well into the melted fat.

07

Once the sugar caramelizes, toss the meat in the sauce until thoroughly coated. Add soy sauce and toss to incorporate.

08

Add Shaoxing wine, water, chopped scallions, sliced ginger, star anise, and bok choy leaves to the pan and bring to a boil. Reduce the heat to low and simmer until the bok choy is cooked through. Remove the bok choy from the pan, cover and simmer for an additional hour.

09

Once the broth has mostly reduced, remove the lid and cook on high heat until thick and syrupy. Toss the dragon meat in the glaze to coat thoroughly.

10

Sandwich bok choy and braised belly in the buns and serve.

DELICIOUS AND PORTABLE. GREAT FOR WHEN YOU'RE ON THE GO!

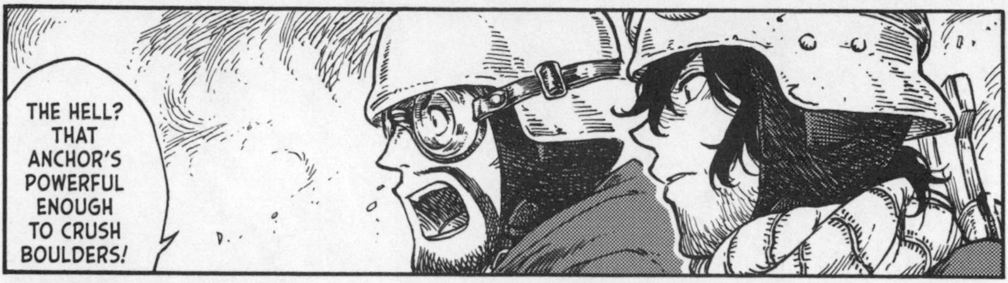
THE HELL? THAT ANCHOR'S POWERFUL ENOUGH TO CRUSH BOULDERS!

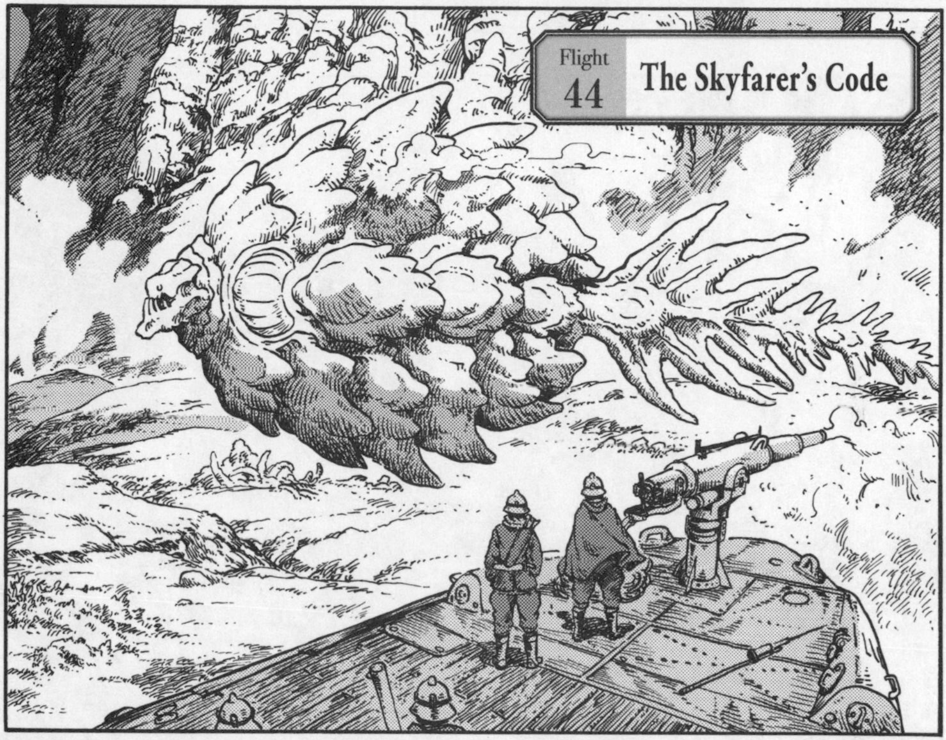
Flight 44
The Skyfarer's Code

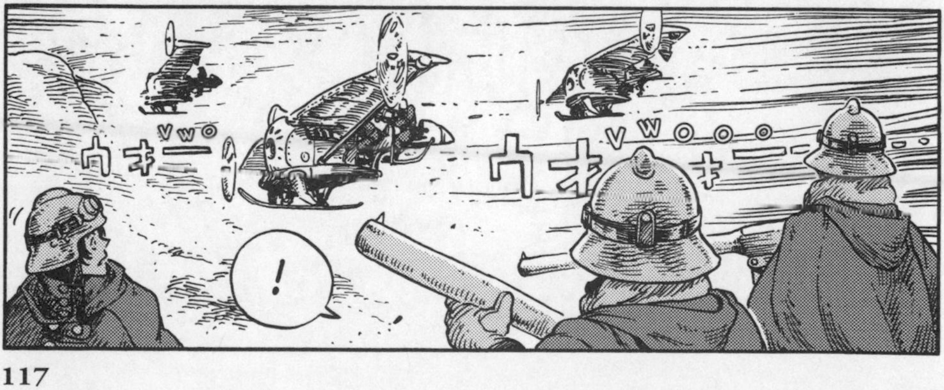
VWOOOO
ウオオーー
VWO
ウオー
!

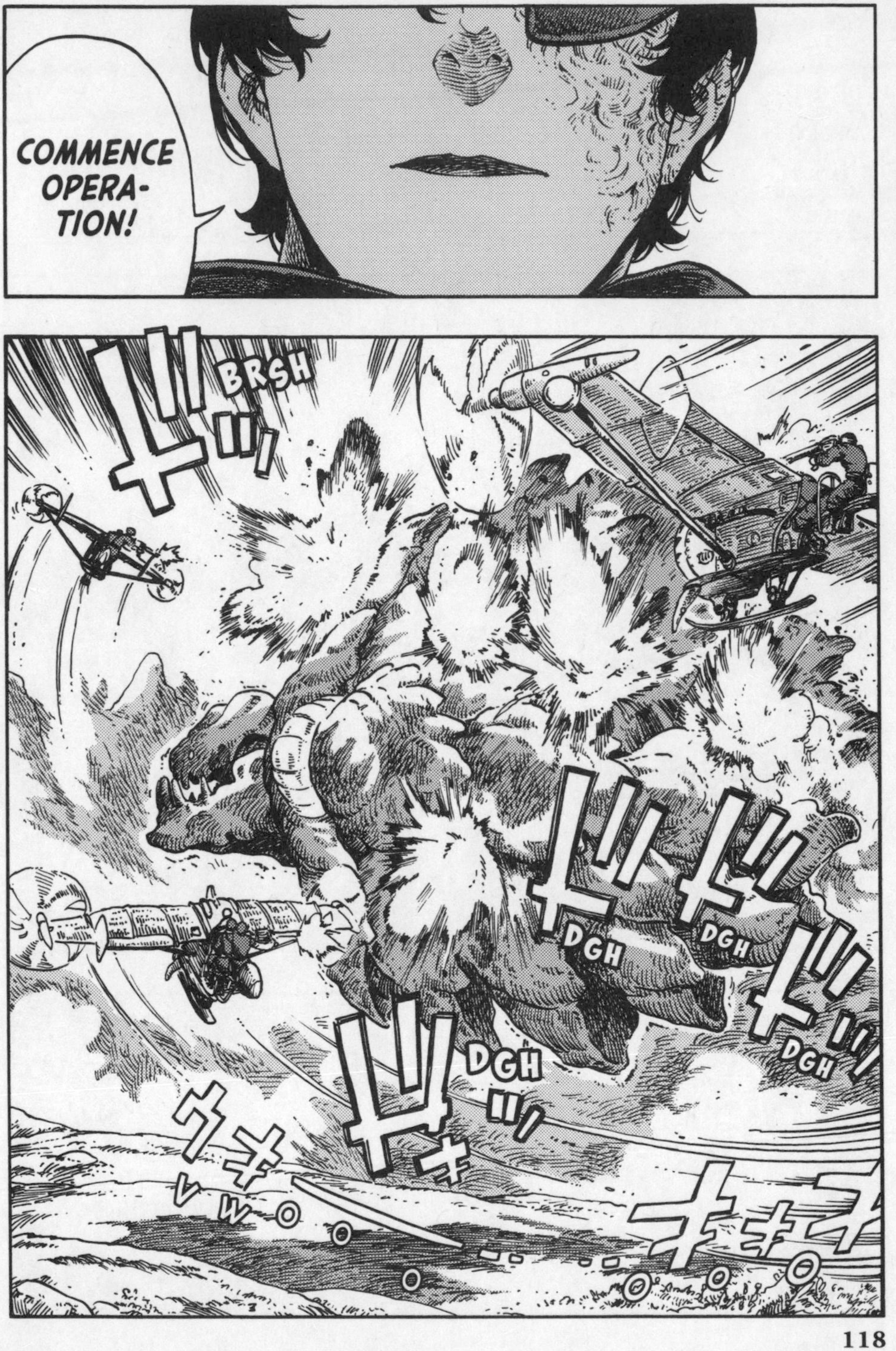
COMMENCE OPERA-TION!
BRSH
DGH
DGH
DGH
DGH

BVVVV
W
IT'S THE SLAY-ERS!
...I KNEW THEY'D SHOW UP.

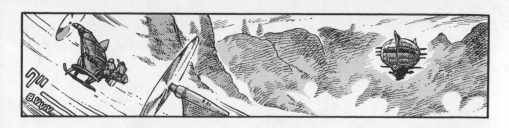

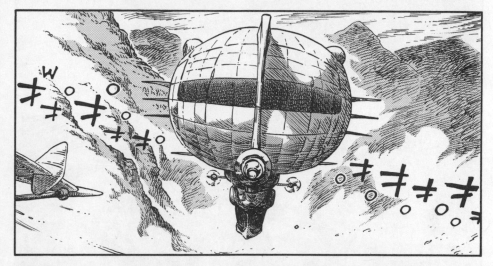

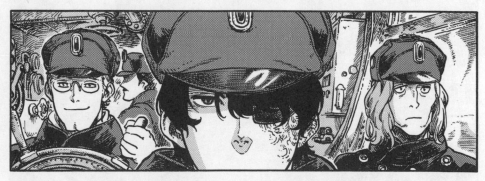

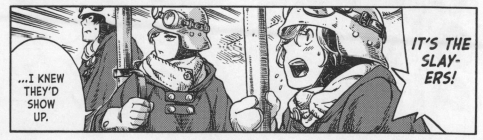

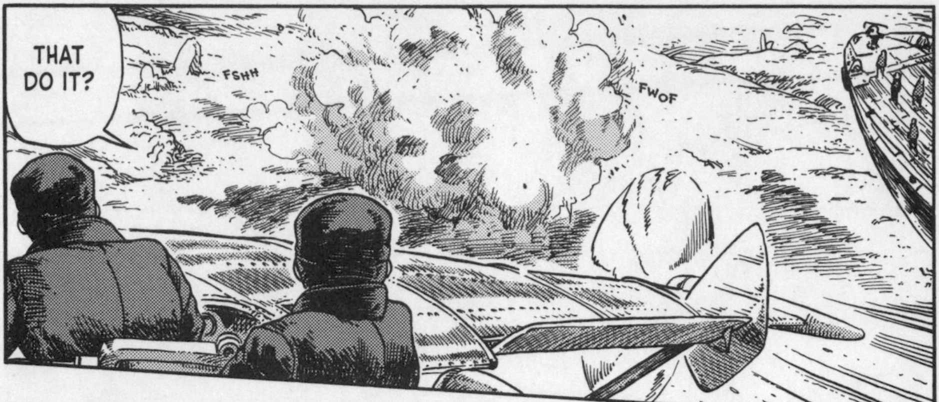
THAT DO IT?
FSHH
FWOF
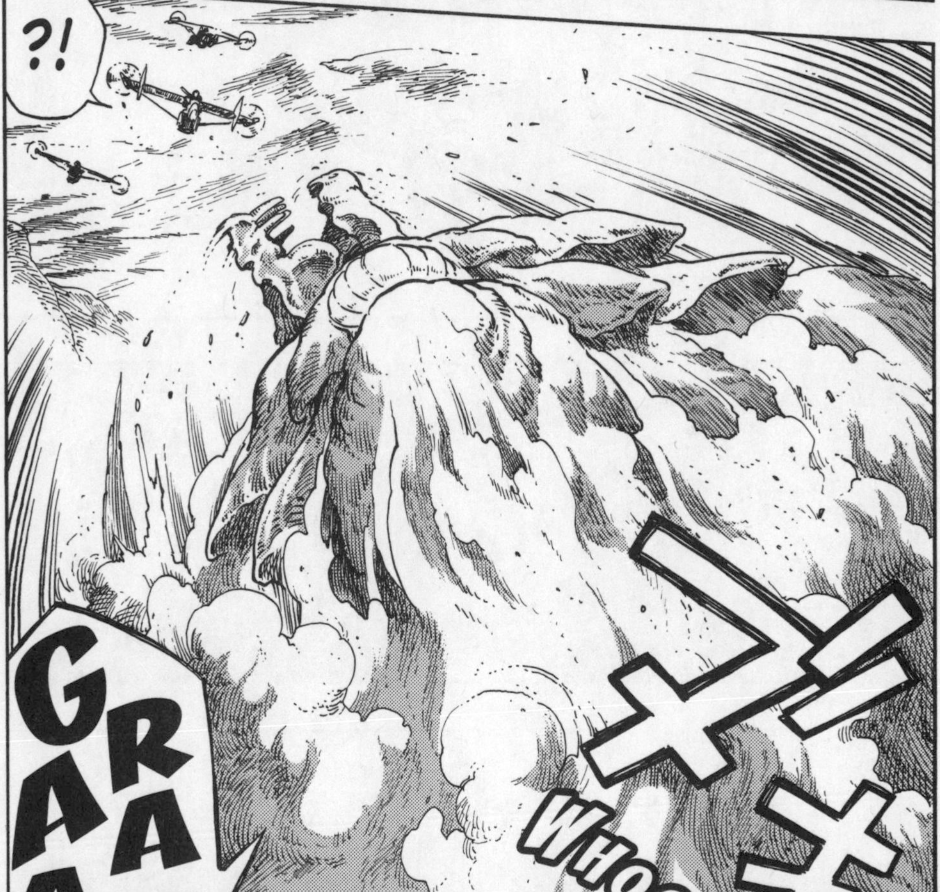
?!
GRAAAH
WHOOSH

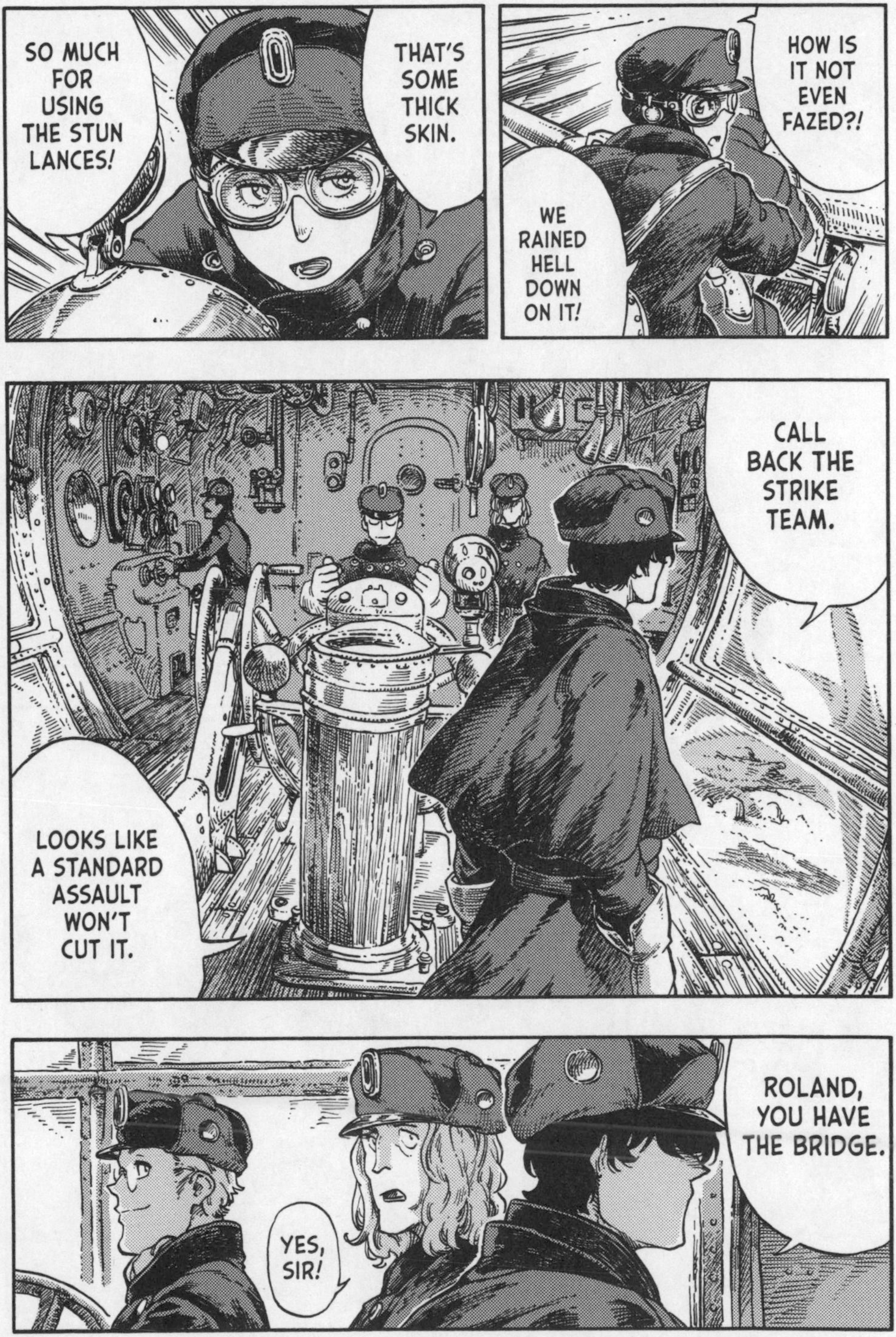
HOW IS IT NOT EVEN FAZED?!
WE RAINED HELL DOWN ON IT!
THAT'S SOME THICK SKIN.
SO MUCH FOR USING THE STUN LANCES!
CALL BACK THE STRIKE TEAM.
LOOKS LIKE A STANDARD ASSAULT WON'T CUT IT.
ROLAND, YOU HAVE THE BRIDGE.
YES, SIR!

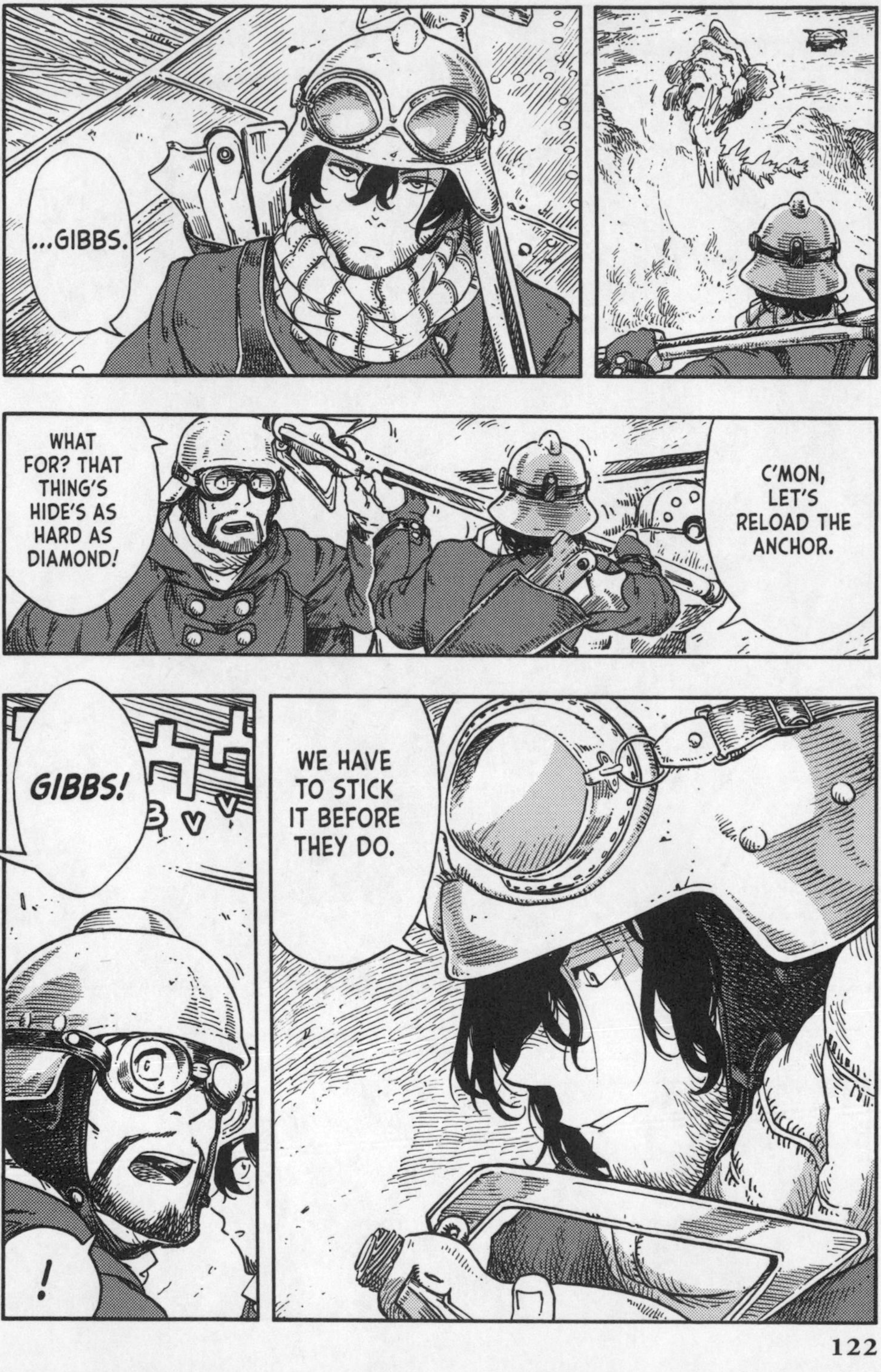
...GIBBS.
C'MON, LET'S RELOAD THE ANCHOR.
WHAT FOR? THAT THING'S HIDE'S AS HARD AS DIAMOND!
WE HAVE TO STICK IT BEFORE THEY DO.
GIBBS!
!

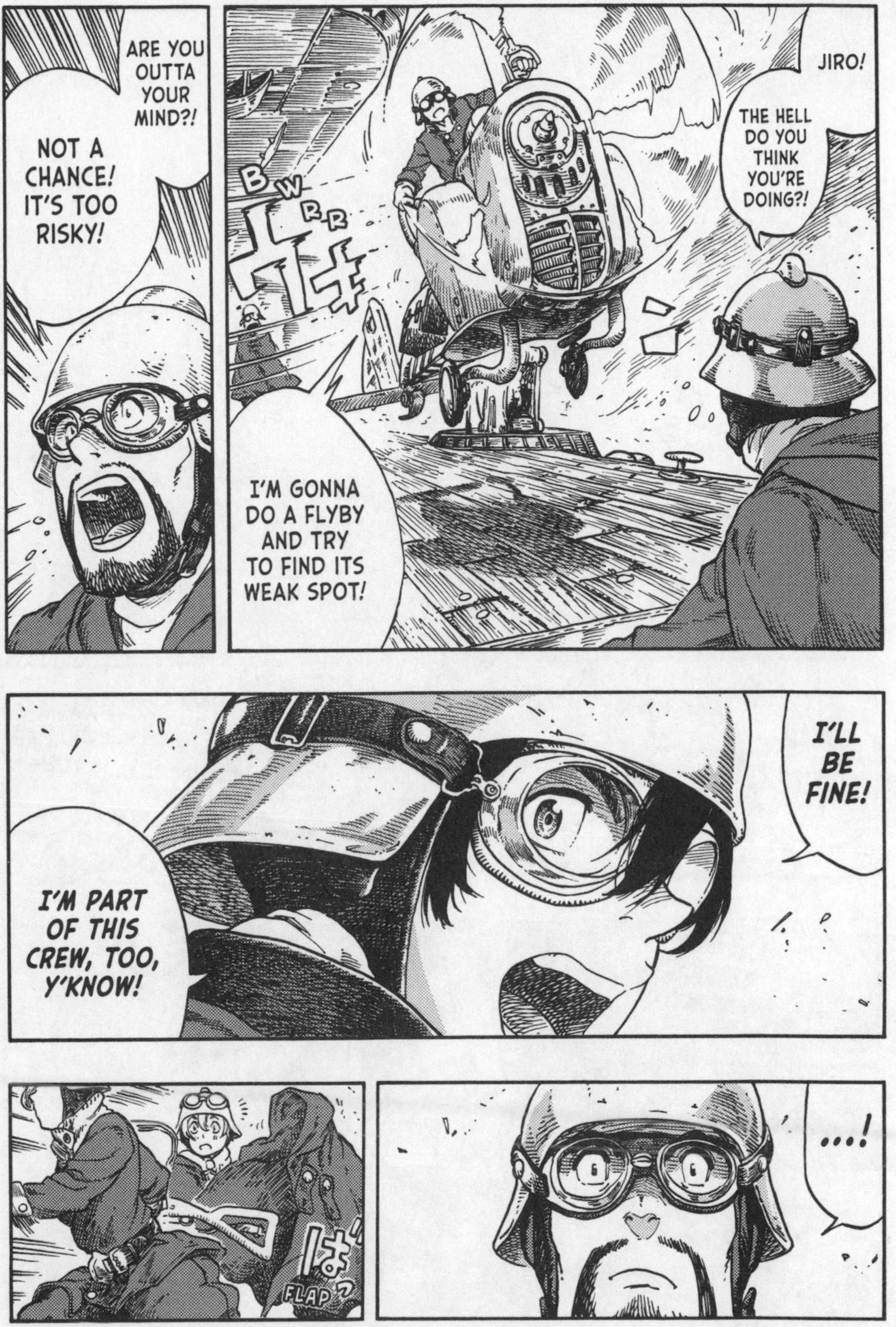
JIRO!
THE HELL DO YOU THINK YOU'RE DOING?!
BWRR
I'M GONNA DO A FLYBY AND TRY TO FIND ITS WEAK SPOT!
ARE YOU OUTTA YOUR MIND?!
NOT A CHANCE! IT'S TOO RISKY!
I'LL BE FINE!
I'M PART OF THIS CREW, TOO, Y'KNOW!
...!
ばっ
FLAP

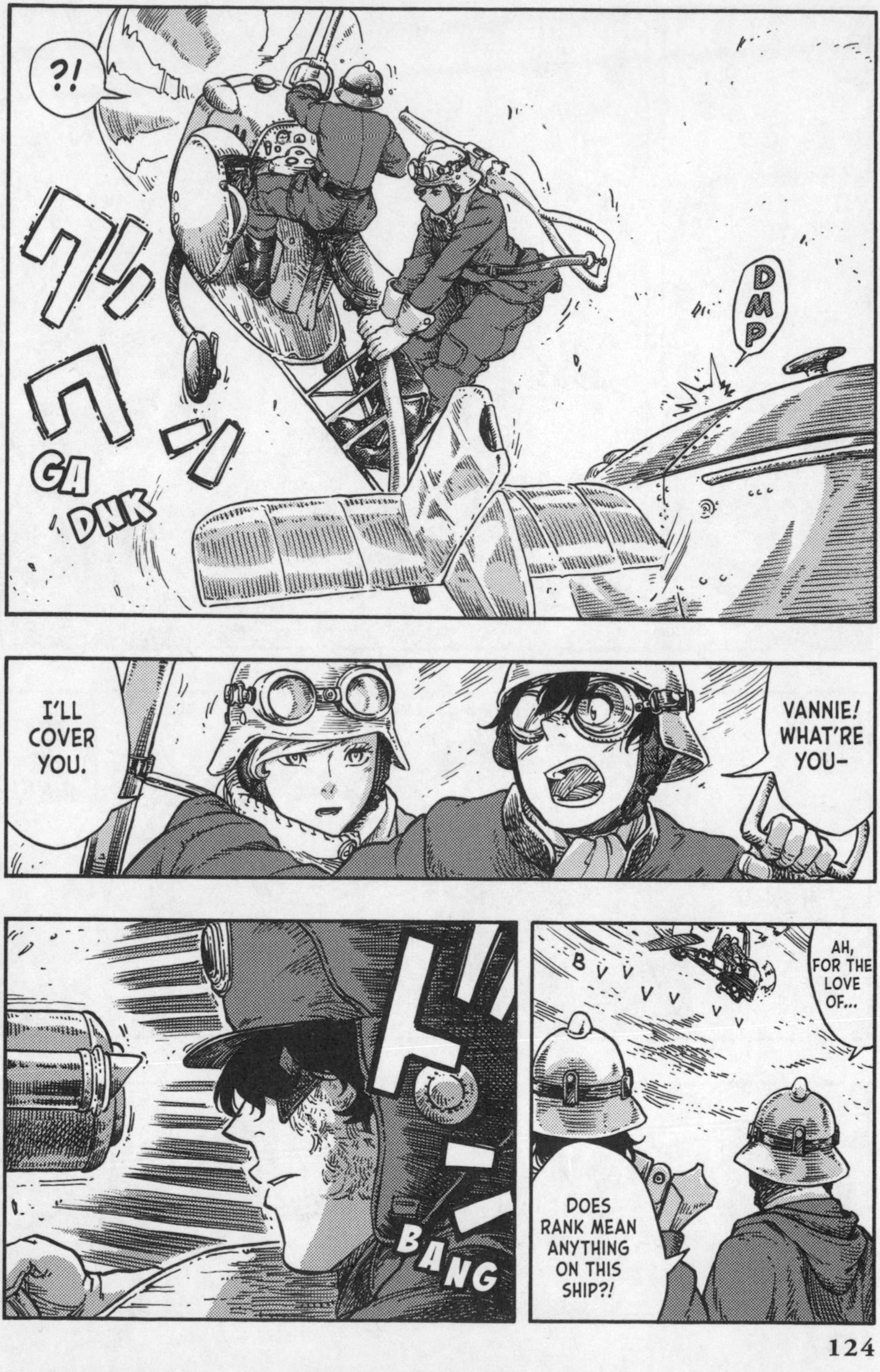

DMP
?!
GA DNK
VANNIE! WHAT'RE YOU–
I'LL COVER YOU.
AH, FOR THE LOVE OF...
BVVVVVVV
DOES RANK MEAN ANYTHING ON THIS SHIP?!
BANG

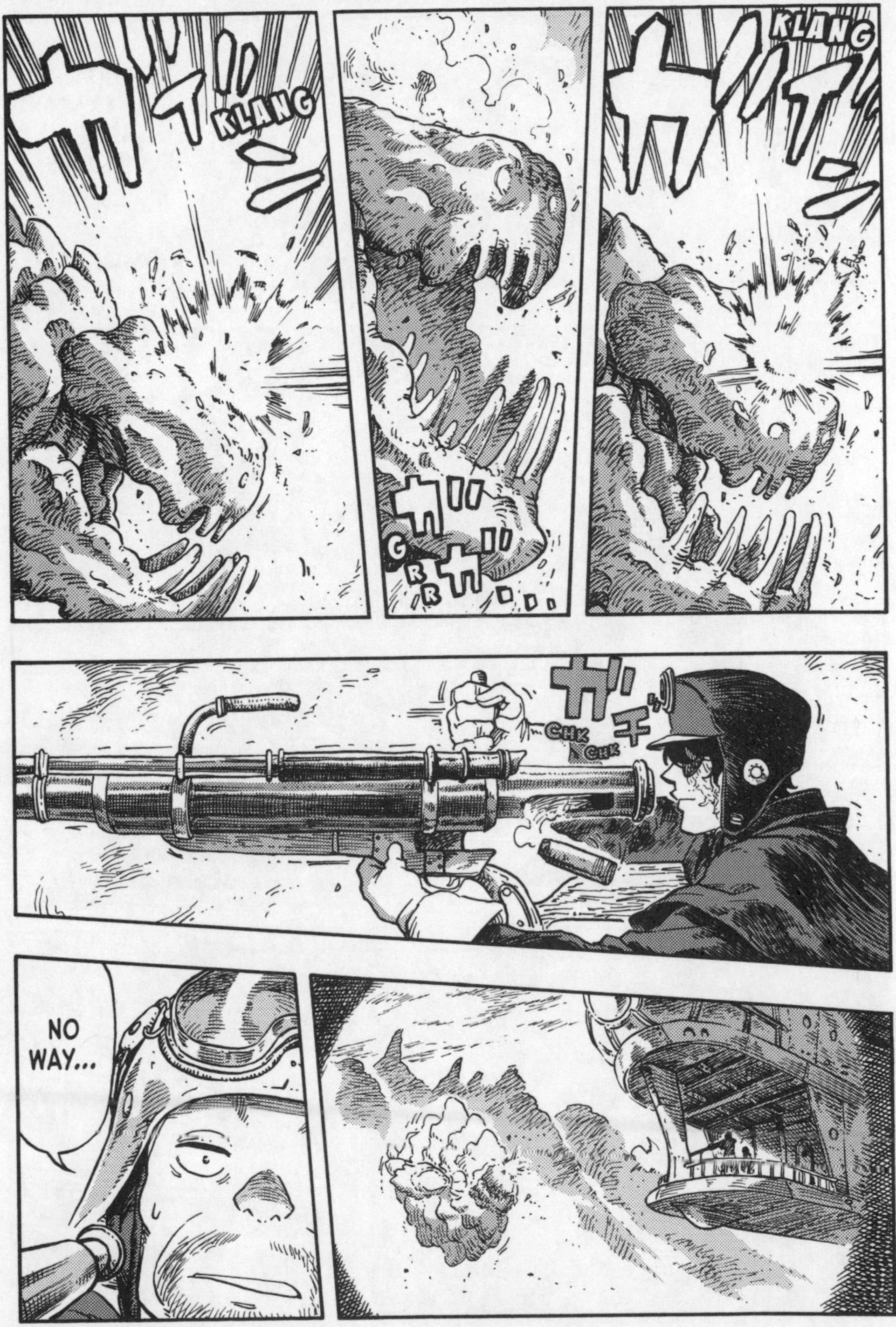
KLANG
GRRR
KLANG
CHK CHK
NO WAY...

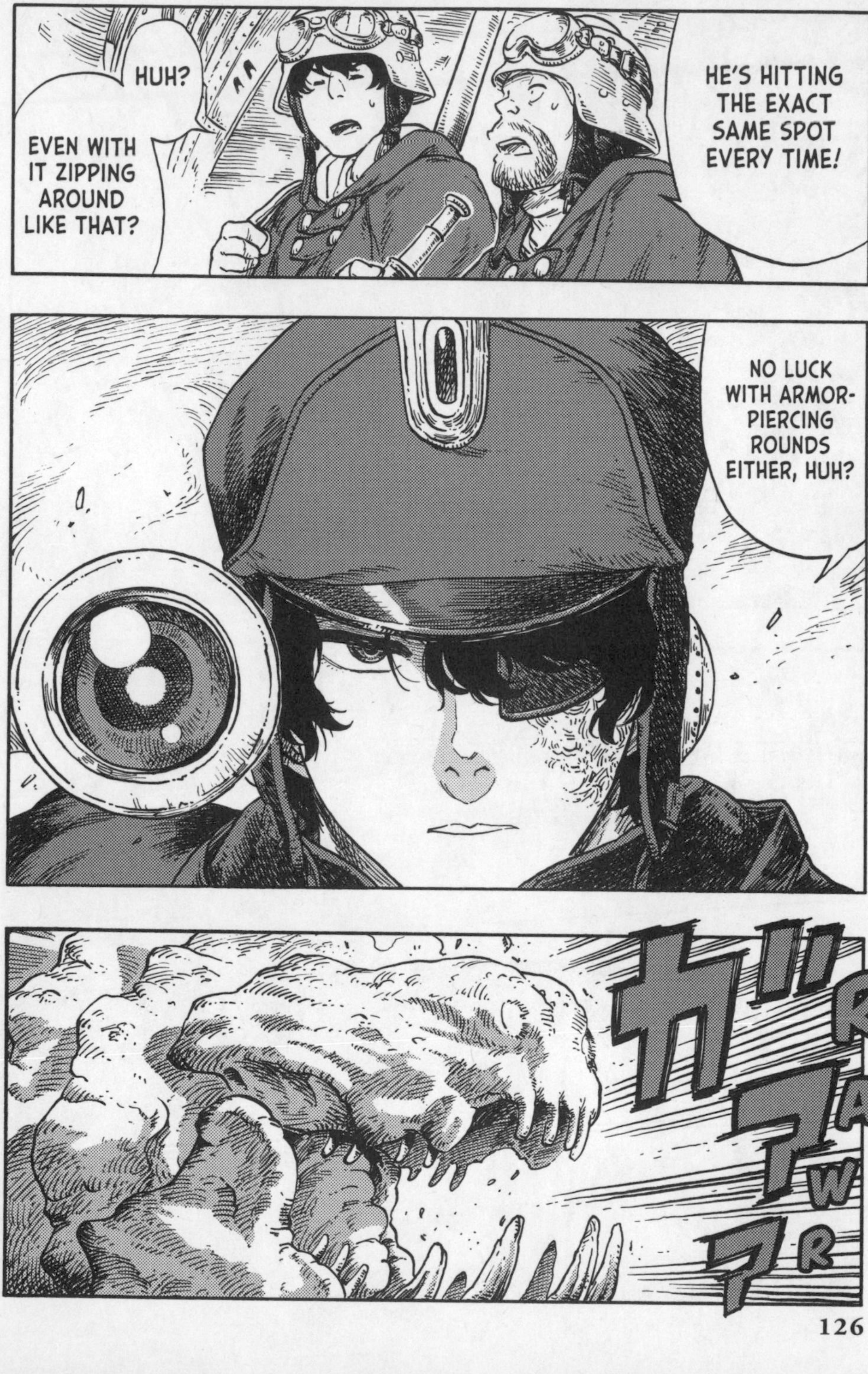
HE'S HITTING THE EXACT SAME SPOT EVERY TIME!
HUH?
EVEN WITH IT ZIPPING AROUND LIKE THAT?
NO LUCK WITH ARMOR-PIERCING ROUNDS EITHER, HUH?
RAWR

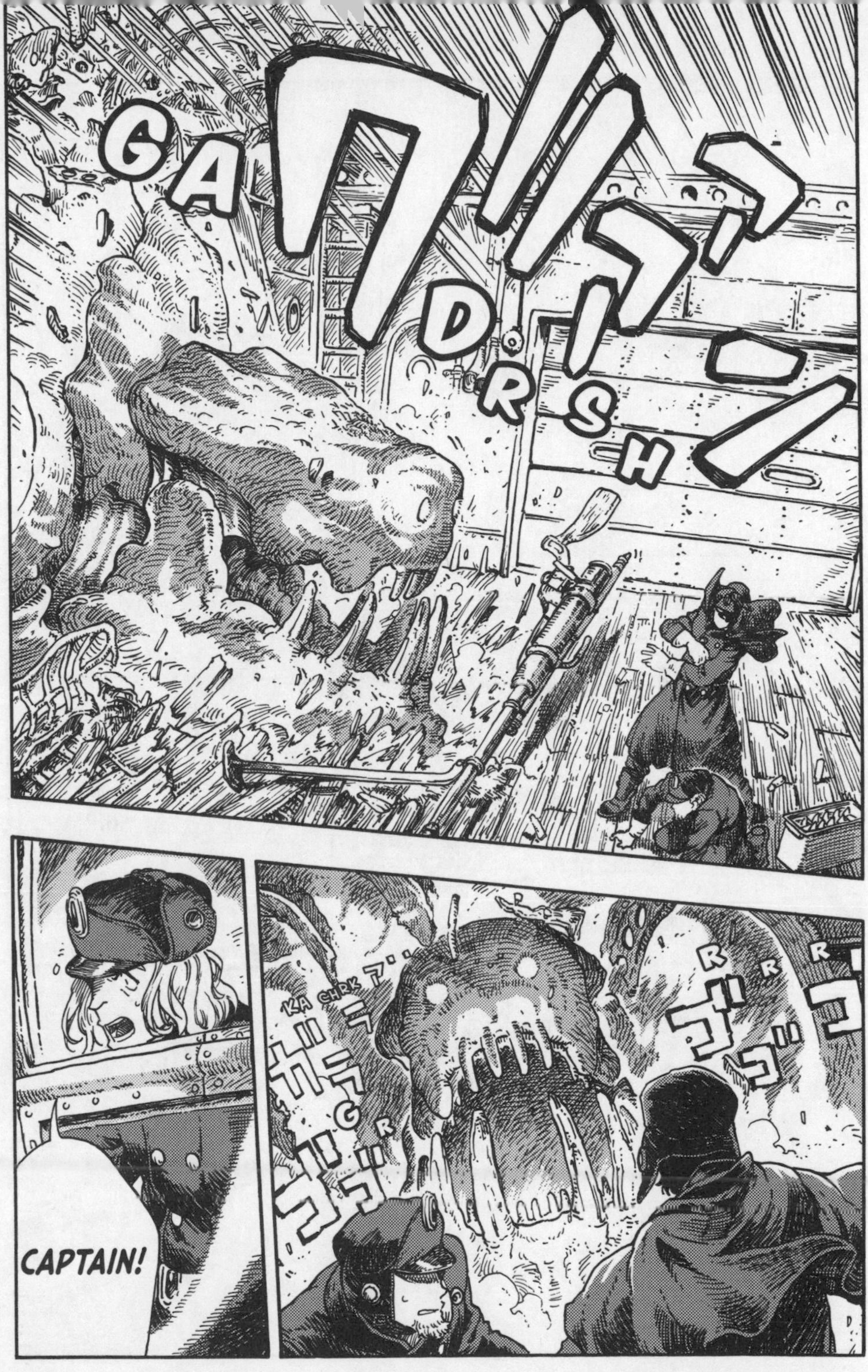
GADRSH
KA CHRK
GR
RRR
CAPTAIN!

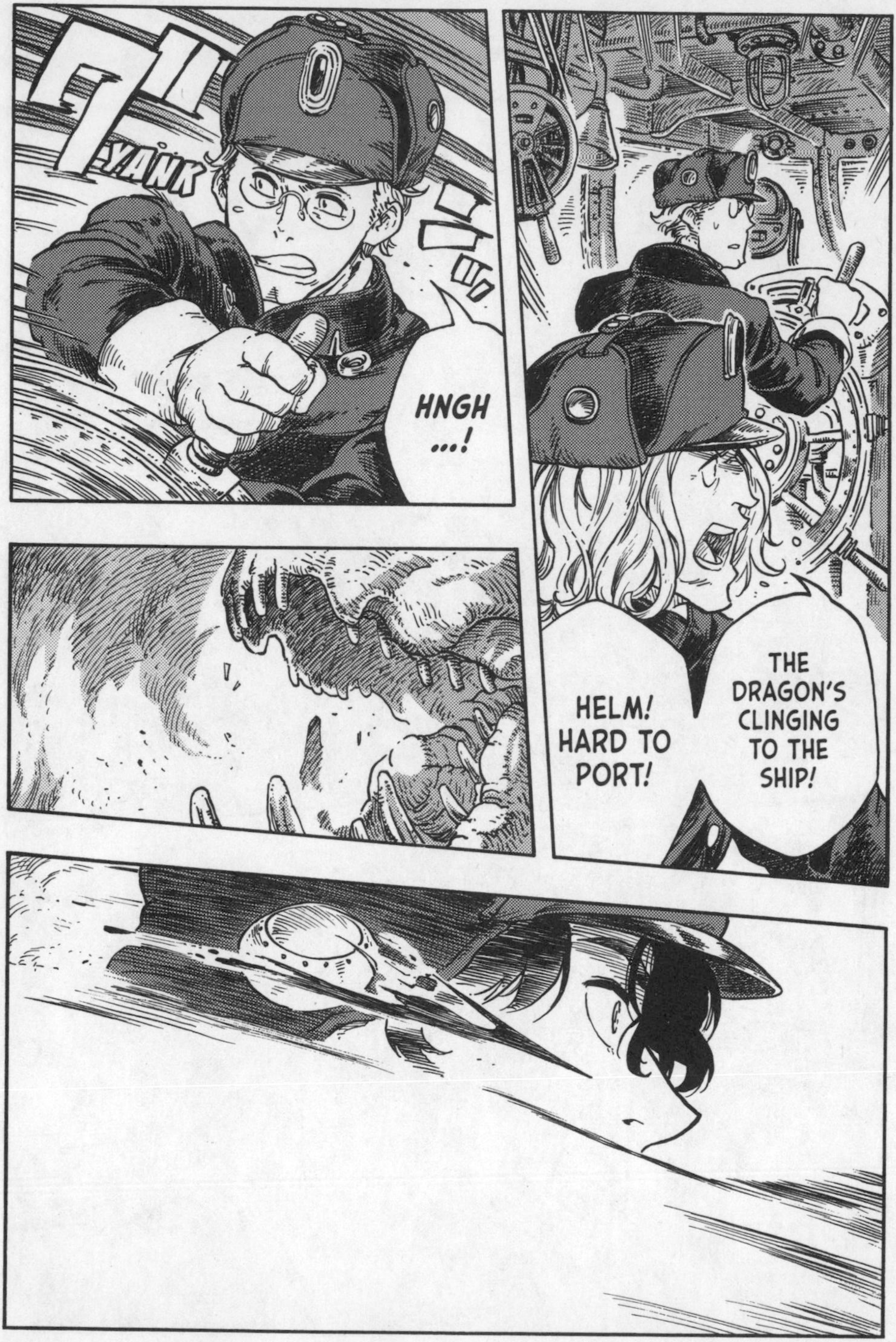
THE DRAGON'S CLINGING TO THE SHIP!
HELM! HARD TO PORT!
YANK
HNGH ...!

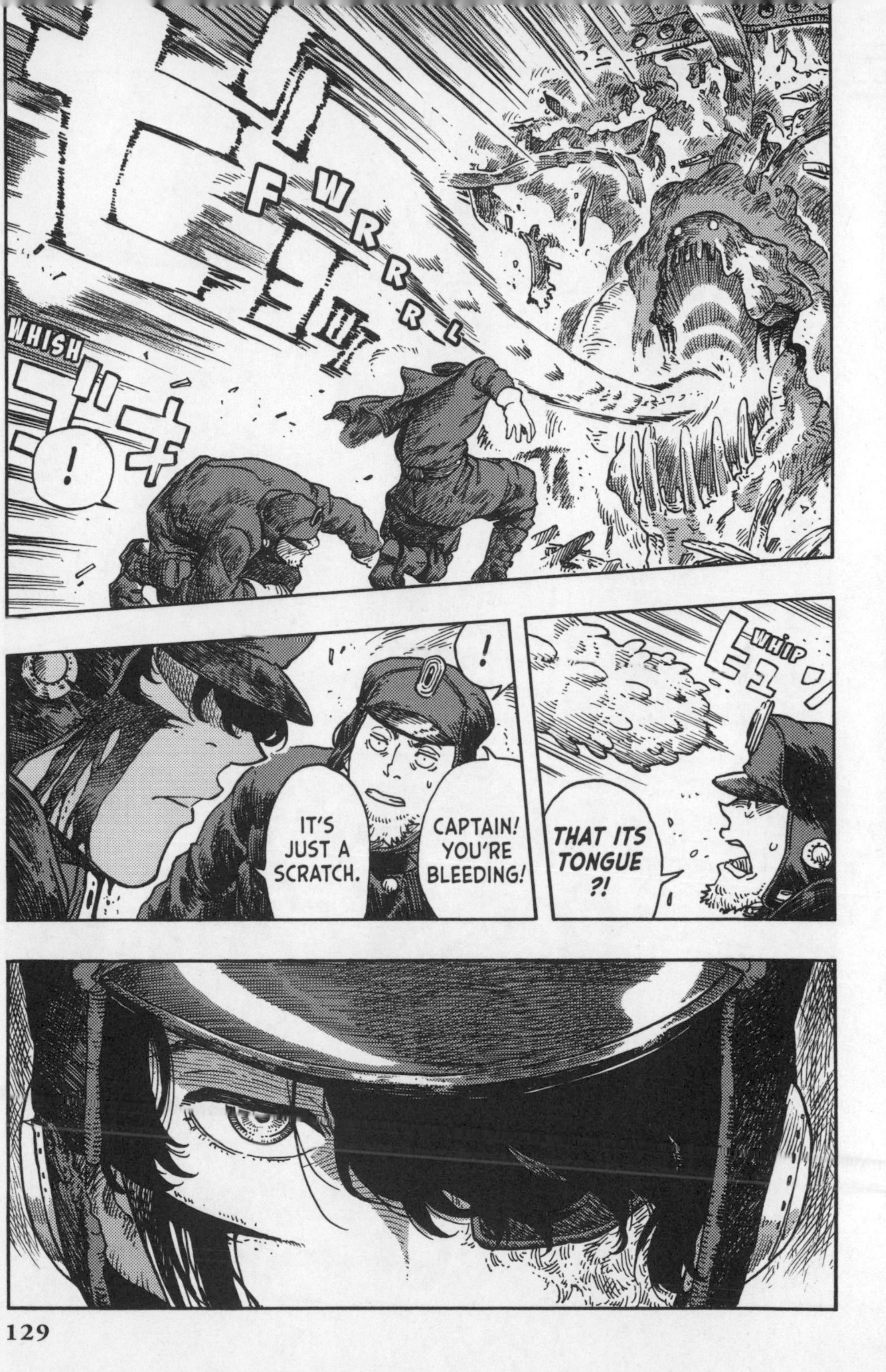
FWRRRL
WHISH
!
WHIP
THAT ITS TONGUE ?!
!
CAPTAIN! YOU'RE BLEEDING!
IT'S JUST A SCRATCH.

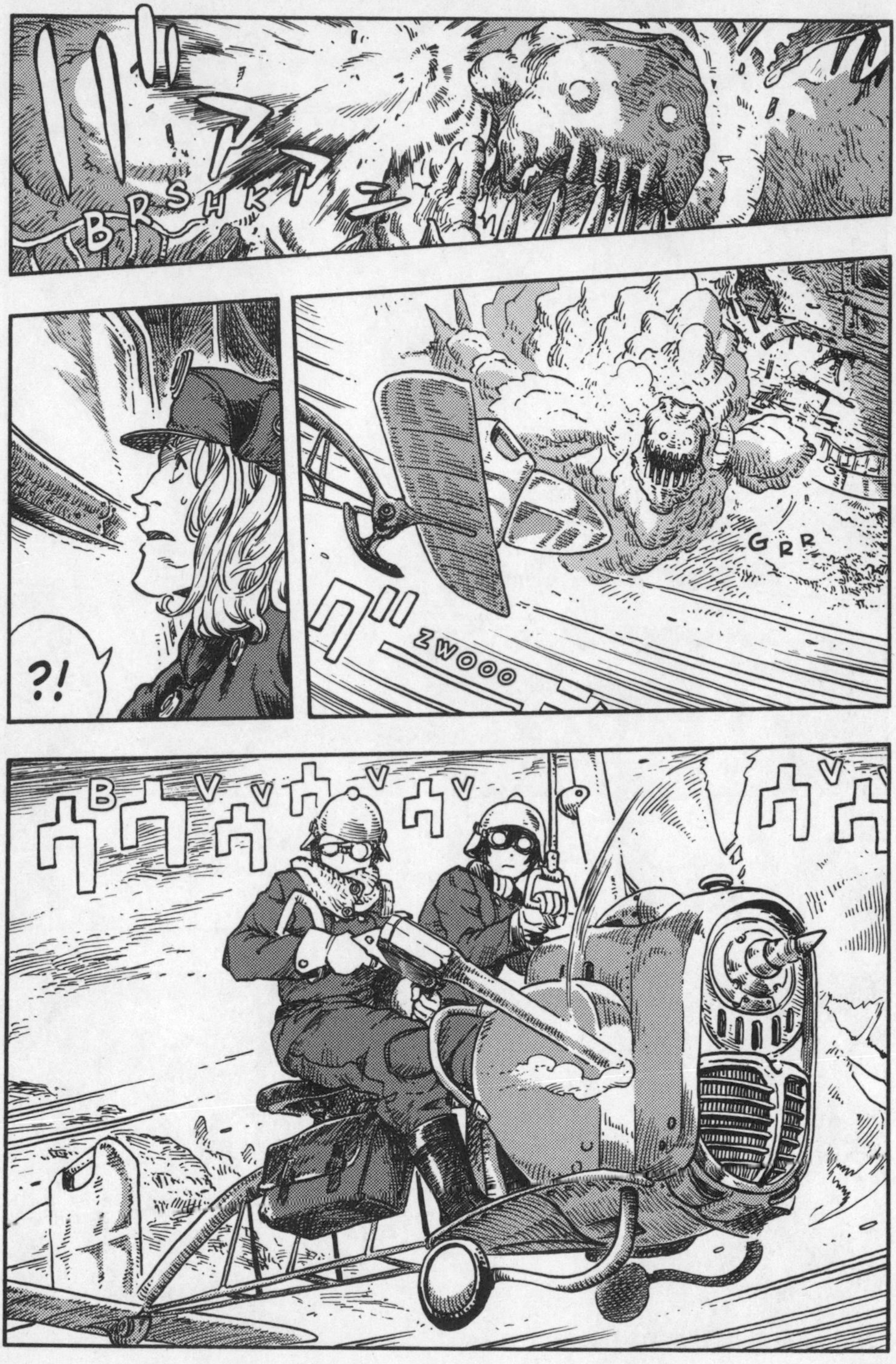
BRSHK
GRR
ZWOOO
?!
BVVVVV

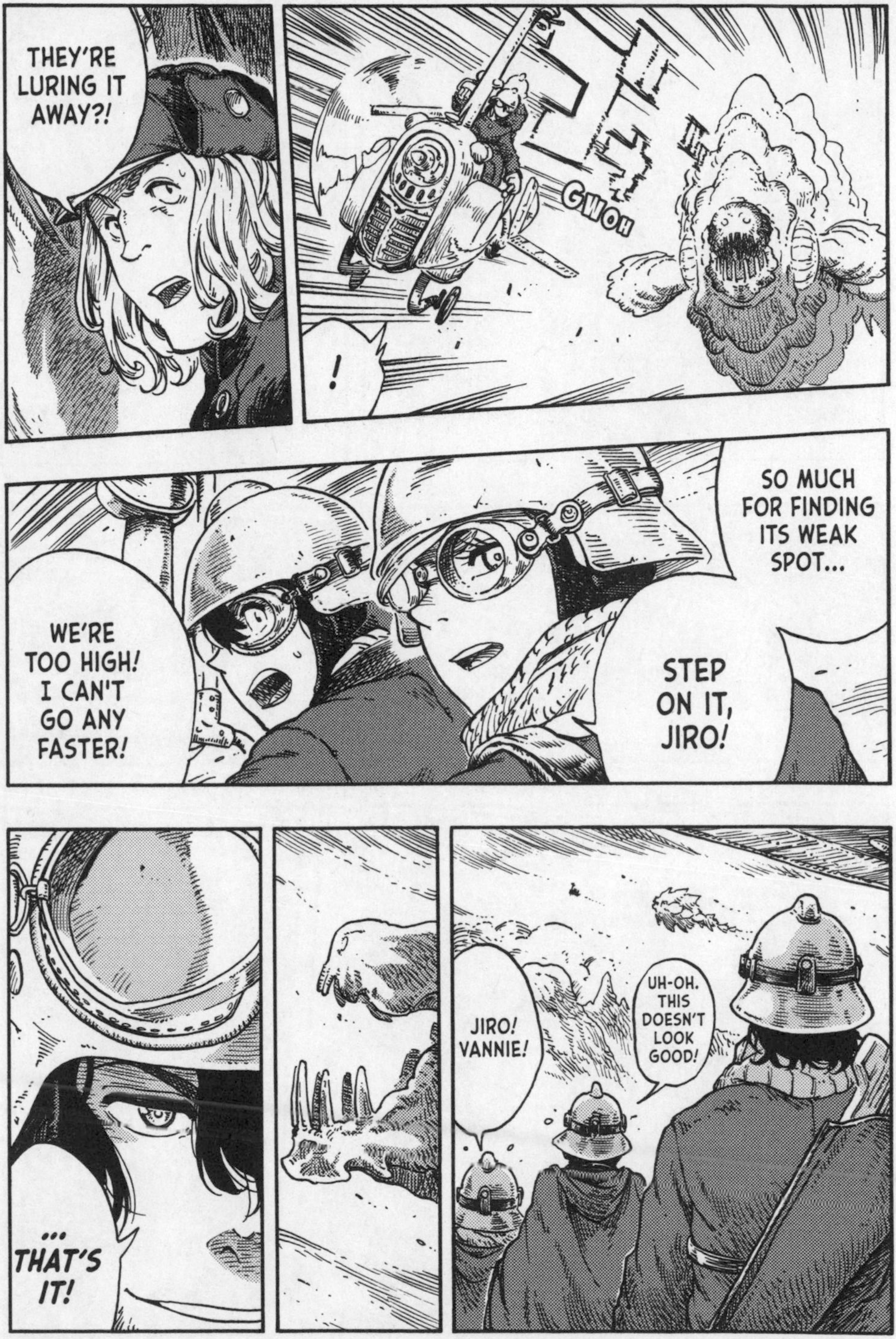
GWOH
!
THEY'RE LURING IT AWAY?!
SO MUCH FOR FINDING ITS WEAK SPOT...
STEP ON IT, JIRO!
WE'RE TOO HIGH! I CAN'T GO ANY FASTER!
UH-OH. THIS DOESN'T LOOK GOOD!
JIRO! VANNIE!
...THAT'S IT!

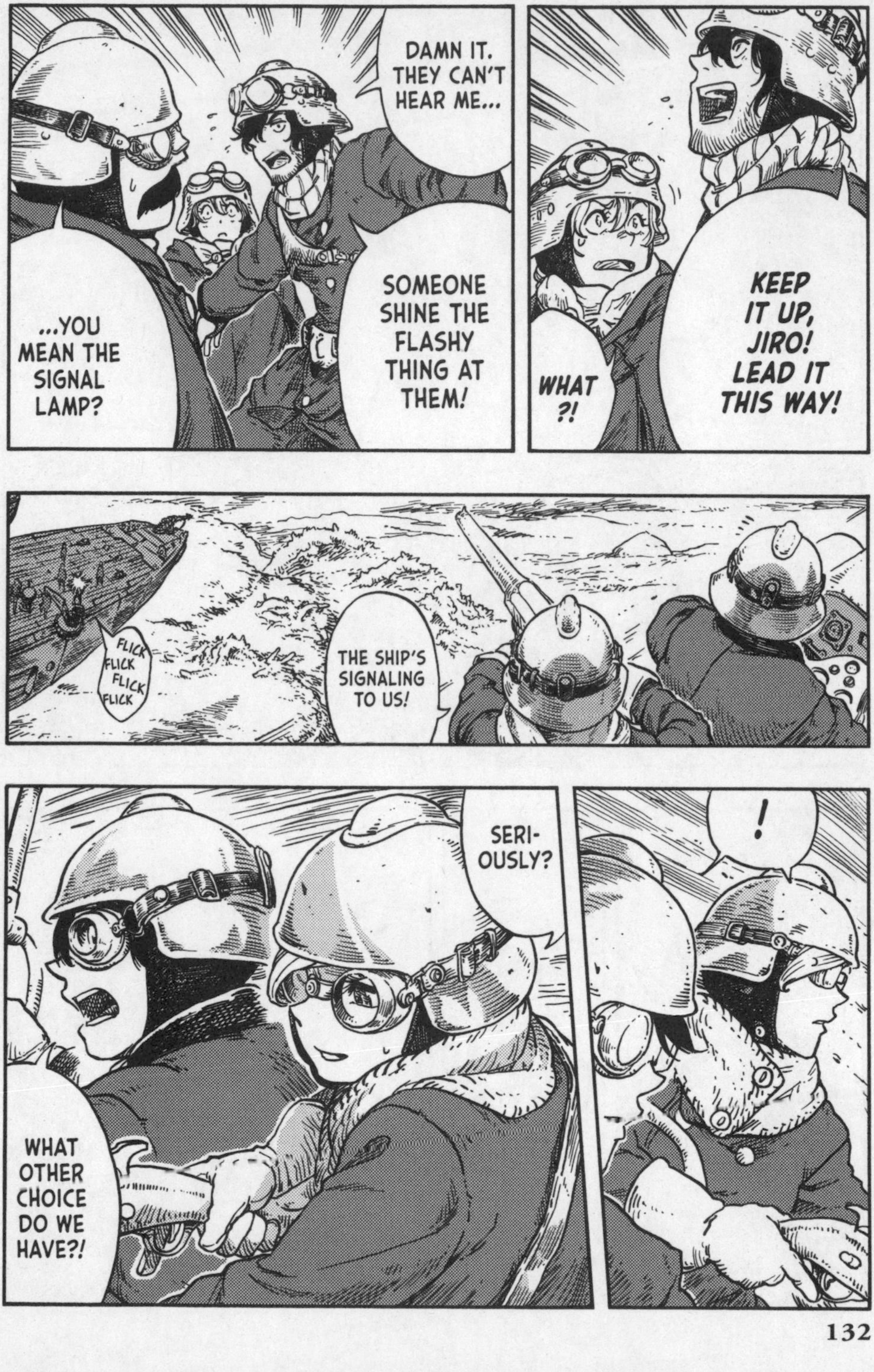
KEEP IT UP, JIRO! LEAD IT THIS WAY!
WHAT ?!
DAMN IT. THEY CAN'T HEAR ME...
SOMEONE SHINE THE FLASHY THING AT THEM!
...YOU MEAN THE SIGNAL LAMP?
THE SHIP'S SIGNALING TO US!
FLICK FLICK FLICK FLICK
!
SERI-OUSLY?
WHAT OTHER CHOICE DO WE HAVE?!

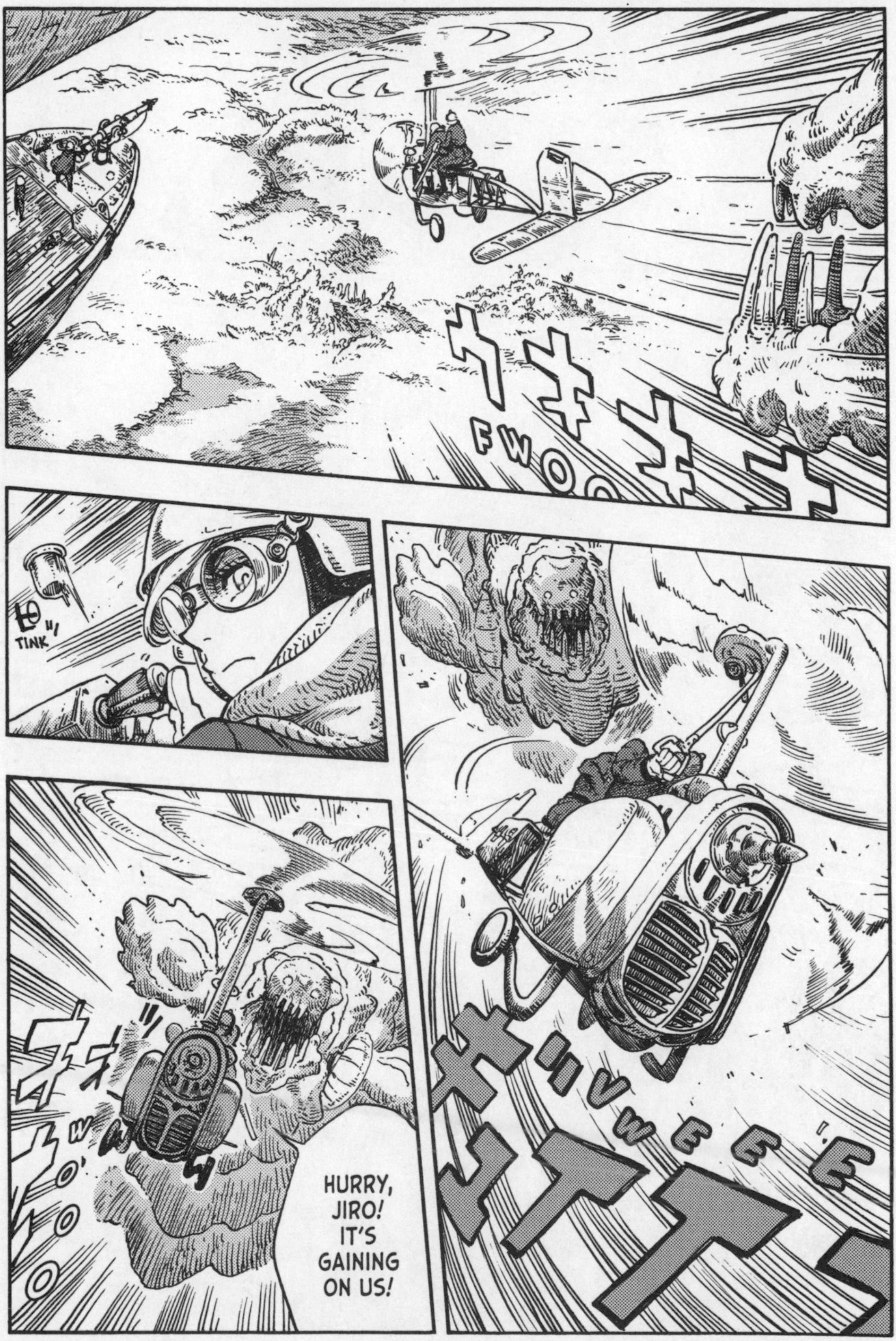
FWOO
VWEEE
TINK
FWOOO
HURRY, JIRO! IT'S GAINING ON US!

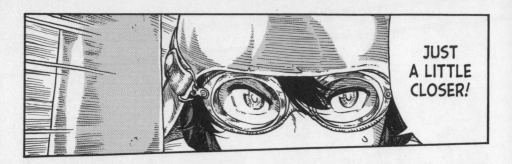

JUST
A LITTLE
CLOSER!

NOW!

134

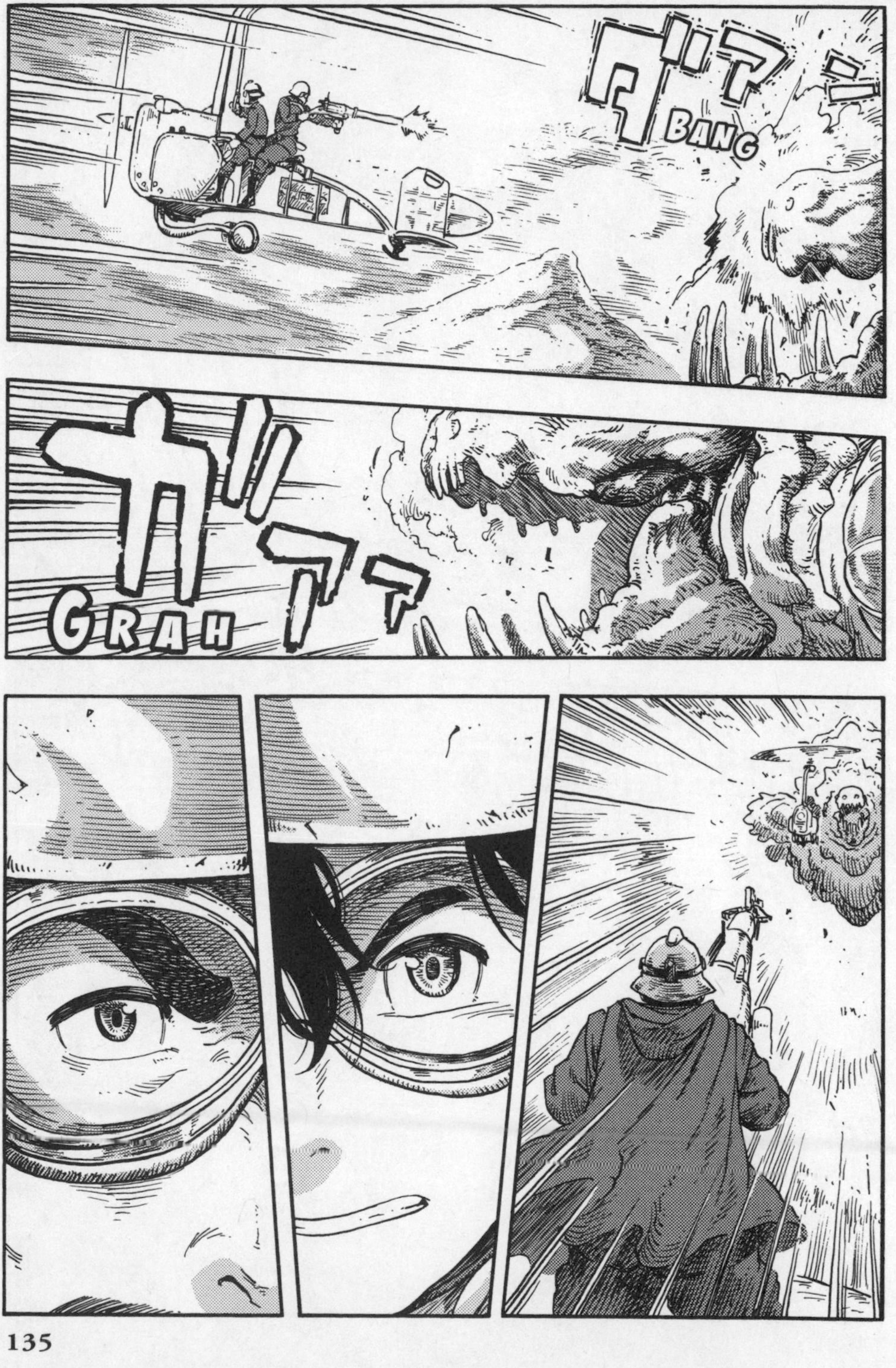
ダァン
BANG
ガァァ
GRAH

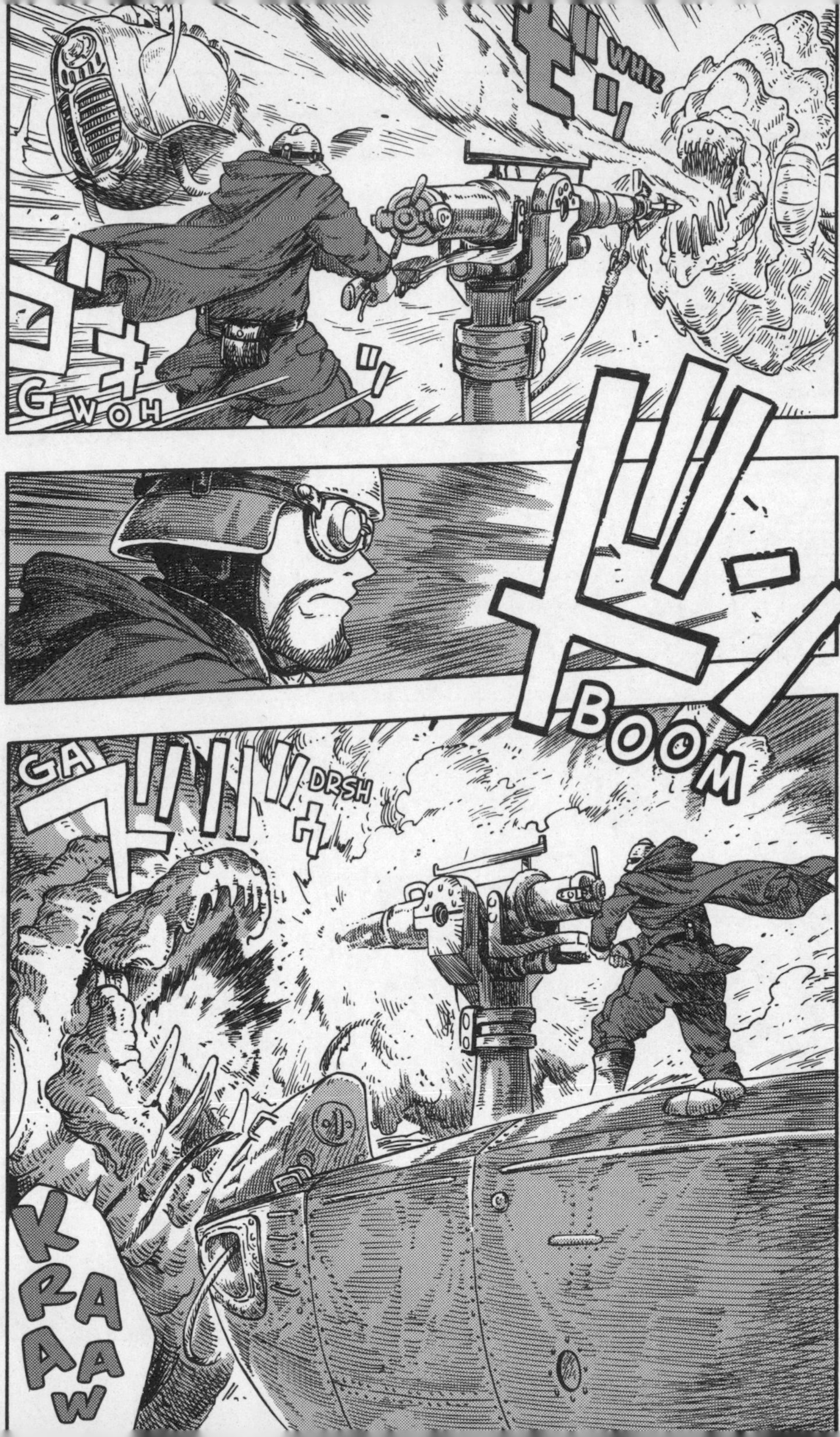
WHIZ
GWOH
BOOM
GA
DRSH
KRAAAW

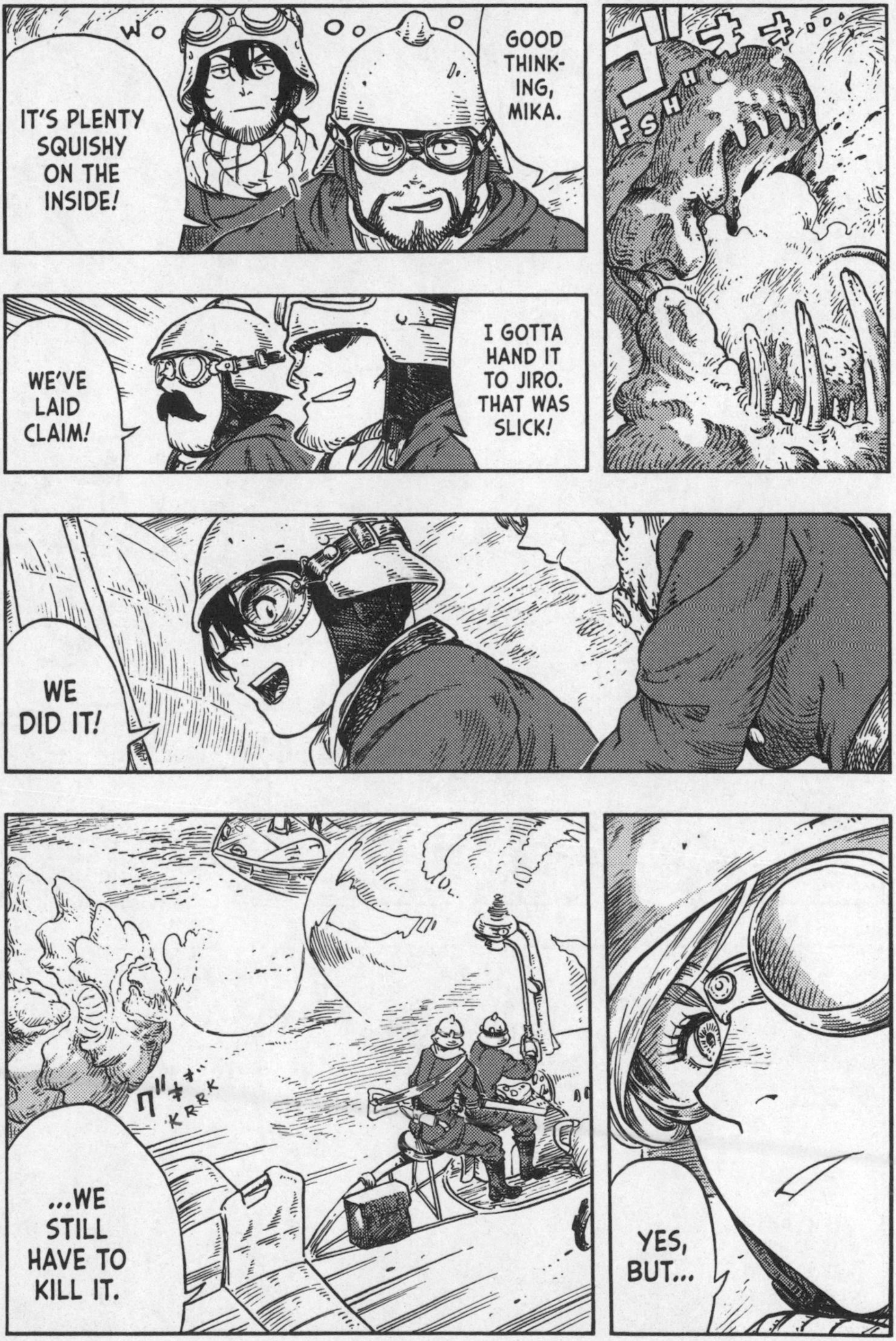
ゴオォ…
FSHH
GOOD THINKING, MIKA.
WOOO
IT'S PLENTY SQUISHY ON THE INSIDE!
I GOTTA HAND IT TO JIRO. THAT WAS SLICK!
WE'VE LAID CLAIM!
WE DID IT!
YES, BUT...
グォォ…
KRRK
...WE STILL HAVE TO KILL IT.

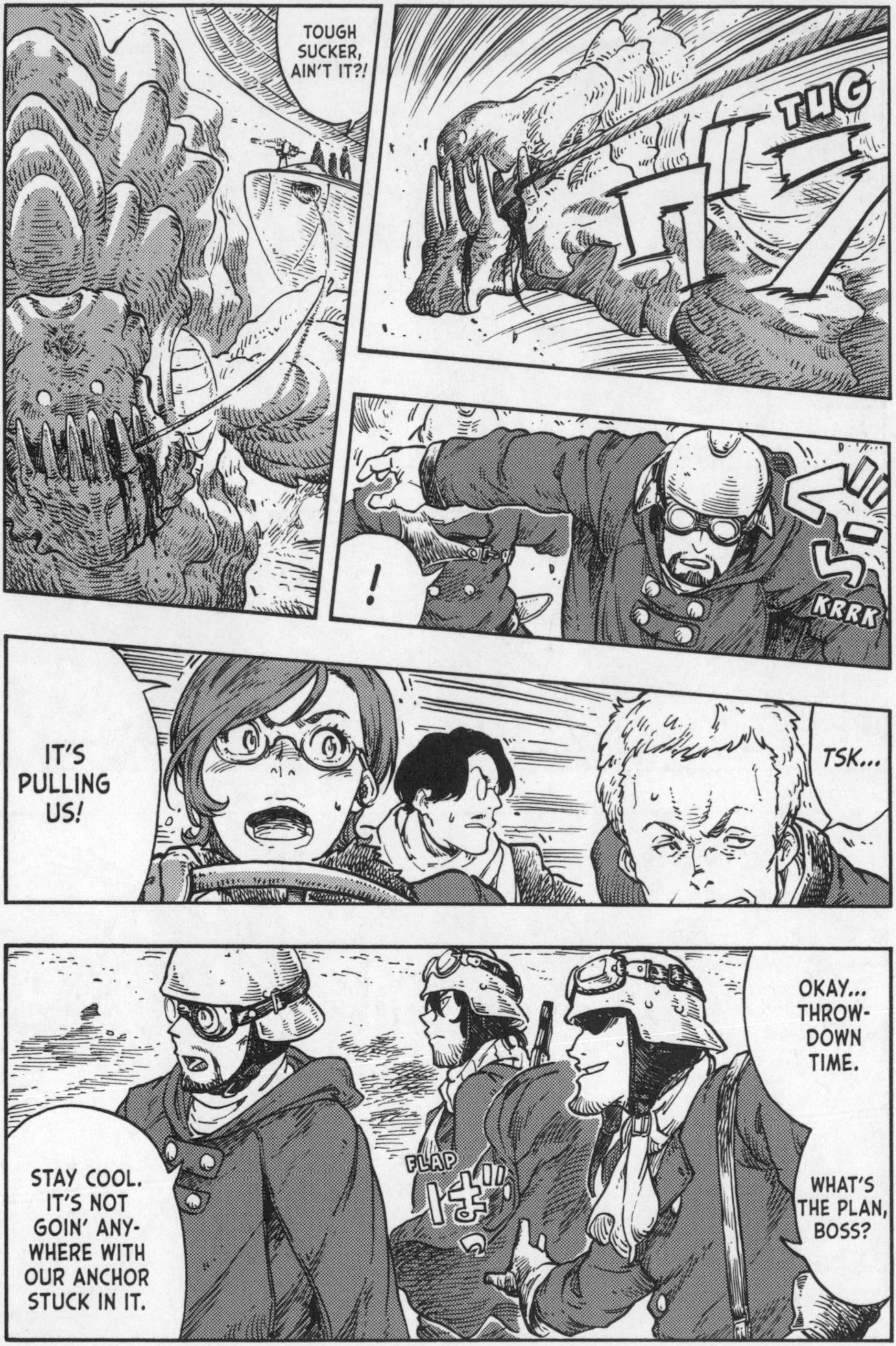
TUG
!
KRRK
TOUGH SUCKER, AIN'T IT?!
TSK...
IT'S PULLING US!
OKAY... THROW-DOWN TIME.
WHAT'S THE PLAN, BOSS?
FLAP
STAY COOL. IT'S NOT GOIN' ANYWHERE WITH OUR ANCHOR STUCK IN IT.

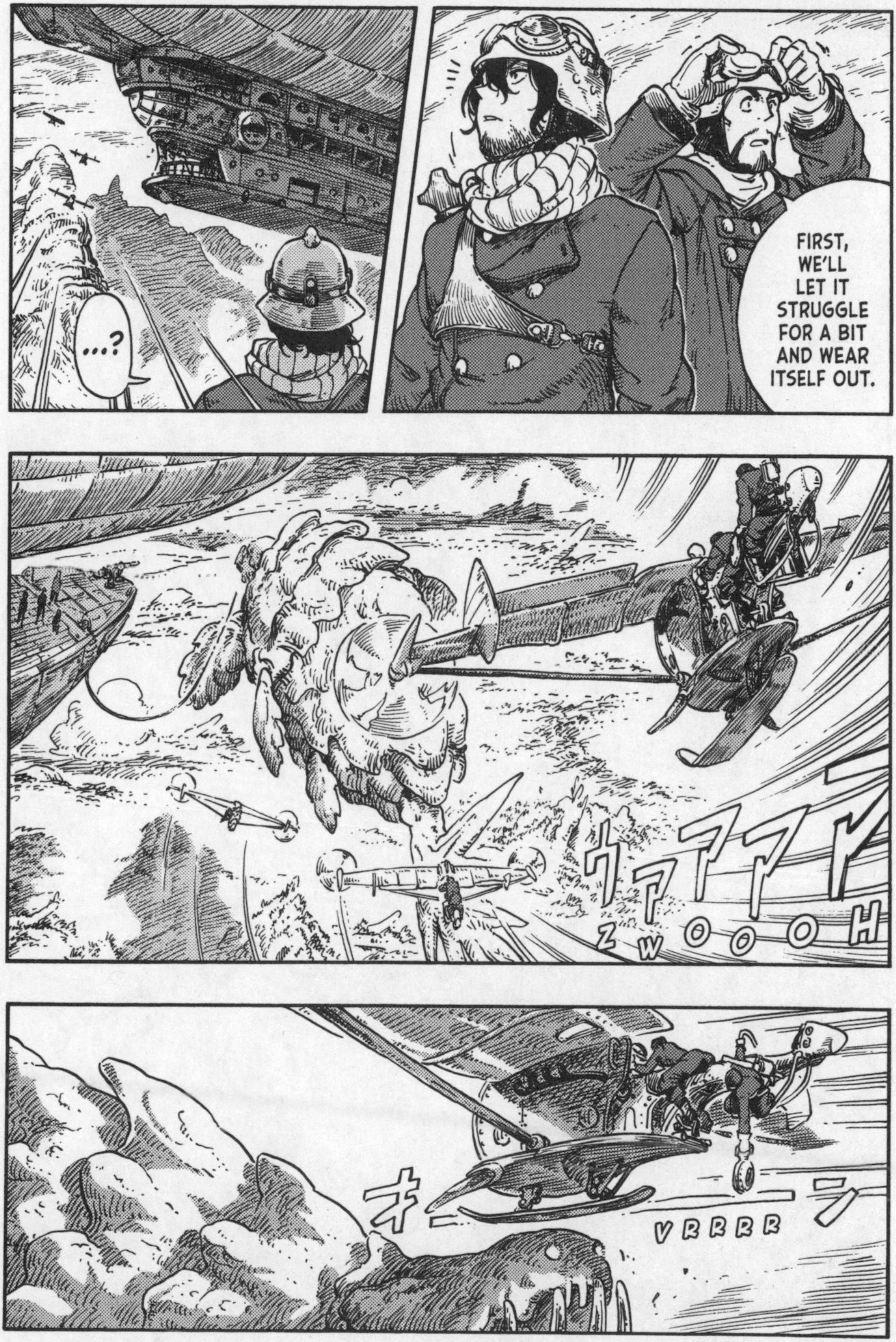
FIRST, WE'LL LET IT STRUGGLE FOR A BIT AND WEAR ITSELF OUT.
...?
ヴァアアァ
ZWOOOOH
オーーン
VRRRR

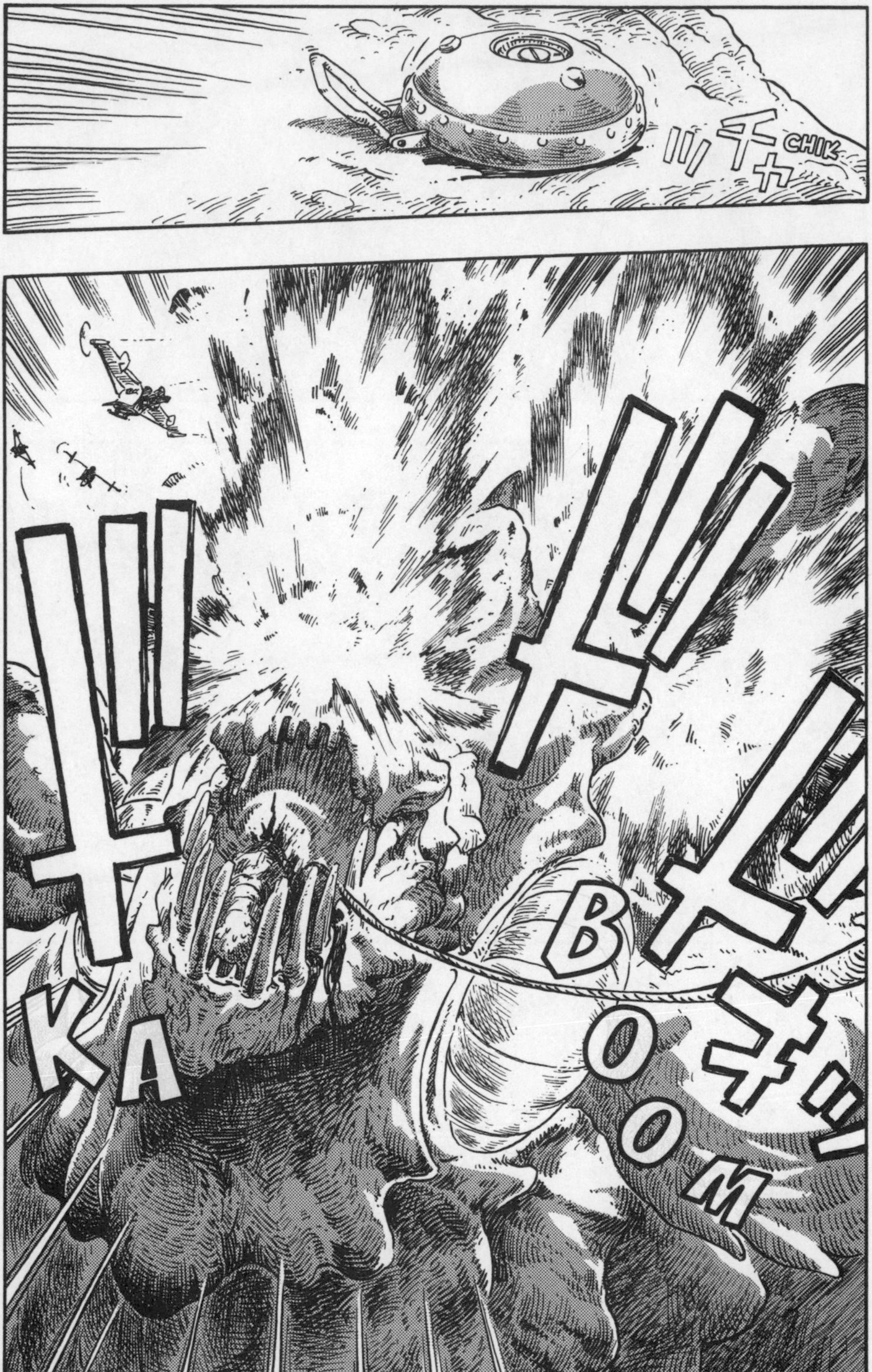

カチッ
CHIK
KA
BOOM

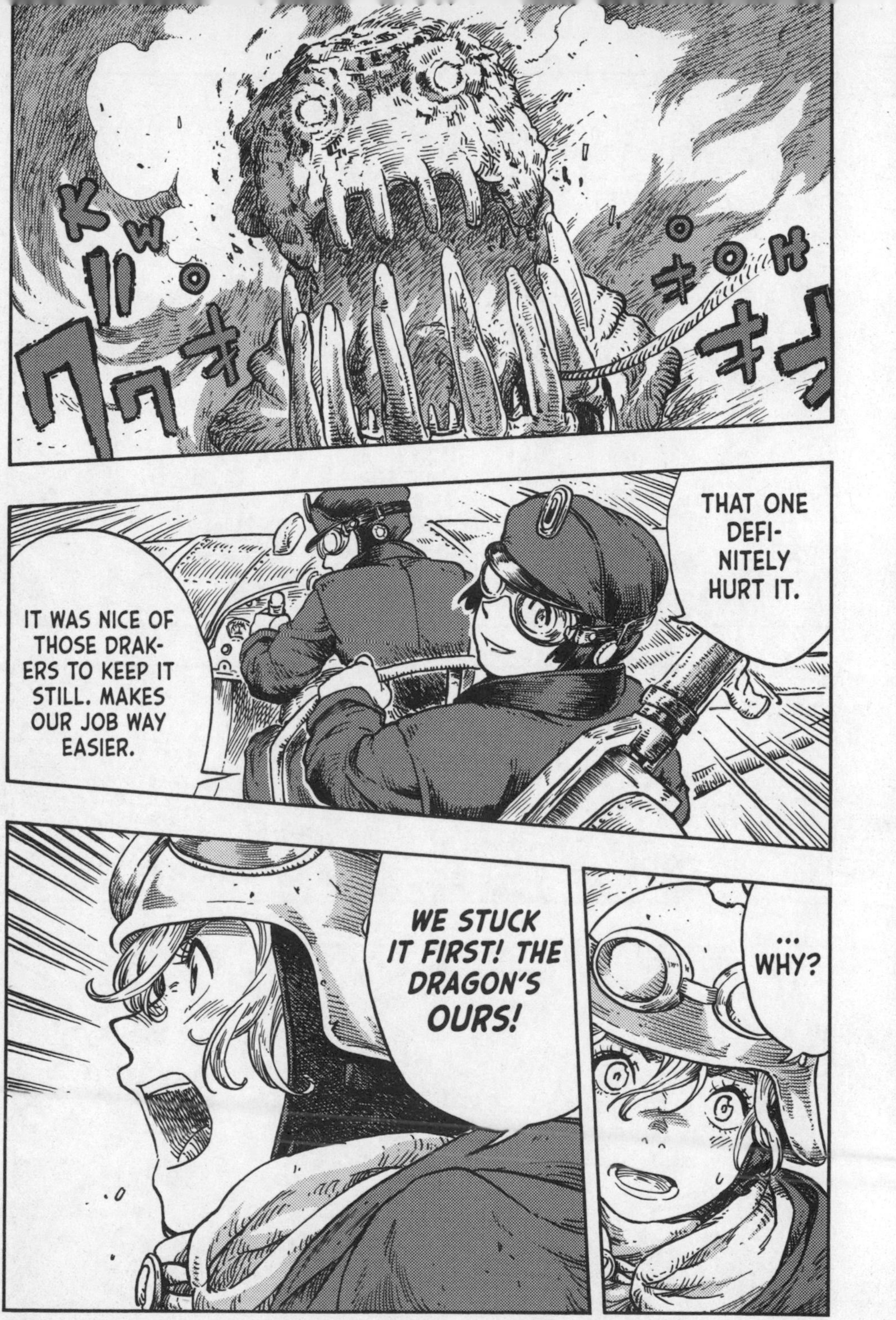
KWOOOH
THAT ONE DEFI-NITELY HURT IT.
IT WAS NICE OF THOSE DRAK-ERS TO KEEP IT STILL. MAKES OUR JOB WAY EASIER.
... WHY?
WE STUCK IT FIRST! THE DRAGON'S OURS!

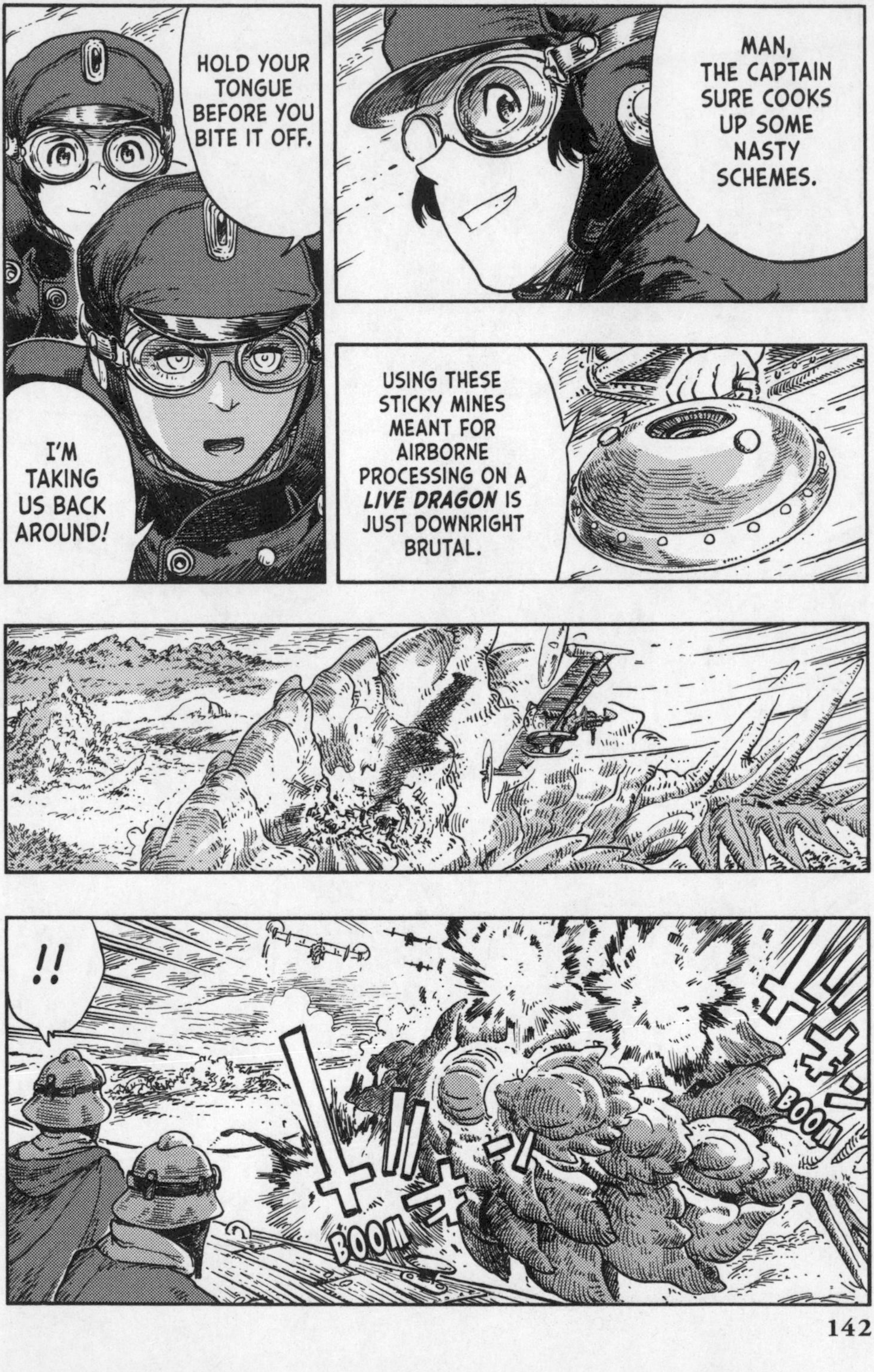

MAN, THE CAPTAIN SURE COOKS UP SOME NASTY SCHEMES.
USING THESE STICKY MINES MEANT FOR AIRBORNE PROCESSING ON A *LIVE DRAGON* IS JUST DOWNRIGHT BRUTAL.
HOLD YOUR TONGUE BEFORE YOU BITE IT OFF.
I'M TAKING US BACK AROUND!
BOOM
!!
BOOM

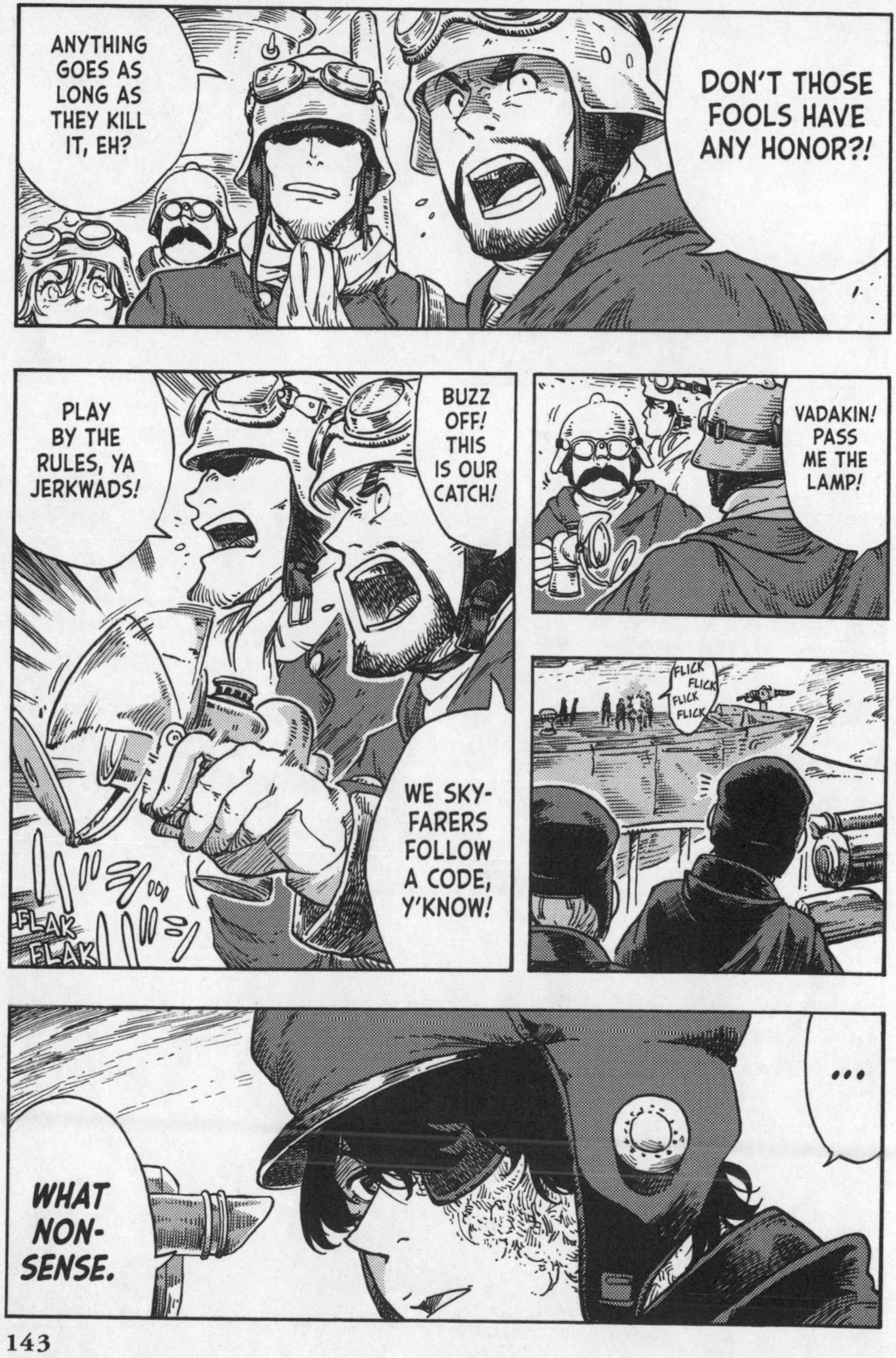
DON'T THOSE FOOLS HAVE ANY HONOR?!
ANYTHING GOES AS LONG AS THEY KILL IT, EH?
VADAKIN! PASS ME THE LAMP!
FLICK FLICK FLICK FLICK
BUZZ OFF! THIS IS OUR CATCH!
PLAY BY THE RULES, YA JERKWADS!
WE SKY-FARERS FOLLOW A CODE, Y'KNOW!
FLAK FLAK
...
WHAT NON-SENSE.

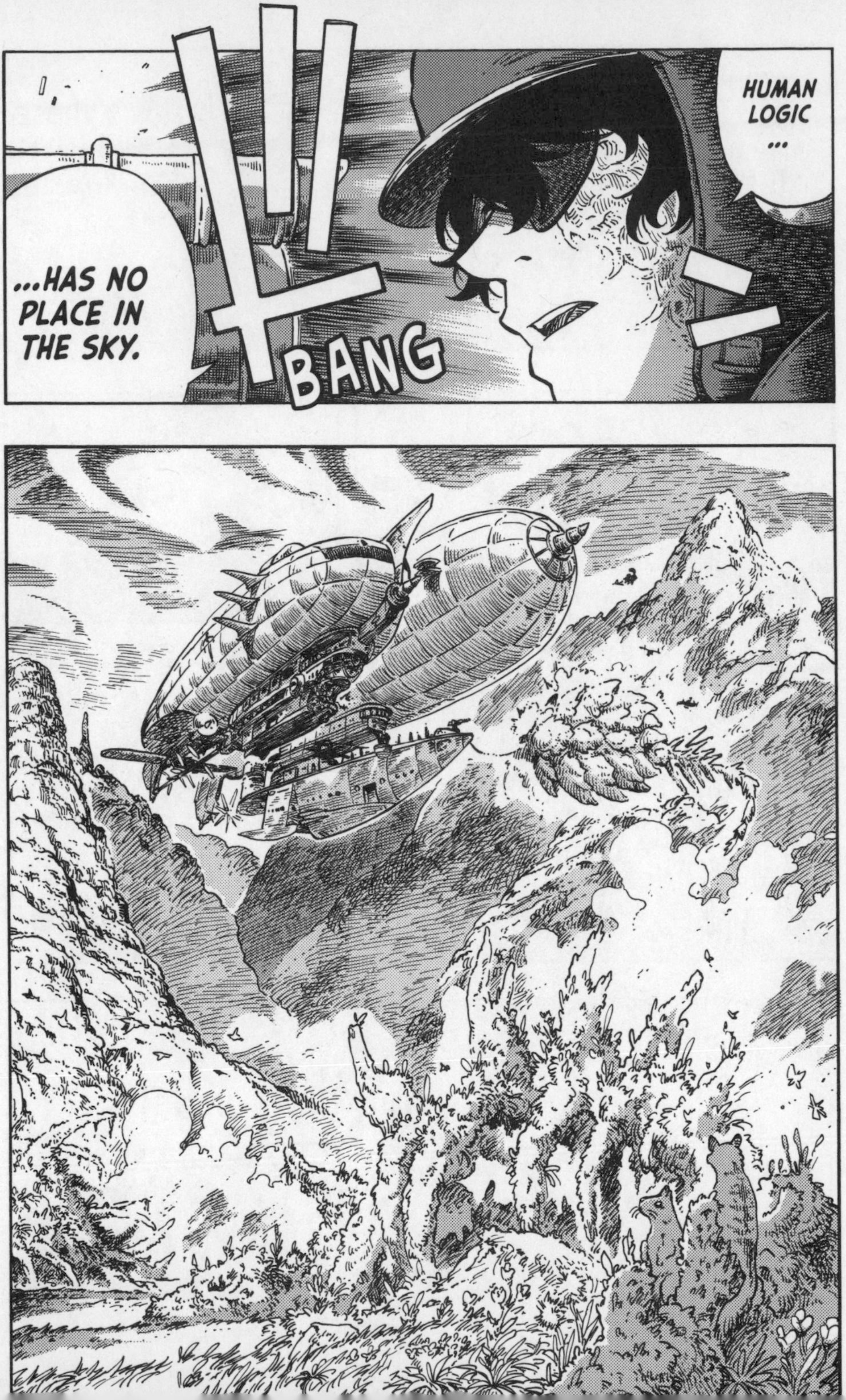
HUMAN LOGIC ...
...HAS NO PLACE IN THE SKY.
BANG

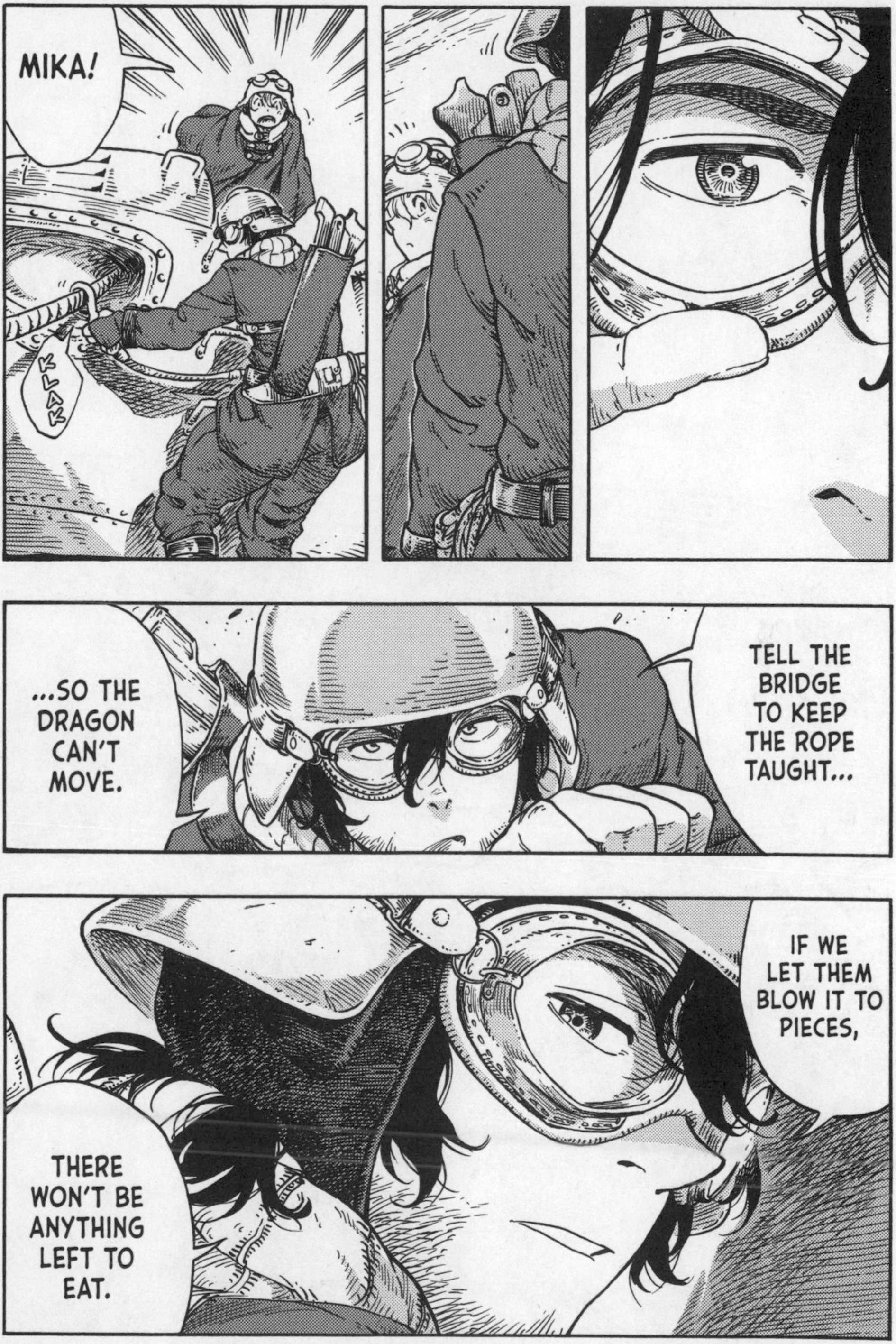
MIKA!
KLAK
TELL THE BRIDGE TO KEEP THE ROPE TAUGHT...
...SO THE DRAGON CAN'T MOVE.
IF WE LET THEM BLOW IT TO PIECES,
THERE WON'T BE ANYTHING LEFT TO EAT.

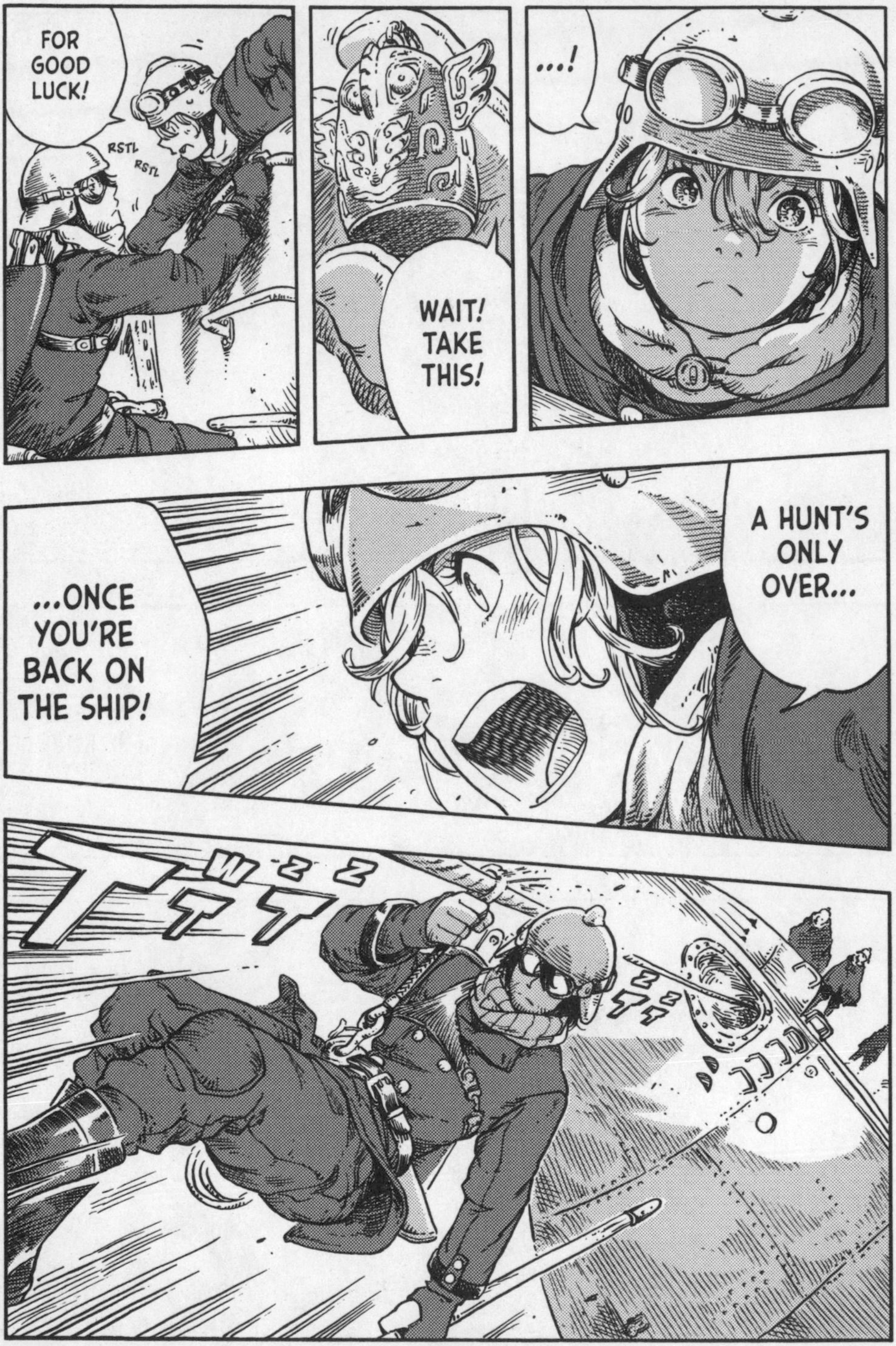
...!
WAIT! TAKE THIS!
FOR GOOD LUCK!
RSTL RSTL
A HUNT'S ONLY OVER...
...ONCE YOU'RE BACK ON THE SHIP!

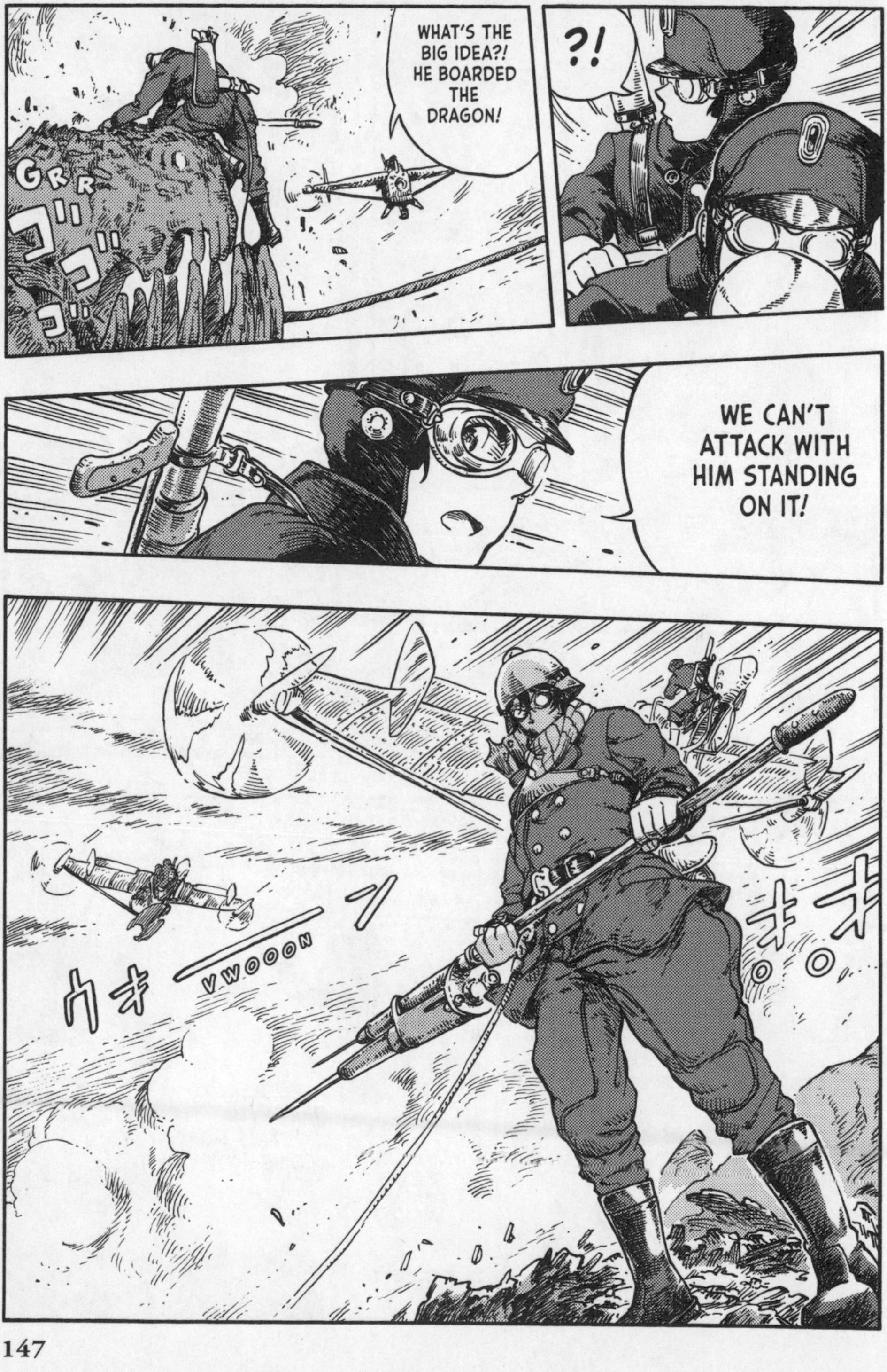
?!
WHAT'S THE BIG IDEA?! HE BOARDED THE DRAGON!
GRR
WE CAN'T ATTACK WITH HIM STANDING ON IT!
VWOOON

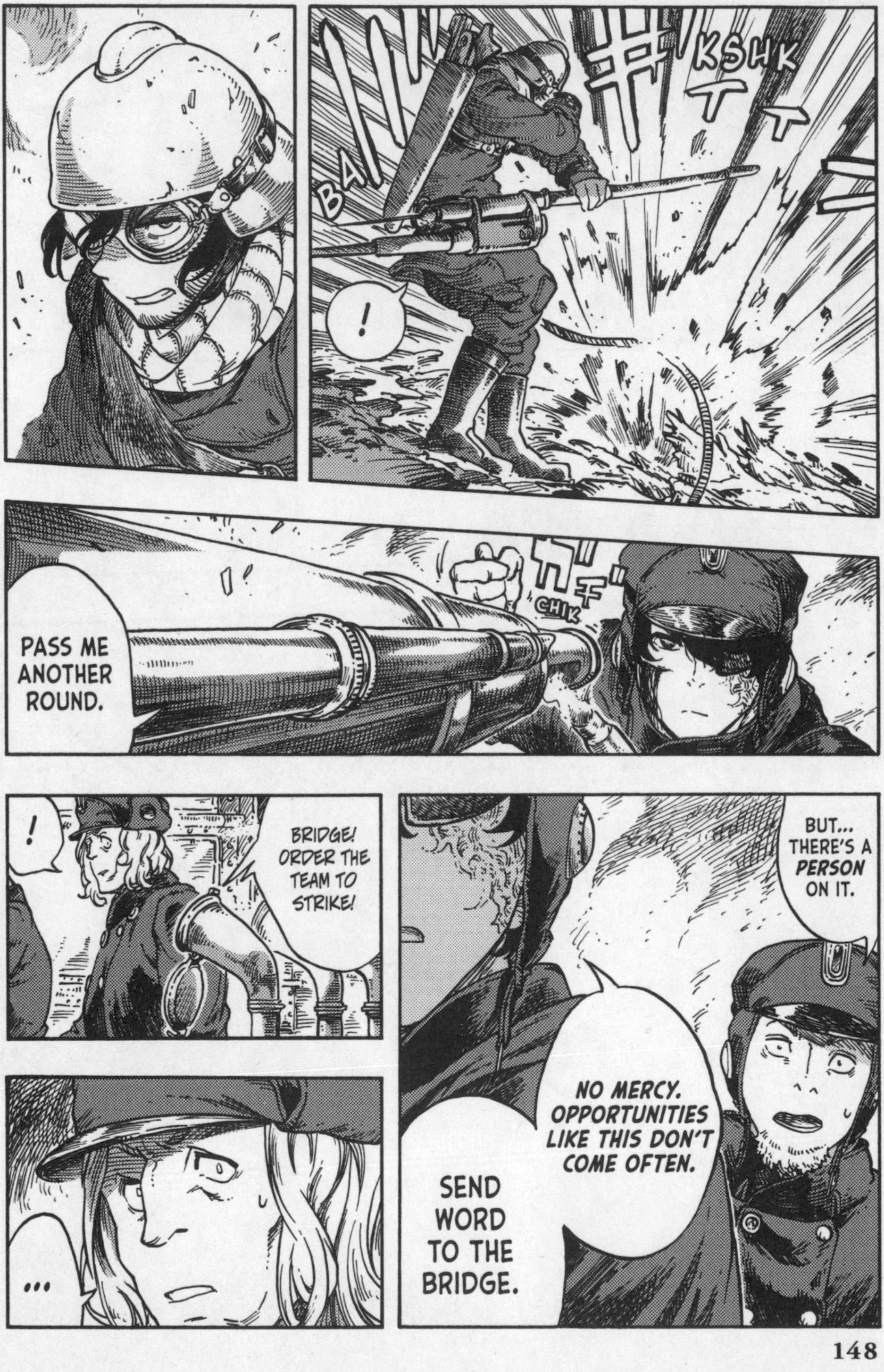
KSHK
BA
!
CHIK
PASS ME ANOTHER ROUND.
BUT... THERE'S A *PERSON* ON IT.
NO MERCY. OPPORTUNITIES LIKE THIS DON'T COME OFTEN.
SEND WORD TO THE BRIDGE.
!
BRIDGE! ORDER THE TEAM TO STRIKE!
...

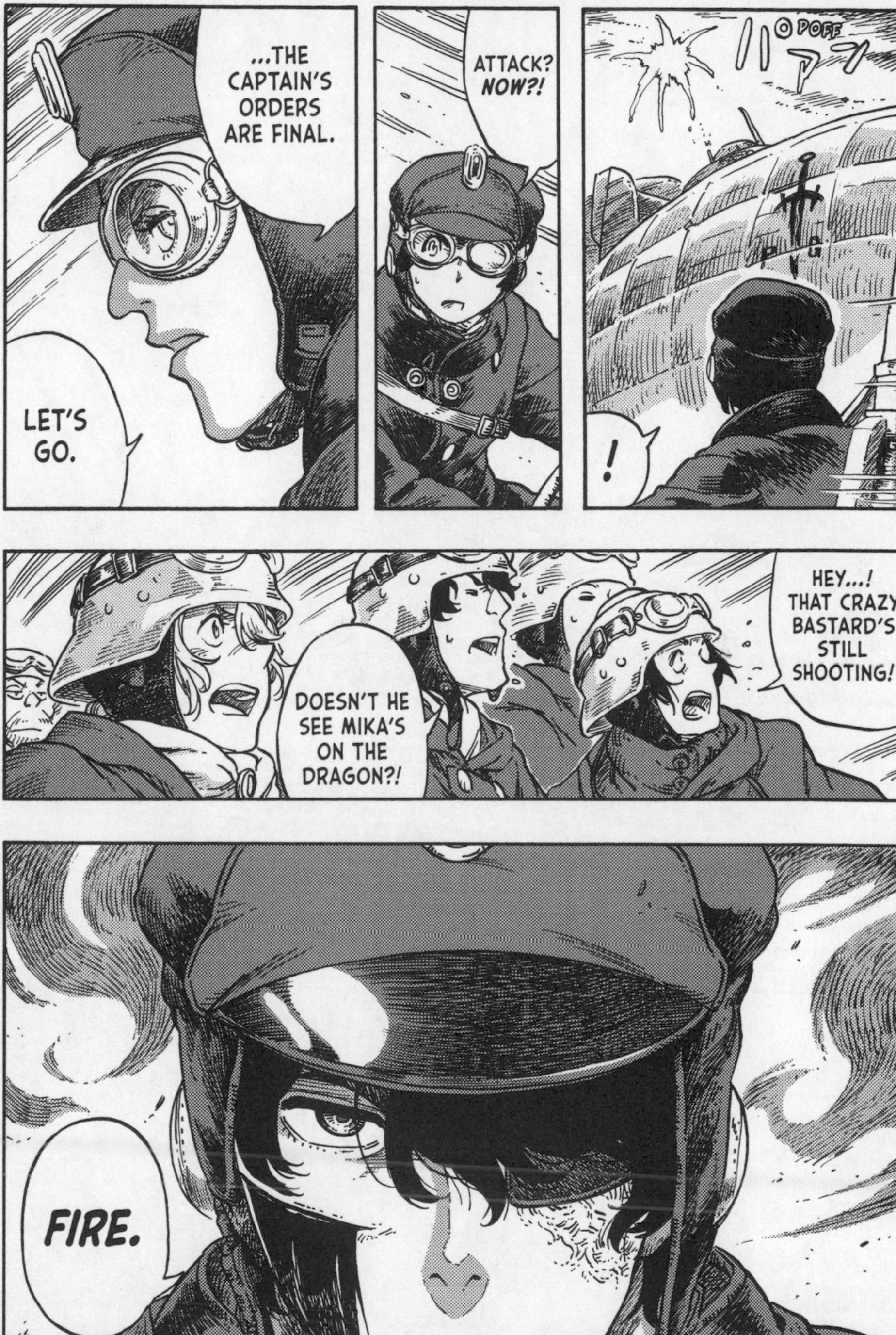
POFF
!
ATTACK? NOW?!
...THE CAPTAIN'S ORDERS ARE FINAL.
LET'S GO.
HEY...! THAT CRAZY BASTARD'S STILL SHOOTING!
DOESN'T HE SEE MIKA'S ON THE DRAGON?!
FIRE.

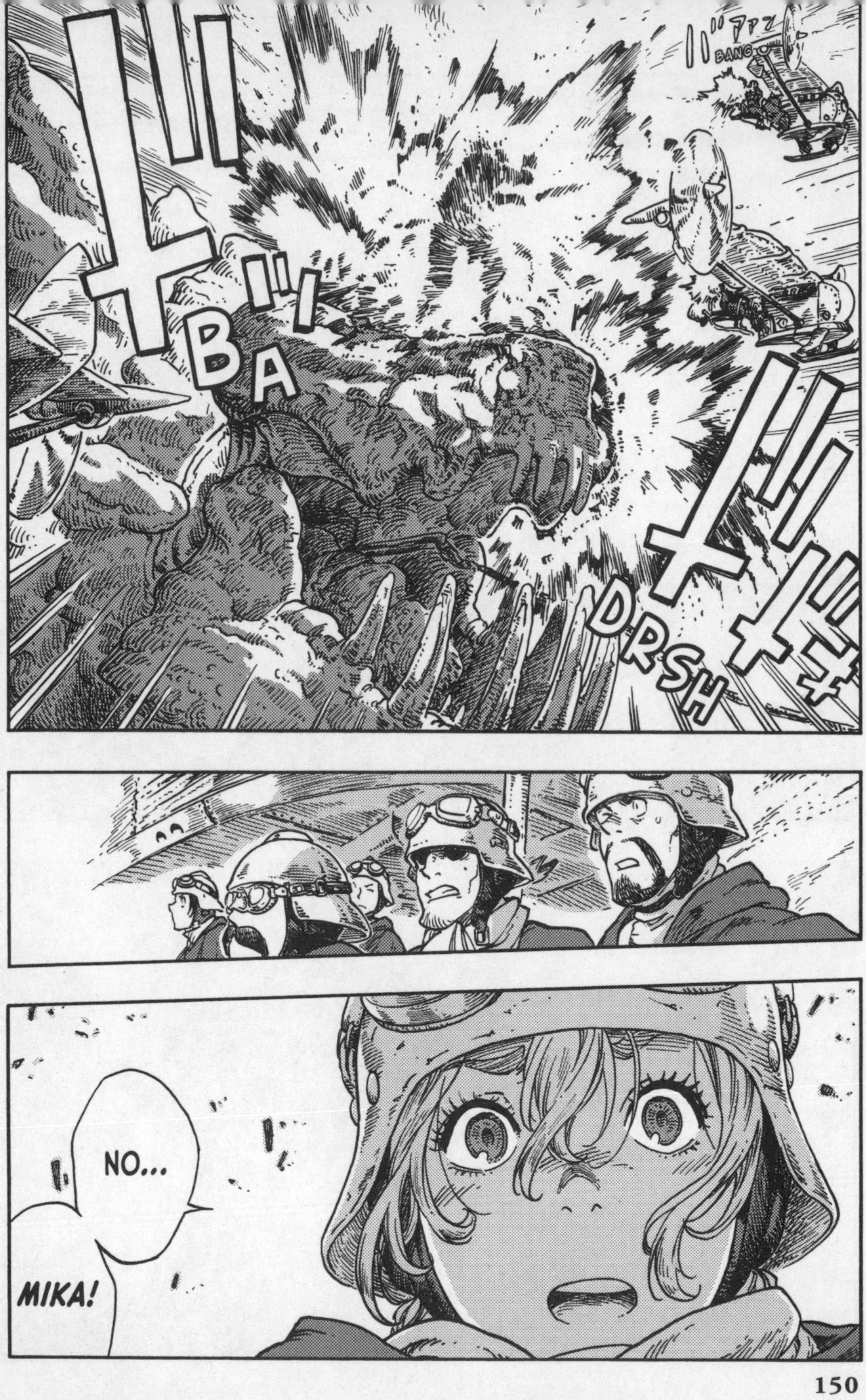
BANG
BA
DRSH
NO...
MIKA!

Flight 45 — Conclusion & Fatty Tian Shan Sashimi

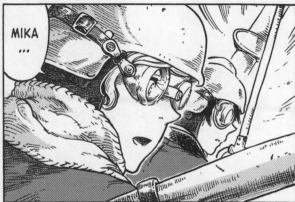

MIKA
...

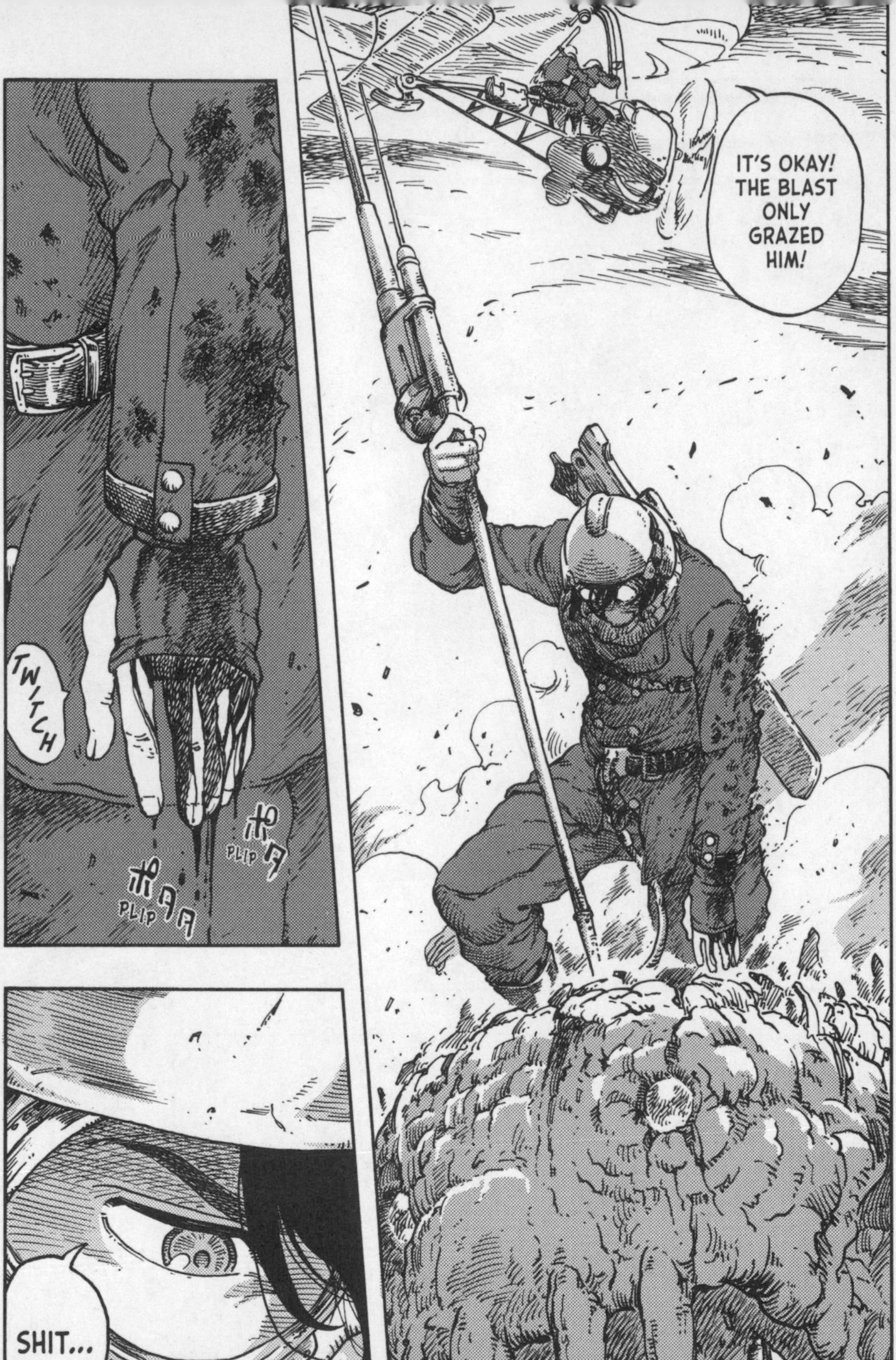
IT'S OKAY! THE BLAST ONLY GRAZED HIM!
TWITCH
PLIP
PLIP
SHIT...

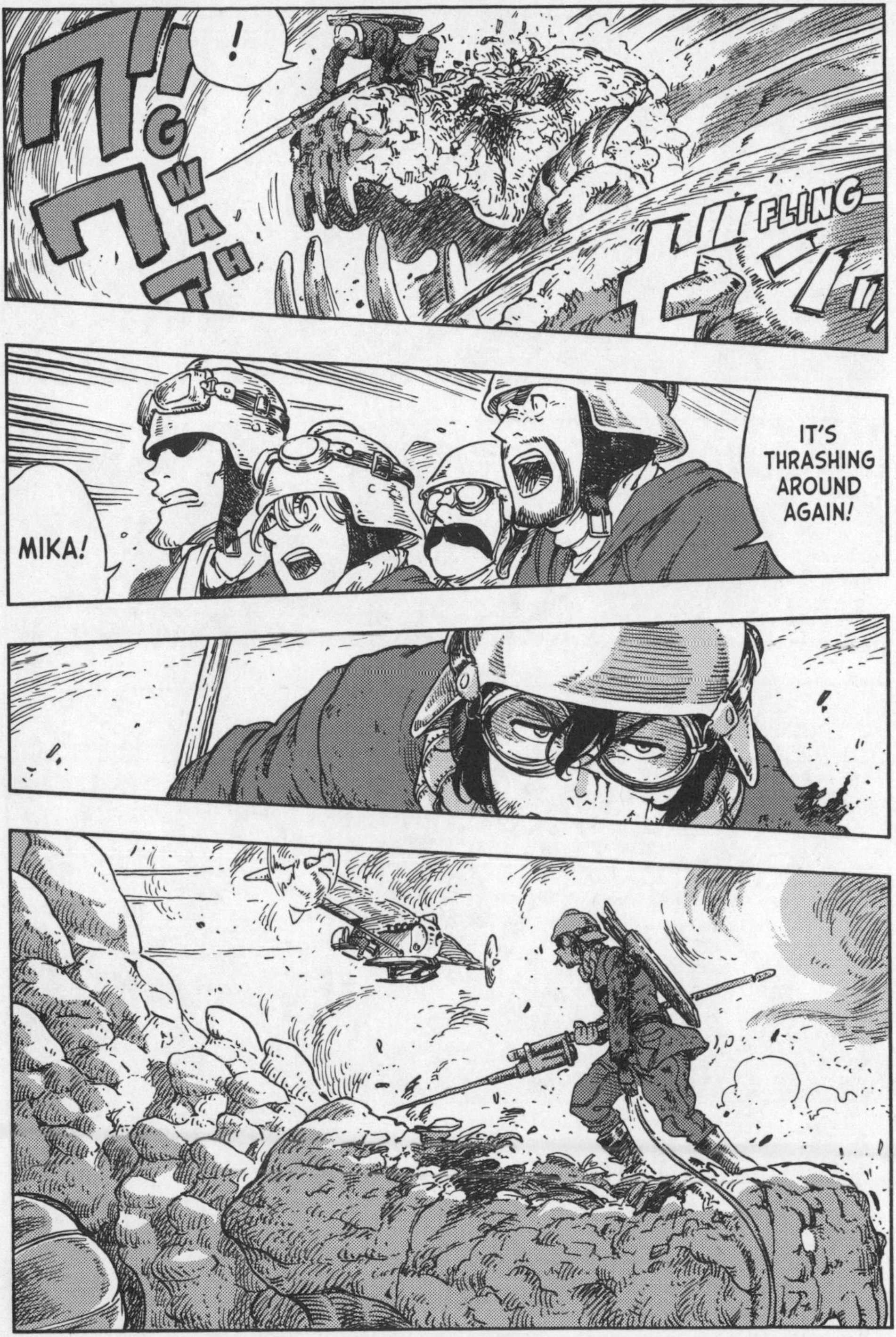
!
GWATH
FLING
IT'S THRASHING AROUND AGAIN!
MIKA!

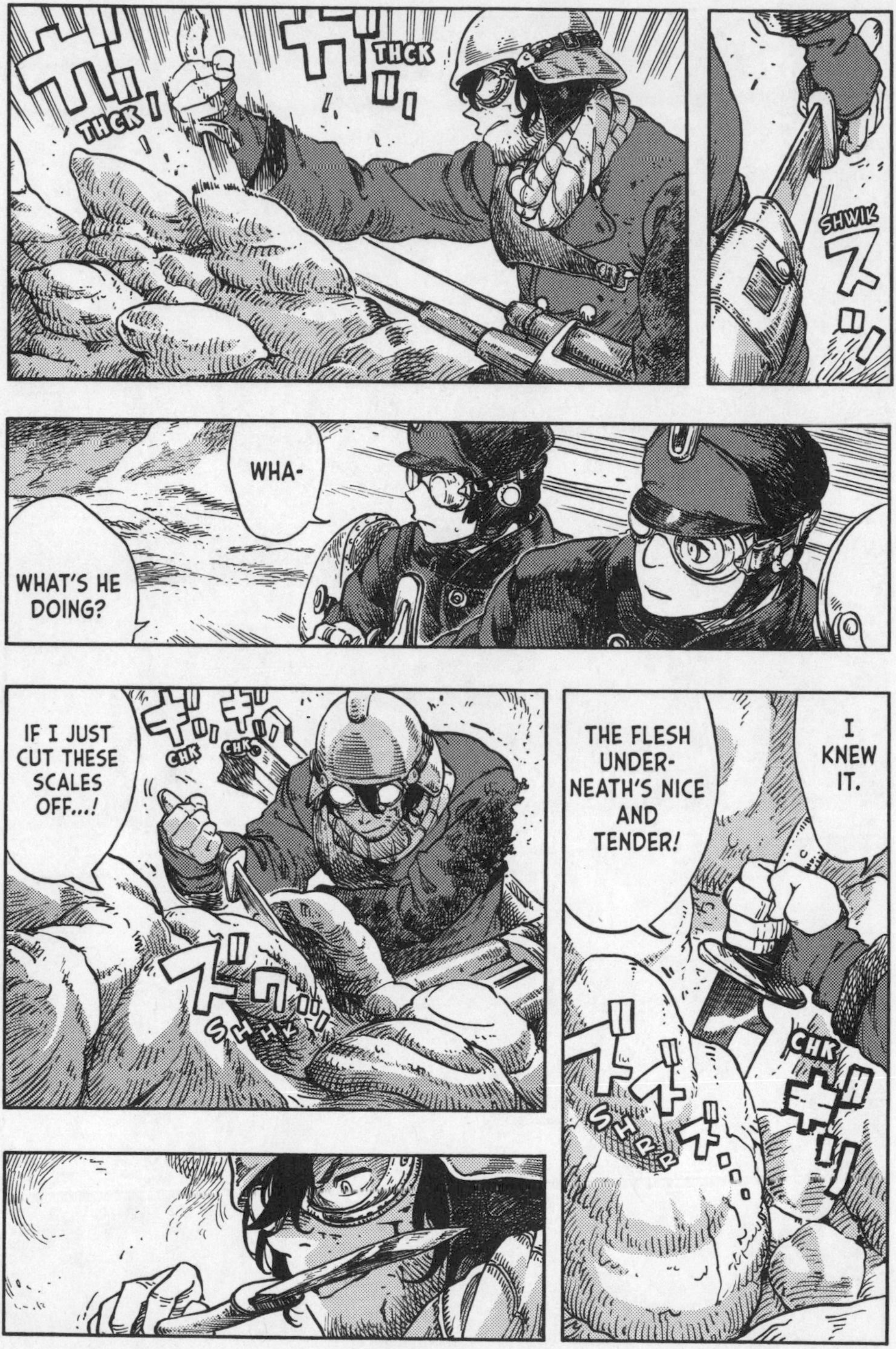
SHWIK
THCK
THCK
WHA-
WHAT'S HE DOING?
I KNEW IT.
THE FLESH UNDER-NEATH'S NICE AND TENDER!
CHK
SHRR
IF I JUST CUT THESE SCALES OFF...!
CHK CHK
SHHK

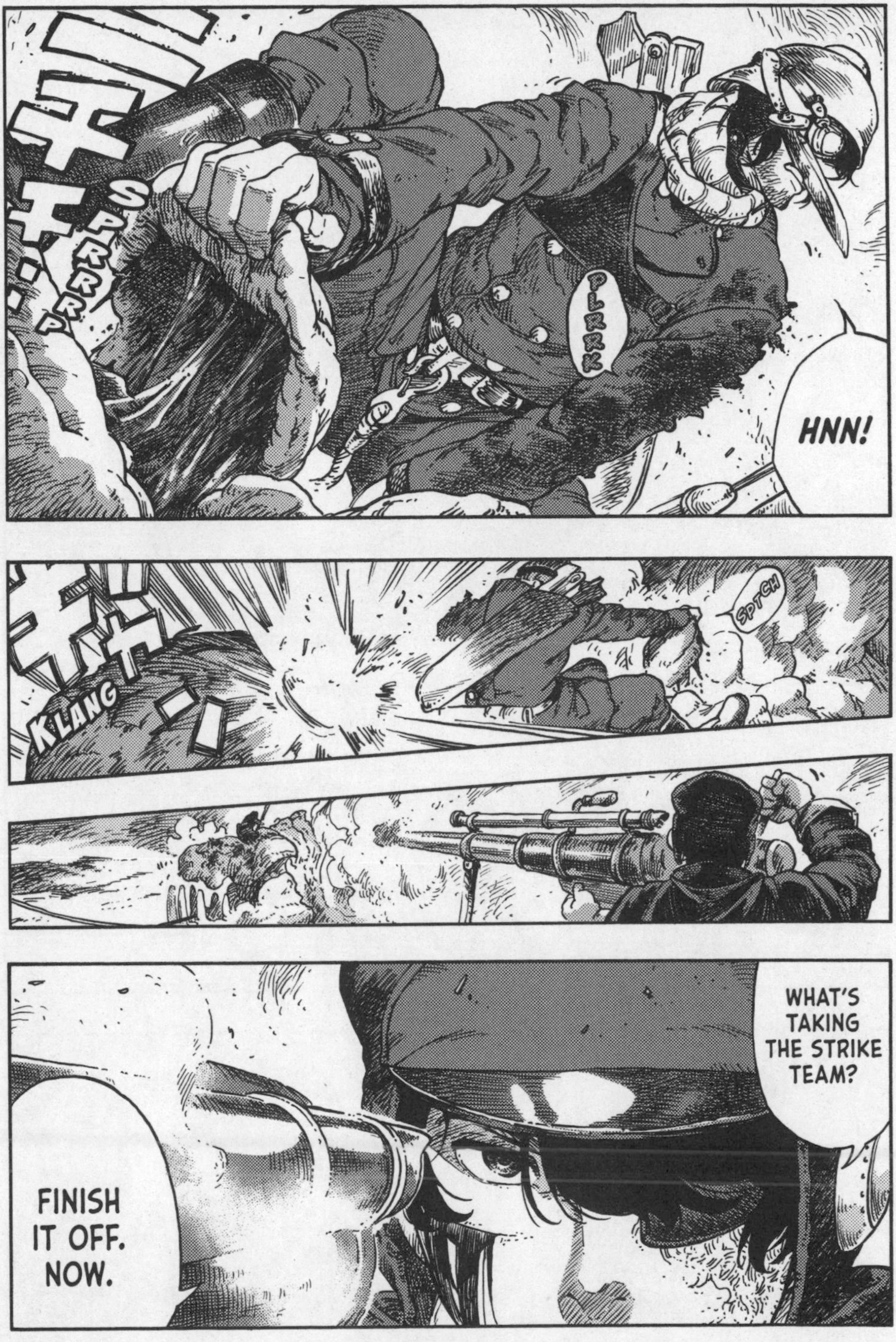
HNN!
PLRRK
SPRRRP
SPTCH
KLANG
WHAT'S TAKING THE STRIKE TEAM?
FINISH IT OFF. NOW.

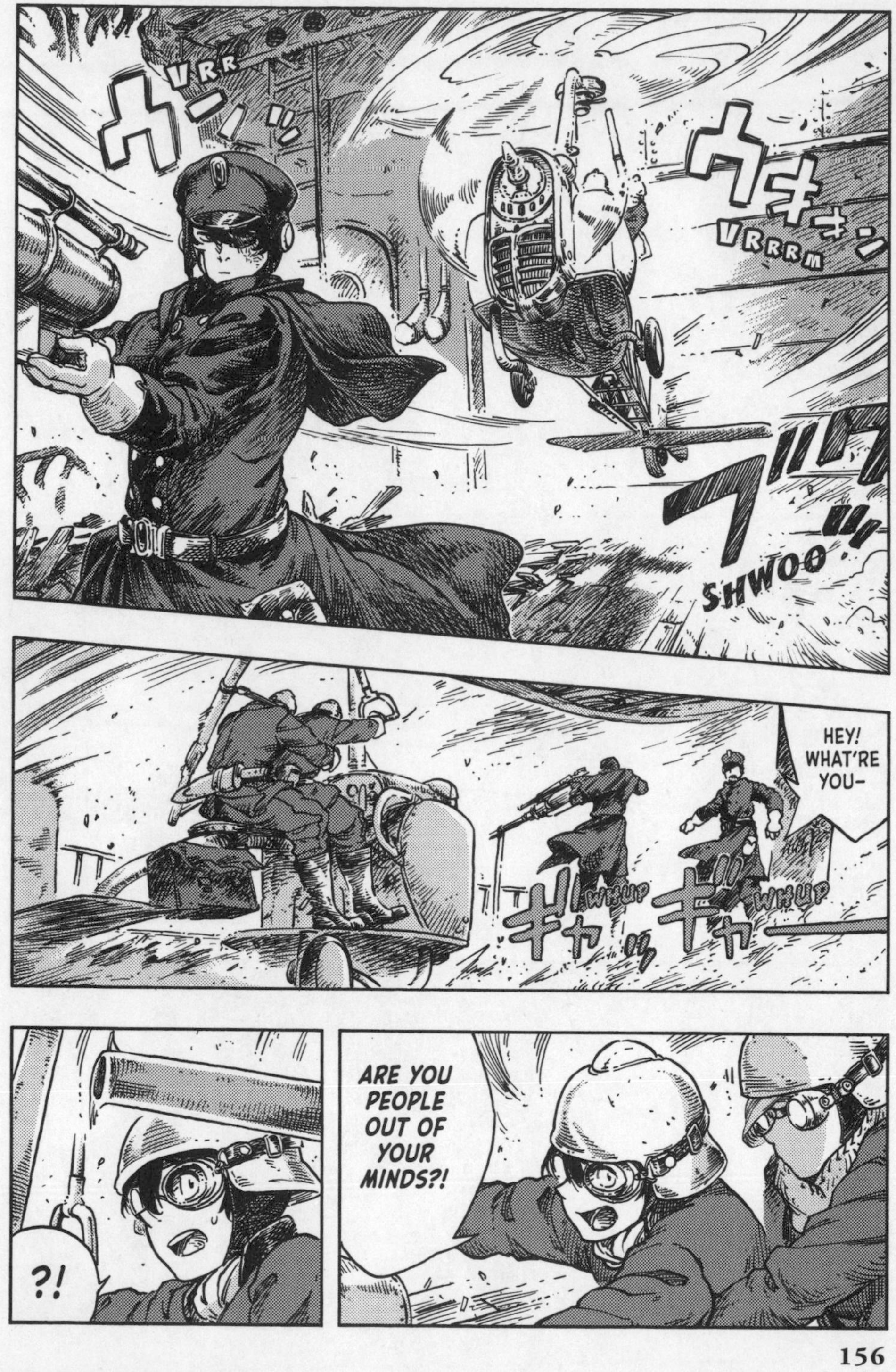
VRRRM
SHWOO
VRR
HEY! WHAT'RE YOU–
WHUP
WHUP
ARE YOU PEOPLE OUT OF YOUR MINDS?!
?!

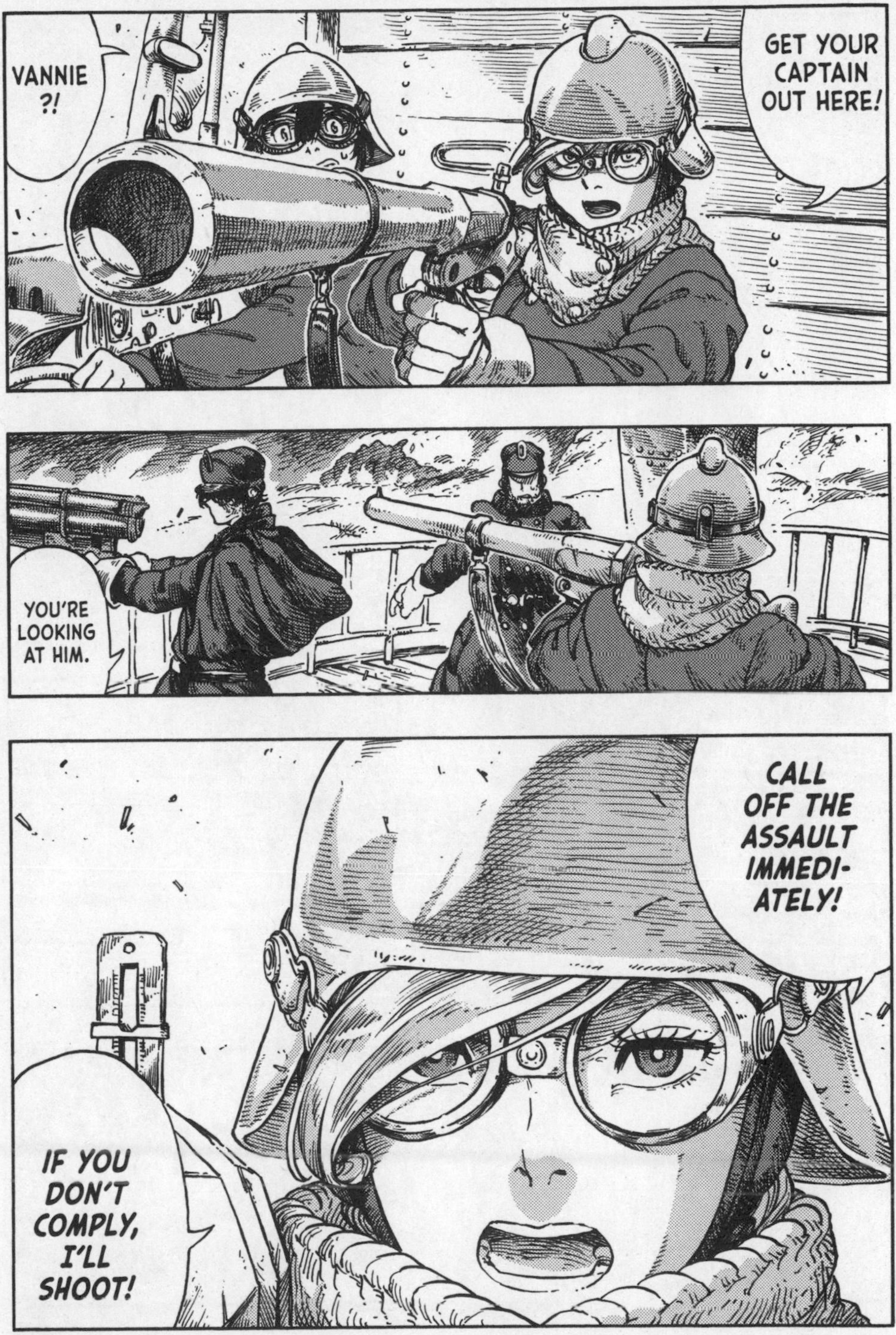
GET YOUR CAPTAIN OUT HERE!
VANNIE ?!
YOU'RE LOOKING AT HIM.
CALL OFF THE ASSAULT IMMEDI- ATELY!
IF YOU DON'T COMPLY, I'LL SHOOT!

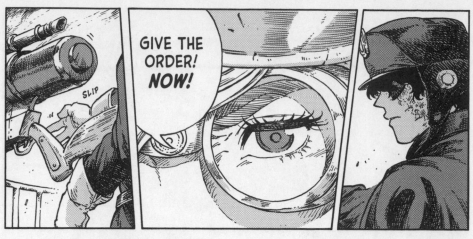

GIVE THE ORDER! ***NOW!***

SLIP

!

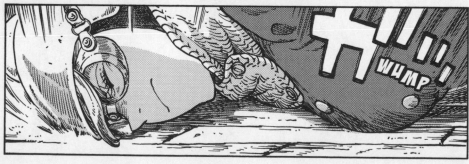

WUMP

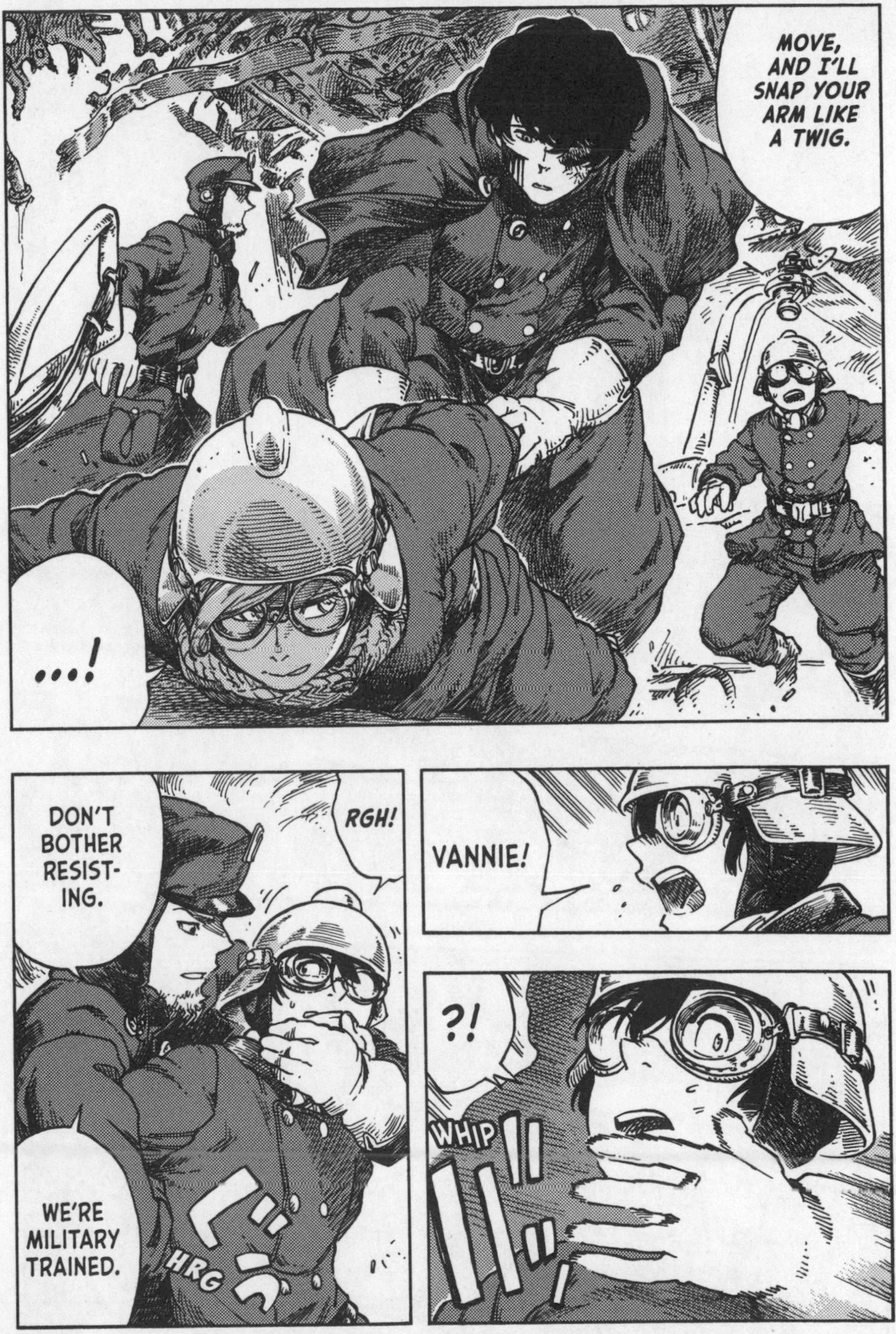
MOVE, AND I'LL SNAP YOUR ARM LIKE A TWIG.
...!
VANNIE!
?!
WHIP
RGH!
DON'T BOTHER RESIST-ING.
WE'RE MILITARY TRAINED.
HRG

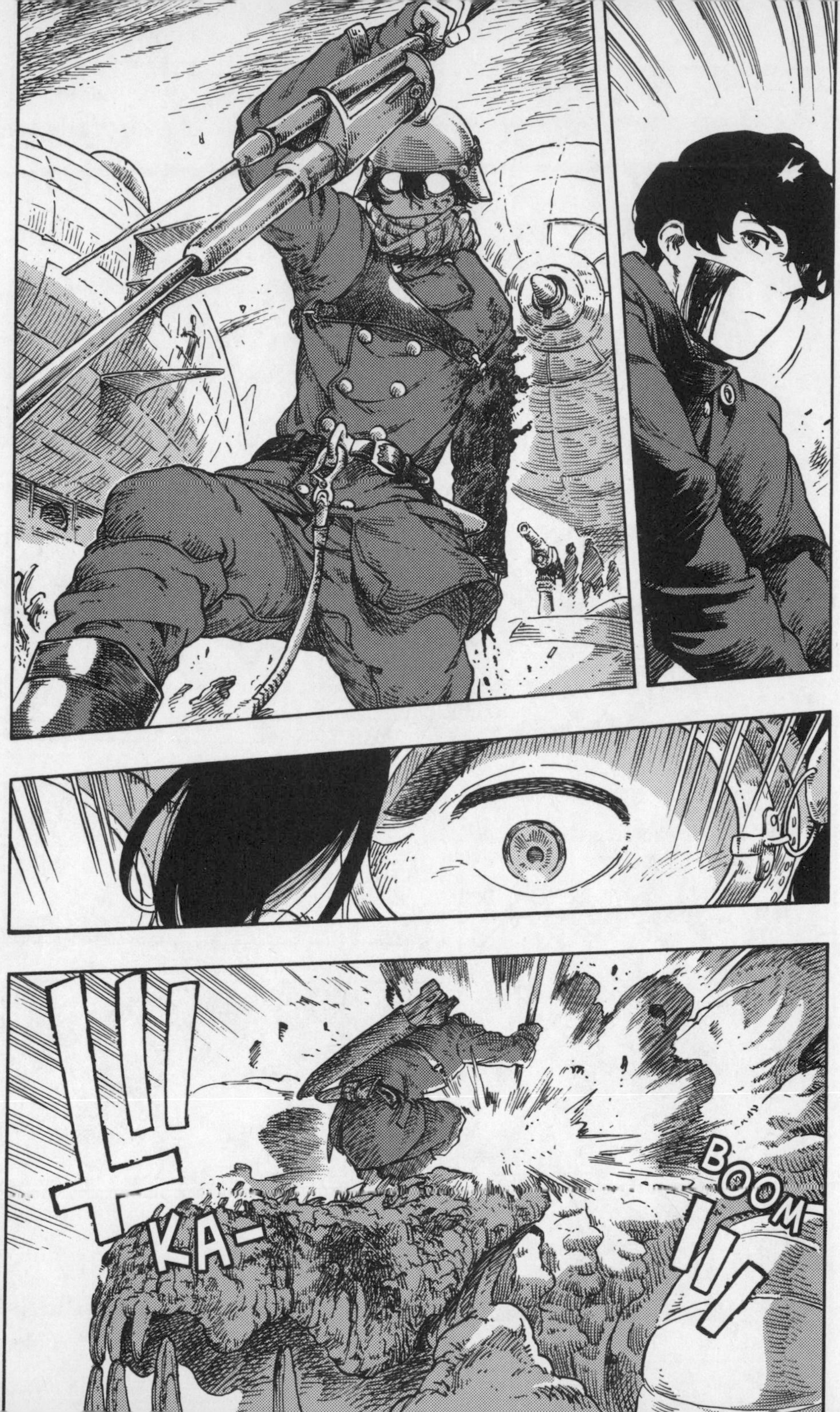
KA-BOOM!!!

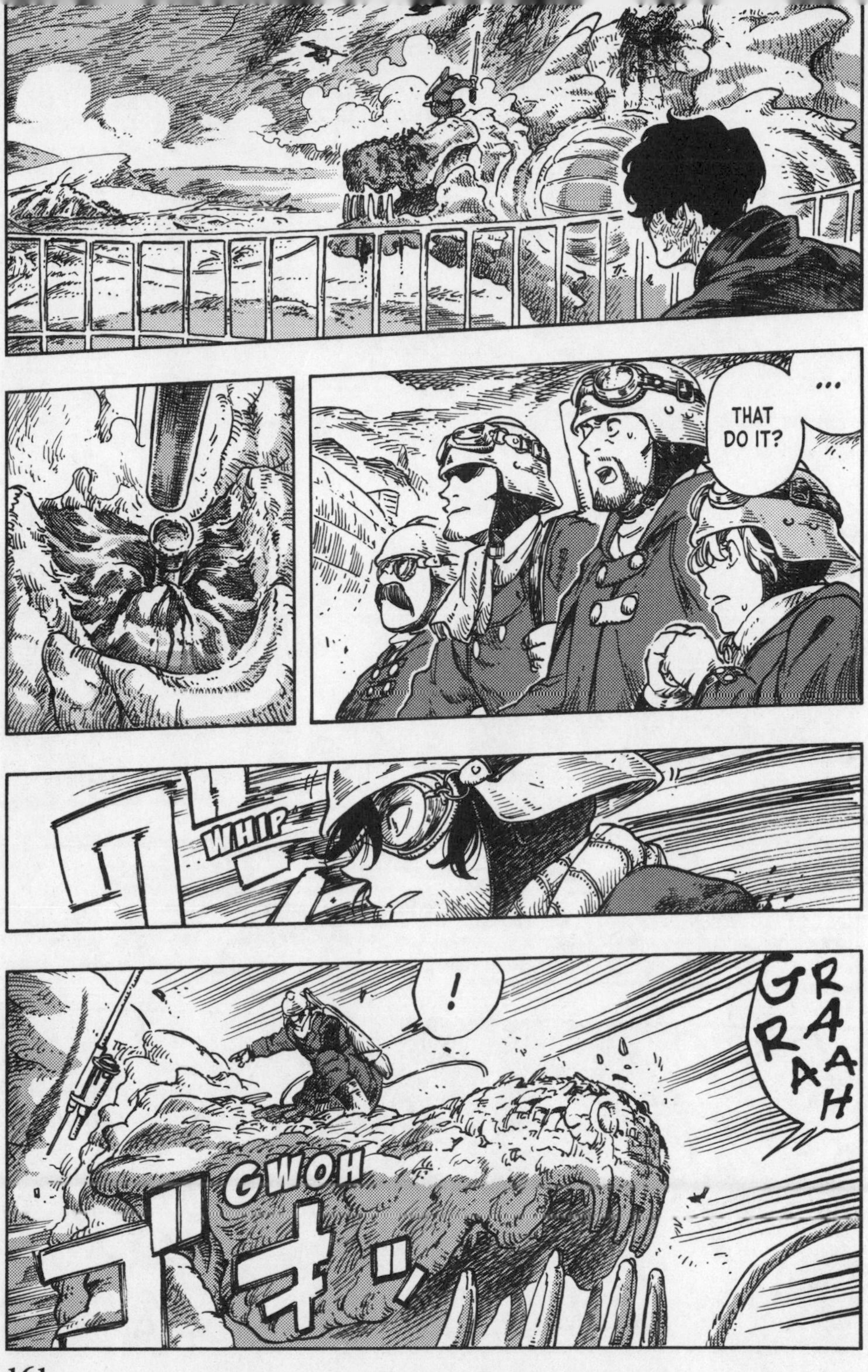
...
THAT DO IT?
WHIP
GRAAAAH
!
GWOH
ゴオッ

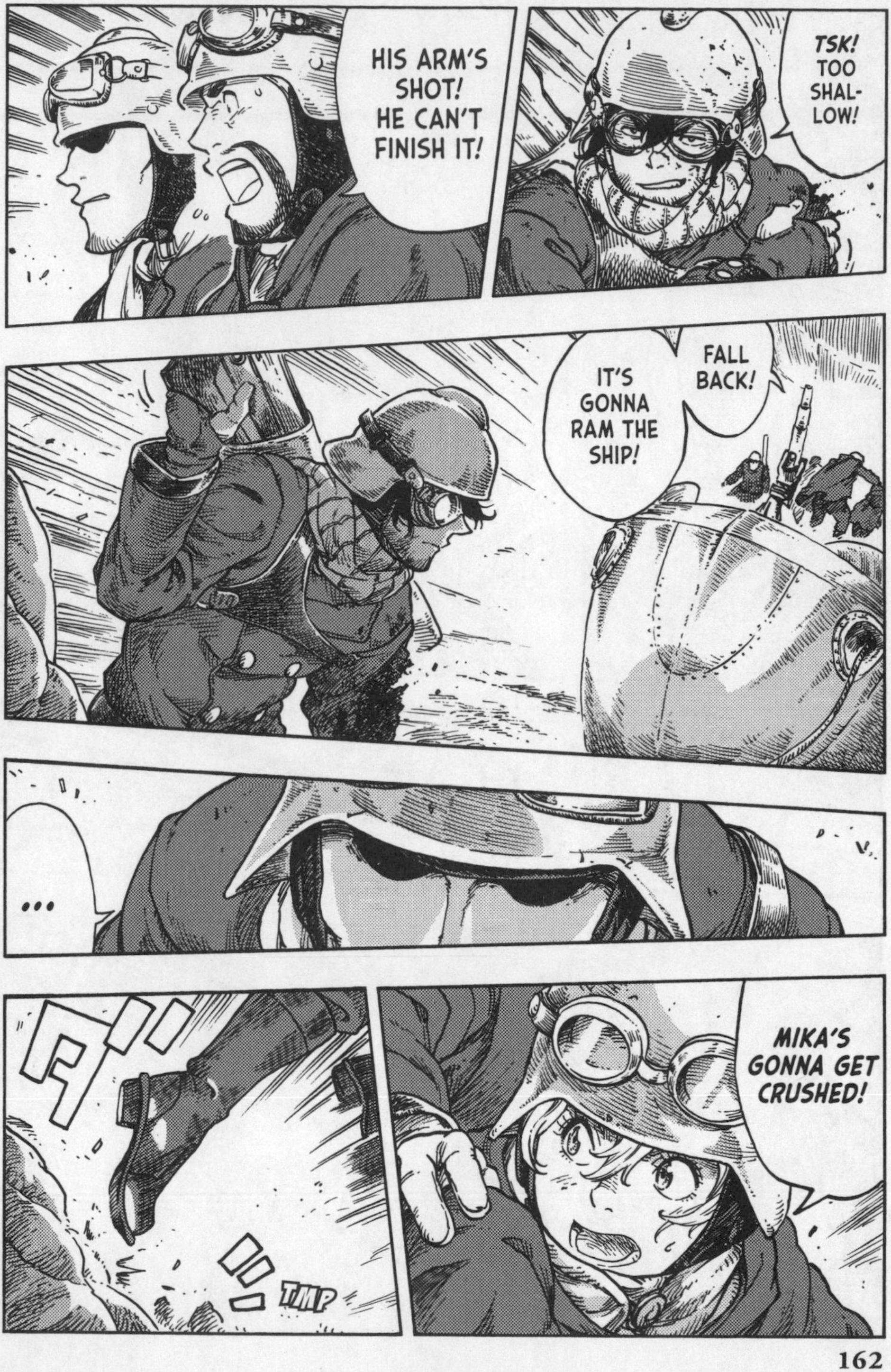
TSK! TOO SHAL-LOW!
HIS ARM'S SHOT! HE CAN'T FINISH IT!
FALL BACK!
IT'S GONNA RAM THE SHIP!
...
MIKA'S GONNA GET CRUSHED!
TMP

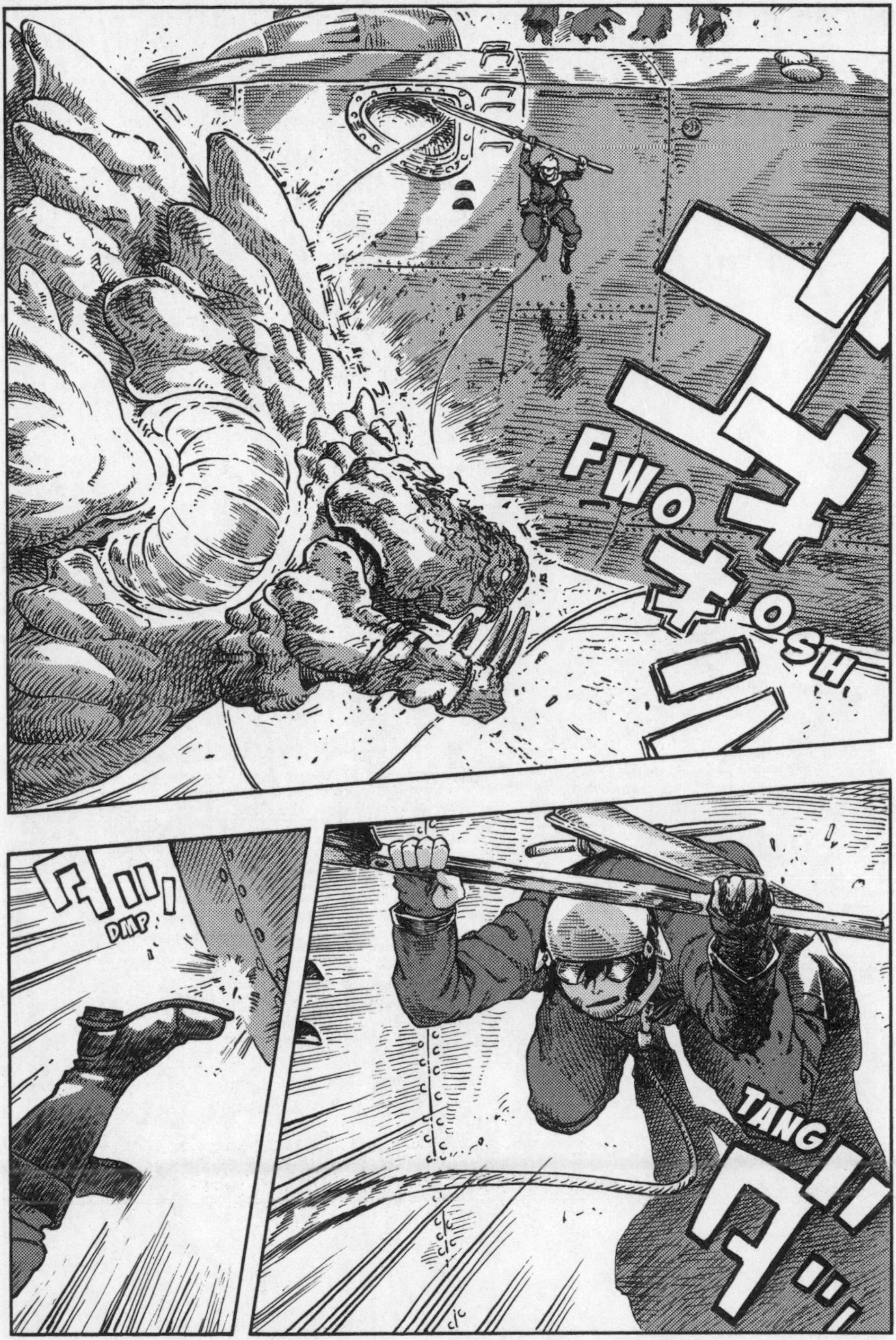
FWOOSH
TANG
DMP

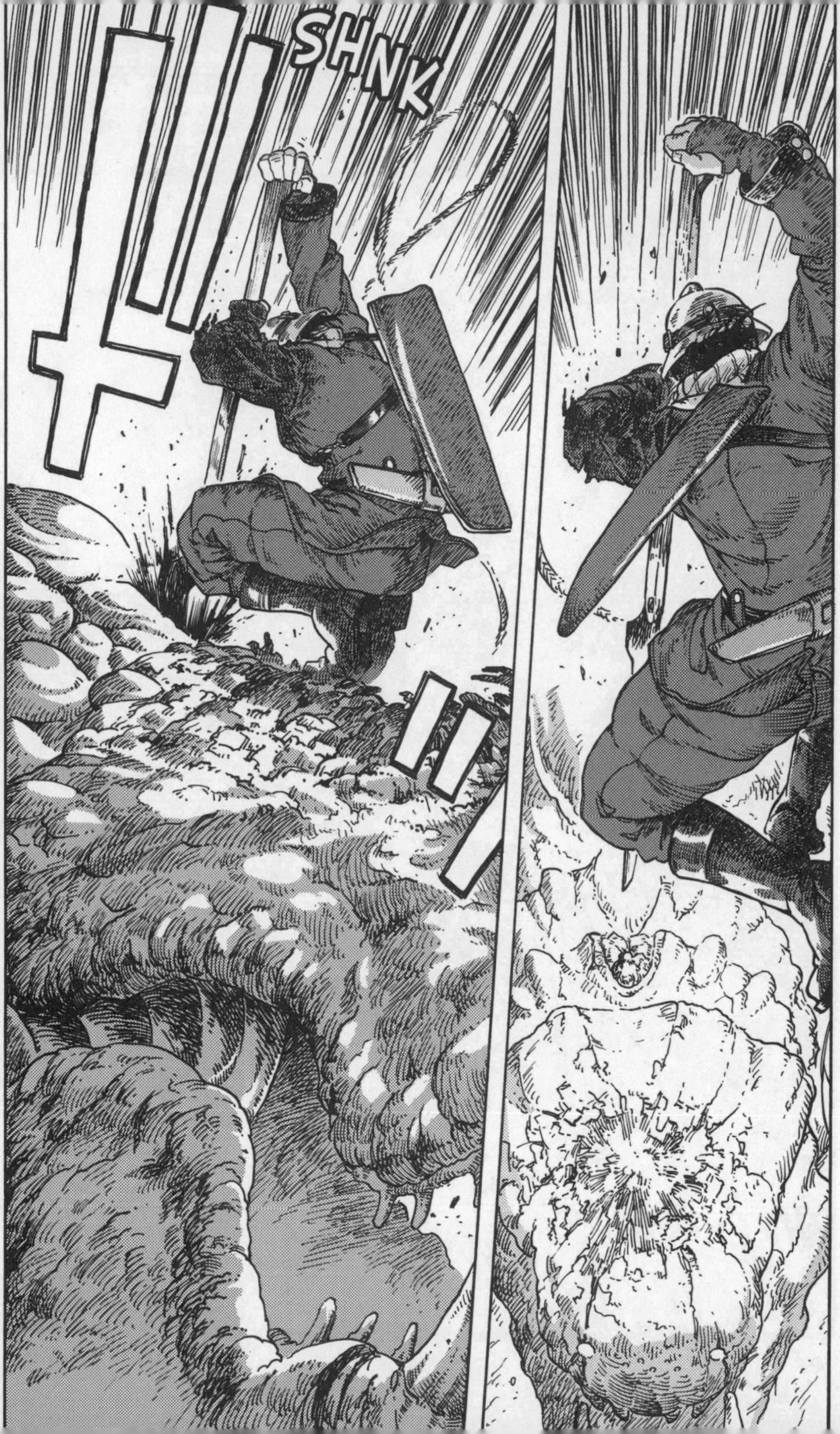
SHNK

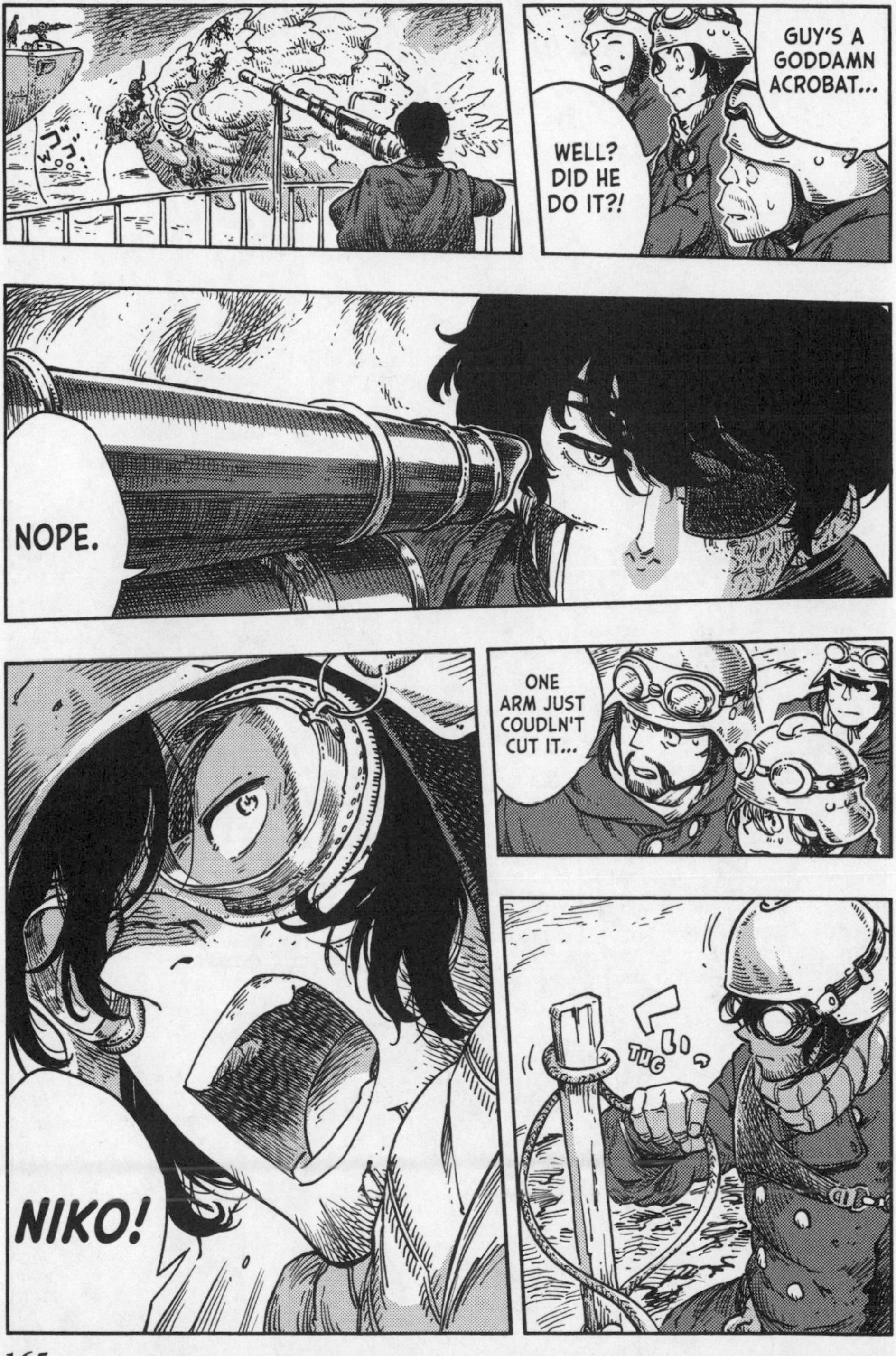
GUY'S A GODDAMN ACROBAT...
WELL? DID HE DO IT?!
NOPE.
ONE ARM JUST COUDLN'T CUT IT...
THG
NIKO!

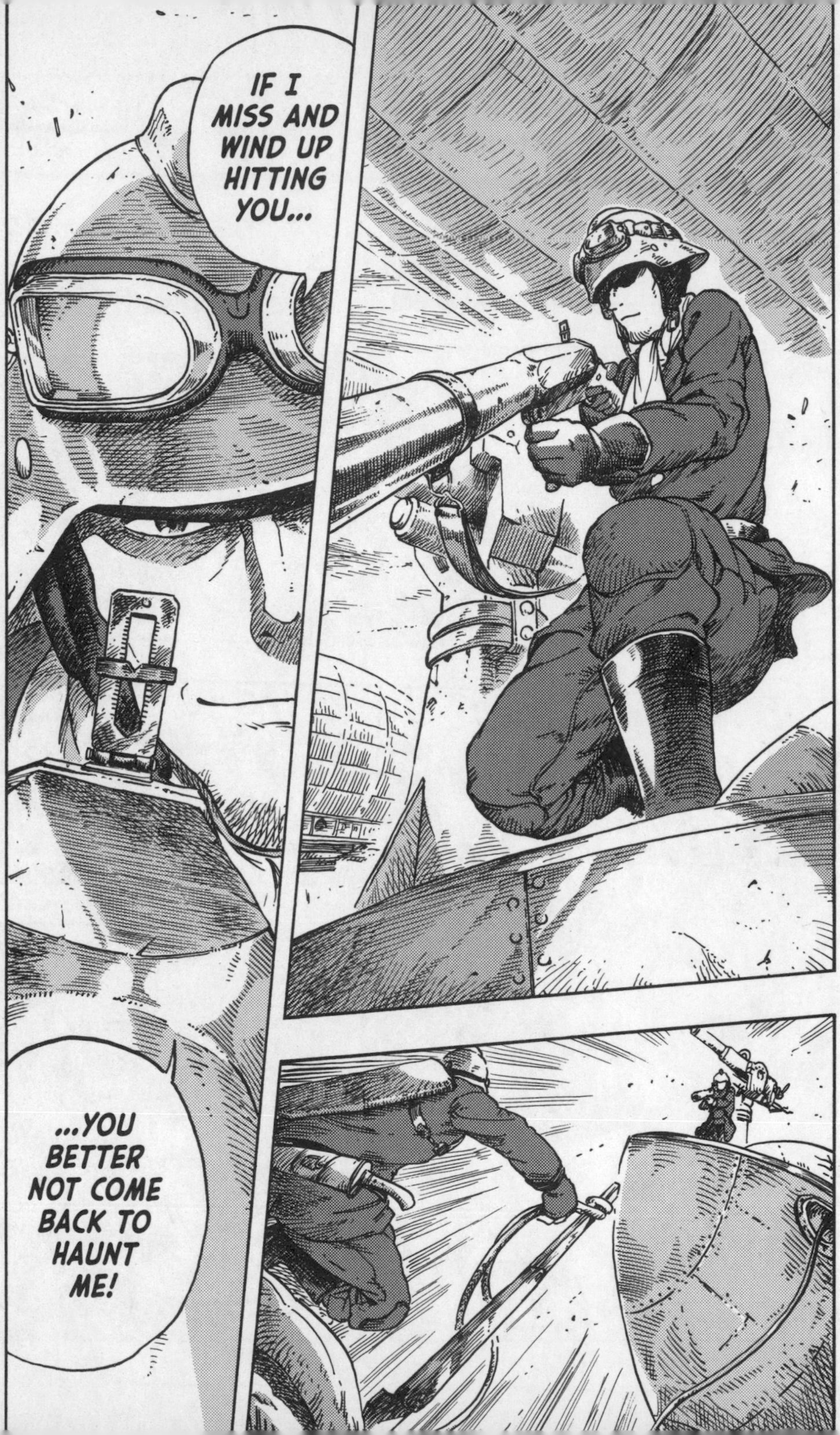
IF I MISS AND WIND UP HITTING YOU...
...YOU BETTER NOT COME BACK TO HAUNT ME!

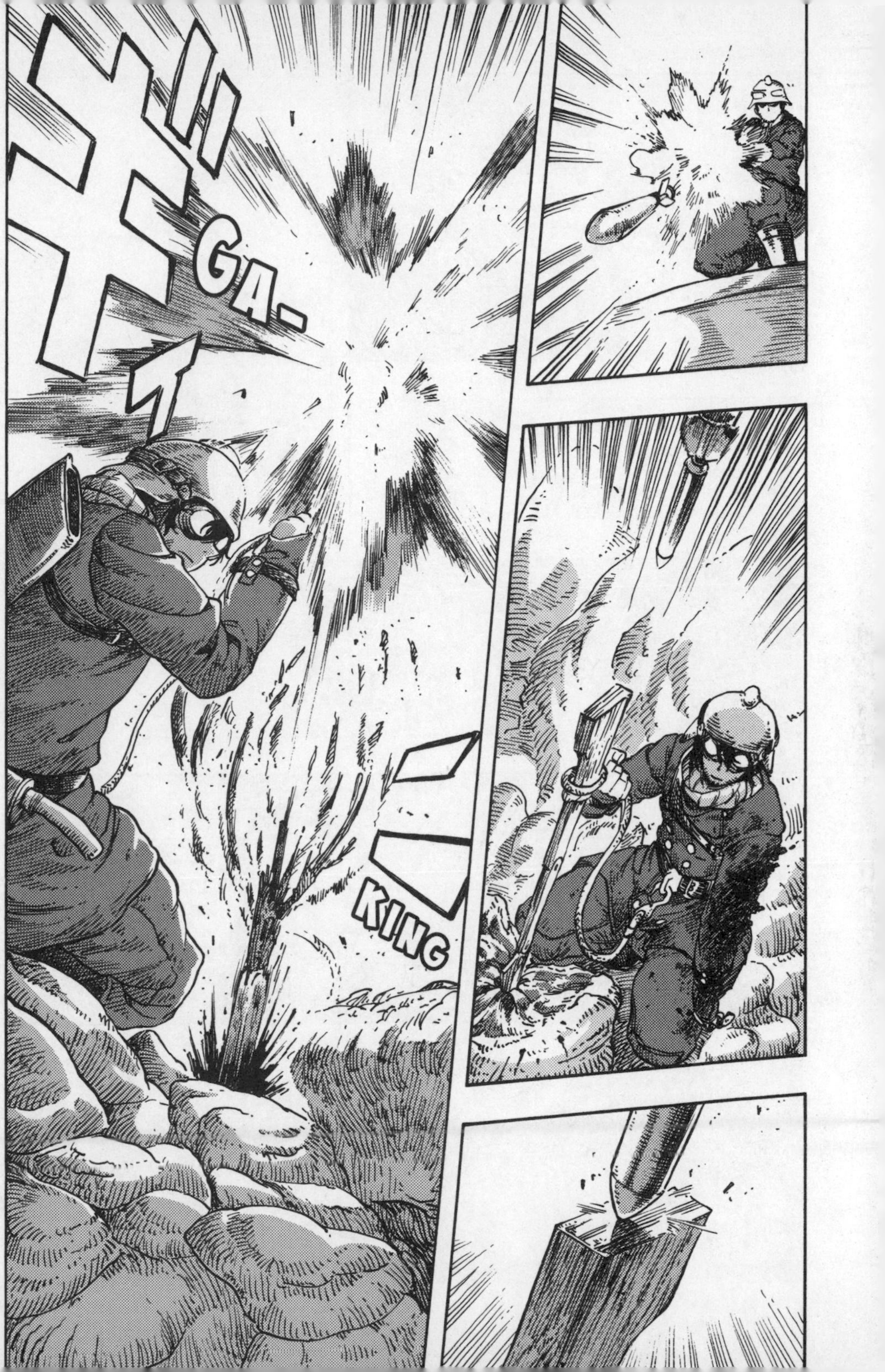
GA-
KING

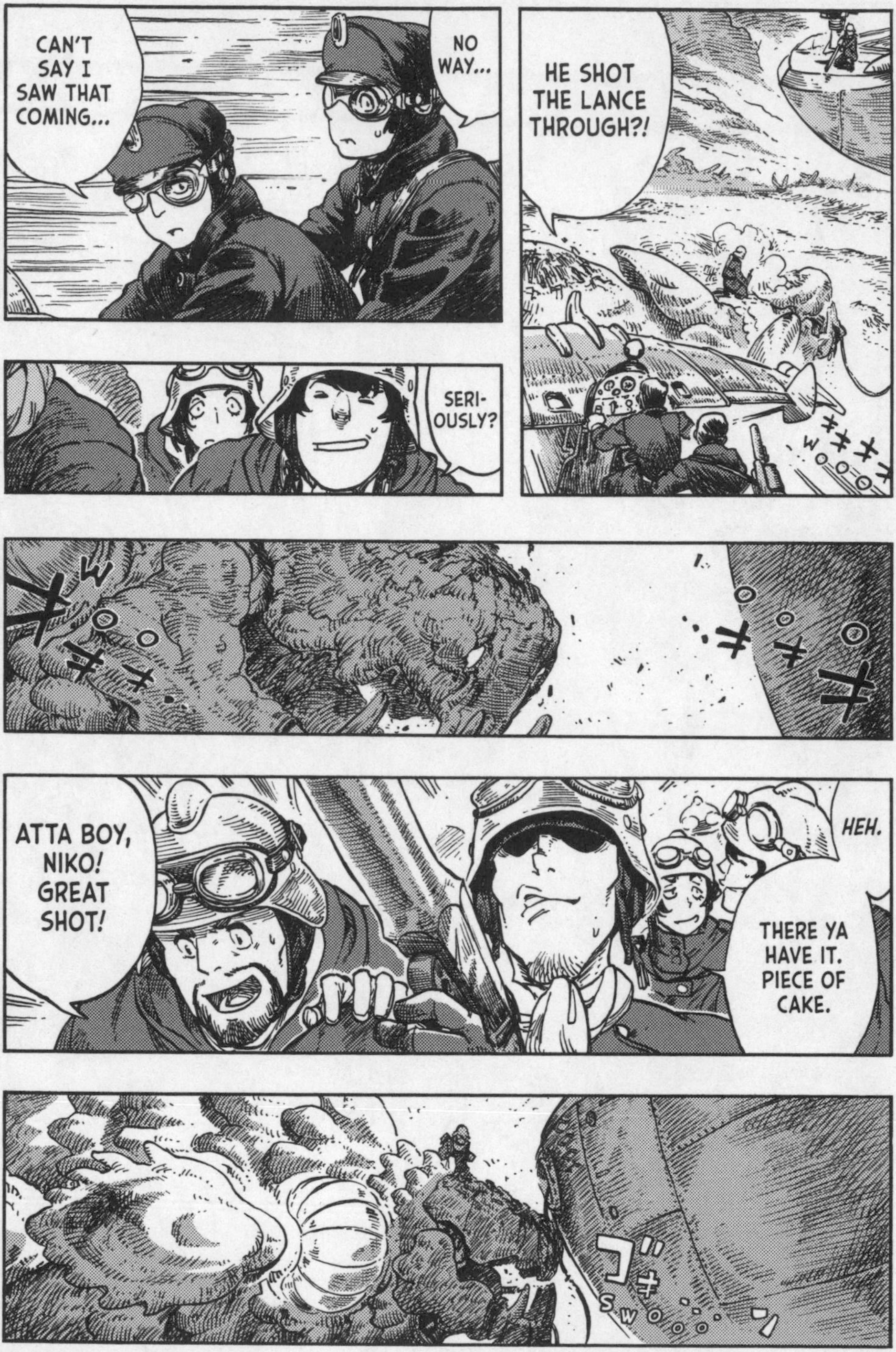
HE SHOT THE LANCE THROUGH?!
WOOOO
NO WAY...
CAN'T SAY I SAW THAT COMING...
SERI-OUSLY?
WOOOO
HEH.
THERE YA HAVE IT. PIECE OF CAKE.
ATTA BOY, NIKO! GREAT SHOT!
SWOOOO

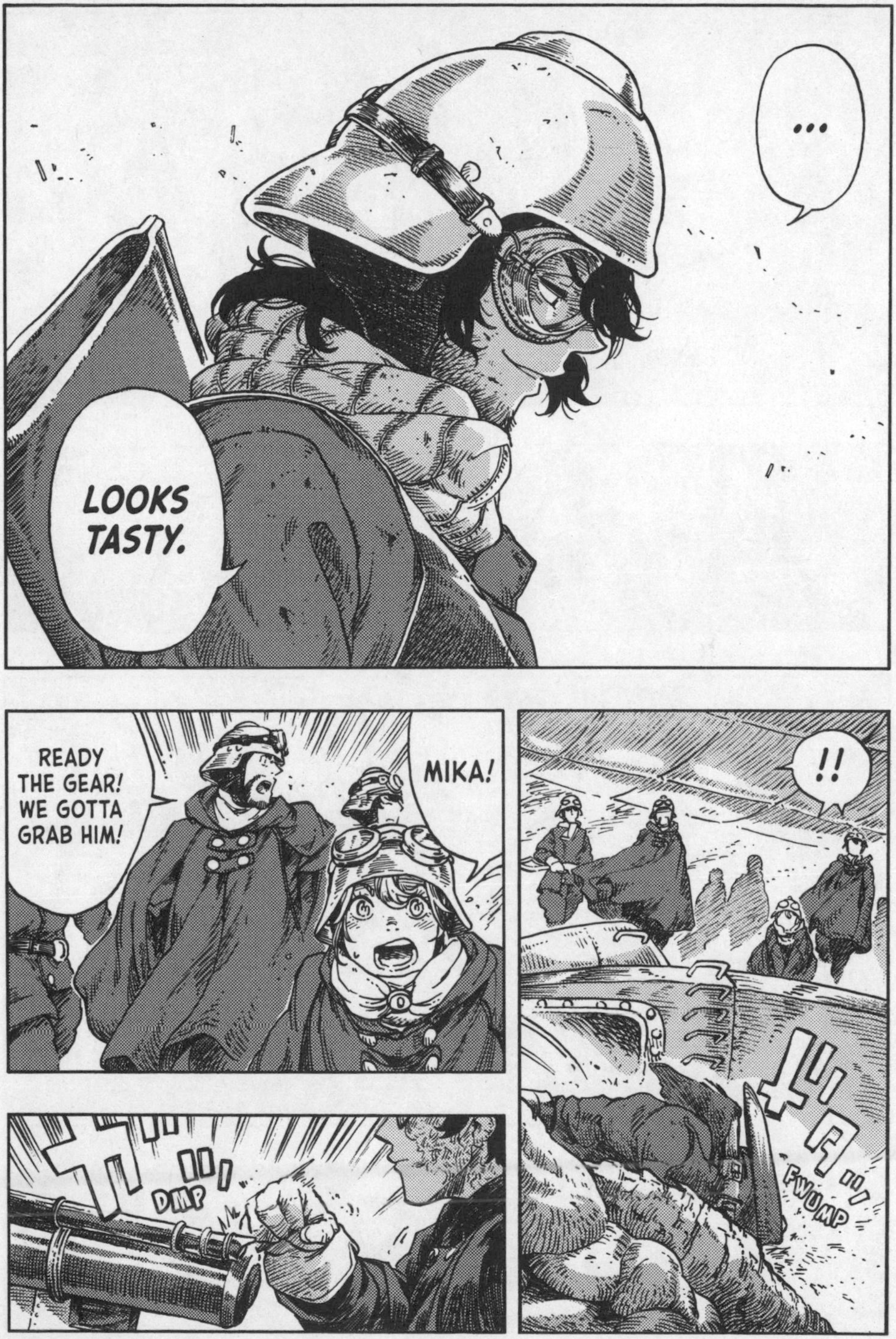
...
LOOKS TASTY.
!!
FWUMP
MIKA!
READY THE GEAR! WE GOTTA GRAB HIM!
DMP

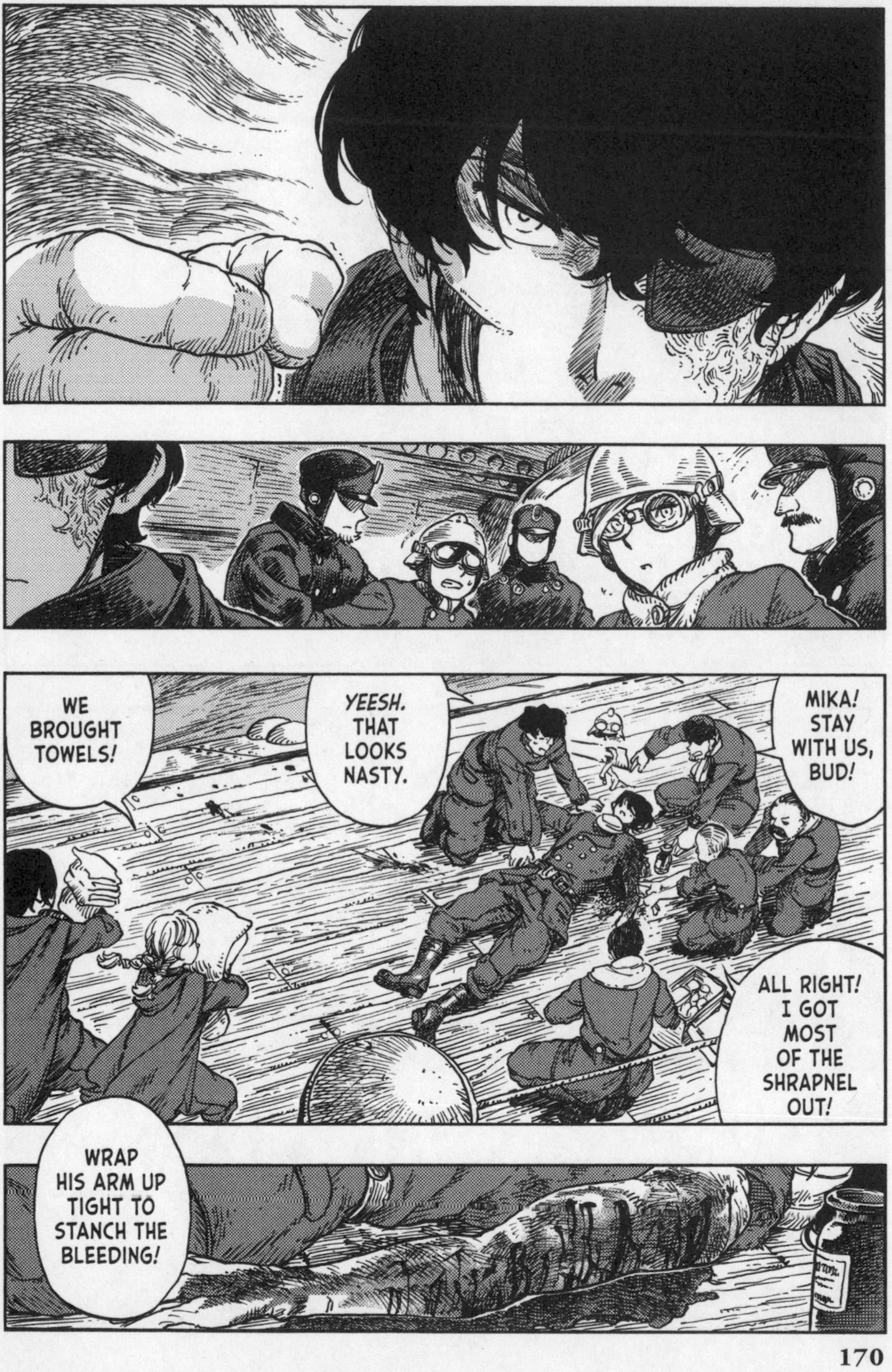
MIKA! STAY WITH US, BUD!
YEESH. THAT LOOKS NASTY.
WE BROUGHT TOWELS!
ALL RIGHT! I GOT MOST OF THE SHRAPNEL OUT!
WRAP HIS ARM UP TIGHT TO STANCH THE BLEEDING!

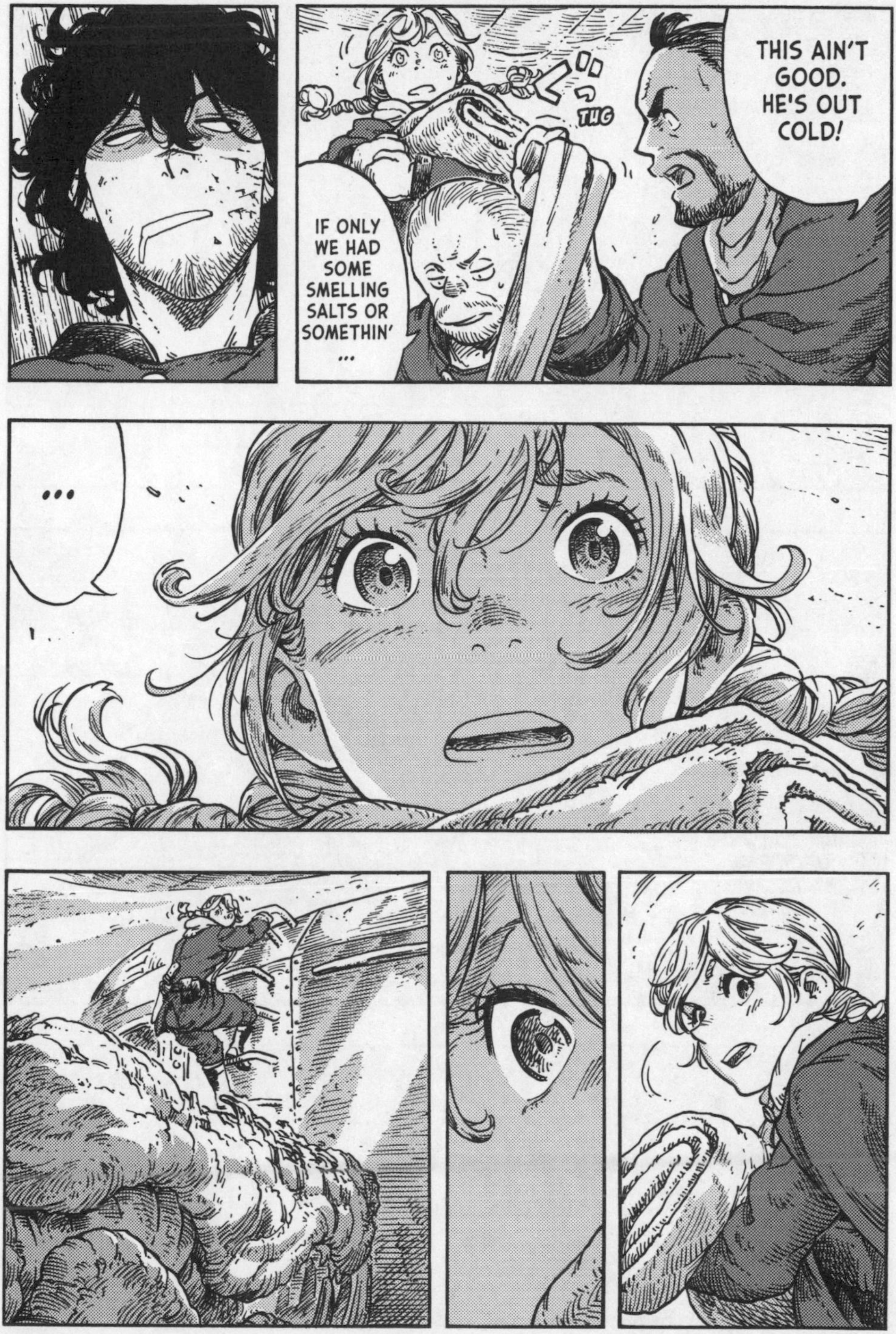
THIS AIN'T GOOD. HE'S OUT COLD!
THG
IF ONLY WE HAD SOME SMELLING SALTS OR SOMETHIN' ...
...

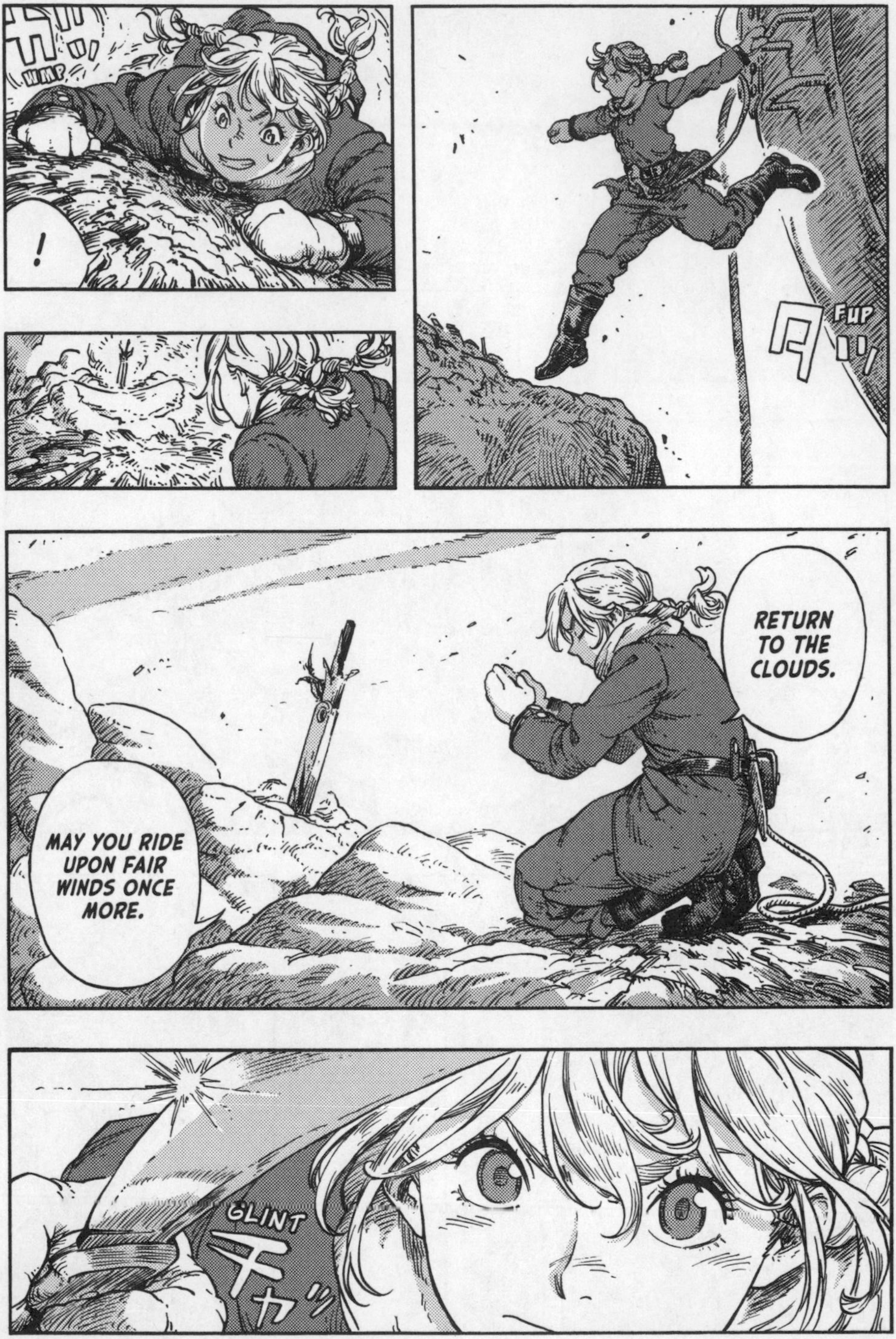
FLIP
タッ
WMP
ガッ
!
RETURN TO THE CLOUDS.
MAY YOU RIDE UPON FAIR WINDS ONCE MORE.
GLINT
チャッ

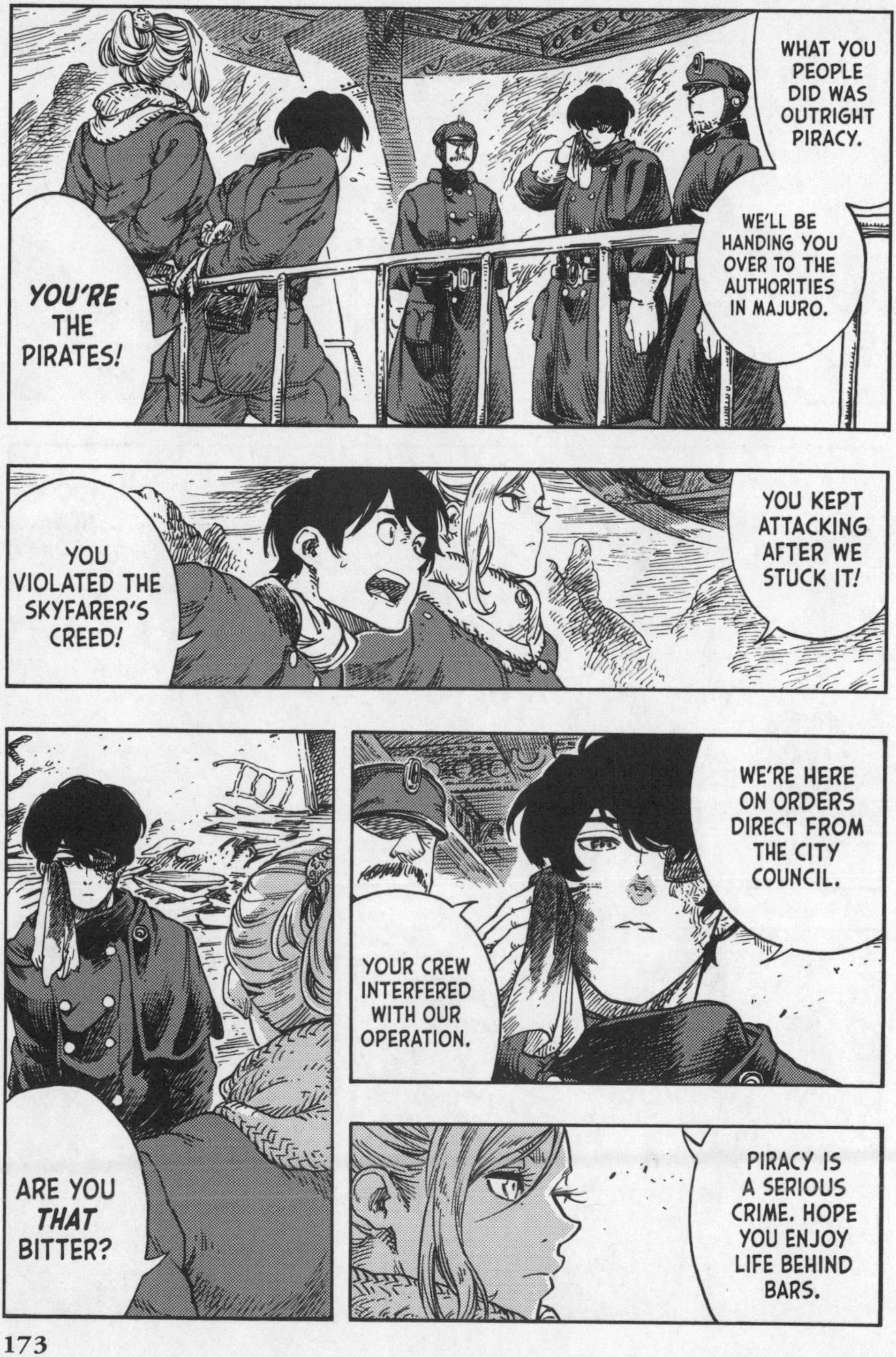
WHAT YOU PEOPLE DID WAS OUTRIGHT PIRACY.
WE'LL BE HANDING YOU OVER TO THE AUTHORITIES IN MAJURO.
YOU'RE THE PIRATES!
YOU KEPT ATTACKING AFTER WE STUCK IT!
YOU VIOLATED THE SKYFARER'S CREED!
WE'RE HERE ON ORDERS DIRECT FROM THE CITY COUNCIL.
YOUR CREW INTERFERED WITH OUR OPERATION.
PIRACY IS A SERIOUS CRIME. HOPE YOU ENJOY LIFE BEHIND BARS.
ARE YOU *THAT* BITTER?

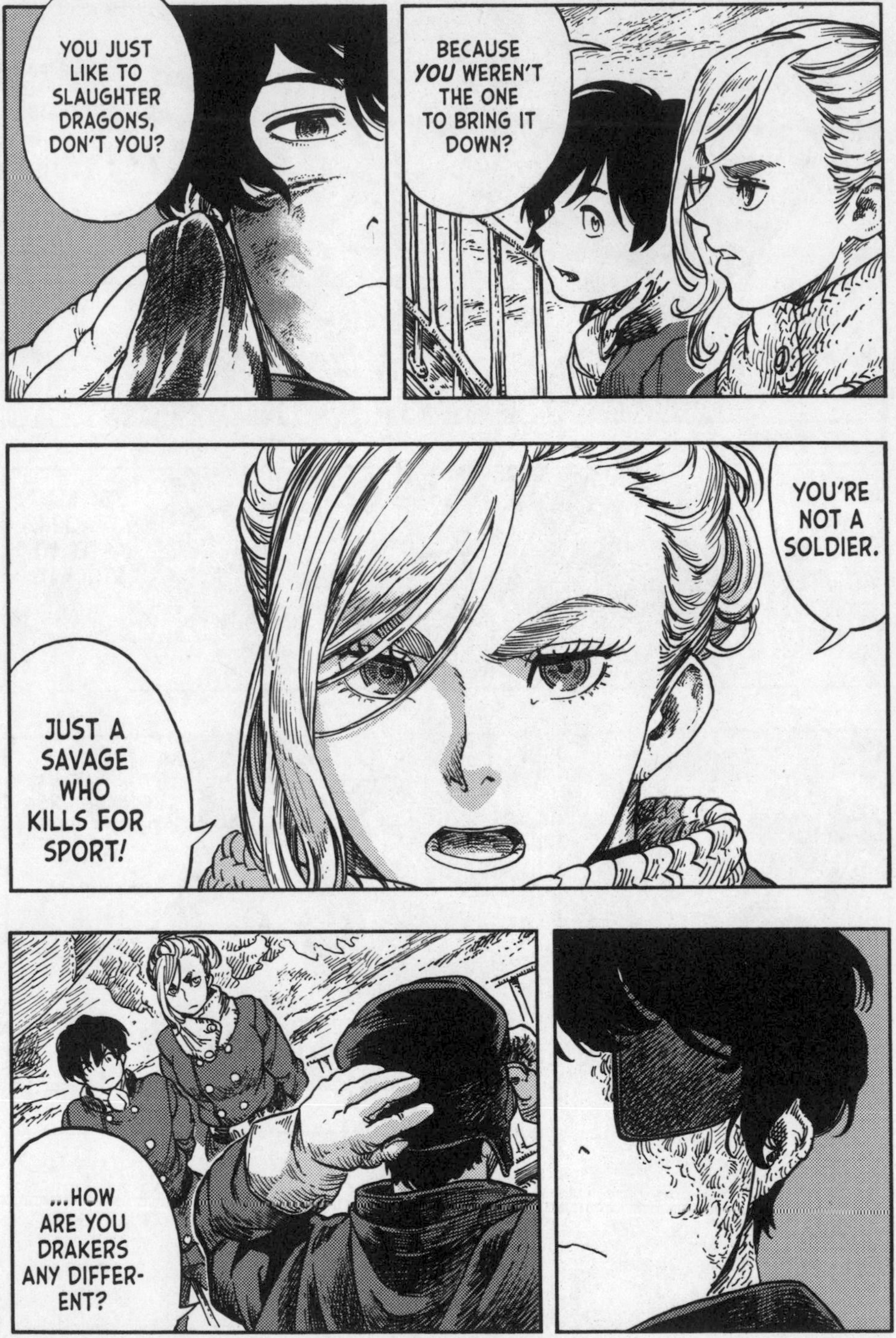
BECAUSE *YOU* WEREN'T THE ONE TO BRING IT DOWN?
YOU JUST LIKE TO SLAUGHTER DRAGONS, DON'T YOU?
YOU'RE NOT A SOLDIER.
JUST A SAVAGE WHO KILLS FOR SPORT!
...HOW ARE YOU DRAKERS ANY DIFFER-ENT?

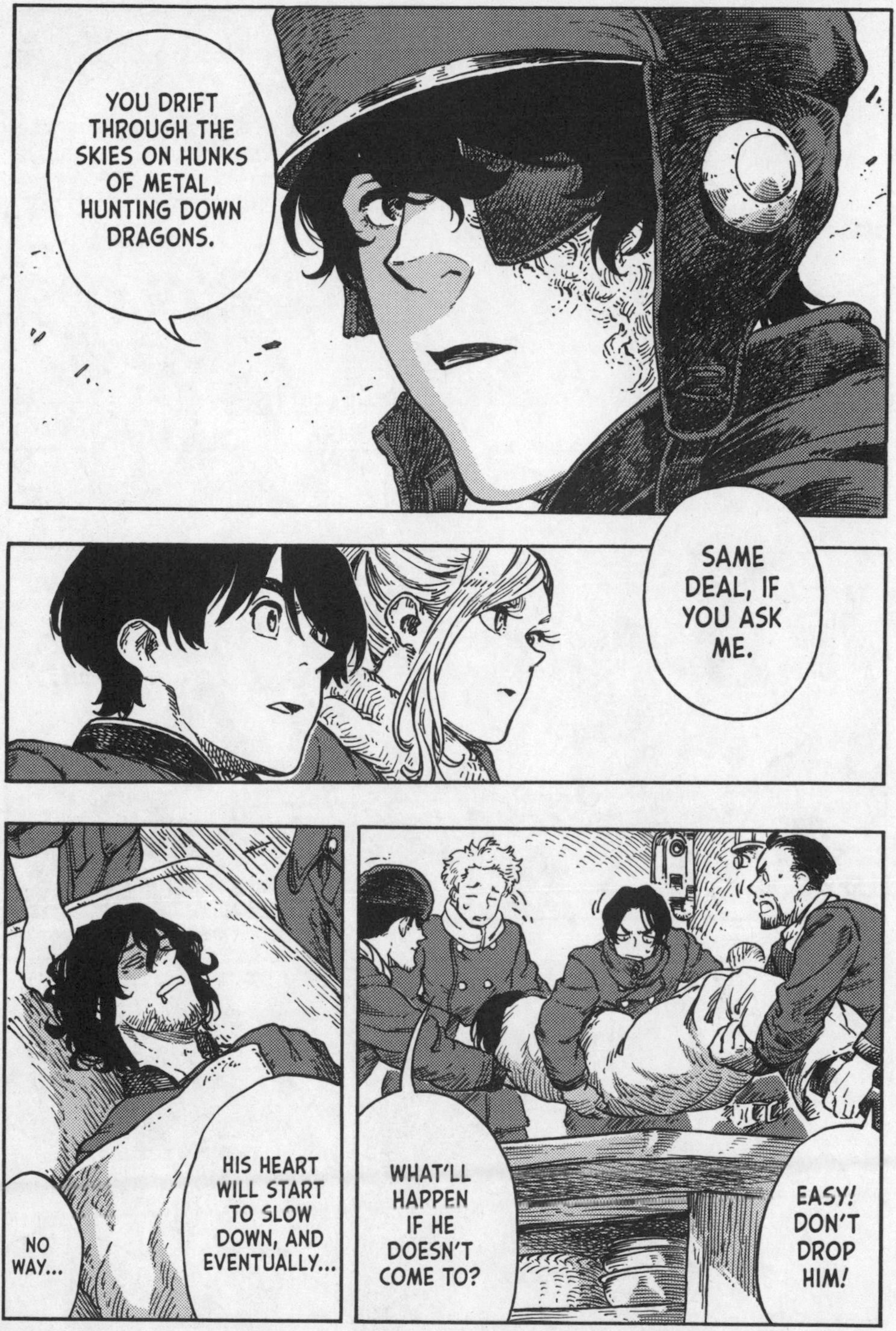
YOU DRIFT THROUGH THE SKIES ON HUNKS OF METAL, HUNTING DOWN DRAGONS.
SAME DEAL, IF YOU ASK ME.
EASY! DON'T DROP HIM!
WHAT'LL HAPPEN IF HE DOESN'T COME TO?
HIS HEART WILL START TO SLOW DOWN, AND EVENTUALLY...
NO WAY...

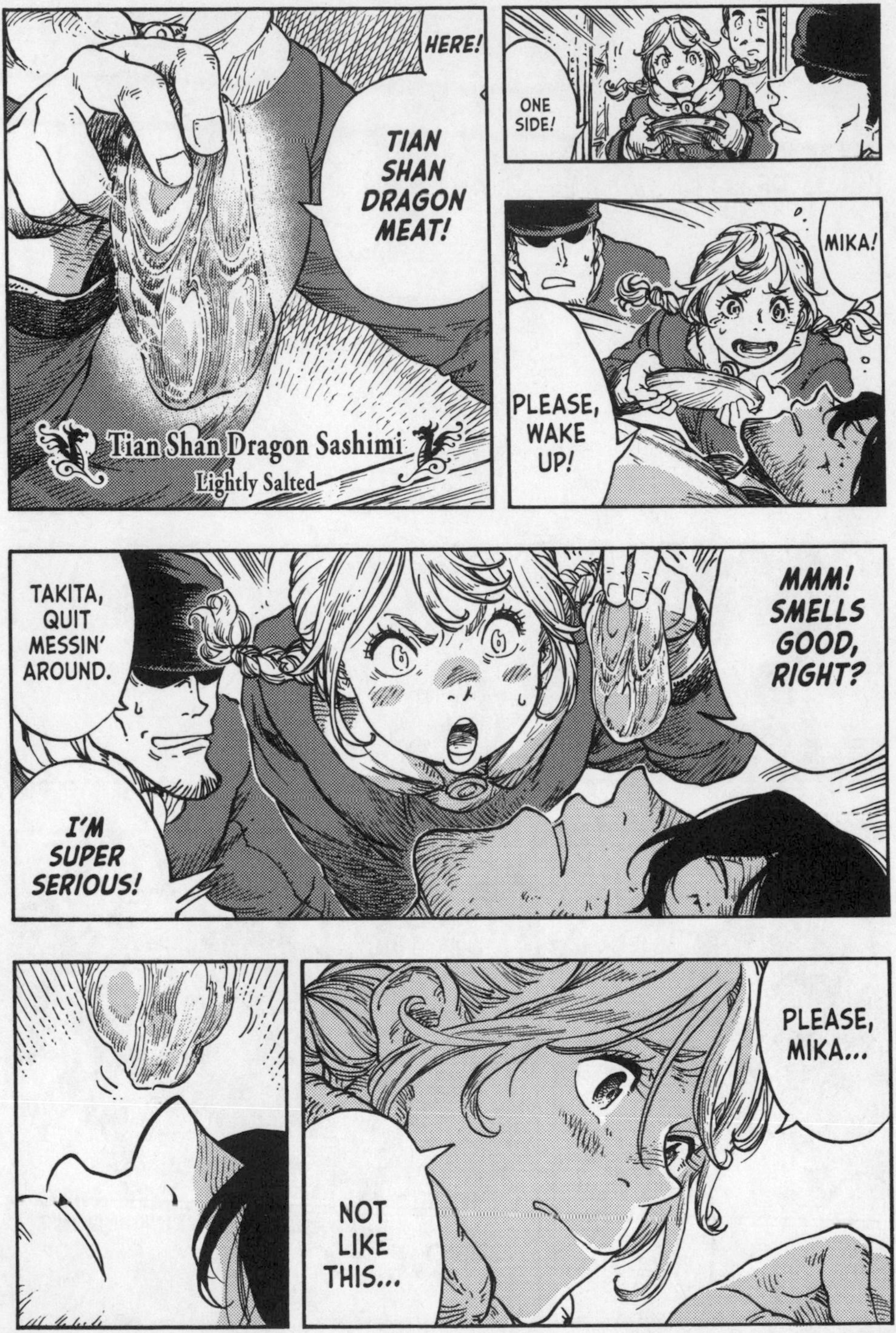
ONE SIDE!
MIKA!
PLEASE, WAKE UP!
HERE!
TIAN SHAN DRAGON MEAT!
Tian Shan Dragon Sashimi
Lightly Salted
MMM! SMELLS GOOD, RIGHT?
TAKITA, QUIT MESSIN' AROUND.
I'M SUPER SERIOUS!
PLEASE, MIKA...
NOT LIKE THIS...

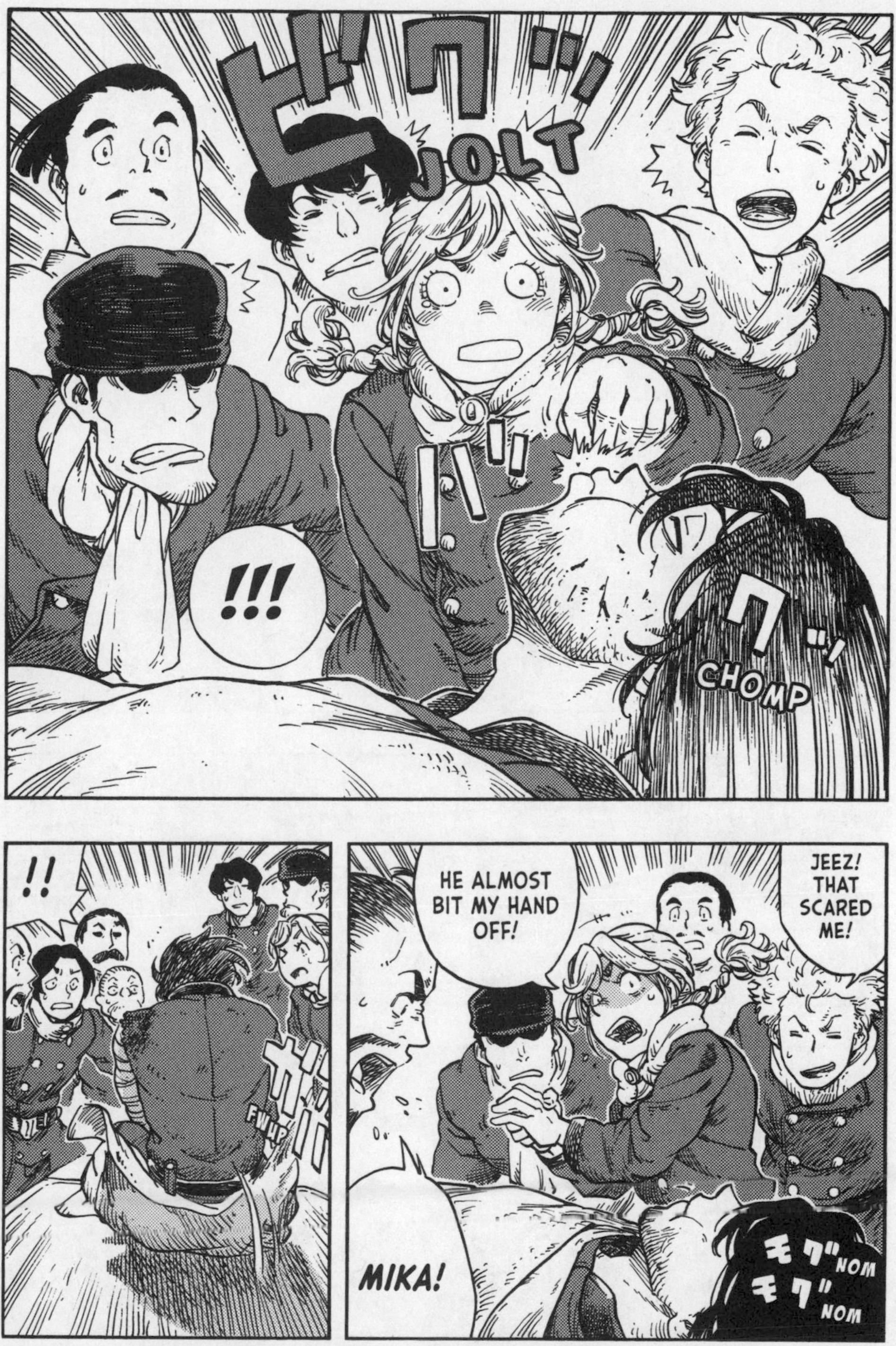
JOLT
!!!
CHOMP
JEEZ! THAT SCARED ME!
HE ALMOST BIT MY HAND OFF!
MIKA!
NOM
NOM
!!
FWUP

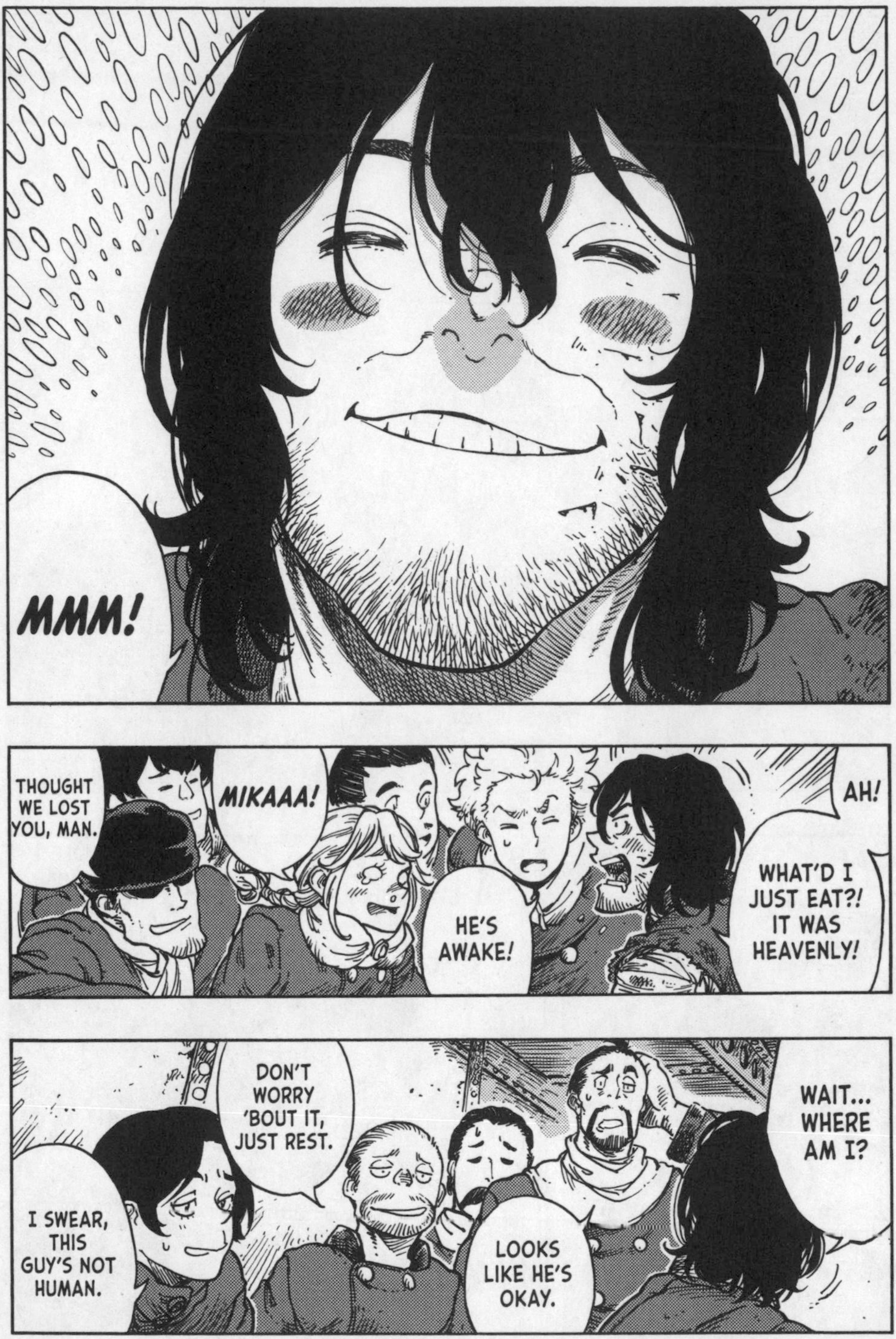
MMM!
AH!
WHAT'D I JUST EAT?! IT WAS HEAVENLY!
HE'S AWAKE!
MIKAAA!
THOUGHT WE LOST YOU, MAN.
WAIT... WHERE AM I?
LOOKS LIKE HE'S OKAY.
DON'T WORRY 'BOUT IT, JUST REST.
I SWEAR, THIS GUY'S NOT HUMAN.

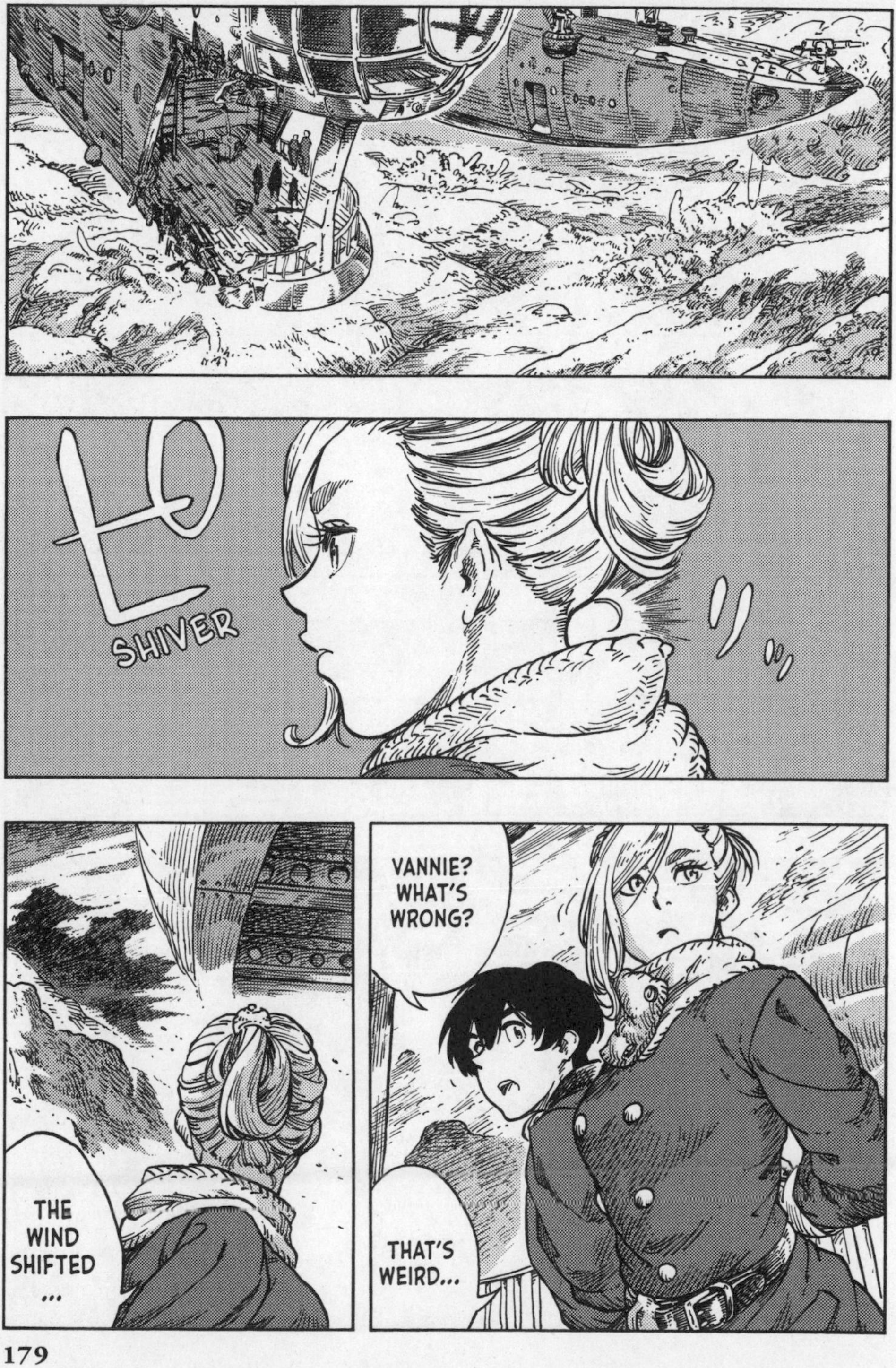
SHIVER
VANNIE? WHAT'S WRONG?
THAT'S WEIRD...
THE WIND SHIFTED ...

オオオオオオ
WOOOOO
ゴロロオオ..
BRRUM
ゴロロロ
GRR
ポッ
PLIP
ポッ
PLIP
サァァァァァ
FSSSHH
ゴオオ..
BRMM

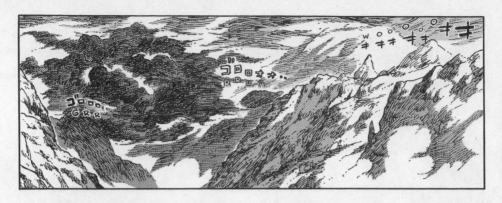

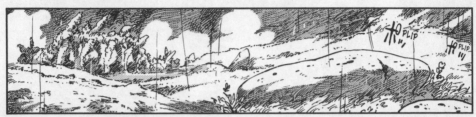

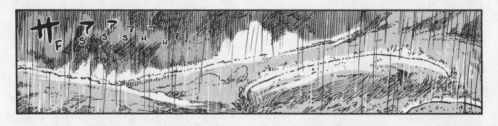

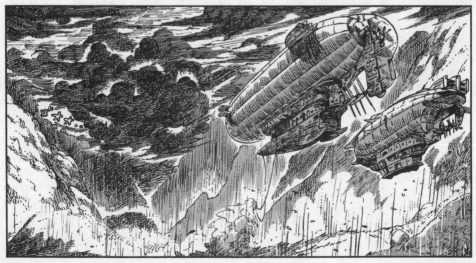

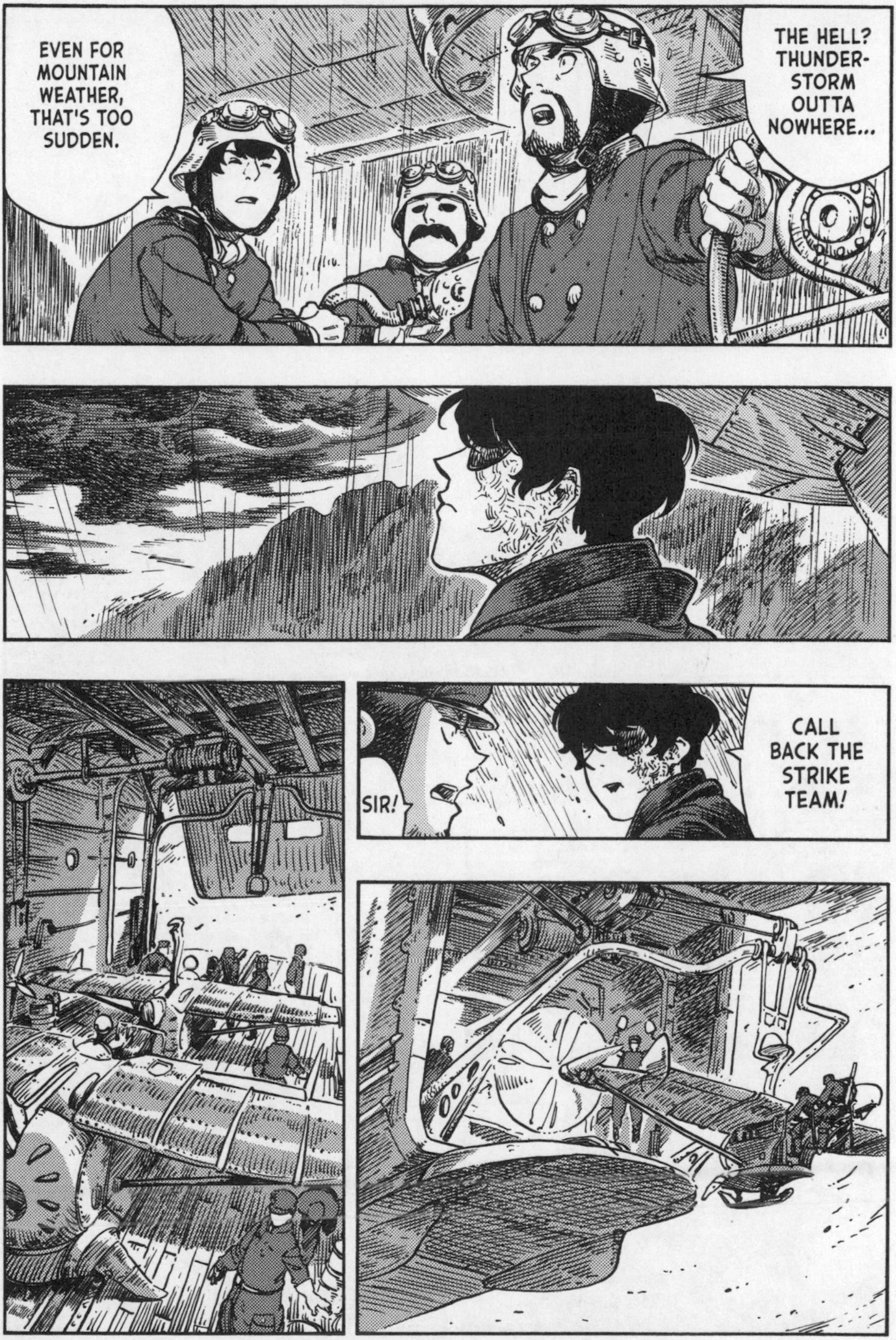
THE HELL? THUNDER-STORM OUTTA NOWHERE...
EVEN FOR MOUNTAIN WEATHER, THAT'S TOO SUDDEN.
CALL BACK THE STRIKE TEAM!
SIR!

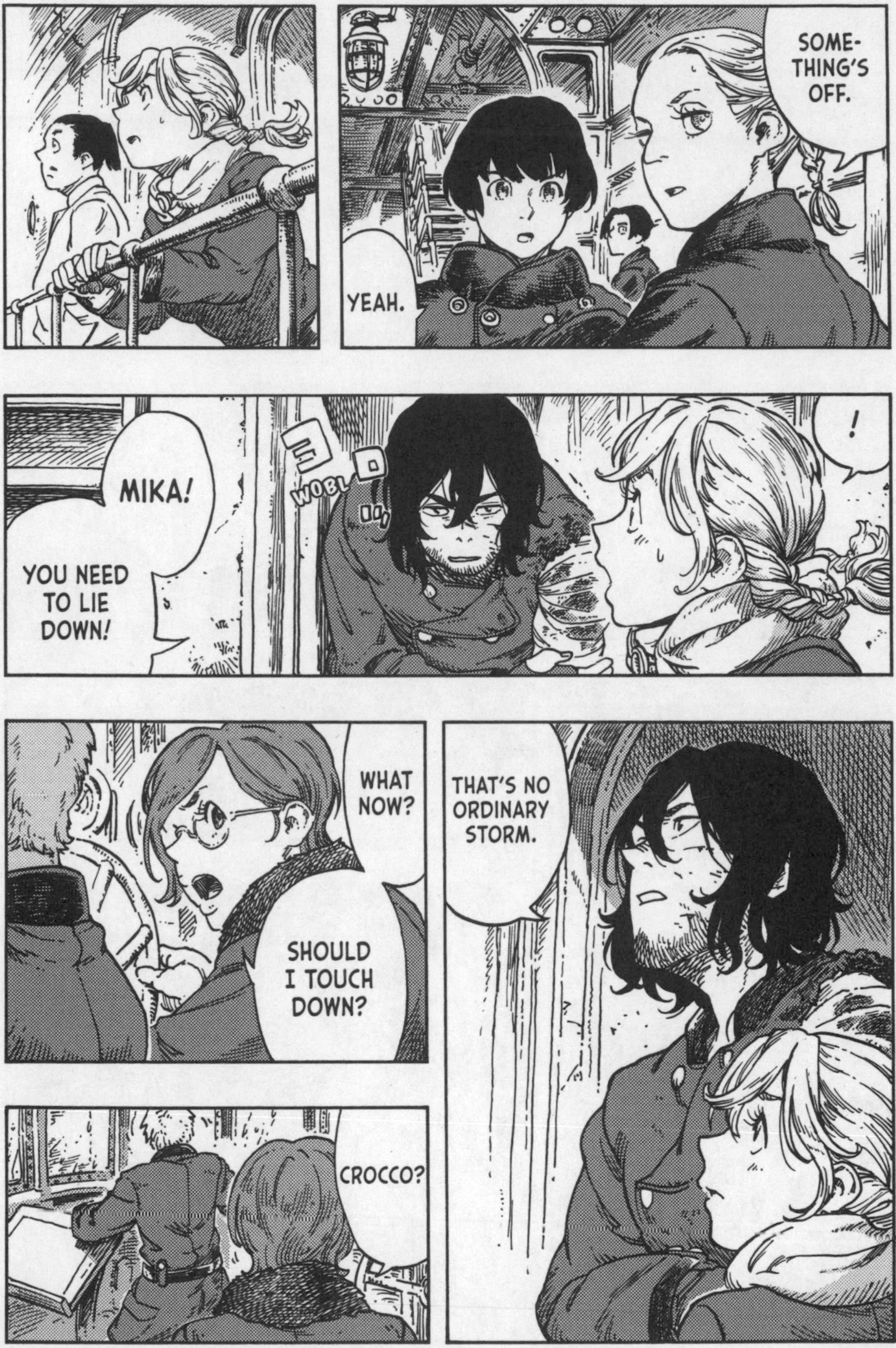
SOME-THING'S OFF.
YEAH.
!
WOBL
MIKA!
YOU NEED TO LIE DOWN!
THAT'S NO ORDINARY STORM.
WHAT NOW?
SHOULD I TOUCH DOWN?
CROCCO?

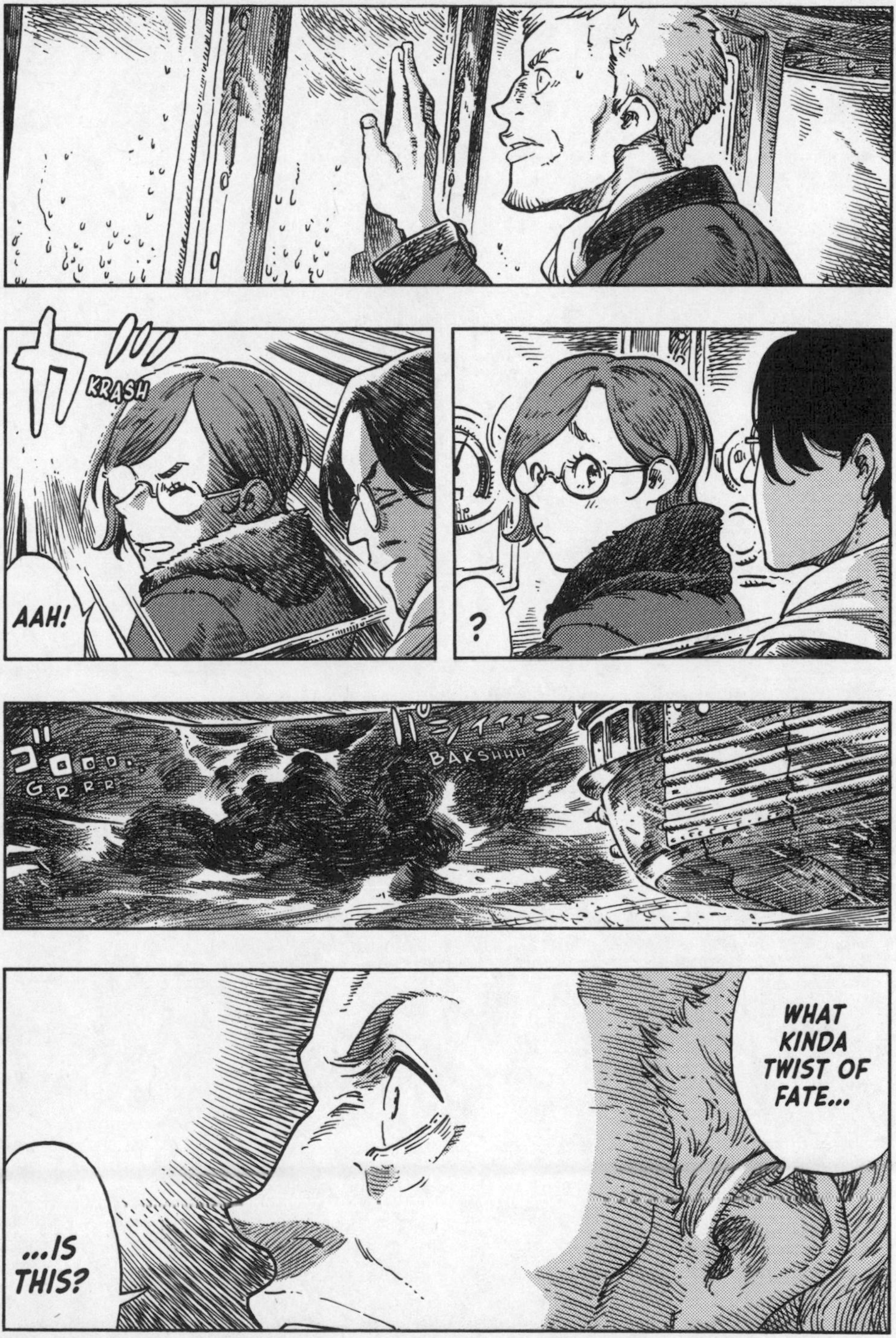
?
KRASH
AAH!
BAKSHHH
GRRR
WHAT KINDA TWIST OF FATE...
...IS THIS?

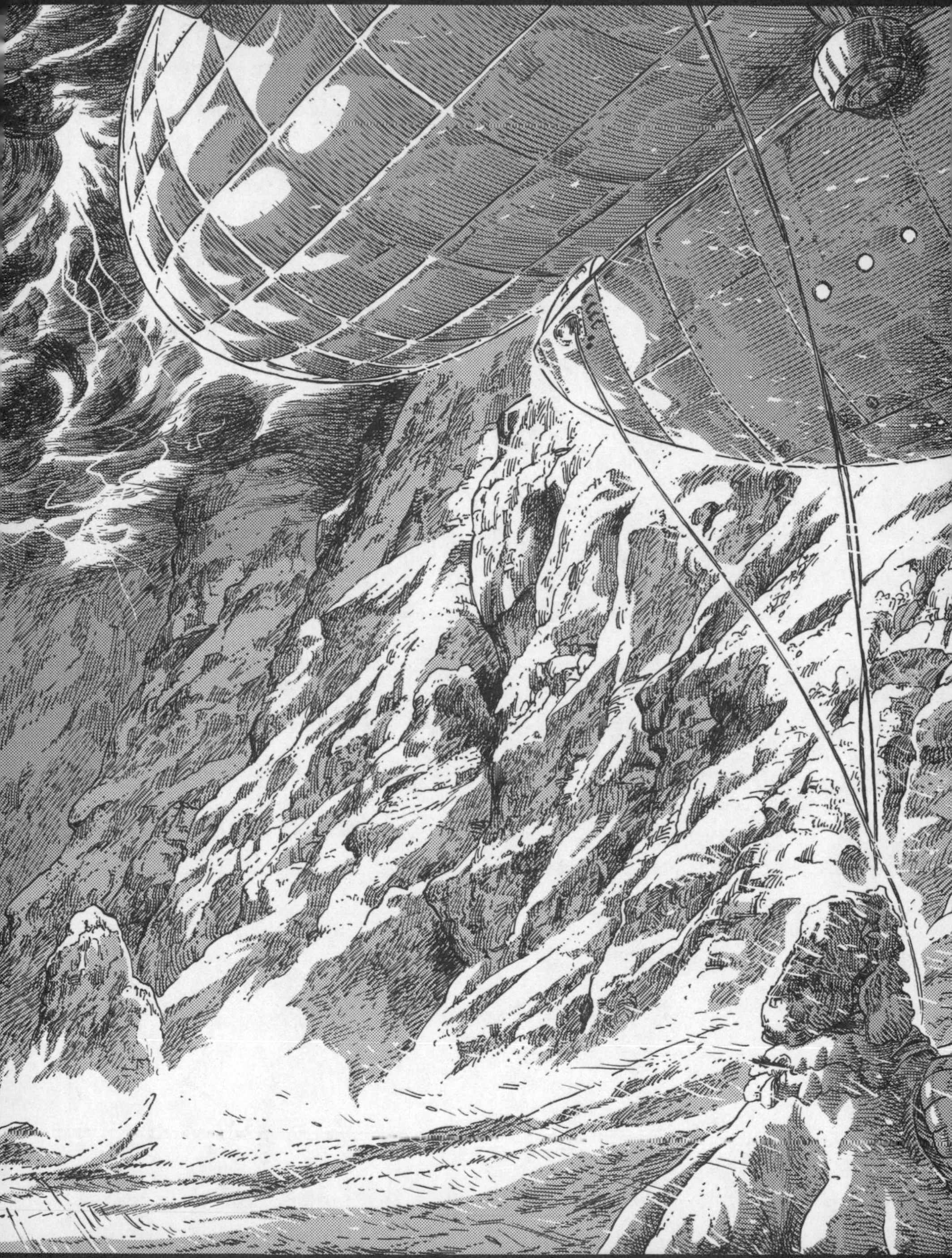

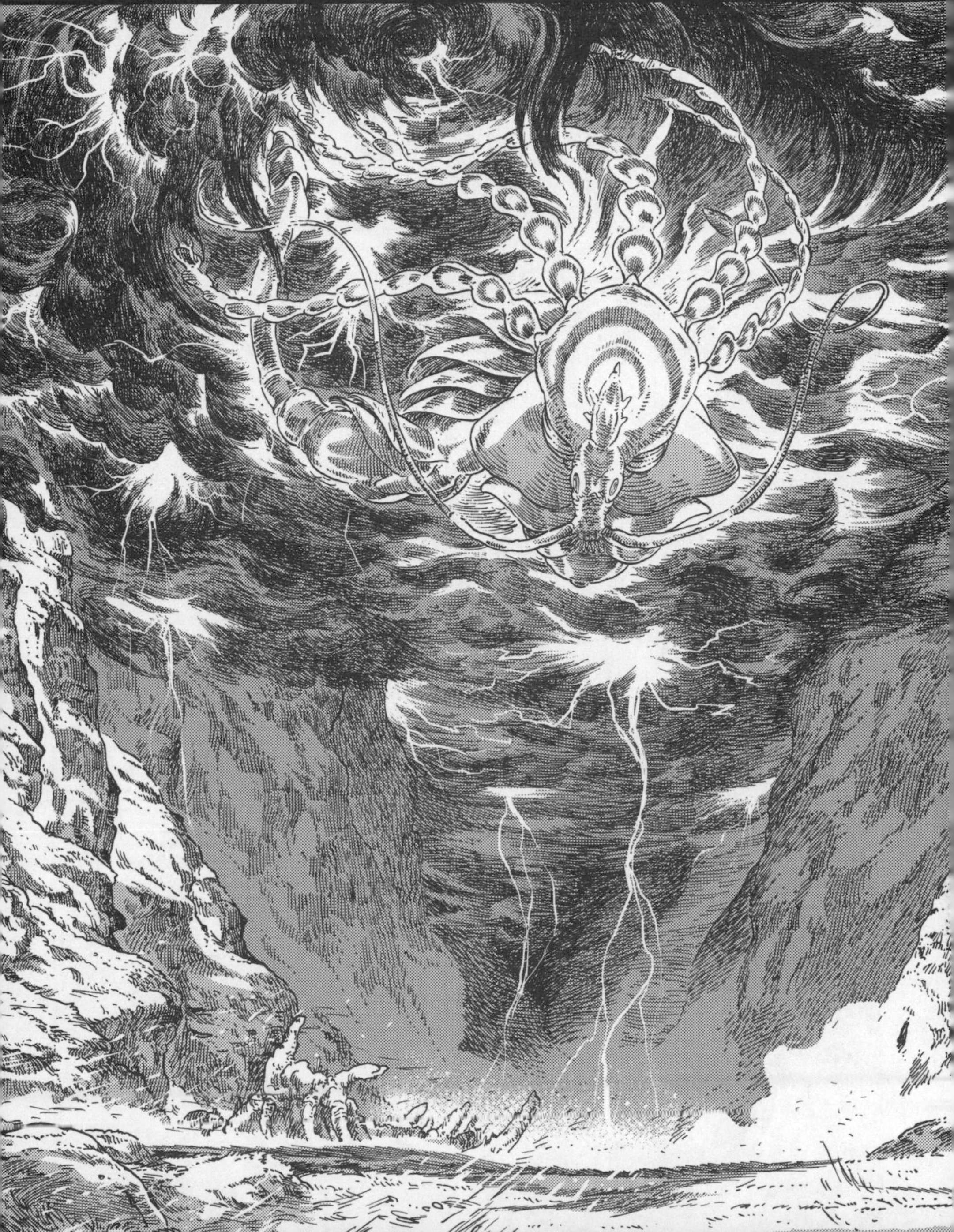

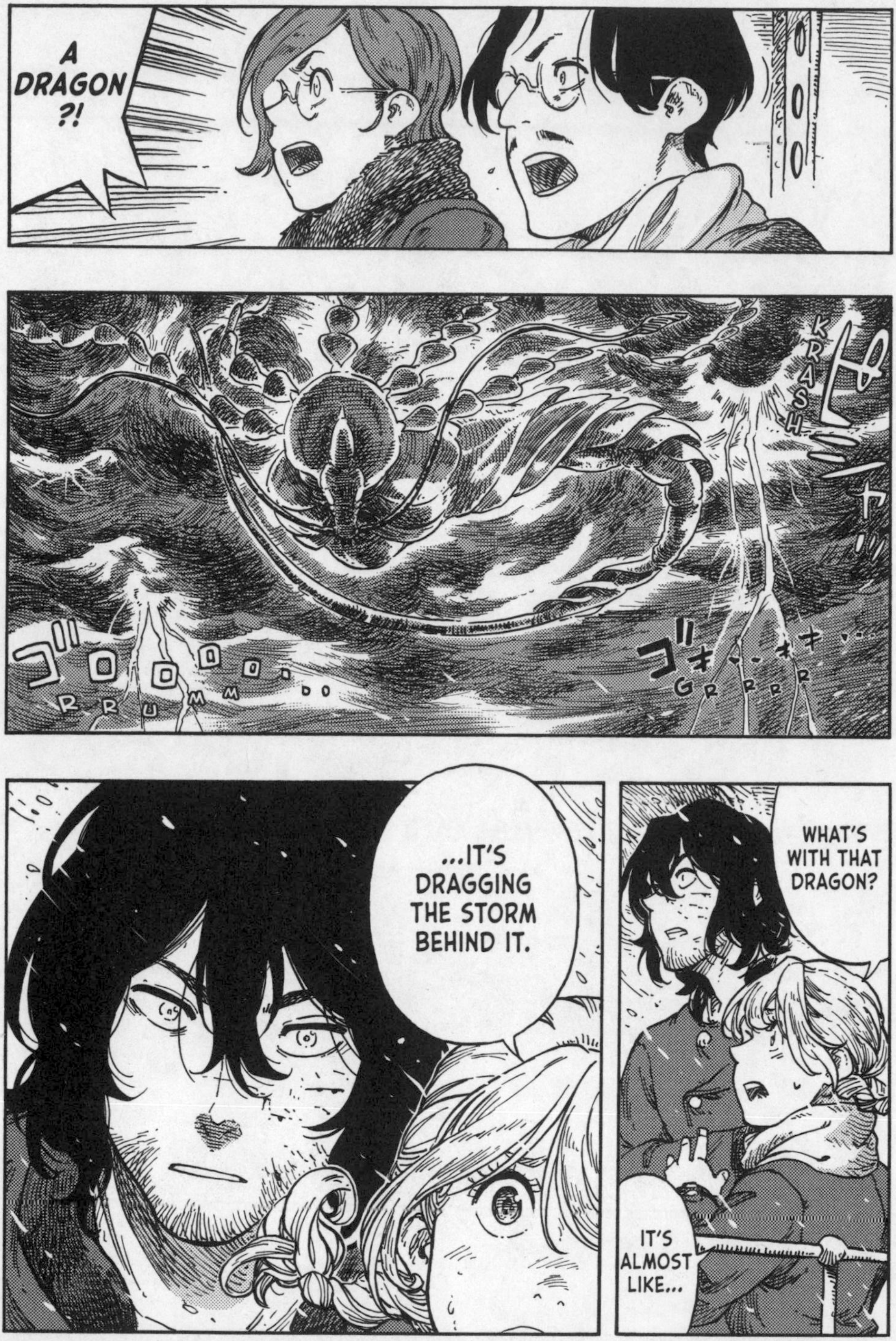
A DRAGON?!
KRASH
GRRRR
WHAT'S WITH THAT DRAGON?
IT'S ALMOST LIKE...
...IT'S DRAGGING THE STORM BEHIND IT.

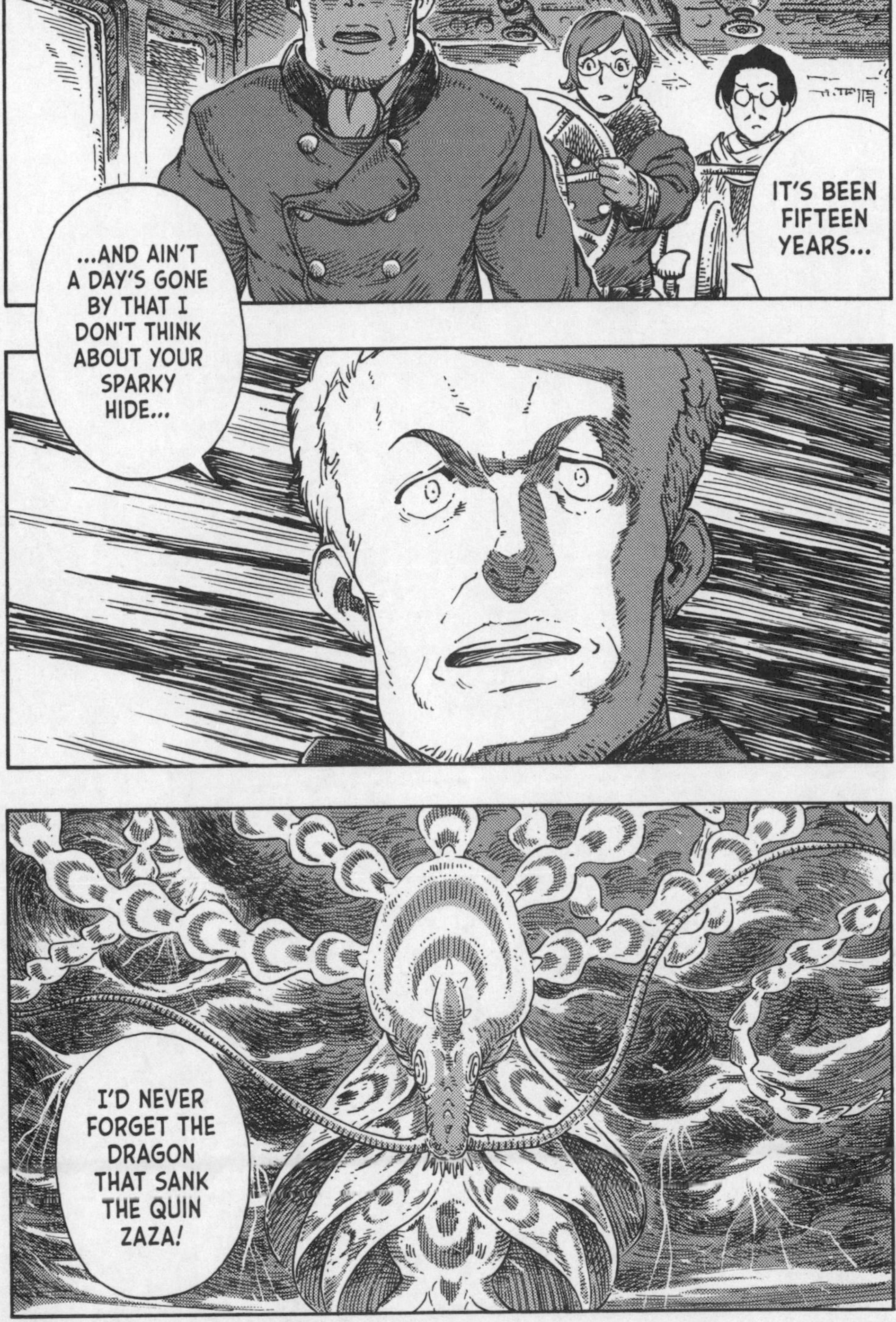
IT'S BEEN FIFTEEN YEARS...
...AND AIN'T A DAY'S GONE BY THAT I DON'T THINK ABOUT YOUR SPARKY HIDE...
I'D NEVER FORGET THE DRAGON THAT SANK THE QUIN ZAZA!

Tian Shan Dragon Sashimi (with seasoning salt)

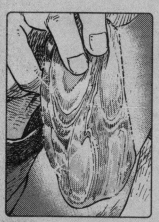

Ingredients

- ✦ Fatty dragon meat: 100 g
- ✦ Salt of choice: to taste

01

Slice dragon meat into 3-5 mm slices.

02

Season with salt and enjoy.

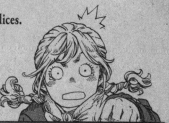

SO GOOD, IT'LL PULL YOU BACK FROM THE BRINK!

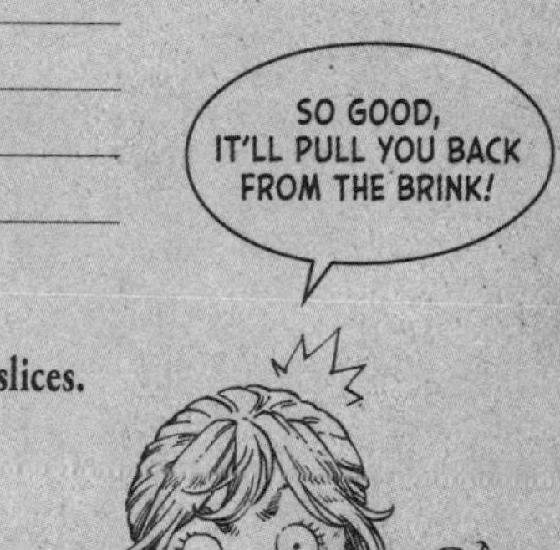

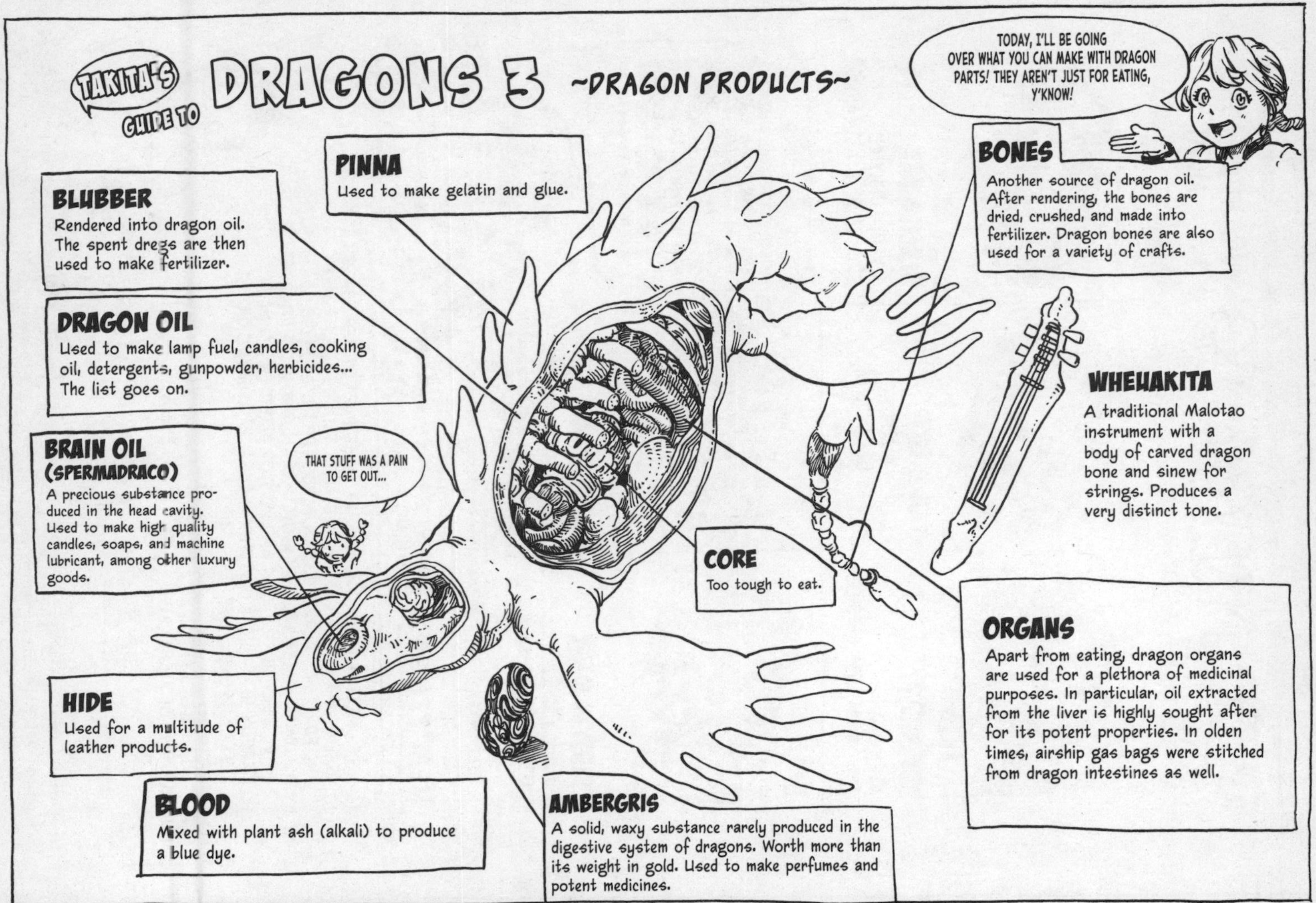
TAKITA'S GUIDE TO DRAGONS 3 ~DRAGON PRODUCTS~
TODAY, I'LL BE GOING OVER WHAT YOU CAN MAKE WITH DRAGON PARTS! THEY AREN'T JUST FOR EATING, Y'KNOW!
BLUBBER
Rendered into dragon oil. The spent dregs are then used to make fertilizer.
PINNA
Used to make gelatin and glue.
BONES
Another source of dragon oil. After rendering, the bones are dried, crushed, and made into fertilizer. Dragon bones are also used for a variety of crafts.
DRAGON OIL
Used to make lamp fuel, candles, cooking oil, detergents, gunpowder, herbicides... The list goes on.
WHEUAKITA
A traditional Malotao instrument with a body of carved dragon bone and sinew for strings. Produces a very distinct tone.
BRAIN OIL (SPERMADRACO)
A precious substance produced in the head cavity. Used to make high quality candles, soaps, and machine lubricant, among other luxury goods.
THAT STUFF WAS A PAIN TO GET OUT...
CORE
Too tough to eat.
ORGANS
Apart from eating, dragon organs are used for a plethora of medicinal purposes. In particular, oil extracted from the liver is highly sought after for its potent properties. In olden times, airship gas bags were stitched from dragon intestines as well.
HIDE
Used for a multitude of leather products.
BLOOD
Mixed with plant ash (alkali) to produce a blue dye.
AMBERGRIS
A solid, waxy substance rarely produced in the digestive system of dragons. Worth more than its weight in gold. Used to make perfumes and potent medicines.

TAKITA'S GUIDE TO DRAGONS 4 ~DRAGON MEAT~

RED MEAT
VERY LEAN.
THE "MEATIEST" OF CUTS.

TAIL MEAT
A CHOICE CUT WITH
A NICE BALANCE OF
MEAT AND FAT.

BLACK MEAT
A VERY FUNKY CUT.
ADORED BY GOURMANDS.

RIBBON MEAT
WAVY MARBLING.
DELIGHTFULLY SAVORY.

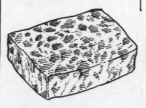

SPOTTY MEAT
SPECKLED MARBLING.
TYPICALLY PROCESSED
INTO OTHER GOODS.

EVERY PART OF THE DRAGON
HAS ITS OWN UNIQUE FLAVOR.
THAT SAID, SINCE DRAGONS
COME IN ALL SHAPES AND SIZES,
IT'S ALMOST IMPOSSIBLE TO
MAKE AN OFFICIAL GRADING
SYSTEM. THE NAMES WE USE
FOR DIFFERENT CUTS ARE JUST
FOR CONVENIENCE'S SAKE.

MEAT PRICES

WHILE MEAT IS EASILY THE MOST COVETED PART OF THE DRAGON,
SEEING AS A SINGLE CATCH IMMEDIATELY FLOODS THE MARKET,
THE FORCES OF SUPPLY AND DEMAND KEEP PRICES IN CHECK,
ALLOWING DRAGON TO BE ENJOYED BY ALL, FROM THE POOREST
OF PAUPERS TO THE MOST AFFLUENT OF ARISTOCRATS. MOST
DRAGON MEAT IN CIRCULATION IS SALT-CURED OR SMOKED TO
EXTEND ITS SHELF LIFE.

IN FACT, OIL SALES MAKE UP
THE MAJORITY OF A DRAKING
VESSEL'S PROFITS.

SO, IT'S
ALL ABOUT
SELLING A
LOT FOR LOW?
NEAT!

Until next time.
See you in volume 9!

DRIFTING DRAGONS

A Kodansha Comics Trade Paperback Original
Drifting Dragons 8 copyright © 2020 Taku Kuwabara
English translation copyright © 2021 Taku Kuwabara

All rights reserved.

Published in the United States by Kodansha Comics, an imprint of Kodansha USA Publishing, LLC, New York.

Publication rights for this English edition arranged through Kodansha Ltd., Tokyo.

First published in Japan in 2020 by Kodansha Ltd., Tokyo as *Kuutei doragonzu*, volume 8.

ISBN 978-1-64651-028-3

Printed in the United States of America.

www.kodanshacomics.com

9 8 7 6 5 4 3 2 1
Translation: Adam Hirsch
Lettering: Thea Willis
Editing: Jordan Blanco
Kodansha Comics edition cover design by Matthew Akuginow
YKS Services LLC/SKY Japan, INC.

Publisher: Kiichiro Sugawara

Director of publishing services: Ben Applegate
Associate director of operations: Stephen Pakula
Publishing services associate managing editor: Madison Salters
Assistant production manager: Emi Lotto, Angela Zurlo

JAN - 1 - 2022